the grocers

the grocers

the **rise** and **rise** of the supermarket chains

Andrew Seth & Geoffrey Randall

**KOGAN
PAGE**

First published in 1999
Reprinted 1999

Kogan Page Limited
120 Pentonville Road
London N1 9JN

Kogan Page (US) Limited
163 Central Avenue, Suite 4
Dover, NH 03820, USA

British Library Cataloguing in Publication Data

A CIP record for this book is available from the British Library.

ISBN 0 7494 2191 6

Typeset by Saxon Graphics Ltd, Derby
Printed and bound by Biddles Ltd, Guildford and King's Lynn

Contents

Contents

Contents

For Edith, Vicky, Patrick, Simon, Christopher, Adrian, Stephen and Toby

Preface

Supermarkets touch all our lives. Almost every household shops in a supermarket, and even those who do not are heavily affected because of the huge and dynamic change that the multiples have brought about in food distribution. It has been estimated in a recent study that an astonishing 2 per cent of an average adult life will be spent inside a supermarket. The stores themselves partly reflect, and partly drive, significant shifts in social patterns – the irresistible growth of self-service; new, global foods availability and sourcing; new feature, storage and display techniques; car-borne shopping; out-of-town centres; the decline of urban as well as rural high streets – the list is seemingly endless.

The four leading UK supermarket groups are successful and admirable businesses, but they have their critics, more today perhaps than they had in their development days. What we have tried to do is, firstly, to tell the stories of how the leading food retailers came to be where they are today. Their paths have been very different, and their individual and intertwined histories are full of unique characters, surprising incidents and unpredictable twists of fortune. As retailing has now become an international business, we set the progress of the UK firms in the context of their European and US counterparts, and do our best to draw strategic lessons from the patterns we have observed. We then go on to examine some of the major issues that have arisen directly from the supermarkets' success; in what has become a topical and often heated debate, we set out the arguments that critics have put forward from a range of vantage points, and try to reach balanced conclusions. Finally, we look at the challenges facing the groups in the future. Some would now say that the formula that has worked so well for them so far may be reaching the end of its natural life, and what is certain is that new, genuine threats to their existence are now appearing.

This is a book the two of us have been intending to write for a long time. In our parallel but very different marketing careers, over almost 40 years, we have witnessed from close quarters the rise and rise of the British super-market groups. Indeed, while one author was learning about and experiencing at first hand their growing power – as brand manager, marketing director and chief executive of a major brand supplier – he was irritated to find that both the mother and wife of the other author were visibly loyal Sainsbury's shoppers, and frequent purchasers of an apparently ubiquitous Sainsbury's own-label brand. Summer vacations in a range of European locations provided the venues for conceptual exploration of the topic and the lively range of discussion which ensued. Local producers' bottled offerings, rather than the wine shelves of the fast-growing number of Mediterranean hyper-markets in the vicinities where we were living, would enhance the intensity of late-night examination of an increasingly successful and European retail phenomenon.

We could not but admire the growth of the new supermarkets but, for profes-sional reasons, were equally impressed by their emergence as leaders in their discipline. As students of business history we would all too often find ourselves lamenting the overall performance of a once-great British industrial economy. Britain had through the 1960s, 1970s and 1980s and has today few world-class businesses to boast of, but we can say with confidence that the four leading British supermarket chains – with the small but innovative Marks & Spencer food operation offering formidable new customer choice and retail challenge – have been world leaders at least through the last decade and probably for much longer. Their stories are worth telling for that reason alone, but they have become an important phenomenon of the late 20th century in their own right.

Because we believe the story we have to tell is so interesting in itself, and of such wide application, we have done our best to paint the picture in an enter-taining and accessible style. In no sense have we sought to produce an academic text, or a technical business monograph. We believe that managers in many retail businesses, as well as those in the grocery trade itself, will find it illuminating. Supplier company managements, now recognizing the need to understand their retail partners, will learn something of value. But well beyond those specific core groups, we believe that the book will appeal to a range of learning managers in all sorts of organizations, and to that hopefully non-mythical figure, the intelligent general reader. We ourselves have found the whole process of researching and writing the book endlessly fascinating, and we hope that some of the excitement as our own learning has developed will be transmitted to you, the reader.

We could not, of course, have done anything without the friendship, co-operation and guidance of many busy and well-informed people who gave their time freely, and were open and helpful with facts and opinions. We spoke at some length to past and present chairmen of the retailers and, with their assistance, to many of their colleagues. We also talked to consultants, analysts, researchers, academics, pressure groups, and indeed anyone with any knowledge of the field. In the process, we gathered far more information than we could ever have used in one book. We can only hope that in summarizing, we have not distorted. We believe that the histories of the main grocery retailers are accurate and as complete as space allowed. We realize that, in such a dynamic and competitive field, some of what we have said will be out-of-date by the time that it is read, and not everyone will agree with all our assess-ments and conclusions. So dynamic is the field, indeed, that just as the book went to press, Wal-Mart announced its take-over of Asda. This is something we had discussed and predicted, despite Wal-Mart's denials just a few months ago. It announces a new phase in the story of British food retailing, and we deal with it in Chapter 3 (The Asda Story) and the final chapter, Future Challenges. The main lessons will, we trust, remain valid. All interpretations and opinions are of course entirely our own, and we alone are responsible for any errors.

Acknowledgements

We can only pick out a few individuals from the very many people who helped us. In first place must be Dominic Payling, at that time a student in the business studies department at Kingston University, who researched and analysed the data on European retailers on which Chapter 7 is based. He deserves particular mention, and it is encouraging that his researches gained distinction status in his final MA marketing examinations.

At Tesco, Lord MacLaurin was a generous and continuous source of practical advice and criticism. His successor, Terry Leahy, gave us valuable time and appraisal. His corporate relations team, led by Andrew Coker, provided much information including photographs, and engaged in significant criticism of some of our conclusions, as well as introducing the authors to Peter Welch of the British Retail Consortium. Lord (David) Sainsbury gave us courteous and strategic insights into the industry at an early stage, and Kevin McCarten, erstwhile Procter & Gamble (P&G) manager and then a new marketing director at Sainsbury's, gave freely of his time as did Sainsbury's most knowledgeable and professional archivist, Bridget Williams, who provided both history and photographs. Tom Vyner, long-time industry practitioner, was specifically helpful on the Sainsbury's chapter. At Asda, Archie Norman was an early counsellor, and set the achievements of the British industry in a strategic, world context. Allan Leighton was informative and helpful, and provided us with the invaluable Harvard Business School case. At Asda we were also helped by former directors Sir Noel Stockdale and Peter Asquith, who gave fascinating insights into the early days. Christine Watts provided facts and figures, as well as trenchant criticism, for Chapter 11.

At Safeway, an old friend, the then Chairman (Sir) Alistair Grant, guided initial work, and his equally constructive successor, David Webster, continued the process. Particularly helpful contributions to the history of the industry were made by Steve Webb at Safeway and we have drawn extensively on the material provided, notably the work of Jefferys (1954). Kevin Hawkins, Head of Corporate Relations, offered friendly criticism of the conclusions in Chapter 11 and help on food safety. At Somerfield, David Simons was a source of practical insight notably into the circumstances surrounding the Somerfield/Kwik Save merger. Ken Morrison, by any standards one of the very great figures of British retailing, gave us a lengthy interview with a series of fascinating personal recollections. At Waitrose, David Feldwick explained the strategy and progress clearly. Marks & Spencer were prepared to tell their own individual story in considerable depth and detail, and Lord Stone of Blackheath gave us a particularly entertaining afternoon at the House of Lords.

From the manufacturing side, we were helped by John Dale, then Chairman of Pedigree Petfoods, by John Millen of Procter & Gamble Europe, and by John Ballington of Lever Brothers. The chapter on the United States would have been quite impossible without the active help, knowledge and encouragement of an old friend and colleague, Keith de Vault, former Vice President of Sales and Customer Relations at Lever Brothers, United States. Nina Lewis, from Richmond Events New York, gave us modern reference material on Stu Leonard's stores. Marcy Gascoigne from the FMI's Information Service in the United States provided excellent baseline material on the US industry as a whole. Business policy Professor Norman Berg from Harvard's Business School was both helpful and encouraging and introduced us to Jim McKenney, also of the Business School, who offered us a series of excellent Harvard case studies, notably those that considered the performance and development of Wal-Mart from its inception until the present day. This gave the US chapter further foundation.

Crispin Tweddell, Chairman of the Piper Trust, is, by any standards, a knowledgeable and strategic player in this industry and his counsel was invaluable, crisp and to the point. Robert Clark is another acknowledged expert in the field and his suggestions and information have always been powerful. Edward Whitefield of Management Horizons was generous with his time and access to their library. Two sessions at the Consumers' Association with a good friend, Director Sheila McKechnie, guided our views on the concluding chapters, and on factors affecting competition. The then Conservative Minister for the Environment, John Gummer, gave us a helpful assessment of the legislation that led to the new retail planning environments post-1993. Analysts Andrew Fowler and Tony MacNeary were notably strong in their assessments of the current players. Professor Neil Wrigley at the University of Southampton's geography department has carried out extensive work into the factors affecting performance and consolidation in the US self-service industry and thus guided our conclusions in the US chapter.

Stephen Locke, former policy director at the Consumers' Association, now at Andersen Consulting, provided important insights, as did John Lett of LPAC, in the areas of planning and environmental significance. Peter Welch, consultant to the British Retail Consortium, participated in two reviews of the position concerning profit margins across the industry – a challenging subject and worthy of a book in its own right, as no doubt the now scheduled investigation by the Monopolies Commission will be finding out for itself. He provided valuable material and appropriate references on the topic, which we have used. A respected colleague from our Oxford undergraduate days, Professor Robert Rowthorn of the Economics Department at Cambridge University gave us a series of challenging, persistent and well-argued insights into the implications for society at large of the retail revolution. Allan Breese, of Taylor Nelson Sofres plc, was generous in providing the AGB Superpanel data that form the Appendix, and giving permission for their use.

Our sincere thanks go also to the very many other people who gave us their time: Clinton Silver CBE, Hugh Walker, J-C Leroux and Sean Ahern of Marks & Spencer; Ian O'Reilly, Tim Mason, Bernard Hughes and Karen Marshall at Tesco; Mike Winch and Roderick Angwin, Safeway; Dominic Fry and Andrew Tasker at Sainsbury; Professor Tim Lang, Thames Valley University; John Beaumont and Steve Barnes of the Institute of Grocery Distribution; Dr Ross Davies and Dick Bell, Oxford Institute of Retail Management, Templeton College, Oxford; Chris Mole, Coopers and Lybrand (now Pricewaterhouse Coopers); Monica Wood, Management Horizons; James Edwardes-Jones, Hoare Govett; Mark Sherrington, Peter Dart, Fiona McAnena and Steve Copestake at the Added Value Group; Professor Robert East and Annik Hogg, Kingston University; Michael Meyer, McKinsey; John Hollis, Andersen Consulting's Smart Store; Hugh Davidson, Oxford Corporate Consulting; Deborah Grant, Verdict Research; Andrew Jeffery, Consumer Automotive Marketing; Nick Jennery, the Canadian Council of Grocery Distributors; and Loudon Seth in Cleveland, Ohio.

Introduction

In our lifetimes, we have witnessed nothing less than a complete transformation of grocery shopping. We can dramatize the nature of the changes by looking at three short scenes. They refer to lives in Britain but would be representative of changes happening across the developed world. In some cases, the situation in United States is specifically referred to for comparative purposes.

A VISIT TO THE GROCER'S IN THE LATE 1940s

Geoffrey walks about a mile with his mother to the shops on the edge of Trowbridge's pleasant but lively town centre. The grocer's is a small shop next to the dairy, and the familiar bell rings as they enter the shop. There is one other customer in the store, and no suggestion of any queue. Mr Wootton, the owner, is an imposing man in a long white apron. He stands behind a wide and ancient wooden counter, on which some of his goods are displayed (today he has some locally produced ham and, unusually for the time of year in these still straitened post-war years, he proudly announces there are tinned sardines). There are wooden shelves covering the wall behind him and the other walls of the shop; on the floor are sacks and barrels, and the shop smells warm, slightly spicy, with hints of the raw products all around. The wealth of assorted food products, haphazard displays, the particular aroma, distinctive style, and colours of his shop are characteristic of the kinds of store that exist up and down the whole of Britain at this time.

Mr Wootton greets Mrs Randall by name, with unaffected politeness and no hint of servility. 'How is young Peter today?' he asks. Peter is the Randalls' elder child, and has been off school with a cold. Anyone can tell that this is a conversation with elements of community ritual about it, but it is one they have had many times before. Time is not of the essence, and they chat for a while about a neighbour who is moving out of the area, but then Mr Wootton picks up his pad to take the order. Mrs Randall orders butter, sugar, salt, flour, baking powder and some caraway seeds (to make a cake). When she pauses, he suggests some of the things that he knows she nearly always buys and might have forgotten. Today, he has some particularly good bacon and, adjusting the machine to the thickness number which he knows she prefers, cuts six rashers.

When the order is complete, Mrs Randall takes only one or two small or urgent items in her shopping basket; the rest will be delivered later by the grocer's boy on his specially adapted bicycle. The bell rings again as they leave the store. Milk and bread have already been delivered by the regular roundsmen. She goes on to the butcher, where there is another conversation, discussion and order (we will ignore the coupons and rationing, as younger readers would probably not believe the details). Sometimes she would call in at the chemist for toothpaste or shampoo. She may go on to the greengrocer, though, like most families, the Randalls grow most of their vegetables and fruit in the back garden or in a locally-owned or rented allotment.

Young Geoffrey is prone to chest infections in the winter, so Mrs Randall makes sure he eats a variety of English fruit: red- and blackcurrants, gooseberries, rhubarb, apples and sometimes pears, occasionally plums and damsons. Geoffrey has never seen, let alone tasted, a banana, though he has seen pictures of them in books. At school, apart from not very edifying school canteen meals, he has milk out of the school-issue bottles twice a day – regarded as crucial to a growing boy's health. He has never heard of aubergines or artichokes, balsamic vinegar, capsicum, coriander, dal, endive, focaccia, granary bread, harissa, or hundreds of other products that we know today. Fresh farm eggs have only recently appeared, replacing the familiar, wartime-imposed dried egg powder, imported from the United States. He will not taste foreign food until he goes on his first school trip abroad at the age of 13, and will not experience Italian, Chinese or Indian cooking until he goes to Oxford at the age of 18. Wine rarely, if ever, graces the Randall-family dinner table, even on special occasions.

A VISIT TO THE SUPERSTORE IN THE 1990s

It is Sunday morning, and Patrick and Debbie strap 2-year-old Jamie into their BMW to go and do their weekly grocery shop. Their South London home is within a 15-minute drive of Tesco, Sainsbury's, Asda and Safeway superstores, but they usually go to Sainsbury's on Dog Kennel Hill. It is nearest, has the biggest store, and so far they are happy with the range and prices. They both work full-time, and on a Friday evening, at the end of a hard-pressed working week, they prefer not to face the crowds in shops, but to spend their evenings together rather than take advantage of the 10 o'clock closing time that all the supermarkets now offer. On Saturday, they are often too busy with Jamie's activities and their own, so they are happy to shop sometime on Sunday.

When they arrive, they park in a large and soul-destroying underground car park – as usual it's crammed to the gunwales with cars. Debbie stops at the tobacco counter to buy a lottery ticket and some stamps and to pick up their holiday photographs, while Patrick struggles with the coin-operated release of a trolley and, on request, as he always does, places a now appreciative Jamie inside the cart. They go into the store, and start at the fresh produce area just inside. In addition to their normal potatoes, vegetables and salad items, they buy fresh coriander, asparagus and a mango. Debbie chooses from four different lettuces, and Patrick is keen to try some Kenyan passion fruit. Jamie's contribution to the decision process is to indicate the satsuma oranges by making one of his unmistakable 'get these right away' noises. His parents capitulate but are hard-pressed to stop him starting to eat one immediately.

As they walk through the aisles, they glance only fleetingly at most of the 30,000 separate items on display. They buy three kinds of bread, meat, tinned and frozen food, spices, milk, fresh fruit juice, plain and fruit yogurt, Italian ice cream, Scots oatcakes, Serrano ham, country pâté, some unpasteurized Brie and Burgundy goat cheese, two sorts of breakfast cereal, bottled water, dishwasher detergent tablets, liquid laundry detergent, and toothpaste in a new dispensing cylinder. The nappies (diapers) take up so much room in the trolley that Jamie, protesting, is forced to decamp. Debbie decides to take him for a drink of juice in the restaurant and orders cappuccino coffee for herself at the same time. She reminds Patrick to buy several frozen pizzas, as Jamie likes them; and before she leaves, she also chooses some ready meals for the freezer – a lamb tikka masala and a chicken with cashew nuts, Szechuan-style. Patrick has developed his wine knowledge, and spends some time browsing among the 400 different wines from 10 countries. When he isn't there, Debbie is quite happy to buy the wines she is familiar with, or to try the special offers, often at less than £3 or £4 a bottle, based on the recommendations on the shelf labels.

They've always been surprised at just how good they are, and also how much they liked the £9.99 champagne they bought for Debbie's last birthday. Usually the Spanish Freixenet at a third of the price is quite good enough for them.

They leave the store having exchanged words with no one other than the till assistants, who are perfectly friendly and efficient but with whom, in common with other customers, they have no relationship other than the commercial one. Still, the process works for them and on the whole, Patrick and Debbie buy almost all their food needs at the superstore. Some of their friends swear by the organic butcher round the corner, but they can't see a lot of difference. For a dinner party, they may go to a delicatessen for specialities, but the new deli-counter at the superstore isn't at all bad and there's been a real effort to shorten the queues there. For top-ups, they have a choice of local Asian-run grocery/off-licences, but often they prefer to stop at the convenience store on the petrol-station forecourt on their way to the cinema or to taking the dog to the park. Debbie does feel that the greengrocer's prices are as cheap or cheaper than Sainsbury's but she wonders whether the quality really is better.

ON THE WEB IN THE 2010s

Patrick now works from home most of the time. On Thursday, his phone/Internet communicator interrupts his personalized daily news bulletin to say 'As-Mart' and remind them to order the food shopping. As he is driving, he decides to wait until he gets home, although he could have connected directly to the Website there and then. When he gets home, he clicks on the As-Mart icon, and seconds later is automatically connected to the superstore's online ordering service. He is greeted by name, and the list of his normal weekly purchases appears on the screen. He checks those he doesn't want.

The store computer makes suggestions: he may be running out of dishwasher rinse gel, non-woven polish cloths, and oregano, and he orders them. It also offers some new products that he will probably like, based on his previous buying patterns. There is a special store offer on a new range of genetically engineered drinking yogurts with some strong health claims. He laughs gently, recalling the scare stories about genetically engineered foods when Jamie and Oliver were children – the world is different today. Wine from areas near the South China Sea is becoming fashionable in London. He checks the full ingredients list, looks at the quoted testimonials from the store's appraisal panel, and decides to give it a try. They compare it to good Burgundy and at one third of the price.

Some of his board colleagues are coming round for a dinner party this week, so Patrick moves to the menu section, and browses. He knows what Debbie considers cooking for these kind of occasions, and is happy he can choose dishes from virtually anywhere around the world; he picks a healthy but quite exotic combination of Vietnamese and Mediterranean foods. The programme advises on suitable wines, and he chooses from the selection offered. This lot probably aren't ready for South China Sea Pinot Noir yet, he reflects to himself. This week the Red Meursault from Drouhin has some specific accolades from the panel and be buys six bottles. All the relevant ingredients are automatically added to his order, and he knows that recipe cards will be included. How on earth do people choose from 22 varieties of bottled water, he wonders to himself, and how can it be economic to bring it all the way to London from the Canadian mountains?

Sometimes, he goes on to look at the books and CDs, or to see what clothes bargains are on offer, but he is too busy now. He glances briefly at the car of the week offer – the new Ford portfolio seem to have begun to dominate the store's range recently – and he ruminates now that Ford have added both BMW and Renault/Nissan to their worldwide stable, whether his 5 series BMW will be featured at a good price in the weeks ahead. The holiday features are pretty exciting too but this is an area to which Debbie, aided by their teenage sons, can do a lot more justice. They still haven't decided where to go for their third holiday this year yet.

When he has finished, he moves to the checkout menu, which shows him the itemized bill, with loyalty discount, airline, car-servicing, holiday and leisure centre validity points, and graduated charge for the home shopping service. The computer asks him if he wants to check his bank balance, as the bill will be debited from one of his three store bank accounts. He does, and looks up his savings account, and his store-managed share portfolio holdings at the same time. The computer notifies him of some new retirement pension products that may interest him, as he has a healthy balance lying idle. He postpones a decision, and logs off. He sends an e-mail to Debbie to remind her to pick up the order on her way home, and another one to Jamie to tell him about the superstore's 'here's your own personal organizer for GCSE candidates' offer. A bit more organization is what our eldest son needs, he reflects, wondering what the multifunctional organizer (cum mobile phone, alarm clock and miniature TV/radio ...) might achieve for his son and heir. Of course they could have had the order delivered into their personalized home mini-kiosk, but the dog seemed to have been taking far too much interest in it, and they didn't want Ruby to develop a complex about it.

You can object to the accuracy of these, particularly the last. The technology to deliver that service is available now; but so few have access to it, and the experiments being run by supermarkets and others are so limited, that for practical purpose all this lies in the future. The point is to show that, in the authors' lifetimes (we are sixty), grocery shopping has changed out of all recognition, and will go on changing. We could have set the pictures in almost any developed country although, as we shall see, there have been differences between the United States and Europe, and between countries in Europe, at different periods. These have, however, been mainly differences of timing, for example, self-service developed very much earlier in the United States than anywhere else, while hypermarkets first appeared in France.

What we intend to do in this book is to examine the changes of the last 30 years, and the roles played by what have emerged as the major supermarket multiples during this period of change. We will look at the comparable position in the United States and Europe. In this introductory chapter, we will describe briefly how the grocery industry in Britain arrived at the point where these chains could take off in the spectacular way they did, pointing out some crucial differences in the United States.

FOOD SHOPPING IN THE 1850s

We are accustomed to thinking of our epoch as one of unprecedented change – rapid and increasing in speed, discontinuous, surprising, wrenching, transforming. Certainly, our lives are very different now from 50 years ago. But we should remember that there have been other periods of dramatic change. The latter half, and in particular the last quarter, of the 19th century was a time of transformation in Britain: many of the features that we associate with our own times first appeared then. (The following section draws heavily on the authoritative work of Jefferys, 1954.)

Of the many parallels, one is people's perceptions of the revolution in shopping. A lecturer in the 1880s could say:

> The epoch of shops is comparatively recent. We are now further removed from the experiences of my youth in these matters than our fathers were from the age of Elizabeth and the Stuarts (ie the sixteenth and seventeenth centuries).
>
> (Thorold Rogers, quoted in Jefferys, 1954)

What Rogers refers to as 'shops' are not what we would recognize by the term. In the middle of the 19th century, retail grocery and provisions came from a variety of outlets. There were grocers selling traditional groceries, from sugar to spices, tea, cocoa and coffee. Farmers would sell fresh eggs and butter, and their own cheese and bacon, in open-air markets. Other outlets included specialist cheesemongers, the ubiquitous oil and colourman, the tallow-chandler and the Italian warehouseman. The exotic-sounding oil and colourman had started as a dealer in colours, paints and oils, but had broadened his stock to include many household stores, such as soap and candles, starch, matches, firewood, brushes, baskets and brooms, petroleum, lamps, linseed oil, beeswax and vegetable wax, colours, gums and resins, and would often extend to groceries such as sauces, pickles and jams, to chemicals and drugs such as soda, Glauber's salts, quack pills and poor man's plaster, and to a miscellaneous mixture of commodities including hardware, ironmongery, china, lampblack, size, ochre, chalk, sand, vitriol, brickdust, and gunpowder and shot. The Italian warehouseman specialized in imported olive oil, nut oil, and items such as macaroni and vermicelli; he might also carry stocks of preserves that duplicated those of the oil and colourman.

Grocers, like other retailers, were skilled craftsmen who had served an apprenticeship. They would own the business, which would pass from father to son, and they would live on the premises. They chopped or ground by hand the cones of sugar, ground and mixed spices, and chose and blended teas. Success depended on reputation passed by word of mouth, and was based on quality of goods and honesty.

We would find the shops themselves unattractive and dimly lit, with no concept of display. Shop windows as we are used to them hardly existed, and indeed were frowned on by many:

> A butcher of the higher class disdains to ticket his meat. A mercer of the higher class would be ashamed to hang up papers in his window inviting passers-by to look at the stock of a bankrupt, all of the first quality, and going for half the value. We expect some reserve, some decent pride in our hatter and boot-maker.
>
> (Macaulay, quoted in Jefferys, 1954)

As Macaulay's view suggests, perhaps unintentionally, the fixed shop retailers, including grocers, catered mainly to the wealthier sections of the population. Although the working class bought some items from the grocer, their incomes were low, and they could afford very little beyond the bare necessities. They would buy from open markets, or in cities from the market halls that were springing up. Until it was made illegal, industrial workers might have to buy much of what they needed from 'truck' shops owned by their employer.

Two final features marked retailing at that period. One was the problem of adulteration and short measure. Where the grocer prepared so much of the final product, opportunities for cheating were always present. The other feature was that prices were rarely fixed and displayed, so haggling (or 'higgling or chaffering') were very much the order of the day.

In the United States, the situation was similar, even perhaps more disorganized; here is an excerpt from 'Stocking America's Pantries: The rise and fall of A&P' referring to lack of organization among US rural food merchants in the 19th century:

> A great deal of time was wasted in looking for articles that were not in place, or had no place. Flies swarmed around the molasses barrel and there was never a mosquito bar to keep them off. There was tea in chests packed in lead foil and straw matting with strange markings. Rice and coffee spilling out on the floor where a bag showed a rent; rum and brandy, harness and whale oil. The air was thick with an all embracing odor, an aroma composed of dry herbs and wet dogs, or strong tobacco, green hides and raw humanity.
>
> (Tedlow, 1990)

We can thus appreciate the force of Rogers's remark. The retail scene described could have existed for centuries, and its main features can be seen in countries around the world. What happened in Britain to change it depended on particularly British circumstances, but the same forces would appear in all developed countries.

FORCES FOR CHANGE

What is specific to Britain in the middle of the 19th century is that the Industrial Revolution had started there earlier than elsewhere. Full industrialization had arrived, leading to the growth of large-scale manufacturing and production. The development of steam power, applied to railways and shipping, revolutionized transport. Britain's dominance of these new technologies, and the opening up of world markets through the adoption of free trade, produced a wholly new economy. The country exported huge amounts of manufactured goods and capital, and imported cheap food.

The effects were clearly wide-ranging, but certain among them were of particular significance for retailing. Firstly, an industrialized working class emerged, living mainly in towns and cities. The workers had mainly steady jobs, and a regular wage. This produced a regular, consistent demand for mass consumer goods. This both allowed and demanded new forms of distribution.

Second, a new, larger, urban middle class appeared, producing another form of demand that existing retail formats were ill-prepared to satisfy. Third, the decline of British agriculture and the availability of cheap food from abroad – such as bacon, eggs, butter, cheese, tea and meat – meant that whole new channels of distribution were needed.

Fourth, mass production techniques spread from heavy manufacturing to the food, shoe and clothing industries. Finally, real income per head increased, almost doubling in the last 30 years of the century. This meant that consumers had the money to spend, and there was a supply of cheap products, of a variety that most people had never seen before.

The scene was set for the emergence of two phenomena that are central to our story: mass-produced, standardized consumer goods; and large-scale multiple retailing.

RESPONSES TO CHANGE – MULTIPLE RETAILERS

Many of the resultant developments are outside the scope of this book; the growth of multiple retailing is central. The earliest multiples were the newsagent firms W H Smith and J Menzies, and the Singer Manufacturing Company, who started to develop chains of shops in the 1850s. Most of the development in other trades came later, in the 1870s, grocery being one of the first.

The numbers of firms with 10 or more branches from 1875 to 1920 are shown in Figure 0.1, and the numbers of food firms with multiple branches in Figure 0.2. Although footwear firms had led the way, by the 1890s food retailers were the largest group, and by 1920 food multiples formed over half of the total.

The multiples relied on techniques that we recognize easily today: 'economies of scale in buying, economies of specialization in administration and economies of standardization in selling' (Jefferys, 1954: 27). In the food trades, bulk buying of imported products on a scale undreamed of by the single retailer, and efficient distribution to a network of shops, were the basis of the business model.

With food buying in particular, the shops needed to be where consumers were – either near their homes or on their journeys to work. Shopping was frequent. There was therefore a limit to the number of customers any one shop could attract. The answer was to take the shops to the customers, and open additional units in new areas. Once the basic model was successfully established, it was comparatively easy to replicate it elsewhere. As more units were added, the economies of scale would increase in the now familiar virtuous circle.

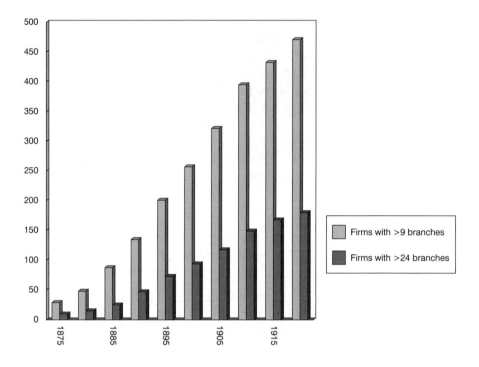

Figure 0.1 *Multiple shop firms 1875–1920*

Although we have said that incomes were rising, they were not yet high. The mass demand was for a fairly narrow range of standardized, acceptable, reliable products rather than a broad selection and variety.

The new shops were basic, with no frills. They relied on low prices, cash payment and effective promotion. The 'decent pride' that Macaulay had taken for granted gave way to plate glass, gas lighting and displays designed to attract passers-by. Amusingly, John Ruskin, the great critic of art and architecture, thought that the failure of his tea shop in the 1870s was at least partly due to his refusal to embrace the new techniques. 'The result of this experiment,' he wrote, 'has been my ascertaining that the poor only like to buy their tea where it is brilliantly lit and eloquently ticketed. I resolutely refuse to compete with my neighbouring tradesmen either in gas or rhetoric!' (quoted in Jefferys, 1954: 37). As the quotation suggests, an important change was that price ticketing became common. This was to have profound implications. Equally profound change was set to affect the stance that retailers took to marketing their products in a whole lot of other respects that Ruskin would have found disquieting.

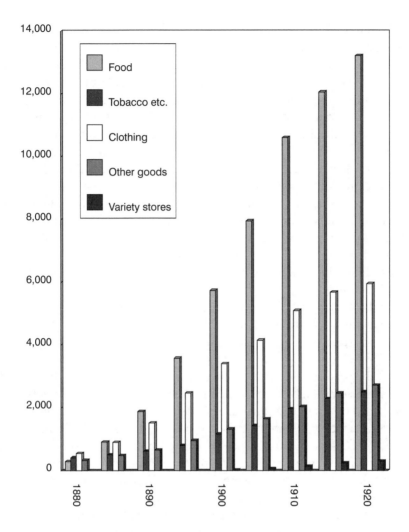

Figure 0.2 *Multiple shops by trade 1880–1920*

PRICE COMPETITION, BRANDING AND RESALE PRICE MAINTENANCE

As price was one of the main appeals of the new retailers, and with the advent of price labelling, it is not surprising that fierce price competition between retailers developed in the last quarter of the century. The quality of the goods on offer had to be asserted by advertising and selling techniques.

A complication was the parallel development by manufacturers of national brands. Mass manufacturing meant that standardized products could be sold across the country. The capital invested in plant and working capital tied up in long production runs and stocks led manufacturers to look for ways of controlling sales. Rather than leave it to the vagaries of wholesalers and retailers, they started to brand their products, advertise them directly to consumers and deliver directly to retailers. National advertising built up the reputation of the brand in consumers' minds, and large sales forces called on outlets, both to sell and also to ensure that the products were stocked and displayed.

These two forces – price competition between retailers, and the desire of manufacturers to control the reputation and sale of their brands – led to the introduction of resale price maintenance. The pressure to maintain agreed prices came originally from retailers, but the manufacturers seemed ready to co-operate (the reverse of a century later!). Thus, by the end of the 19th century, food retailing had been transformed, and many of the features we think of as peculiarly modern had been established: multiple retailers, national brands, price competition, and resale price maintenance.

We should not exaggerate. The trends had been established, but the penetration of multiple retailing was still small. By 1900, multiples accounted for perhaps 12 per cent of total retail sales of food and household stores, rising to just over 20 per cent by 1920 (Jefferys, 1954: 30). What they represented was the future.

In the early years of the 20th century in more urban parts of the United States, things had not moved very much farther forward. Serious anxiety was expressed in the report to the House of Representatives by the Industrial Commission on the Distribution of Food Products: 'On the whole nine-tenths of our cities are behind the distributive experience of the best fed communities for want of proper facilities for bringing producers and consumers together at some convenient place or places at regular times' (Tedlow, 1990: 188).

But the really big and important changes still lay ahead and it was here and in the 1930s that unsung heroes but great US innovators, Saunders and Cullen in particular, could really claim to have led the world into a new retail age. By 1931, the forces of consumer marketing in the United States had changed from small-scale marketing to 'a large scale fully capitalistic business'. This revolution was not yet the supermarket, neither the concept nor the name being yet a reality, but the chain store. Chain ownership, management of retail outlets, and backward integration were what was generally meant by the 'revolution in distribution' until the 1930s.

However, as early as 1916 in Piggly Wiggly Memphis, Tennessee, the daring and inventive Clarence Saunders had established the first self-service store, promising his customers that he would 'slay the demon of high prices'. It took till 1930 for the supermarket to become a serious factor. King Kullen of 171 Jamaica Avenue in Queen's, New York, declaring himself with something less than total constraint as 'the World's Greatest Price Wrecker', challenged US chain store owners of the day to 'read these prices and weep'. In his famous 1930 proposal written to the Presidents of both Kroger and A&P Stores, the heavy hitters of the time, Michael J Cullen had used the most confident and populist language to forecast the effects of his monstrous stores and his, low cost, self-service, advertised prices approach. 'Nobody ever did this before … nobody ever flew the Atlantic either until Lindbergh did it … it would be a riot. I would have to call out the police and let the public in so many at a time. I would lead the public out of the high priced houses of bondage into the low prices of the house of the promised land. What is your verdict?' (McCausland, 1980). Cullen ended looking for help and support to make his vision happen. The response from Kroger and from A&P was an identical and speedy 'No'. So off went Cullen to found King Kullen in the city of New York, and 15 stores after his first in Jamaica Avenue. The new revolution was finally happening whether Kroger and A&P liked it or not. It was to take rather longer in Europe.

THE CO-OPERATIVE SOCIETIES

Over long periods, most working-class families lived at subsistence level, with very little cash to buy food and household necessities. Often, they felt at the mercy of unscrupulous retailers. A unique British solution, which was to have an important influence on retailing in Britain and to spread around the world, was the co-operative. Although there had been earlier attempts, such as joint buying by a group of weavers in 1761, the modern co-operative movement was founded by 28 impoverished weavers in Rochdale, Lancashire, in 1844. The Rochdale Society of Equitable Pioneers was set up as a mutual aid group, and as its first initiative founded a grocery shop.

The Rochdale principles, which set the tone for later developments, were:

- democratic control, with each member entitled to one vote regardless of shareholding;
- membership open to all, irrespective of class, race or religion;
- payment of only limited interest on capital;
- distribution of surplus earnings (to be known in Britain as the dividend, or 'divi').

By selling at fair prices (around the market level), the co-op would both serve the needs of its shopping members, and earn surpluses for reinvestment as well as for the dividend.

The Rochdale society was successful, and soon added a flour mill, a shoe factory and a textile plant. The model was rapidly copied, and throughout the rest of the century the number of societies and members rose continuously. By 1863 there were over 400 societies, with 100,000 members; by 1881, membership was 547,000 and retail turnover was over £15 million. In 10 years both figures doubled, and by 1900, membership reached 1,707,000, sales £50 million. By the outbreak of war in 1914, the figures were 3,053,000 and £88 million.

Each society was separate and autonomous, a strength in these early years of expansion, but later to become a serious weakness in the face of competition from centralized multiples. They belonged to a co-operative union, so could exchange information, and their buying power was enhanced by the foundation of the Co-operative Wholesale Societies (CWS) (in 1863 in England, and 1868 in Scotland). The CWS was both a food processor and wholesaler acting on behalf of its member societies. Interestingly, it was an early pioneer of an international approach, setting up a buying point in Ireland in 1866, and a depot in New York as early as 1876. Other depots followed: Rouen in 1879, Copenhagen in 1881, and Hamburg in 1884.

The retail societies were in these early years concentrated in the industrial North of England and Scotland. Their members were overwhelmingly working class, and the range of goods on offer reflected the need for basics. They usually started with groceries and provisions, later expanding to other foods, meat and tobacco. Eventually, they would broaden their range to cover almost any consumer need, a 'womb to tomb' service (for decades until the 1970s they were the largest funeral directors in the country).

The co-ops clearly met a real need, and continued to expand. By 1915 they probably accounted for almost 20 per cent of grocery and provision sales, and over 10 per cent of household stores. Their buying power, through the CWS, and their responsiveness to local needs meant that they could compete effectively not only with individual rivals but also with the growing chains.

THE INTER-WAR YEARS

In Britain, as elsewhere, the years from 1918 to 1939 were marked by severe economic volatility, with depression and the slump interspersed by rising prosperity. Britain's industries, too, faced new challenges. As other nations, particularly the United States and Germany, developed rapidly, the UK's century-old dominance of basic manufacturing industries came to an end, and many previously thriving areas saw decline and decay. Unemployment was very high in some areas and industries even outside the slump of 1930–34. Generally, incomes continued to rise, but not for everyone.

Socially, the country was changing too. The rate of increase in population slowed, and the size of the average family and household declined. More widespread education, the not unrelated rise in the circulation of newspapers, and even the influence of advertising began to make the population more homogeneous, both regionally and as between classes.

Both a contributing cause and a reflection of this homogeneity was the increasing standardization and branding of consumer goods. This process had already started in the previous century, as we have seen, but it spread in volume and range. The smaller households did less of the food processing themselves, and instead bought small amounts of branded products in tins, packets and containers.

A further trend was the shift in population to the southern half of the country, where towns and conurbations grew fast. Anyone familiar with Britain will recognize the huge growth in the suburbs shown by the housing built in the 1930s, as the middle classes escaped the run-down city centres to live in the typical 'suburban semi'.

For the grocery industry, these influences served to reinforce the trends already established. The number of multiple shops continued to increase, from 7,880 in 1920 to 13,118 in 1939. The larger firms grew by acquisition and merger as well as organically. Between 1924 and 1931, several firms merged with Home and Colonial to form a group with over 3,000 branches, while International Tea grew to over 1,000.

As incomes rose, and as manufacturers expanded their range of standardized products, it followed that the variety stocked by retailers continued to grow too. The tendency for food processing to be carried out increasingly by manufacturers or wholesalers contributed to the deskilling of the grocer, as did the spread of resale price maintenance. On the other hand, the need for *business* skills increased. The grocer no longer needed to be an expert on preparing bacon or spices, but did need to be able to keep records of a much wider range of stock, to understand accounts, to negotiate with salesmen, and to display and promote goods.

Shops became larger and more hygienic. Window displays developed as an important way of attracting customers, while inside the shop cabinets and showcases as well as shelves were used to display packages. As price competition was limited, service became a weapon; home delivery became widespread in this period, not just confined to the wealthy.

Naturally, small specialist shops remained, though in smaller numbers, as did the village store selling a very wide range of goods. More and more, however, the general pattern was established.

> Dealers trading in fair-sized shops and surrounded by marble counters, shelving and glass showcases stacked with half a dozen makes of breakfast cereals, a dozen types of jams, packages of various choices of biscuits, varieties of sugar and blends of tea, and literally hundreds of samples of branded condiments, sauces, pickles, spreads, food beverages, gravy mixtures, essences and powders, were representative of the bulk of the trade in the 'twenties and 'thirties, as was the very full service they were prepared to provide for their customers.
>
> (Jefferys, 1954: 135)

The co-operative societies reflected these general patterns. They expanded especially into the Midlands and south of England, the number of individual members rising to 8.5 million by 1939. While this figure may be misleading (due to multiple membership and non-buying members), we can say that in 1938 there were some 1,100 societies trading in about 24,000 shops.

Like their commercial counterparts, many societies merged to form larger units, and others joined federations. This allowed the bigger groups to extend their activities, for example to baking and laundry. The greater size also led to economies of scale in operations, and many societies introduced standardized techniques to control a number of outlets.

THE WAR AND GOVERNMENT CONTROLS

During the Second World War, the government introduced not only rationing, but very detailed controls on prices (in this, Britain was similar to many European countries, but radically different from the United States). Many of these controls remained in place for years after the war, when the British economy was in a severely damaged condition. The purpose of these controls was to ensure that goods – particularly food but also clothing and furniture – were distributed fairly to all sections of the population. Their success can be judged by the fact that the population as a whole was *healthier* at the end of the war than at the beginning, despite existing on what we would regard today as a meagre and limited diet.

A second major factor affecting the trade was a shortage of manpower. Large numbers of men were conscripted into the forces, or directed into industries and services of national need. Women, too, were heavily involved in the war effort, replacing men in factories and on the farms. When the school-leaving age was raised to 15, this diminished the supply of cheap junior staff. As a result, the numbers employed in the trade fell rapidly, and services were cut back.

Apart from this, the whole grocery industry was, in effect, frozen for the duration of the controls. While this was frustrating and limiting at the time, it had some benefits, since no new competition could enter. As the country emerged from war, wherever goods were still rationed or in short supply, the existing firms were, in effect, in a position of monopoly. As Jefferys put it, 'The established wholesalers and retailers could hardly put a foot wrong and only the completely incompetent firms, once evacuation [of the civilian population, especially children, away from cities] and bombing had been weathered, were likely to fail' (Jefferys, 1954: 106).

Even after the war, controls on some goods remained, and planning regulations were strict. New shops were allowed only in new housing areas, or to replace bomb damage. Property prices were inflated and rents high. The costs of refurbishment were also high (as the prices of materials and equipment were much higher than pre-war), and likely to be uneconomic with price controls still in place. Until the economy started to move, and controls were relaxed, the trade remained more or less static.

THE POST-WAR YEARS

The British economy, almost bankrupted by the war effort, was slow to recover. Retailers were, however, looking eagerly for ways of improving their business. The source of ideas and inspiration was often the great modern economy that had actually benefited from the war, and which was now by far the strongest and most innovative in the world – the United States. Two inter-linked ideas which were to transform the grocery scene came from there: self-service and supermarkets.

One of the effects of war, and of other developments such as the raising of the school-leaving age, was to reduce the pool of cheap, available labour. Anything which would help with this problem would be welcome, and self-service, though novel, met the bill perfectly. The idea had started in the United States as early as 1916, as we saw, and took off in the 1930s; by 1965 it was more or less complete. The earliest conversions to self-service started in Britain in 1947, and such was the success of the experiment that numbers grew rapidly (see Figure 0.3).

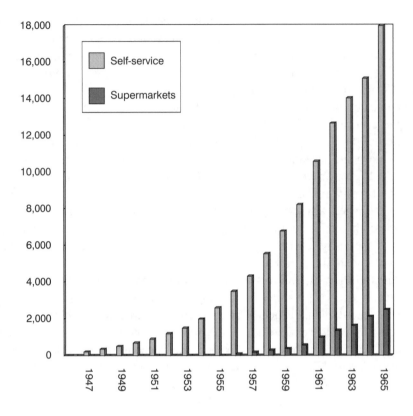

Figure 0.3 *Self-service and supermarkets 1947–66*

Although self-service could be used by any store, it was adopted most enthusiastically by the multiples. The efficiencies and cost savings added to the multiples' growing advantage. This advantage really began to work for them in this period, and their growth towards dominance started to take off, as Table 0.1 shows.

Table 0.1 *Multiples share of grocery sales*

Year	Percentage
1950	20
1957	22
1961	27
1966	36
1971	44

Source: Beaumont and Webb,1982

The other secret that the chains discovered in these decades was, of course, that size matters: the larger they made the store, the better they were able to capture the economies of scale.

THE 1970s ON – SUPERMARKETS, SUPERSTORES AND HYPERMARKETS

As grocers discovered the gains from increasing size, they began the trend that continued for decades: the total number of shops declined, but the average size increased. In one year alone, 1978–79, the multiples closed over 350 shops smaller than 5,000 square feet, and opened 60 of more than 10,000 (Tanburn, 1981). Over the period 1971–79, the total number of grocery shops fell from 105,283 to 68,567, a decline of 35 per cent; for multiples, the decrease was 45 per cent.

The logic of size was applied remorselessly by those who recognized its potential, and new types of store began to appear – superstores (25,000 square feet or more) and hypermarkets (50,000 square feet or more). Figure 0.4 shows their growth.

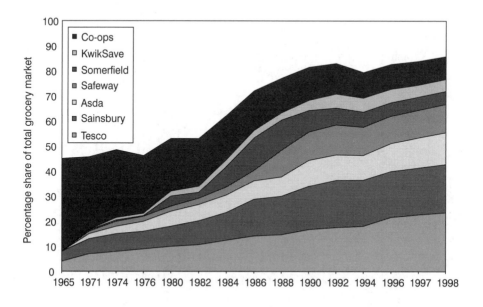

Figure 0.4 *Shares of total grocery market, all main players*

Figure 0.4 summarizes the dramatic transformation of the British market. We can see that:

- the biggest single player in 1965, the Co-operative movement, shrank from over 35 per cent to less than 10 per cent of the market;
- the 'independents and others' sector , which started the period with more than 50 per cent, ended at under 15 per cent;
- the big winners were Tesco and Sainsbury's, followed by Asda and Safeway: together these have now won some two-thirds of the market.

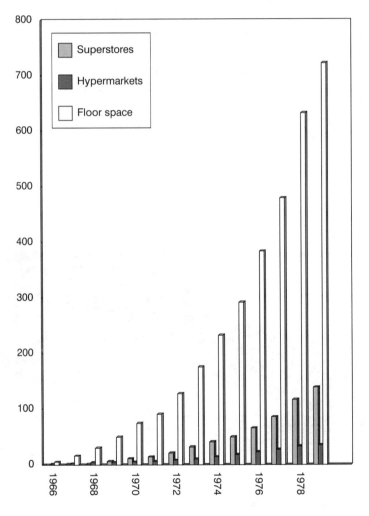

Figure 0.5 *Superstores and hypermarkets*

The following chapters tell the stories of these winners, who so changed the face of the British grocery scene. The stories of Europe and the United States are told in Chapters 7 and 8.

INTO THE ACRONYM JUNGLE

All areas of human activity seem to develop their own TLAs (three-letter acronyms, sorry). In grocery retailing, we might hear someone say that, while DPP is OK, it is not applied in SM at present, as all their energies have been going on CRP and CM, but POS data have been invaluable in DSD. EDI was a tremendous help, particularly when they moved to CAO and, even better, CSO. ECR has brought it all together.
For the uninitiated, here is a brief guide:

CAO Computer Assisted Ordering: using POS data to help the retailer order accurately.
CM Category Management: managing a whole category of similar products as a unit, rather than as separate products. Practised by both retailers and manufacturers, preferably in partnership.
CRP Continuous Replenishment: a system in which the retailer supplies the manufacturer with warehouse shipment and inventory data, and the manufacturer supplies products directly based on those, rather than on the retailer's purchase orders.
CSO Computerized Store Ordering: a further development of CAO, with less human input; can be automated, or allow some judgement depending on category.
DPP Direct Product Profitability: allocating all relevant costs (eg handling and storage) to each product , rather than relying just on gross margin.
DSD Direct Store Delivery: in Britain, an intermediate phase, from delivery by manufacturers to wholesalers, to delivering direct to stores; now mainly superseded by deliveries to retailers' distribution centres.
ECR Efficient Consumer Response: introduced in the United States in 1993, an initiative to get manufacturers, wholesalers and retailers to co-operate in improving the efficiency of the supply chain. Spread to Europe in 1996; most major players are involved.
EDI Electronic Data Interchange: a proprietary system allowing buyers and suppliers to communicate electronically, extensively

used in the grocery industry (and many others) for ordering, query resolution and, to a lesser extent, invoicing. Will probably be assimilated into the Web via extranets.

EDLP Everyday low price: a policy of limiting special promotions and temporary price reductions in favour of a generally lower price level.

LFL Like-for-like: the increase in sales, usually on a year-on-year basis, from the same store base (ie excluding growth from new stores or acquisitions).

POS Point-of-sale; nowadays, the till.

ROCE Return on Capital Employed: a measure of profitability (see Case Study, 'How Profitable Are Food Retailers?', in Chapter 9).

SKU Stock-keeping unit: (eg one flavour of one size of one brand).

SM Space Management: the use of computerized models to describe the effect of different shelf layouts, to try to optimize use of space.

A NOTE ON THE SALES AND MARKET SHARE FIGURES USED

Data on grocery sales and market shares are published by several different organizations, including the Institute of Grocery Distribution (IGD), Audits of Great Britain (AGB), A C Nielsen, and Verdict. As they use different definitions, and are produced from different sources, the results are also different.

Since we wanted as long a series as possible, we have adopted as our basic source a set going back to 1965, produced by Robert Clark, a retail market consultant. His figures are calculated from official statistics, company results, and data from publications from the Economist Intelligence Unit and Corporate Intelligence on Retailing. We believe these to be sound and accurate, and best represent the performance of our target companies in grocery retailing.

The total market data include all sales by mainstream grocers, but *excluding* CTNs (confectioner-tobacconist-newsagents), specialist food shops (such as bakers, butchers etc.), off-licences (liquor stores) and chemists. They also *exclude* VAT.

For each grocery retailer, the sales are all sales through their UK food or superstore outlets: that is, they include non-food sales in supermarkets and superstores (eg Sainsbury's Savacentres), but exclude sales through non-food outlets (eg Sainsbury's Homebase).

Differing total market size and sales figures, and therefore shares, are produced when some or all of these are included, as they are in some other series. The general pattern remains much the same, though there may at times be an apparent change in rank order of the various players.

1

The Tesco story

There once was an Ugly Duckling,
With feathers all stubby and brown,
And the other birds in so many words
Said 'Tchk! get out of town ...'
'Who, me! A swan? Oh ... go on ...'

Danny Kaye

Tesco is today the UK's leading food retailer. It was founded as a private company 70 years ago in the stalls of London's East End markets by one of retailing's truly amazing characters, Jack, later Lord, Cohen, who took on later and happily the sobriquet 'Slasher Jack'. It was he who took the company public and who stood firmly behind the renowned Tesco retailing policy in the early years of self-service of 'pile it high and sell it cheap'. During the 1980s, led by Ian MacLaurin, Tesco went on to establish itself as a reputable no. 2 in the UK market. It became undisputed market leader in 1995, at the same time extending its reach into the markets of western and central Europe.

Few retail stories in recent years can capture the imagination the way the change and development of the Tesco business can. It is not often that a company is able to break free from a limited heritage to the extent that Tesco was required to in the years post 'Checkout'. This kind of breakout, when it happens, usually features expensive mistakes and often risks outright failure. Tesco's progress has not been easy or predictable. The confidence that has followed was not easily won. Ten years ago the bravest of forecasters would not have seen in Tesco a recognized market leader on any of the standard market measures – volume, profitability or innovation. But leader it is. On most key measures ahead of the long-time, dominant front runner in UK retailing – Sainsbury's – for the moment Tesco seems determined to hang on to its hard won gains, and has strategies in place to make its lead permanent. Its achievement has been a spectacular transformation of a once virtually derelict business concern. Five years in first position is a short time, as it knows, and the market is now changing to become global, which presents an even more withering challenge ahead. But Tesco is making the pace here as well, and few doubt its capacity to be the UK's leading company when global considerations start to change the structure of the market. Indeed if a global alliance were to be needed to place Tesco in the front rank of world retailers in the years ahead – as well it may – Tesco would enter such a relationship holding many of the key cards.

THE FOUNDER AND THE EARLY YEARS

The Tesco founder, Jack Cohen, is the stuff of unadulterated business legend. Born in 1898, son of a first-generation East European Jewish father, Avroam, Jack Cohen learned his trade the hard way and in unforgiving company in the rough and tumble mêlée of the street markets of East London, in Hoxton, Hackney, Whitechapel and the Caledonian and Essex Roads. Cohen was quick-witted, a natural trader with a gift for buying below the market price and selling at a quick profit. He was the entrepreneur nonpareil, with a head for figures, an intuition for a good deal, and there were few kinds of business risk capable of scaring Jack off. The name Tesco arrived by chance early on in Jack's trading days. T E Stockwell was a partner in the tea-importing company from whom Cohen would buy tea in packets at 9d (old pence) per pound and sell it in half-pound packets for 6d.

Tesco, the name of today's billion-pound grocery colossus, was nothing more glamorous than a combination of Stockwell's initials and the first two letters of Jack's name. Tesco Stores was founded as a private limited company by Jack Cohen in 1932. Jack's business prospered. 'Always keep your hand over the money and be ready to run' was a favourite Cohen admonition. It was sound advice in the markets where he learned his business.

Cohen knew how to make small selling spaces work – the market stall gave Cohen a base from which he expanded to a further stall in Tooting in 1930, and then to his first stores in Becontree and Edmonton a year later. They were important in more ways than one. Cohen's new 500 sq ft stores were veritable minnows compared to the Co-ops, Sainsbury's and even the Allied shops with whom he was competing. But Cohen was no longer mired in his East End grassroots.

He had moved upwards socially to the middle-class suburbs. Not that this ever changed Jack's dealing approach to business. Ian MacLaurin told me of Cohen buying a consignment of 'Flying Bird' Danish cream from a half-sunk ship and sending it off to his shops with this instruction – 'Take off the labels, get a tin of Duraglit from the shelves to clean off the rust and sell these for 2d a tin.' His customers couldn't get enough of it. It was typical of Cohen's eye for a bargain and for his unshakeable lifetime conviction that it was low prices and nothing else that moved business fastest. The product at Tesco was distinctly secondary – a legacy that took Jack, or at any rate his successors, a long time to live down.

After the war years, some new and well-known figures joined the founder, some more permanent than others. Jack did not take advice easily. Hyman Kreitman, Cohen's son-in-law, was a thinker with an eye for innovation. He would clash fiercely with 'Slasher Jack', his maverick father-in-law, who was as tight-fisted about all aspects of business costs as he was pathologically prone to cut prices. Daisy Hyams, another formidable personality in an era when women rarely achieved prominence, arrived to run purchasing. Jack and Daisy were a famous dynamic duopoly with a reputation across the whole food industry. By the mid-1950s Tesco had 150 small and physically unimpressive stores, most of them on self-service formats. In 1957 Cohen announced results, profits of £500,000, a record, and a signal of the progress he had made over 30 roller-coaster years. As the supermarket revolution arrived, Cohen opened his first Tesco supermarket in 1956. But in all conscience Cohen was singularly ill-equipped in either visionary or operating terms as a leader to handle this level of radical change. Big trouble lay ahead.

COHEN'S DILEMMA

Cohen's problem was that he was running a one-man band. He viewed himself as a figure of Napoleonic proportions, who was, to all intents and purposes, the company Tesco. The company revolved entirely around the business methods, style and predilections of its unusual founder. Cohen's modus operandi had barely changed since Jack had learned to make successful deals in Hoxton market in the 1920s. Cohen had applied all the intuition and bravura he could muster to growing Tesco. He liked to be a buyer, using cash to purchase companies to generate volume growth, irrespective of whether they were well fitted for tomorrow's retail environment or indeed, often, of how much he might be asked to pay for them. Cohen's trading instincts were heady growth medicine, but as a new retailing culture took hold, and innovation and customer service began to matter, his policies began to be seen for what they were – a ragbag of tactical approaches to moving volume through an unprepossessing assortment of old-fashioned and increasingly uncompetitive outlets. It was the most limited of models, with initiatives confined to pricing tactics, and although Jack himself would have hated to admit it, quality and innovation did not feature prominently, if at all, in the Tesco armoury of trading weapons.

A further significant problem was the Tesco management philosophy and structure – it simply did not exist. Cohen was prepared to accept that he needed financial minding to keep him solvent, but he kept it at all times firmly in an advisory capacity. A degree of derring-do and genuine flair was detectable among his managers, who liked to believe they could behave as free-spirited buccaneers and were rarely incommoded by any systematic controls that could prevent them doing so, if they wanted. At the top, however, Jack liked to have his own way. There were few rules, and no coherent trading information to plot the way forward. Kreitman's skills were used sporadically, and the arrival of Leslie Porter, husband of Cohen's daughter Shirley, geometrically increased the scope for family board dissension, since Porter too had ideas about instilling modest order into Tesco's business behaviour. Planning was, however, foreign to Jack's nature, and there was no method or discipline in Tesco's trading approach. An assignment to Tesco's HQ was known engagingly among the Tesco other ranks as a voyage into the 'snake-pit'.

As the competition were developing attractive and large outlets which were appreciated as a shopping experience, and took custom away from the high-street counter stores, Tesco's unruly collection of undistinguished trading locations was seen for what it was – cheap, cut-price bargain basements where price was a lone redeeming feature and the only customer buying rationale. The business was now on the slide, and Cohen's team knew this well. In 1960, Hyman Kreitman, prevented for too long from playing any coherent policy-making role and fed up with his father-in-law's increasingly irascible lack of any form of plan, resigned. Tesco could not go on this way for much longer.

Cohen, of course, would not have agreed. He saw no reasons to change what he had regarded, for most of his trading life, as a winning formula. He was out on the trail buying stores, using this exciting tactic to be first in the land to achieve claimed 'national coverage' which, with the acquisition of Irwins stores in 1960, he had indeed accomplished. Irwins were Merseysiders, and Cohen was proud to announce that Tesco, unlike anyone else in food retailing, had 'gone national'. The claim was a vapid one, since the company had no pretensions to national organization, and indeed it brought in its train more management problems for Cohen's unstructured Tesco team. The board were engaged in a constant running argument about expansion, while recognizing there were organic problems which they had not begun to tackle. At least Tesco were beginning to play a part in the new supermarket game – at the end of 1961, comedian Sid James opened their flagship (16,500 sq ft) Leicester store. It was many times bigger than most new supermarkets and comprehensively dwarfed the traditional Tesco offering. But by now Cohen had found another exciting war to wage, one that would serve to burnish his combative image as a 'knight in armour riding to the aid of hard-pressed consumers' and strengthen his own and the Tesco price-fighting reputation for years to come.

RESALE PRICE MAINTENANCE AND TRADING STAMPS

Resale price maintenance (RPM) had long been a feature of British and world retailing. In the 1950s a Swiss philanthropist, Emil Duttweiler, mounted the early challenges to RPM from which today's powerful Swiss own-label Migros chain was born. Resale price maintenance had been promoted and protected by brand manufacturers who saw it as a way of maintaining the widest brand distribution at a level of margin from which everyone, even the smallest traders, could make some profit. It was not in the consumer's interest, however, and the more efficient retailers began to realize they could do better without it. It was an improbable Jack Cohen who took up the gauntlet, personified as a life-sized modern St George slaying the 'robbing people monstrously' RPM dragon.

The price maintenance case: 'unless one has constant prices the goods deteriorate because prices go below economic levels' was hideously flawed. Its days were numbered when Edward Heath's resale prices bill passed through Parliament in 1964, despite furious resistance from manufacturers, most notably the confectioners Cadbury and Rowntree Mackintosh. Cohen's reputation as the poor shoppers' champion vaulted, and his Tesco traditional 'pile it high, sell it cheap' message was given a highly visible fillip. He had revolutionized retailing, giving it 'the green light for the most intensive retail development the country has ever seen'. But sadly Jack Cohen's Tesco was a lot less well positioned than most of his competitors to exploit the undoubted strategic market opportunity.

Leslie Porter's energies at the Cheshunt headquarters had at last begun to instil some business order into the wayward concern. Home and Wear development provided some necessary Tesco product growth, often at rather better margins than their range of foods could command. But Tesco was incapable of reaching the standards set by a confident Sainsbury's, which was moving from quality high-street locations into purpose-built new southern supermarkets. In the north, Asda was meanwhile building its mammoth stores and selling at low prices. The two challenges magnified the Tesco problem. Tesco now had margin and food-quality issues on their hands simultaneously. With no food reputation, Tesco were forced into an ill-considered push for margin improvement through higher consumer prices. Everyone could now see this as the beginning of the end – Cohen's classic trading methods eroded by profit requirements. A decision had been made to use trading stamps in Tesco, defying the agreed policy UK retailers had taken together. Cohen defended his decision to jump ship, saying merely that 'stamps seem to be what shoppers want, so we will be here to provide them'. It enabled the Tesco driving imperative for growth in an expanding market to push ahead.

Stamps were one growth engine through the late 1960s and 1970s, and the first steps to building Tesco's own-label brand was another. As with store appearance, however, there was no attempt to build quality into the brands and in retrospect they were probably lucky to adopt two unknown names (Golden Ring and Delamare) for the nondescript new ranges. They were well below Sainsbury's equivalent, and performed badly. But Cohen was back on the buying trail once again, this time acquiring, with his own unfathomable business logic, the chain of Cadena Cafés. This was followed by 300 Victor Value stores, not an altogether happy purchase either, but one which took Tesco's complement to over 800 UK stores. Sadly, most provided a pathetic shopping experience, and many of these stores would disappear in the years ahead.

Cohen, reaching his seventieth year, was knighted for services to retailing in 1969 and, thoroughly against his will, relinquished the Chairman's role to become Life President – a predictably futile attempt to put the boss out to grass. Yes, younger people had to be given their chance, said Jack, but like St Augustine he went on, 'Not yet, oh Lord!' The endless boardroom bickering continued, now to be joined by a new player, Ian MacLaurin, from Malvern College, who had been taken on by Jack in a pretty informal way as the very first Tesco management trainee. While sales doubled in the first half of the

1970s, profits deteriorated. Kreitman – who had returned – resigned once again and was succeeded by Porter as Chairman and then by MacLaurin as his Managing Director. Were the pair of them capable of sorting the Tesco problems out, particularly with the irrepressible father figure, Jack, still hovering in the wings?

THE NEW TEAM – CHECKOUT

Tesco certainly had a battle on its hands. By the mid-1970s the risk of collapse was staring it in the face. Its real prices were higher than its cut-price reputation persuaded customers they might be. At the same time, Tesco quality – always known to be poor – was actually much worse than any perceptions. Tesco was between a rock and a hard place. Cohen's unique intuitions, his dealing ability and buccaneering tactics had reached the end of the road. Radical reform was needed and it would clearly take time. Few aspects of Tesco's strategy or operation did not need comprehensive overhaul. The board had concluded – after lengthy deliberation, uncompromising advice from strategic consultants (and further bouts of the well-known brand of all-in-the-family wrestling that was a known feature of Tesco corporate behaviour) – that it should relaunch the Tesco business. It decided to base this on a consumer re-presentation to be called 'Checkout', which was intended to make the Tesco offer inherently more competitive and better value. It would use the revenue from the elimination of trading stamps to pay for worthwhile price reductions. Checkout was a marriage of inspiration, strategy and good luck – well timed but, importantly and unusually for Tesco, brilliantly executed. It was a watershed in Tesco fortunes and destined to take the market by storm.

The targets for Checkout were to bolster Tesco's market share and strengthen poor customer and store loyalty, by improving the company's appallingly weak brand image and store delivery. The speed at which a good response came from customers genuinely surprised the new team. Ambitious targets had been set but most were achieved with a lot to spare and soon they were operating at twice the levels of growth at which Checkout had been targetted.

The nature of the challenge moved. From making market share gains and improving its customer reputation, Tesco now needed effectively to service unanticipated high-store throughput. With their notable lack of systems, this was not easy. While Tesco's initial results from Checkout were outstanding, there was genuine doubt – among suppliers, competitors and in the City – whether Tesco logistics and distribution competences were robust enough to sustain initial gains. Sainsbury's response, 'Discount 78', took time to materialize and did not stop Tesco momentum. A new competitive phenomenon, offering substantive customer choice, had arrived in the market; one which was not to disappear for years to come. The home team had successfully arrived at first base.

RESPECTABILITY – PROGRESS THROUGH THE 1980s

It was now possible to plan ahead – a management luxury Cheshunt had never previously enjoyed. A cadre of new functional directors, all professional managers, were put in place (Malpas, Gildersleeve, Tuffin, Darnell). They worked as a cohesive team, setting out to integrate new, consistent approaches. Nothing like this had been seen before in the intensely pragmatic and self-help Tesco culture. Tesco implicitly obeyed Cohen's price-slashing maxims, but operating in an administrative fog meant they rarely knew which prices were being cut, by how much or where. Enterprising store managers had followed their hunches, personal initiative being rewarded in a bravado culture. Tesco had to impose uniform policies for a range of operations – smacking of central control that would transform the way it did business. Managers had resisted control as a matter of course. Now, in short order, systems for: pricing, stock planning, suppliers and the product range, buying, own-label performance and quality, and importantly even management training began to be established. Laissez-faire was dead and gone – MacLaurin, Malpas and the Tesco team knew it. Fortunately, results went on pushing steadily ahead.

Strategy, marketing, systems, a new approach to learning and training – all contributed. But the crucial Tesco problem was its ragbag of stores, lacking character, most of them too small and quite unbelievably scruffy. They were of no real help in fighting the new supermarket battle, but equally they could not be upgraded overnight. Firstly, Tesco simply didn't have the cash. New and good sites were hard to come by, and would be competed for tooth and nail by all their rivals. MacLaurin confronted two sides of a store conundrum. He needed the new quality sites to take on Sainsbury's, Asda and the others. He had to eliminate the disgraceful physical assets that were carrying the Tesco flag and destroying its still recognizable price-fighting reputation. MacLaurin had no choice – sort out the stores or pack up your tent.

Again a considerable reversal in style took place. The characteristic Tesco attitude where it bid for and secured a new site was to ignore planning regulations. Regulations from wherever they emanated, like all kinds of rules, were regarded by Tesco as a nuisance. Sometimes a retrospective fine might result, but it was worth paying these for a quiet life. Pragmatism of this sort naturally did not endear Tesco to the planning authorities, who began to use the only weapon they had – withholding building permission. Noisy fights on appeal broke out regularly with Tesco being known as the most cavalier and irresponsible of the operators.

Porter and MacLaurin set out to rid themselves of their cowboy reputation, and started building relationships with local authorities and the planners who controlled the pace of expansion. This helped the company from the 1980s onwards to build a coherent and attractive store base, establishing Tesco as a quality entrant, particularly in the new, big out-of-town superstore sites that were especially attractive to the UK's universally car-borne shoppers. While Tesco started a long way behind Sainsbury's in penetration, and below Asda stores in size and quality, an evolutionary policy was adopted, creating a base for expansion and a reputation for size and quality in a rejuvenated business. From being at a scale and size disadvantage to Sainsbury's, Tesco were able to catch up and eventually even to begin thinking about moving ahead.

Respectability had arrived. The signs of change were all around and Tesco had a new and different feel. Many reforms were recent, and there remained doubts as to their durability. It was inconceivable to view Tesco as a potential leader but after Checkout there were times when the Tesco market share was indeed bigger than Sainsbury's. Tesco were a decent second and committed to getting ahead. A big difference was the conversion to team management under MacLaurin and Malpas. They maintained the Tesco reputation from Cohen's days of being open-minded willing listeners, experimentalists, open to supplier initiatives, prepared themselves to try novel approaches. This was very different from the autocratic, command-and-control style so brilliantly operated by Sainsbury's. The suppliers were never in any doubt that they liked Tesco better. But they had always known that Sainsbury's on the other hand would make things work. Now if only Tesco could compete on this dimension ...

CONSOLIDATION AND MATURITY – THE LATE 1980s

So while there were still questions, the change was that Tesco was providing good answers. Cohen's harum-scarum acquisitions policy was replaced by cool strategic appraisal of what was available. Victor Value was sold to Bejam for £5.3 million and an ill-starred Irish foray, 'Three Guys' was called off. Tesco's store requirements were clear. 30,000 sq ft with flexibility, and Tesco-branding, together with the classless warmth that was individual and could compete with the best Sainsbury's or a rejuvenated Safeway offered. By 1987

Tesco was ready to make a hostile purchase of Hillard, a north-eastern concern that everyone suspected would, in any case, fall to one of the majors. Tesco paid £228 million for Hillard, and with a big boost to morale, beat out Sainsbury's in the process. The integration of the 40 Hillard stores was efficient, a feather in Tesco's commercial cap, a sign of the company's growing maturity. It gave it confidence for future acquisitions. The company was flexing its muscles, perhaps, for the first time, embryonically aware that market leadership might one day be an achievable vision but that organic growth per se might not be enough to make it happen. Leadership still seemed a very long way off.

In marketing too, the company began to refurbish a tarnished image. Own label had always been the feeblest of propositions in Tesco, and was never seriously regarded by manufacturers such as P&G, Unilever, or Mars. That Tesco has retained an attitude of open-mindedness about manufacturers' brands is well recognized. Nevertheless a programme of systematic upgrading and innovation with the Tesco brand was to produce increased reputation and rich rewards through the 1980s, with the Tesco own-label share moving steadily to 40 per cent of their sales. This share increase may substantially be attributable to the food manufacturers' own weakness in not exploiting their own research and development programmes with enough determination, so leaving the centre ground to retailers, particularly of course to the newest of the contenders, Marks & Spencer.

INNOVATION IS GIVEN ITS HEAD

One unexpected example of initiative was Tesco's precursor adoption of the Healthy Eating programme in the mid-1980s. This had been an area characterized by inertia, where preserving scale economies and the brand status quo drove increasing internecine market arguments. Tesco decided to take the bull by the horns and implement an ingredients' labelling approach which took competition, the main food companies (Unilever, Nestlé and Heinz) and indeed the civil servants in the Ministry of Food unawares. Their astute early reading of consumer opportunity was then followed by the rest of the market in double quick time. Other European markets had made significant progress and Tesco reasoned, correctly, that the UK consumer was ready for it. Perhaps most relevantly, it established Tesco alongside Sainsbury's, Waitrose, and even Marks & Spencer as a company capable of taking seriously food quality and aspirations where nutrition is concerned. New ground was being broken – this was a league in which the company had not hitherto played.

Tesco then followed this in 1988–89 by a second, even less predictable initiative. Of major UK retailers, Tesco might have been viewed as perhaps the least likely to promote environmentally-safe or green initiatives. The company's profile had always been more downmarket and price-dependent than Sainsbury's or Safeway, and there was a sense, a residue of the Cohen generation's hoopla and razzmatazz, that the Tesco stores' offer, while invigorating and entertaining, was less considered and rational than that of many competitors. In fact, this issue was handled with moderation and maturity, noticeably devoid of the more extreme environmental preaching that had been seen in German retailers through the 1980s. For Tesco it was a reputation-building initiative, achieving high levels of promotion and editorial comment ('the greening of Tesco'). In future, Tesco would make social customer propositions with a lot more confidence and at the same time be recognized as the first to make them happen.

Unsurprisingly then, we arrive in 1990, with MacLaurin's Tesco team in fine shape, and self-belief rising visibly. On turnover up by more than 50 per cent over the three years to 1990, profits had more than doubled, and operating margins had passed the 6 per cent barrier. Tesco was achieving volume growth of more than 3 per cent, adding space at almost 10 per cent and delivering solid value growth increases year on year. By any standards these were handsome results, a tribute to the Tesco management's abilities to ride a strong growth market. The company was entitled to regard itself as one of the strongest long-term growth players and the stock market rating was responding very positively. Perhaps the only modest dissatisfaction might be that, despite all their efforts through the decade, and a rapidly rising market share performance (to 10.5 per cent by 1990), the business lagged permanently, or so it seemed, behind its long-established rival, Sainsbury's, who had itself seen its market share rise strongly in the late 1980s. Indeed, looking at the market at the time it is hard to find a loser, since from lower starting points Safeway, Asda, and Kwik Save all registered market share increases. The Co-op, a sliding Gateway, and an endemically weak independent sector are the only visible losers through this period.

The *Guardian* put it best: reporting Tesco's 1990 results it noted that:

> a decade ago Tesco was the modern equivalent of a music-hall joke. But now it is Tesco which is laughing – all the way to the bank … at the end of the seventies Tesco began discarding the 'pile it high sell it cheap' philosophy on which the chain had been built … then it discovered what much of British industry has been learning; that people are often prepared to pay for better quality, are often more concerned with service than with price and there's often more profit in worrying about quality and service than in bribing customers with low prices. The transformation of Tesco is a remarkable success story.

> (Powell, 1991)

Remarkable it had been, but the transformation was not complete; there were some important hurdles ahead.

MACLAURIN'S TEAM – A STRONG BOARD

By 1990, it appeared Tesco had depth of management experience at the top level – a platform from which to move forward again. Perhaps the best place to start is with the leadership team that was by then in place. Ian MacLaurin, knighted in 1989, had led the Tesco board for more than 10 years. His principal contributions have to be recognized at human levels and it is the establishment, leadership and development of the Tesco team that will be seen as his lasting achievements. David Malpas, at MacLaurin's right hand throughout, was the planner, strategist and the man responsible for making Tesco marketing a force with which to be reckoned. Malpas was the strategic thinking power in Tesco's renaissance, but he too could point to concrete and substantial market place achievement. With the help of seasoned campaigners such as John Gildersleeve – originally Marketing, latterly Trading Director – and David Reid, an experienced financial head, Tesco had a committed team that was experienced, had 10 years together and perhaps most importantly was at the same time listening to their own people and to the market, but capable of speaking with one voice. The same could not be always be said for all their competitors. Tesco also, perhaps alone of the big four, was beginning to create its own long-term succession; it had the reputation of wanting to attract good young people and of giving them room to develop when they were brought aboard.

THE EARLY 1990s – CAN TESCO GO ON GROWING?

However, the early 1990s were not plain sailing for the industry or indeed for Tesco. 1991 and 1992 were bleak trading years and the early figures for 1993 again showed they were losing customers vis-à-vis their 1992 levels. It is a little appreciated truth that it is often just at the time when confidence is highest, when strategies seem most clearly established, and when the track record of success stretches back for longest that implementation of change may be most required. There were talks of a crisis at Tesco, and those same City analysts who had been the strongest of backers now started to become more dubious, suggesting that Tesco and MacLaurin personally, after almost

20 years, were 'losing the plot'. Did Tesco have a strategy to respond? There were widespread doubts.

The doubts were well founded. For most of 15 years, Tesco had pursued a single-minded and winning strategy. It had been able to move steadily forward from the days of 'pile it high, sell it cheap' and a reputation for tactical thinking that verged on sharp practice. The combination of improving demographics among its shoppers, credible own-brand development, and high-quality out-of-town superstores had altogether changed the face of the Tesco organization. But 'catching up is hard to do' and the fact remains it was still cheaper and seen as cheaper than Sainsbury's, its image was better but still lagging, and by 1992 it seemed policies to correct the balance had reached something of a dead end. The Tesco profile was younger than Sainsbury's, but it was also less educated, less aspirational and less well off. It had hit a brick wall, having got as close to Sainsbury's as the present approach could. Redirection was needed and, given the recession, needed fast.

THE EARLY 1990s – NEW LEADERSHIP AND NEW STRATEGIES

In response to this decline, research was undertaken to throw light on the reason for the fall-off in customer numbers. It showed Tesco customers wanted innovation, but they also wanted better value and better service as well. The plan to carry this out became the responsibility of Terry Leahy, the Marketing Director. The significant programme of innovation that Tesco now put in place under his guidance was as important to the health of the business in 1993 as Checkout had been in 1978. The day of opportunity had arrived for Leahy earlier than expected. The headline of the innovation drive was simply to create better value and better service. As with many retail initiatives it was not a single 'home run' advantage that the team generated. The components were:

- Tesco's new 'value lines', key to operating in the recession;
- the 'one in front' cut-the-queues initiative;
- a positive approach to new store formats and sites, eg Metro, where Tesco led the way;
- the loyalty card launch (see 'The Pursuit of Loyalty' on page 39); and
- further aggressive pursuit of the non-food profile.

These were concrete initiatives that were, in sum, to prove critical. Tesco had used consumer research in a salutary way, to determine the nature of the problems the business faced but to map a forward direction as well. These customer panels have now become an organic part of the Tesco forward development process – there is one taking place in an area of the country every working day now, and the learning potential of these sessions for the business has been enormous.

Tesco took the recessionary market of the early 1990s with pinch-hit singles which got their business moving. Service advantage was at the root of the change. In retrospect, it is astonishing that others allowed Tesco to appropriate unique service advantage – but they did. Cheshunt were engaged in root and branch overhaul, while the main competitor was 'off the boil', apparently uncertain about how to take an era of undisputed leadership forward, without a strategy that produced innovations, and lacking the focussed operational lead present through most of John Sainsbury's years, of single-minded hierarchical control. Tesco remained true to its heritage of low prices so critical in recessionary periods. Value Lines in 1993 would, in due course, be succeeded by the 'Unbeatable Value' approach on 600 lines in 1996. Although reluctant to lead any wholesale market reduction in margins, the well-established consumer value profile was known to be a key contributor to Tesco's ongoing growth.

Despite the problems that had been agitating the City, Tesco's long-term market share had gone on rising – by 2 points in the five years from 1989. The reason was the store opening programme, with at least 30,000 sq ft of floorspace, and flexibility to increase beyond; Sainsbury's had a more conservative policy. Tesco was still opening 30 stores a year, in what was to turn out to be a forward-thinking approach, with attractive designs both lively and warm, and while their personality lacked the consistency of Sainsbury's and the prestige of the best Safeway or Waitrose, they were personable and increasingly classless – a social parameter that the new meritocratic people at Tesco had cleverly identified as important. It was the world they came from, that they understood, a message classically right for its time. 'We should aim to be classless, to provide the best shopping trip, to be the best value ... to remain relevant by responding to changing needs ... the natural choice of the middle market by being relevant and serving them better ie customer focussed' (Mason, 1996). It was a strong and different message.

Meanwhile relationships between Tesco and the Tory ministers were now good. It was well known that MacLaurin supported Conservative thinking, and shared a consuming interest in cricket with the Prime Minister. It was therefore a source of genuine surprise when the eager and determined Environment Minister, John Gummer, began a planning initiative which, in 1993, for the first time, set out to arrest the out-of-town shopping phenomenon on which most of Tesco's growth had been built. The laissez-faire performance of

British planners had been a singular exception to the European norm, entirely at variance with the dirigisme of France, and other developed European practice. Few now doubted the need for some control. But the move took the Tories away from Thatcherite free-market thinking which viewed high-street communities as apparently irrelevant. Through the 'get on your bike' – or get in your car – 1980s, it had looked as if they did not have the stomach to make the change. Tesco and others thought the new policy was unnecessary market interference. But in truth it was late in the day to be considering the role of the high street – the policy die had been cast long before the new law was placed on the statute book. While the Tesco property team in particular were well placed, with a solid 'land bank' of sites – that others did not have – from which it could continue expanding, everyone in retailing could see that that life had changed, and in their terms, not for the better.

INNOVATIONS FOR A NEW REGULATORY ENVIRONMENT

Tesco acted at speed to convert change to the highest measure of competitive advantage. While mounting a committed policy defence of out-of-town super-stores in public statements, and improving access and service through the provision of low-cost or free public transport and more parking, Tesco backed both horses, quietly recognizing that the planning change might be necessary and, if it was, would represent a watershed for the industry. If government felt the high streets were capable of renaissance and if, as seemed possible, even the mighty car's days were numbered, they would listen to the signals. They had begun to open high-street stores; the first, in June 1992, called Tesco Metro being in Covent Garden. The wheel was turning, with a vengeance. Leading a modest reversion to 1950s shops was the industry's principal inno-vator. Of course these were not the old all-purpose counter stores – changes had happened in the interim and there were major superstore sites where the family shopping was done. But the new Metros were a sign of changing times, and represented attractive opportunity for new Tesco to create designs that enhanced urban shopping experience. Tesco's reputation had moved ahead again and the change was not confined to urban high streets. As the years passed, Tesco modified its approach to out-of-town shopping and, for the country or semi-rural high street, provided a new Compact store. Once the petrol forecourt offer was in place, a new 'Express' format offered a selection of foods to the car-borne shopper paying for petrol. Gummer's PPG6 had halted the drive out of town.

Opinions differed as to how permanent this might be, and already decades of laissez-faire meant two-thirds of food was bought out of town. But Tesco was positioned for change were it to happen, and in so doing could be seen as a good citizen as well as the keenest of business innovators. Innovation was not confined to store format. The recession showed consumers were again getting anxious about prices. The proportion of food spend in the family budget had been declining for years. Tesco led the industry's move to reputable but tightly priced generic lines, confidently branded Tesco but with lower prices. Value lines came later. If the market needed lower prices, Tesco knew where its roots lay. Recognizing the primacy of value to the consumer, it would be there to provide it. The speed of the move was impressive and helped to stunt the arrival of the new 'hard' discounters at birth. At the same time Tesco possessed a diversified consumer base, ripe for experiment, and this encouraged it to try out longer shopping hours, new product areas and ultimately distribution methods – often ahead of competition. Alongside a retained reputation for value and a recognizable focus on service, Tesco was making innovation a source of ongoing advantage.

Simultaneously, Tesco moved to decrease dependence on foods, through extending home and wear (and specifically the Items brand) – non-food areas with volume and good margins – home entertainment, eg CDs, where for too long the public had waged ineffectual war against cartel prices and overblown margins. The price promise was made a prominent feature, and Tesco value was promoted in growth sectors such as sport and home leisure (Leisureworld). With more and more bravado, Tesco (along with Asda) took on the manufacturers of specialist branded items who were selling at ludicrous margins. For example, in clothing, big names such as Levi and Nike have been openly challenged by Tesco cut-pricing. Fresh and chilled foods continue to provide the main focus for product development, and service counters are becoming a feature of the new stores in many of the formats including Metro. It was a delicate balancing game – enhancing quality and good service, while maintaining a price position with a sharp cutting edge – a bridge that Tesco appeared now well able to straddle.

The Tesco approach to consumer marketing was growing up. For too long it felt it was in the shade of the vaunted expertise of the consumer goods' manufacturers, with their fleets of well-versed marketing and brand managers. Now, with a record of innovation and clout of their own, the baton was passing to the retailer. All but the best of the consumer marketing companies were to find marketing initiatives wrested from their grasp by retailers happy to fill an innovation vacuum with their own ideas for products. Their capacity for innovation was significant – annually Tesco can introduce 5,000 new and relaunched lines – and the size of superstore ranges (say 30,000 items) with the speed of measuring success meant that the branded manufacturer was often left uneasily off the pace. The weaker and soon the majority of these proud companies even turned to making products for the chains – the distributor's own brands. An astonishing reversal of fortune has been accomplished, nowhere more visible than in the market for foods. It is clear today; food development initiative lies with the best retailers, the most influential having been Marks & Spencer, once famous as Britain's leading clothing supplier. Tesco's own-label has certainly prospered, and while its store loyalty remained well below Sainsbury's, its pace of growth was fastest in the market by 1996–97.

MARKET LEADERSHIP

Leahy's new managers were a confident breed, their capabilities nowhere better demonstrated than with the new Tesco Clubcard launched in 1995. It had been clear for some time that loyalty cards made sense and that costs could be paid for by increased consumer volume, but longer term it was the profound strategic grasp which information from a recordable and manipulable consumer data stream that really mattered. Tesco did not invent the card nor were they first mover, but in retrospect they executed its introduction bravely and brilliantly, getting the timing right, stealing and – to their great surprise holding – the initiative away from Sainsbury's, attracting wide visibility, and having banks of Japanese-style churning (regular repeated innovating) improvements ready as competitors reacted. The extent of Tesco's advantage with loyalty cards surprised everyone.

THE PURSUIT OF LOYALTY

'I don't want loyalty. I want *loyalty!* I want him to kiss my ass in Macy's window at high noon and tell me it smells like roses. I want his pecker in my pocket' (Halberstam). Tesco is one of the most down-to-earth of companies but something more subtle and businesslike than this crude expression drove MacLaurin and Leahy's team when it voyaged purposefully into the brave new world of consumer loyalty cards.

In February 1995, Tesco launched the first national supermarket loyalty scheme. It was not cost-neutral and 1 per cent discount on purchases was the concrete proposition which it put on the table, but it talked at the same time of customer and store values and was couched in rich overtones of emotive persuasiveness. The card was envisaged as a way to re-create the relationship that the local shop had with customers 50 years ago (see Introduction, p 1 – A visit to the grocer's in the late 1940s). Tesco said simply and nicely in the language of every little helps that it was 'a way of saying thankyou to our customers', which indeed it was and was so perceived by hosts of grateful Tesco customers. In a real sense, however, it was not and has not been a loyalty card at all. It reimbursed customers for their shopping at Tesco, but the customers who intrinsically did best were not the most loyal, but those who bought the most – and by no means all of it necessarily at Tesco. Minimum entitlement thresholds have, in fact, been quite an issue and, under pressure, qualifying limits were lowered.

Not all its competitors shared the Tesco enthusiasm. Safeway had been there already, working quietly to develop its expertise for many years – I can remember Alistair Grant proudly telling me about this as early as 1992. Sniffily, down at Stamford Street, they called it 'a Green Shield Stamp way to offer value', and it is well known that the Sainsbury's ethic had always been pathologically opposed to such short-term and irrelevant inducements. Asda and Morrison were content quietly to watch from the sidelines but Tesco was visibly on to a launch that was a winner, an innovation that paid its way. Within a month they had 5 million card customers, and penetration increased by 200,000 households – a measured response that provides yet another irony. This is a case of new users growing the business, the very antithesis to repeat business, generating more custom from existing users or any increase in loyalty.

Tesco's management was genuinely astonished to be given so clear a field and could not believe its good fortune. When in 1996 the antici-pated Sainsbury's riposte (the Reward card) finally arrived, Tesco were armed with Clubcard Plus which landed on the market, not entirely by chance, on the very day that Sainsbury's launched Reward. Clubcard Plus was modelled on a Carrefour idea; consumers were encouraged to hold deposit accounts to earn 5 per cent interest in Tesco – a neat way of maintaining the innovation behind the card and building a retail banking brand through consumers who used Clubcard to pay for groceries. Gains in business were powering ahead strongly. Ten million members make Tesco the biggest loyalty card player, and a stated 'like-for-like' growth of 3 per cent was attributed to Clubcard. It appeared that Tesco was riding the crest of a wave.

However, the prime rationale for the card has yet to be realized. There were early signs, and they still persist, that the company fell victim to information overload in their customer data bank and few consistent signs yet that the card is able to take meaningful catalytic advantage of the one-to-one relationship that potentially exists between company and customer. As a behaviour driver, therefore, the Tesco loyalty card still has a process mountain to climb. 'There are huge virtual warehouses of information about customers, that just don't seem to be used,' said Robert Clark recently. The gap, according to Robert East at Kingston University, is the absence of demographic data about the customers. Researchers at the Added Value company confirm that the segmentation approaches that Tesco have so far been able to apply are too complex to make the findings usable – but they too know the marketing potential is enormous. As with all worthwhile innovations, the Tesco scheme has been widely copied and improved upon. Boots the Chemist is a case in point, their smart card a genuine advance, already a highly popular element in perceptions of sensitive and generous customer service. Sainsbury's, slow to start, have plunged in with a vengeance and Reward is both differentiated from and more heavily promoted and advertised than Clubcard.

What happens now is an absorbing question. The supermarket chain that everyone agrees has come closest to sorting out information application for consumers is still Safeway – it has targetted families with children successfully with its ABC card. However, even this successful tactic can be characterized as slow and steady single-shot warfare, when simultaneous repeat fire at a series of designated and evolving targets is what this weapon is capable of delivering. Will Tesco be able to innovate sufficiently and generate segmented consumer information that can give it this capability? Will Safeway have the resources and commitment to build advantage from its present narrow but genuine base? Tesco moved quickly and effectively to gain the initial advantage but three or four years later, the challenge is to create leadership of the process which it knows only too well it has not yet achieved. At its simplest, therefore, the question is – will it now create what it set out to achieve in the first place – a widely accessible and distinctive Tesco *loyalty* card?

Clubcard was a winner, growing to nearly 10 million subscribers. The Consumers' Association rated it emphatically a 'best buy'. From a platform where growth had outstripped the market, the 1995 sales gains were enormous. The William Low purchase, on top of growing volume, was enough to bring Tesco long-coveted market leadership by the end of 1995. The lead then widened in 1996, to two share points, £2 billion in sales, a not inconsiderable difference, equivalent to the entire sales volume at the time from Waitrose or Morrison's highly successful store chains.

ACQUISITION AND EUROPE

Tesco had timed Clubcard well, but performance had been further enhanced by the acquisition of William Low's stores at the end of 1994. Low operated in Scotland and the north-east and provided Tesco with 57 good stores which, with 45 in Scotland, doubled Tesco's share north of the border where it had traditionally been under-represented. Once again, Tesco beat off competition in the William Low purchase and had become a lot more expert in managing acquisition in the process. Moving Low to the Tesco format and brand were put in hand quickly, with synergies and rapid growth resulting. Overnight William Low became Tesco, Low service became Tesco service, the improvements were visible and Tesco had reaped the benefits.

The company had, in fact, been back on the well-known acquisition trail already. In 1994, Tesco achieved full ownership of 104 French Catteau stores, and it was clear that the company knew they needed a twin strategy of increasing domestic market share in the UK, while pursuing growth opportunities in Europe. Initially they went to northern France, a move that was not to succeed, since three unprofitable years later they had retired with a very bloody nose. It is not difficult to see that while France held significant prospects for Tesco, Catteau was marginal and difficult to manage for them. This was followed by a change of plan – a move to areas that perhaps Tesco could dominate, through a presence in the growing markets of central Europe. They took a stake in 50 Global shops in Hungary first, followed by purchases of interests in Polish Savia, and in Czech and Slovakian companies. MacLaurin, by now a member of the House of Lords and dealing with leadership issues in English cricket, told the author that he for one felt that the Eastern European move was better considered and had stronger strategic justification than had France – 'Tesco knows a lot which will help set up strong retail trading companies in a fast growing East – it's not dissimilar from the UK 20 years ago.'

Tesco had also strengthened its Irish presence, buying, at a price which at the time was felt to be expensive, Weston's ABF stores. The going has not been entirely smooth in Ireland, yet Tesco has handled the market well and is a leader. It is now moving faster than its national competitors outside the UK and if it gets even a majority of the decisions right, it can create an attractive future profits stream, and a hedge against declining long-term purchases of UK food and an often predicated loss of UK retailer margins.

It is interesting to note that as Sainsbury's moved west, Tesco, a follower in retail investment outside the UK, are moving east and south. MacLaurin is clear this was a result of strategic analysis. In the early 1990s, Tesco studied the potential of US purchases or alliances. They concluded that the good chains were too good for them to add value, and the bad were so awful they would have a battle on their hands to survive. Hence the move east. It seems to have left Tesco with the better forward options as the market turns global in the 21st century.

THE SEARCH FOR EFFICIENCY

Perhaps Tesco had again been lucky with timing, with the existence of the land bank, and had stolen another march. By 1996, the industry level of superstore openings was tumbling to the lowest level for years, barely above the 26 stores an ambitious retail trade had opened in 1986. The acquisition of Low moved Tesco's own openings up strongly in 1995, by which time they had 545 stores, many more than Sainsbury's. In 1996, however, the number of new openings scarcely moved. The tide had turned and energies now turned to re-equipping current stores to generate store traffic and efficiencies – where Tesco still had considerable room for improvement, against the best benchmarks, Sainsbury's best-performing stores.

This highlighted an area of endemic weakness that Leahy's new team needed to address. Huge strides had been made in two decades to catch a once impregnable Sainsbury's. The fact remains that by 1996, a riproaring year for Tesco and a poor one for Sainsbury's, Tesco still needed a third more space, 15 per cent more superstores, and contented themselves with sales per square foot that were 15 per cent worse than Sainsbury's in a bad year, and even below Marks & Spencer. This would become an issue of credibility for Tesco, and it was no doubt a compelling reason through the mid-1990s as Tesco continued to surprise the stock market with quality overall results, that Sainsbury's price/earnings ratio was rated consistently above the new market leader's. (This has now changed and the stock market has recognized it.) Tesco responded to the new challenge, taking the lead with initiatives in ECR (efficient consumer response), and ensuring that they expanded EDI (electronic data interchange) with suppliers. The core task was systems change, and store efficiency was becoming the crucial determinant. Though Tesco started behind, rapid progress to raise store densities was achieved: 4 per cent in one year 1996–97, over 20 per cent in five years. The performance gap vis-à-vis Sainsbury's was now beginning to narrow.

THE ROLE OF CUSTOMER SERVICE

Tesco's new Chief Executive noted, 'We cannot and do not rest on our laurels.' The provision of better customer service had Leahy as major architect, and is a challenge Tesco is happy to pursue. In 1997 he told me,

> This obsession with our customers, their needs, and how these must be changing means that you should not expect us to go on opening large edge-of-town superstores long after the need for new ones has passed. Expect … continual evolution: expect us to provide a mix of formats in different locations … to meet special needs of customers in each location.
>
> (Leahy, 1997)

This open-mindedness in the face of perceived future change remains Tesco's most engagingly attractive trait. To the author it has been a characteristic, holding Tesco together in both the best of times and the worst of times – compelling confirmation of business maturity, of a profound capability to cope with market upheaval. Open-mindedness can become sloppy thinking and lack of strategy, and Tesco needs to be watchful – but I see precious little evidence of this happening. Indeed the new guard seem as hungry, every bit as anxious as their predecessors from the Checkout days.

A further sign is its consumer mission: the view of the customer that drives Tesco forward. In overall terms, it wrote, prior to the launch of Clubcard,

> We should aim to be positively classless, the best value, offering the best possible shopping trip. This will be achieved by having a contemporary business and therefore one that remains relevant by responding to changing needs. We should aim to be the natural choice of the middle market by being relevant to their current needs and serving them better ie customer focussed.
>
> (Mason, 1996)

The signs were in 1997 that the service obsession is penetrating customer consciousness and that it is getting through in store. Listening plays a large part in refining the approach.

Overall, there had been through most of 1997 a decline in those shoppers who did the majority of their shopping in out-of-town superstores. Erstwhile Environment Minister Gummer's desires were apparently being fulfilled. However, Tesco's share of visits edged up to 13 per cent, with no competitor above 10 per cent for comparison. Tesco's traffic densities – sales per square foot – were still moving ahead with competition static. Total consumer spend had declined overall, and Tesco, indexed at 136 to the average (100) was below Sainsbury's 140, both well ahead of all others. Tesco shoppers were driving a greater distance so that Tesco drew half its business from shoppers living three or more miles from the store. Tesco store loyalty, aided by the card, was now matching the best benchmarks – recognition that the brand had genuinely strengthened. A further indication of the strength of the brand is to measure the positive reasons shoppers give for choosing a particular store. Tesco customers offer seven positive reasons while their competitors achieve, at best, around six. This confirms rich brand strength in a market where competitive positions can change quickly, but where Tesco is changing for the better.

1997 had, in any event, been a good year for the industry, and for Tesco. Significant new areas for product expansion were being staked out. Having established a major share of the petrol market by squeezing the industry's forecourt margins, the year saw the two big retailers challenging the banks, with Sainsbury's being the first mover. Shoppers at Sainsbury's and Tesco were quick to spot the advantages of banking while they shopped. They liked the competitive deposit rates too – so much so that Tesco misread demand and found servicing customers difficult. Perhaps what was most significant was that it was once again Tesco who had taken one of the key steps, using its Clubcard Plus to make its offer flexible and more attractive than its rivals. To all intents and purposes Tesco had used Clubcard to enter the bank-card market, and indeed it was not long before the Tesco Visa card was itself on offer at very competitive rates. Along with noticeably better deposit rates, it confirmed that Tesco and banking had come to stay. The well-known clearing-bank inertia only had itself to blame. As this book goes to print Tesco have announced a further interesting product range initiative – a move to market 'Tescooters' as a first move into the automotive market, where once again it seems dealer margins and complacency may be threatened by the more ambitious British retailers – another market opportunity ready for plucking.

If the high-street banks were not already worried, they must have seen the writing on the wall when the Labour government's new mass tax-free savings scheme, hardly a public relations winner, was targetted at increasing numbers of tax-free savers by encouraging them to make savings happen, not in the banks, but at their local Tesco or Sainsbury's. If new Labour had taken Tesco's interests to heart, it was no surprise when Tesco themselves announced their helping hand for Labour's Welfare to Work scheme by offering 1,500 new jobs to young people, the largest company-sponsored decision at the time. A new, more co-operative relationship had dawned and there were those who saw a link between Blair's new Labour and Tesco's classless society. Things had come a long way from Jack Cohen's maverick and independent-pricing stances, and the years of bad-tempered planning argument. Amazingly, Tesco were now a recognizable part of the new establishment. Substantial support for the government's Millennium Dome project at Greenwich, where Tesco is a keynote company contributor, was to follow.

THE DEVELOPMENT OF A NEW CULTURE

Events had changed in other ways too. Twenty years ago, the author attended a dinner of Lever and Tesco directors with Leslie Porter and Ian MacLaurin. Wives were present. As happened in those days, an intemperate and bitter Tesco argument had broken out late in the evening when a Lever wife confessed in reply to Porter's questioning that she 'rarely ever saw a Tesco manager in the store she used'. MacLaurin – a long way off from Leslie Porter at the other end of the dinner table – was hard pressed to defend Tesco practice and a graceful evening descended into utter and riotous disorder.

The 1997 report shows how far the business has travelled; sales have risen by a handsome 15 per cent, profits by over 10 per cent, the accent is firmly on the goal of first-class service and the means to deliver it – the institution of 5,000 customer assistants designed to offer customer service wherever and whenever it might be required. Earlier, Terry Leahy had spoken of 'a constant striving to improve our offer to the customer – you have to involve the whole business. You have to be very supportive of people, encourage them to take risks and that means accepting failure which is easy to say and hard to do. You have to be prepared for the failures as well as the successes in order to innovate.' In the intervening years, Tesco has aspired to be, and perhaps now is, a people business. Both the content and the tone of voice have changed out of all recognition.

Morale is high and the new team have the bit between their teeth. As he went off to run English cricket, MacLaurin felt his successors had a platform which might keep them ahead for a few years. Bright new faces had appeared on the board at Cheshunt: Tim Mason in marketing, a product of the Tesco management development process; Lesley James to run personnel – both of them Tesco managers with long service, each capable of a further 20 years on the board. They worked alongside people of deep experience like David Reid – a financial director who had piloted Tesco through many new developments and was ready to develop a range of other new global positions for them – and John Gildersleeve, a rough, tough character who knew products, stores and suppliers like the back of his hand. Under the 42-year-old Leahy's guidance, Tesco had contrived to manage its succession from the MacLaurin/Malpas era with confidence, a far cry from the rocky ride a young Ian MacLaurin experienced taking the reins himself 20 years earlier.

THE IMPORTANCE OF TEAMS

Ian MacLaurin's Tesco career began and ended with cricket. He is fond of relating how he joined. Already in possession of a job he was on tour with Old Malvernians and met Jack Cohen in the bar of the Grand Hotel, Eastbourne, where the Tesco owner was wont to have family holidays. Jack gave him his business card and a few days later 'out of curiosity … I wasn't really thinking of joining them!' MacLaurin met Cohen. The old man learned that he was already in a job paying £900 per year – a lot of money then. Jack offered him £900 for six months' work, saying, 'If I like you after that you can have £1,000 and a car.' The car was a clincher for MacLaurin, who joined Tesco as a first-ever management trainee. It was a misnomer, of course – there were no trainee managers and no training at the time. Tesco at that time would not have known what training was. Shortly afterwards he was on his way to became a store manager which is where on-the-job training really took place – in all the retailers – at the time.

MacLaurin was at Tesco for the critical years and was a witness to the major culture change that took place. His own management style is visible, straightforward and consensual – like a good cricket captain's. He concentrated throughout on team building, first internally and then externally. Internally, the quality of the board, and the steady development of Tesco's people capabilities and disciplines are among his significant accomplishments. It may not always have been the most knowledgeable competitor but it was certainly the most cohesive. But externally as well, in the relationships with planning authorities and the large store crusade at the end of the 1970s so critical to Tesco's future development, he was able to create inter-locking teams rather than antagonistic relationships. Tesco was one of the earliest to make supplier relationships capable of themselves being seen as joint team exercises. The best supplier teams, often those with young, go-ahead managers, uncluttered with the processes and constraints of the past, were some of the quickest to see the potential of shared information and brand/store strategies. The link between business and social and sporting team relationships was always pretty visible there too.

In the 1980s, Tesco had several strong sporting teams, including a mixed team of men and women golfers that were well able to take on the more universally male supplier company teams, and give them a good hiding in the friendliest of environments, where the supplier team – win or lose – generally picked up the tab. Suppliers queued up to escort the Tesco golf teams to exotic sun-drenched venues round the world, and were quite happy to be seen to lose on the course to the Tesco competition – which wasn't difficult – providing the orders remained big and the prices stable.

As he stood down to hand over to Terry Leahy, Ian – now Lord MacLaurin of Knebworth – was invited to take over the Test and County Cricket Board, a post for which he was seemingly well equipped. The challenge here is even greater than pre-Checkout Tesco – as he set off for Australia at the beginning of 1999 he knew that England hadn't won an Ashes series against Australia through five encounters. He felt that morale was a key element, however, and started to make changes pretty quickly; one of them, reputedly, being to insist that the players were moved to more presentable hotel accommodation, even if it meant he had to foot the bill from his own pocket.

Terry Leahy, MacLaurin's successor, took over in March 1997, at the age of 42, after a period of considerable innovation and success as Marketing Director. Educated at St Edward's College, Liverpool and UMIST, where he read management sciences, he is a modern business leader; has a serious, even scholarly appearance; and both archi-tecture and the theatre are two of his consuming interests. Of course Leahy has inherited a team culture, and his task will be to strengthen and deepen it which, I assess, he will have both the time and the incli-nation to do. Tesco marketing has come of age under his guidance and is now leading the industry. Leahy has given its marketing a hard, practical edge. Once again, it is customer service and the contribution marketers can make to its improvement that fire Leahy's passion. Consumer research and a culture that encourages new ideas from everyone also shows that Tesco has become a lot more democratic and developmental than it used to be. Of course, to create positive learning advantage from the Tesco team will take many more years of committed endeavour but one senses that Tesco do have it on their agenda, at the very top.

Leahy's Liverpool boyhood has made him into a committed, lifelong Everton supporter. 'That's the one thing at home that's mandatory,' he says. Tesco may be on to a winning business formula but its leaders seem to have an uncanny knack of picking the most daunting and uphill assignments where their sporting affiliations are concerned.

THE FUTURE

And the future? Tesco has come a long way, and was called by the *Financial Times* 'one of Britain's top companies' following 'astonishingly good 1997 results'. Excellent progress continued in 1998 and the position reached would 10 years ago have been surprising, 20 years before quite inconceivable. The industry Tesco faces offers tougher challenges ahead. Home shopping, where Tesco has a development in place, may render expensive sites redundant. Unravelling would be difficult. The food business is itself in decline. Capable competitors stand ready to move faster than Tesco – Marks & Spencer who have already set new standards for prepared meals, Sainsbury's with a century of food quality from which to build. Store efficiencies show Tesco still behind, and if the market now stagnates, the gap is one they may never quite make up. The acquisition record has been patchy.

Catteau has been sold to Promodes, a sign that Tesco has found advanced West European markets too hot to handle and that it is much too late into a mature European game, long dominated by French and Germans. Alliances will be hard to come by and competed for hard by the ever smaller group of world grocery retailers. The Tesco brand, though it has been well handled and has depths it could not have contemplated 10 years ago, is at best an embryonic plant. The management team, committed and willing to take risks to stay ahead, is not yet fully battle-hardened. Finally, Tesco will have to fight the next decade in a global industry, where there are seasoned players (Carrefour,

Ahold, Metro and certainly Wal-Mart) with many more years of transnational experience and learning than even an accelerating Tesco possesses. Tesco's renowned flexibility will be challenged as never before. While it has 20 years of managed change behind it and a sizeable lead on the home front, tomorrow's battles will be fought with new weapons demanding new skills, against competition it has not encountered before, and taking place a long way from Cheshunt's homely and convivial corridors.

Against this Tesco can now offer cultural cohesion and a retailing track record, over 20 years, second to none. It is a deserved leader, has held on, and has the 'feel good' factor strictly on merit. The City likes the Tesco story – one where volume gains, service quality and innovation pay for cost increases and at best flat margins. The store complement, approaching 600, is an advantage in a constrained UK market. So is flexibility through site expansion and format in town and country. Tesco has moved ahead to make Clubcard work, and building loyalty from a strong database is an encouraging sign. There are very clear signs today that it needs further initiative so it is probably to the further developments of the card and information-driven service innovation that it must now look. Leahy's service drive is practical and well understood by the people in his team. Teamwork at Tesco is visible: learning has moved ahead with speed, and internal promotion is now the norm – although there are still signs that vacancies at key levels are proving hard to fill quickly. Empowerment is no empty word at Tesco these days.

Externally, it is positive that Tesco is looking outwards and has opted for Europe and the developing markets of the Far East, which now look a better bet than the United States, and are certainly preferable to being stuck at home, waiting for the invaders to strike. But these are early days. There is a vibrancy and willingness to listen and learn in the Tesco process, which is rewarding internally and attractive to suppliers and prospective partners. The new team are mightily aware of the priority of the Tesco brand, and of the need for a much more precise definition of its genetic code. 'Every little helps' is a start and strengthening the brand essence is being tackled. If it is done well, it will be hard for more regimented or more marginal UK competitors to match Tesco's consumer story, though it does seem that sooner or later Sainsbury's must try. The harshest critics concede that Tesco, whatever its shortcomings, is unafraid of continuous change. The business deserves high marks for managing a succession from one strong team to another, and Leahy has a record as a credible architect of change. If success attends Tesco's future strategies, it will be said of it that, like Wednesday's child, it worked hard for its living, and I suspect that the teams that created this excellent company will be entirely happy to have this said of them.

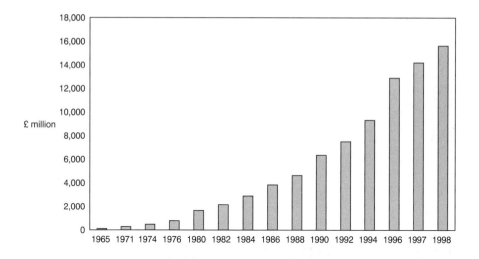

Figure 1.1 *Tesco sales 1965–98*

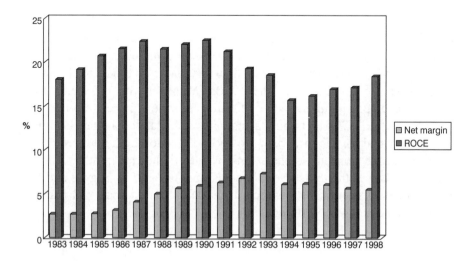

Figure 1.2 *Tesco net margin and return on capital employed 1983–98*

2

The Sainsbury's story

There's a divinity that shapes our ends,
Rough-hew them how we will.

Shakespeare, Hamlet

Sainsbury's is the doyen of British food retailing, an organization founded more than a century ago in the time of Gladstone's premiership. Throughout its long reign it set the standard for food quality and fresh produce, pioneering the self-service revolution in the 1950s. Managed for 125 years by a succession of powerful Sainsbury family chairmen, it became a public company in the 1970s. It is now a major British Public Limited Company (PLC), relegated for the time being to second position in the domestic food sector. However Sainsbury's has extensive related interests in other retailing areas, including both Homebase in the UK and, through its Shaw's and Star supermarkets, a significant presence in the affluent east coast US markets, which it first entered 15 years ago.

A COMPANY IN TRANSITION

Sainsbury's is unique in British grocery retailing. It is the story of one single family that spanned an entire century and more, and that became a dynasty and then an institution. From humble beginnings as a small store selling butter and eggs ('the best butter in the world' founder John James Sainsbury claimed), it went on to create a uniquely powerful food brand, and a retail empire that literally dominated UK self-service food retailing over two decades. Sainsbury's diversified into new retail markets at home, and entered the United States through the sophisticated east coast markets in the early 1980s. The story covers four Sainsbury generations and six family chairmen, but as a family history it was completed in 1997, following David Sainsbury's retirement from the board. Lord (David) Sainsbury of Turville's great-grand-father opened his Drury Lane store in 1869 – but in 1999 for the first time, 128 years later, there is no one named Sainsbury as chairman, and no Sainsbury sits on the PLC board. Does it matter? The retiring chairman, speaking to the *Financial Times* before he took office in July 1991, was quietly confident; he suggested, 'This is now a very highly professional business with very good managers. The success of the business isn't dependent on a fifth generation coming in.' His predecessor agreed with his cousin wholeheartedly – 'It doesn't matter if there's a Sainsbury at the helm. What matters is to keep the ideas and principles.' It had been ideas and principles that had taken Sainsbury's to a position of pre-eminence in British retailing, a unique place in the national psyche, influencing many British lives – a fascinating story.

Nearly 10 million customers visit its stores weekly. The company's early visionary thinking, its persistence with established values, and the consistent leadership that produced outstanding growth and profits over a century make this an unusually well-integrated enterprise. Surprisingly, and obviously painfully, the unthinkable happened and it has been forced to cede market leadership to a short-lived upstart of a mere sixty years standing. Today it is having to confront massive change, with less experienced hands at the wheel, and without much time to digest and plan. Yet Sainsbury's remains a modern colossus. Many consumers still refuse to believe it is not the supermarket leader, so often the case with once dominant ideas that have imperceptibly slipped. First floated as a public company in 1973, Sainsbury's today is a company in thoroughgoing transition. Whether it can command the new vision, strategy and differentiation to reposition itself again as national food leader in the domestic, not to say the world markets in which it competes remains to be seen. We are right at the beginning of a new chapter in the Sainsbury's story where its proud history is at best a hazy guide to future performance.

JOHN JAMES SAINSBURY – FOUNDER

John James Sainsbury started the business in 1869, his twenty-fifth year, with his even younger wife Mary Ann at his side. The chain's reputation for high-quality fresh food at low prices was established from the outset and remained utterly constant. John James displayed the message 'quality perfect, prices lower' on his stores in London and the Home Counties. The Sainsbury pair knew all about retailing focus. They were committed through an exacting working day to levels of hygiene and cleanliness that set tremendous benchmarks. Their butter, eggs, bacon and cheese set the product standards in the central London area – the street locations where the business began. John James knew about tight prices too, but it was quality that set Sainsbury's apart from the competition (Lipton, Maypole, Home and Colonial). Sainsbury bought direct from quality producers, but was able to extract lower costs from these same producers through his rising volumes. The *Financial Times* commented admiringly and not for the only time on 'this wonderful efficient distribution company, coming from humble origins'.

While growth slowed through the war years, by 1928 when John James died, he had built the strongest of foundations, turning over £6 million from just 182 provision shops. The competition needed 1,000 stores for sales just twice this amount. The seeds of Sainsbury's legendary footfall efficiency – number of shoppers and rate of purchase – were being planted. Meanwhile, the succession plan had been meticulously prepared, as all Sainsbury's succession plans were, and John James's son, having begun work for his father as a schoolboy, graduated to the position of right-hand man by the outbreak of the First World War. He himself was destined to run the trading business with equal success and consistency until a second world war was itself imminent.

THE FIRST MR JOHN

Under Mr John's guidance, Sainsbury's business quadrupled between the wars. He took the company into new locations outside London, moved the product range ahead into meat and packaged groceries, but his greatest achievement surely was to take the initiatives to build the first elements of the powerful Sainsbury's brand reputation. The enduring commitment to quality which John James had instilled as Sainsbury's birthright was the bedrock. Sainsbury's grew handsomely in London, where population itself was growing at twice the national rate, and expanded through acquisition into the Midlands.

No particular hurry ever seemed to attach to the expansion process. There was no conceivable prospect that the family could ever contemplate losing control of their unique company. So they took their time, adding what they called the new 'links in the chain' as good new sites became available. Choosing them was one favourite occupation of the chairman. Like his father before him and a generation of Sainsburys in their infancy or yet unborn, Mr John liked to be intimately involved in all the details of his company. It was an attractive, some might say, a necessary characteristic, and, again, of course, it ran in the family.

ALAN AND ROBERT SAINSBURY

John's son, Alan, a thoughtful and visionary future influence who could no doubt have done many things in his life, had joined the company in 1921, at the age of 19, 'because my mother said it would break my father's heart if I didn't!' For a time three generations were there together, underscoring Sainsbury's now enviable consistency. On John's retirement in 1938, the *Grocer's Gazette* described an 'empire of high class provision shops', noting the style of leadership as 'unapologetic dictatorship', a trait one might consider to be deep-rooted in Sainsbury family genes. So it fell to Alan, credited by many as the architect of the modern business, and his brother Robert to pilot the company through war years and into the self-service era. War curtailed growth – it was 1954 before turnover recovered to pre-war levels. Meanwhile, however, the new Sainsbury's leaders had been studying the US trends. They noted the rapid growth of the new stateside 'supermarkets' and the motor car's astonishing capacity to accommodate a week's shopping. Mr Alan believed the same idea might work in Britain and set out to find out if indeed it would.

But again, the leadership was patient and did not force the pace. In no hurry to convert the stores quickly, or to sell the full food range, the first self-service store opened in Croydon in 1950, and was a rip-roaring success. Yet by 1960, only 10 per cent of stores were self-service, a figure that by the end of the third Sainsbury generation's reign had still graduated to only half their stores. One visualizes strong-minded owners taking their time to think and to plan coherently, who believed if they offered quality and managed efficiently, time would be on their side. But the message was crystal clear. Sales and profits of the new self-service store were double those of the traditional counter stores which had served to grow the company uniquely through its first operating century. Conversion to self-service was one legacy of the period. A second was the appearance in 1959 of a new poster advertisement stating 'Good food costs less at Sainsbury's.' One hundred years and three generations had not altered the founder's proposition, but product quality and a growing reputation had enhanced its credibility and by 1969, when another John, (Mr J D as he was then known,) took over the reins, it provided a platform that left the company securely placed for a more competitive self-service era.

THE SECOND MR JOHN – THE MOVE TO PUBLIC OWNERSHIP

Yet again, Sainsbury's had found a leader with an intimate knowledge of grocery, a long apprenticeship in the stores, and the highest personal commitment to command Sainsbury's fortunes for most of a quarter century. John had joined the company in 1950, and the board in 1958. Ten years later his own first board of directors was to contain no fewer than seven family members, the newest his cousin David, a Columbia MBA, as Finance Director, and quite unlike cousin John in his approach. But in any case, for none of the Sainsbury's board was it 'business as usual' – radical moves lay ahead for the family business which were to change it out of all recognition.

Sainsbury's was opening as many of the new larger stores as it could afford, and now with a greater sense of urgency. By the 1960s the first signs of serious quality competition began to appear, improbably from a company in the north called Asda, who were themselves building massive stores to a clear formula demanding 40,000 sq ft of space. Meanwhile, much closer to home, Jack Cohen's unpredictable Tesco employed speedy and indiscriminate acquisition tactics to build a widely trumpeted national presence. To cope with the faster pace of expansion now required, the family decided to float a minor part of its equity – still, however, retaining 85 per cent of the shares in the family. It was the London Stock Exchange's biggest offering, and unsurprisingly was over-subscribed 34 times. Nearly one in four Sainsbury's employees applied for the share issue, and 1 million shares were set aside for them. 'It would in no way affect the control of the company, its established trading policy or its style and philosophy of management,' said John Sainsbury, announcing the flotation in October 1972. The offering was unfortunately timed, however, and the 1970s oil crisis saw the shares tumbling fast. Engagingly, Sainsbury's suggested that its stockholders should hold on, remarking that 'paper profits aren't real nor are paper losses!' The instruction was in fact correct. The business emerged from the crisis a lot stronger and much more cost-effective than before.

The 1970s were the start of a series of truly great years for Sainsbury's. Sales per branch doubled through the decade and sales per employee went up

25 per cent. In fact, though the *number* of shops declined, it was the efficiency of the new self-service conversions that created huge and cost-effective growth. But John Sainsbury's board was meeting restraint from a deeply irritating source – it simply could not get enough good new high-street sites. Never a man to mince words, J D observed, 'It was taking three years to get planning permission for a single new shop.' The battle for sites, both with the town planners and with Ian MacLaurin's reinvigorated Tesco, was now on and in earnest. Sainsbury's fought the new planning process tooth and nail, calling the planners' decision process, or in its view, lack of one, 'a vivid indication of a lack of identification with the consumer'. Sainsbury's uncompromising stance was a conceptual posture not to be lost on a new and very different cast of government that was arriving as the decade of the 1970s ended.

It is Tesco, its needs much more pressing, who is credited with first appreciating the store development potential that existed out of town. But if MacLaurin led, Sainsbury's were quick to follow and to make these new locations work. Cambridge in 1974 was one notable success, and it remains today a fine Sainsbury's store. Yet it was never part of the Sainsbury's plan to match the largest stores in size. Its average size moved ahead steadily to 18,000 sq ft but only eight stores exceeded 25,000 sq ft – very much smaller than a normal Asda. There are the usual signs of inherent family conservatism of wanting to make things work before venturing too far afield. New sectors were opened, such as delicatessen in 1971, clothing – with modest results – and bakery.

In 1980, however, Sainsbury's remained seemingly unconcerned about non-foods development. It stocked a mere 7,000 lines in total, many less than competition, attributable in essence to its profound concentration on food. Its ability to develop sales across a wide food range in its own brand was a uniquely impressive phenomenon. This added further efficiency, and built Sainsbury's market place reputation. Nearly half of Sainsbury's weekly shopping was from its own brand portfolio – a figure that had even the best worldwide retailers gasping in astonishment. Customers, increasingly persuaded by the store's growing reputation for the best food quality and control, appeared simply not to notice the limited range. Quality was emphatically preferred to width. In keeping with the Sainsbury's store image of the time, the Sainsbury's customers of the day knew exactly what they were doing. It was a formidable mixture.

Finally, Sainsbury's, in keeping with its evolutionary expansion policies, did not seek country-wide coverage. The market leader of the 1970s and 1980s remained insignificant in the north, and noticeably absent from the Celtic fringe. While it advertised for new sites, adoptions were steady, not hurried. The impression at the end of the 1970s was that Sainsbury's were a classically well-drilled regiment, with a firm hold on the more affluent customers, market shares that approached dominance in the prosperous south-east, an enviable own-brand reputation, and systems technology and cost-effectiveness at levels of best national and even world practice. Leadership stayed firmly in family hands, and the family knew what it was doing. This was a company that could stand comparison with the best food retailers in the world.

The launch of Checkout by Tesco could have been the first serious national price competition that Sainsbury's experienced. Timed deliberately to coincide with Jubilee promotions that Sainsbury's were planning, Tesco's abandonment of trading stamps – a novelty that had been consistently and scornfully rejected by Sainsbury's – and simultaneous aggressive price moves put serious marketing questions to Sainsbury's management for the first time. Sainsbury's had a further problem when industrial disruption threatened its supplies. That Tesco had at long last regrouped was regarded as a faint possibility, though the rather brash Tesco 'publicity coup' was downplayed by Sainsbury's management. Holding its fire, Sainsbury's hit back hard in January 1978 with 'Discount 78' – reducing prices on 100 key items by as much as 15 per cent. Sainsbury's achieved a 25 per cent sales increase over the previous half year, and AGB showed their share moving up two clear points to 10.8 per cent. Chairman John Sainsbury claimed Discount 78 was 'the most important marketing strategy since we established our unique own-brand range'. 'Don't play with the tiger' was the chairman's unstated but uncompromisingly militant message that Sainsbury's wanted Tesco and other aspirants to leadership to receive and digest.

EXPLOITING STRENGTH – THE 1980s

'Implacable' or 'immovable' were words competitors could apply to Sainsbury's. It did not court popularity with the industry, with government planners, in the media and emphatically never with suppliers, who were used to being starved of relevant information, but moved with wariness in awe of Sainsbury's formidable power to shift entire markets. Even for the strongest of their branded suppliers, Sainsbury's wielded a big stick. They felt they could take on the leading manufacturers, and brooked no argument when they failed to get their way.

One example was in the growing fabric softener market that was moving volume but not generating profits for the two key manufacturers (Unilever, and Procter & Gamble). It offered even worse profits for Sainsbury's, who holding the only worthwhile 'own-brand' had reluctantly to sell it at low margins because of brand-leader Comfort's 'simply unacceptable' high volume/low margin pricing. Sainsbury's buyers were given the charge of teaching this brand leader a meaningful lesson. Within a year, differentiated but legitimate pricing, and penal destocking and distribution policies had reduced Comfort's share in Sainsbury's stores by more than a half, while in other (non-Sainsbury's) stores, Comfort's share had continued to grow quickly. The move, against a manufacturer (Unilever subsidiary Lever Brothers) of formidable brand power and the deepest of pockets, was a sign of impending change to market power.

Implacability was a trait by which Sainsbury's were happy to be recognized. While Sainsbury's buyers and managers made few friends, there was little doubt through the 1980s who was starting to call the shots, and setting the pattern for increasingly uncomfortable negotiating sessions with the brand owners. Few holes in the company's defences could be detected. There were clear rules and procedures that might not be broken and adherence to rules was what John Sainsbury expected, and, wherever he went, was what he got. J D's regular but normally unannounced store inspections, sometimes landing by helicopter on the store roof, became a legend. If he liked what he saw, store staff were warmly congratulated. If he didn't, and J D was a man who knew what he wanted, they were left in no doubt where and when improvements would happen. After nearly 20 years at the helm, the leader's recipe was working well. Sainsbury's were perceived to be developing a stranglehold on the UK grocery scene. When paparazzi caught the new Prime Minister out shopping in Sainsbury's Cromwell Road store, a sense of natural and national harmony existed, supported by pictures of Mrs Thatcher with her Sainsbury's shopping trolley, full of Sainsbury's own brands. The Iron Lady wouldn't go anywhere else, would she? She knows what she's doing. Strength seeks out its equivalent.

J D's last five years in office are a profound tribute to an organization that unashamedly aspired to dominate, and left nothing to chance. J D had seen Sainsbury's transformed from a medium-sized, regional family business into the highest quality professional public company. The results spoke for themselves. Not only was Sainsbury's undisputed market leader, it held on firmly to all the market control levers. The Sainsbury's brand dwarfed retail competition, increasingly challenging the best that manufacturers' brands could do. The company's logistics, its systems and distribution effectiveness were well ahead of industry benchmarks. Costs were firmly controlled, and in all areas of cost-effectiveness, Sainsbury's was seen to be the business to beat. Pricing initiatives were frequently initiated by Sainsbury's competitors, who were more dependent on pricing advantage for their own growth. But they took these steps in the knowledge that if Sainsbury's did not like the pricing initiative, they might find themselves rapidly 'living on borrowed time'.

Brand manufacturers were no different – they were treated in exactly the same way. Even those with strong brands and open investment policies needed Sainsbury's powerful store disciplines to drive their growth. Sainsbury's was simply the biggest volume driver the market had known. Finally, Sainsbury's own staff were in no doubt where their own future lay. They belonged to a tightly managed and winning retail team. They could see for themselves in their own pay packets – and generous stock option schemes, fuelled by an upwardly mobile share price – that the future with Sainsbury's was indeed a bright one. Sainsbury's shop managers, trained in this relentless environment, if offered the chance of the same job with a competitor, even at a higher salary, thought carefully before accepting. Life was tough, hours were long, standards were uncompromising and home lives were limited, but it was a world that was comprehensible and rewarding, and anywhere else looked distinctly second class by comparison.

LORD SAINSBURY OF PRESTON CANDOVER – SCALING THE PEAKS

The Sainsbury's Annual Reports for the years 1987–92 are mystically predictable, and provided brilliant shareholder returns. Little ever changes in these reports, and when it does, it is to record yet another mountain scaled triumphantly by a group of happy Stamford Street climbers. Sales increases are always in double digits, with the best years simply staggering – 25 per cent growth in a maturing market, in two of these years. Profits are dependability personified. In no year do they drop below a 20 per cent increase on previous year's levels. Earnings per share (EPS) are a benchmark for the best British companies – only in J D's last year, 1992, does EPS drop below the 20 per cent yardstick the company appears to have set itself. In these annual reports, neat graphs portray ascending numbers, ascending higher and higher, leaving mortal competition gasping for breath. Well-informed investors at this time regarded Sainsbury's less as an important retail foods company, more as the market's well-oiled retail moneymaker. The reports are formatted with mechanistic efficiency to a recognizable formula, rooted in orthodoxy, predictable in its every aspect. The chairman features strongly, pictured talking to 'staff', 'a member of staff', 'a customer' and latterly even 'Len Such from Basingstoke depot' – surprisingly and individually named as a member of the team. Penetrating eyes glint at each of them. The chairman's comments are terse and to the point – describing measured achievement and apparently predestined progress. Questions do not arise. Sainsbury's price advantage (claimed as 2–3 per cent less than larger competitors) is restated as a litany. The 'leading retailer' produces the market's best margins, as one expects, and again as expected, provides the best computer technologies, backing the best logistic systems. Record share increases are a normal occurrence, but there are late signs (1991–92) that the going is getting tougher. 'Future challenge' and 'as competitive as ever' are phrases that begin to be used. Almost wistfully, the normally trenchant J D laments that 'innovations that we pioneered are now ... industry standards' – a harbinger of more embarrassing confessions to come. Was he, after 42 years, a little less confident than his all conquering demeanor suggested?

Nonetheless, J D's (by now Lord Sainsbury of Preston Candover's) final year was further tribute to an outstanding performance, with little visible sign of the choppy water ahead. True, sales were up only 12 per cent, poorer than previous benchmarks and EPS had actually dropped (to, sic, 17 per cent!) for a third year. Margins are a breathtaking 7.9 per cent – what do non-UK retailer readers make of this, one wonders? Return on capital at 21 per cent is 'good' but – aspiring price controllers and assorted busybodies please note – 'certainly not excessive'. Market share grows a shade, 20 new stores are as usual opened, including a Sainsbury's first in Scotland, and the largest in Southampton. What is more, 30 per cent of the UK is still out of reach of a Sainsbury's store – an opportunity for organic growth not available to competitors. The Sainsbury's brand ('better than leading brands') has more than 7,000 lines. UK suppliers, in a long look back to John James's policies, are happily still 'favoured'. Finally in this best of all worlds, customers have 'choice, convenience and comfort' at performance levels second to none. Sainsbury's staff, increasingly numbered as happy shareholders, know why they work in the finest of retail companies. Quite a valedictory in this the best of all possible worlds.

1992 – COUSIN DAVID TAKES THE REINS

Lord John handed over the company to his cousin David in November 1992. In more ways than one, the company had reached a watershed with his departure. David had been on the board for 25 years, yet, as it now seems, all hell broke loose as soon as he took over the reins. Sainsbury's fortunes experienced change, and the new chairman's six years were anything but easy. Why did so sudden and traumatic a change occur? Why does Fowler, a highly respected analyst, asking the question, 'Has the Sainsbury's chain, finally, turned the corner?' and outlining the cost of 'the 5 year loss of form in 1993/97' note the 'visible scars of under achievement' and still query whether there might be significant unrevealed damage 'below the waterline'? This is a reversal of fortune of quite unimaginable proportions. How could it happen and happen so quickly, with so strong a performer, and how too can loss of form endure for five whole years, indeed right up to March 1999 when the *Financial Times* headline is 'Sainsbury fails in drive to lift flagging sales'? This is the question that needs addressing, recognizing as Sainsbury's leaders have sensibly pointed out since time immemorial, that it is *long-term progress* that matters, and in a company of Sainsbury's size and longevity, five (six or even seven) years is a *remarkably short* time.

The change that took place with J D's departure was an enormous one. J D had established his commanding and investigative personality on the whole company, and his departure was bound to leave a huge vacuum. The new leader, though of the same Sainsbury generation, was a different character, broadly and humanely educated, an unashamed intellectual and in many eyes the essence of a modern business leader. While he was to be the sixth family chairman, he was never going to be capable of exercising the kind of control-and-command leadership that so many of his predecessors had done, and with so much obvious enthusiasm. The world had changed. Whatever happened, whatever happens subsequently, Sainsbury's in its turn was destined to change markedly.

CHALK AND CHEESE

Founder John James had six sons who all worked for the family business including the eldest, John Benjamin, chairman for 28 years. Then his two sons Alan and Robert worked as joint general managers together, Alan becoming chairman in 1956. Robert was then briefly chairman, before Alan's son, John D (later Lord Sainsbury of Preston Candover) was chairman from 1969–92. Robert's son David (Lord Sainsbury of Turville) then took over, retiring prematurely in 1998, a first-ever unexpected happening in the top echelons of management of the group. For a century-and-a-quarter, succession had been admirably managed – smooth, seamless takeovers through four generations, with polished results – providing their own ample testimony to the achievement of consensus through planning ahead and successfully organized hand over arrangements.

David, last of the family chairmen, said before he took over, 'This is a highly professional business ... its success isn't dependent on a fifth generation coming in.' But the latest succession was, by some margin, Sainsbury's least congruent or harmonious handover of power. Which is not surprising given the organic differences between David, a modernizer, and cousin John, a recognizable Conservative who has given substantially to the party and establishment causes, notably the Opera House – of which he was chairman – and the National Gallery's own Sainsbury wing. David is a bird of different hue. Now a Labour minister, he was a founder of the SDP (Social Democratic Party). The very richest of this rich family, he remains a democrat living in Notting Hill, gives substantially to charity from his whimsically named Gatsby Trust, has numerous perfectly classless interests and is eminently normal and approachable.

They are deeply contrasting personalities. John the autocrat created a precise organization with military level efficiency where his orders went at all times unquestioned. The approach having run its course could not continue and David's consensual style should have been a perfect antidote. He played the role of philosopher-king, subscribed to analysis, encouraged talk on an equal footing, and set in hand company-wide change programmes (eg the ill-fated Genesis.) The patient refused the medicine and widespread lack of confidence ensued. Sainsbury was seen to have taken its eye off both its market and the competition, and at times its new chairman's heart seemed elsewhere, which indeed it subsequently proved to be.

David accepted a job at the Department of Trade and Industry, handing over to Dino Adriano, the former Homebase CEO, with Diageo's George Bull becoming chairman. After many unfortunate new Labour industrial appointments there are hopes that David Sainsbury may yet play John the Baptist to Blair's leadership. But there is no love lost between the two Sainsbury cousins. John was dismissive of David's retailing abilities and, given his own painstakingly accurate in-depth knowledge, he must have been most difficult to succeed. David's own comment (recorded in the *Spectator* in May 1998) when asked whether John would be speaking in the Lords after retirement, was, 'Hardly ... after all he doesn't really believe in the right of reply.' This may show what he felt he had experienced as John's group finance director for nearly 20 years. John said in turn that it was immaterial if a Sainsbury was at the helm. 'What matters is to keep the ideas and principles.' Of course there is no doubt he was quite right to believe and say this and strong companies are those that believe in and possess both.

But Sainsbury's plc have learned a fundamental lesson the hard way. Company succession planning today is substantially trickier and needs more careful consideration than in the simpler days of Sainsbury's founder, John James, and his son the first Mr John.

We can recognize that the seeds of many of the problems faced by the new chairman were, with hindsight, apparent well before the last years of his predecessor's reign. In particular, for a team with a mission, a stated 'passion to innovate' John Sainsbury's company had been losing the desire, the capability to tackle new things and convert them to business advantage. The new leader himself understood this, as is clear from his contributions to the post-1992 annual reports where the case for innovation case is persuasively argued. In the 'Best Butter in the World', published in 1994 for the 125th anniversary, David Sainsbury outlined the case for 'consistent values ... with a passion to innovate'. The innovations in recent years, though numerous, are either minor in scope (innovative architecture, reduced fat products, energy efficiency) or relatively undifferentiated (customers' changing tastes, staff opportunities, extended hours). There is a sense in which Sainsbury's seems to be listing formal competences with no passionate belief in their relevance. Alongside the approaches to innovation, it was at the same time losing the ability to deliver in a much more competitive market. This was a once great family enterprise, now a huge public company that had, compared to its distinguished past at least, simply lost its cutting edge.

COMPETITION – THE SAINSBURY'S RESPONSE

A key factor was the competition in the market. Through J D's later years as chairman, Tesco under MacLaurin and Malpas's leadership was for the first time becoming a coherent force. In 1993, stung partly by City criticism of recent performance and doubts as to whether progress could be maintained, Tesco decisively nominated its own succession, some years before MacLaurin's retirement, and remitted Leahy to redefine Tesco's increasing competitive advantage. Given the radical change that was happening at the top in Sainsbury's, the Tesco timing could not have been better. It was followed by spirited redefinition of service advantage, important innovation (Clubcard), and a major acquisition (Low) all of which caught Sainsbury's new management on the run. Tesco also hoarded a sizeable 'land bank' which when the boom was lowered by 1993 legislation, provided once-off structural advantage against Sainsbury's. Elsewhere, in 1990, Archie Norman took over Asda, redefined strategy and, using enlightened management alongside a well-crafted City story, restored Asda to its 'value' heritage. Tesco and Asda were hot news in a market where Sainsbury's was collecting its thoughts and re-creating strategy. In essence, Sainsbury's was doing little more than marking time. Some of David Sainsbury's own actions, it must be said, did not help his cause. His failure to land William Low should be forgiven – if Sainsbury's had wanted Low, it was the outgoing chairman's responsibility to ensure this was poised to happen. The reverse was true – MacLaurin had the ball in Tesco's hands. The move to take a major holding in Giant Foods (United States), a very bold one looked at now, was confirmation of a long-accepted US strategy at Sainsbury's, designed to create geographic scale, and generate world-scale learning. The unavoidable impression was that David persistently believed in the US supermarket. Subsequent events, ie accelerating US retail consolidation, show now that he may well have been right. The abrupt 'dismissal' of loyalty cards – painfully retracted – was unfortunate, and Sainsbury's has had to eat its words. Finally, for a company that prided itself on the best logistic systems, the moves to a new stock replenishment procedure ('Sabre') in 1993 was temporarily at least a disaster, causing business damage and a distinct loss of confidence in Sainsbury's vaunted systems. The market's surprise and City disappointment inevitably followed.

But at the end of the day it was management shuffling and visible senior management indecision which caused the biggest uncertainties. The top strategic and operating positions on the new board were initially offered to Tom Vyner and David Quarmby, J D's two established and most trusted lieutenants. This was a return to old Sainsbury's behaviour patterns, a well-intentioned but vain attempt to maintain a steady and even pattern of succession. It did not work. Quarmby, seen as a systems innovator par excellence, left quickly, seemingly ill at ease in the way the new structure was shaping, and perhaps disappointed by the results of the new supply system. Vyner, exemplar to a fault of the hands-on Sainsbury's management style, whose penchant was for determinedly effective trading and buying, was persuaded, apparently very much against his will, to stay on longer than he had intended.

Meanwhile, key strategic issues such as a brand and customer proposition no longer as clearly positioned as they had been, were simply not being addressed. The company's market position was drifting, but more significantly there were big things that were not even on the agenda. Strategy was not being tackled. The new chairman was having second thoughts but he took four years to replace Vyner in the central operating role. The result was the loss of five years in appointing an integrated top team. Adriano and Bremner are now in place – initially with Sainsbury himself retaining the role of chairman, now with David stepping down and George Bull, erstwhile chairman of Grand Met taking over. He is the first non-Sainsbury to hold the top position in the former family business. Whether the new team is permanent, whether the experience will be adequate, and whether more importantly, it can craft a strategy that revitalizes the business is not certain. It has a huge job on its hands. It may be playing its cards close to the chest but so far there are few visible signs of substantive change or strategic progress.

THE 1990s – THE KEY ISSUES

There are three ways in which the apparent post-1992 change for the worse in performance could have happened at any time. At one level they are simply a reflection of a business with traditional strengths needing to redefine strategic advantage in times of high change. These three areas are: the Sainsbury's core positioning, the Sainsbury's brand and the Sainsbury's customer. Each conferred significant strategic advantage in the past. But as times change so does the rationale for core advantage.

The notion 'Good food costs less at Sainsbury's' was a core tenet, having been an unchallengeable and heartland family belief for a century. On this platform John James built the franchise, and with it subsequent leaders – notably Alan Sainsbury and then J D, in 1978 – had triumphantly continued to repel all boarders. There remained a widely held perception through the 1980s that Sainsbury's food quality was better. If not actually cheaper than its main rivals as it was wont to claim, which Sainsbury's emphatically wasn't, consumers gave it the benefit of the doubt and, granted pricing equivalence (versus Tesco, less probably vis-à-vis Asda, but certainly against Safeway), Sainsbury's commanded the heights of 'best food value'. By the 1990s, perceived food quality standards were no longer so clearly demarcated. Marks & Spencer, and Waitrose in the normal course of events, and all three majors from time to time were perfectly capable of challenging Sainsbury's pre-eminence. Along with pricing parity, key elements of Sainsbury's difference had been eroded once and for all. In retrospect Sainsbury's management was quite unwilling to believe this had happened and preferred to go on relying on history, and believing its own internal publicity. When it did understand what had happened it had no idea what the strategy to respond to the issue was going to be. Today's leadership is beginning to recognize this need, but the position is now deep-rooted. Recovery is therefore a much more significant challenge.

The second key change is related and concerns the Sainsbury's brand, a phenomenon of epic historic strength. Consumer perceptions had altered. Perceived quality, while still appreciated, was no longer a unique Sainsbury's product strength. Behind every great brand resides product or functional advantage. Alongside perceptions of mere product parity came mutterings of disquiet that the emotional values of the Sainsbury's brand were becoming drab, dated, more conventional, colder, less open-minded and exciting than competition. Given the faith in Sainsbury's loyal shoppers to the Sainsbury's brand, and perceptions that the breadth of the product range was certainly not an advantage, Sainsbury's own-brand offer was becoming less attractive. Sensing this, Sainsbury's launched stand-alone brands with new names – eg Novon, Gio – but these lacked, on the whole, any major advantage, enjoyed mixed fortunes, and are unlikely to represent a long-term approach. The company's response to back-pedal on its long-term intention to make the Sainsbury's brand pre-eminent in its own stores has in turn created internal and customer uncertainty. Today Sainsbury's own-brand penetration remains significantly higher than key competitors – a tribute to the persistent brand building of early years. But the direction remains unclear, and there is lack of apparent vision in the development process.

Finally the Sainsbury's consumer – an enormous strength for the company, since Sainsbury's always appealed, more than its rivals, to discriminating, more knowledgeable customers. It was a distinctiveness that had been built faithfully by successive managements over many decades. Recent trends show Sainsbury's differentiated core following has inhibited them from attracting new, younger family shoppers. Sainsbury's has one of the lowest levels of child presence in the market, and its weakness among pre- and young-family segments is, unsurprisingly, compensated for by strength among retired, and 'empty nester' groups. Its strength among older customers is reinforced by a continuingly higher penetration among ABC1 shoppers (a critical precursor group), but an inability to attract the large C2 group, where Tesco makes its strong appeal. In the end it is the ability to retain and grow loyalty that matters most, and Sainsbury's has maintained its overall core appeal – but it has now been matched, initially to its surprise, in top position by Tesco for the first time ever. Such a change 10 years ago would have been dismissed as improbable. Once again, the response to market change and competitive challenge is not yet obvious.

To summarize therefore, the radical change in fortunes for the Sainsbury's business from 1992–98 stems from a wide range of effects, some immediate, others long in the making. The change had little directly to do with events of 1992–93 but are deep-rooted. Fundamental changes to the company's positioning, brand and customer base had been taking place for some years. These, along with market and competitive pressures that ebb and flow at any time, precipitated *the appearance of rapid even overnight change of fortune.* To repeat, however, what matters for any company is not its apparent, or even its 'real' operating performance over a short period, but its competence to secure and maintain long-term differentiated advantage. A winning strategy is what is going to count for most. How and when is this going to happen?

RESTORATION OF LEADERSHIP

Stock markets have a propensity to overestimate their winners – long after they have lost the art of winning – and to underestimate their emerging heroes or recovering stars. Can Sainsbury's play such a role in the years ahead? It is to enduring strength that we should pay most attention, and to give Sainsbury's its due, it has always stressed the long-term strategic viability of its actions. The company has sometimes been alone in the market in measuring itself against long-term performance standards, a sign of mature business confidence.

Sainsbury's capacities in the UK market remain second to none and it should still be considered the UK world player with most potential even if it currently does no better than head the world's second division. Alone of the UK big four it has possessed a recognizable long-term strategy, and US acquisitions show recognition that it needs to get footholds elsewhere to compete with the best global retail companies. Dino Adriano, the group's chief executive, confirms its commitment to Sainsbury's US presence, but there is a slightly defensive ('just in case you're wondering why we're here') ring to the defence. Shaw's and Star Markets are in affluent New England, where many retail developments are born and they are both sizeable, giving Sainsbury's a good second position to Ahold-owned Stop 'n Shop in Connecticut, and US \$4 billion in US sales. They have now lost their stake in Giant to Ahold, an immensely powerful world-retail player whose achievements have made Sainsbury's lack of progress all the more obvious to neutral (US) observers. Frequently in its recent past Sainsbury's have cannoned up against the key Dutch major (Ahold) with Sainsbury's invariably coming off worse. The US belief is that in the US at least Sainsbury's has tried to run their US companies to a UK formula which hasn't worked, whereas Ahold has used more imagination in learning flexibly and developing the local methods when it best suited them. Sainsbury's by contrast does not really seem to be participating in the rapid US consolidation movement, and have suffered from the (public/private) comparison of funding vis-à-vis privately held Royal Dutch Ahold.

Allied to its US outlook, Sainsbury's – again alone of UK majors – has diversified in the home market. It has the potential to build long-term UK leadership from a retail portfolio which could ultimately dwarf competition. Thus Savacentre's 13 hypermarket sites, with huge per store areas, offer Sainsbury's a chance to exploit the UK hypermarket opportunity – Reading is one excellent example of this. Traffic constraints and other pressures suggest there is future potential – so while current Savacentre results disappoint, they are a solid vote for an alternative future. (Additionally, while outside our terms of reference, Sainsbury's presence in DIY with Homebase is powerful and there is promise, with the Texas acquisition, that the chain could build pre-eminence, justifying the original Sainsbury's consumer promise – 'a distinctive store experience' – albeit now in the mundane world of tin sheds.) This versatile portfolio is more of a hedge against both food dependency and the British market than any competitors have.

Sainsbury's unwillingness to hold land and become a genuinely national chain has sometimes been hard to fathom. Singular strength in London and the south is balanced by low Celtic and northern presence. Acquiring large sites and permission to build is trickier since 1993, which makes organic growth a tougher proposition. Acquisition – with Morrison either the very best or perhaps the only UK-based candidate – is a route to correct this and since it could, in one bound, restore market leadership this would have the highest priority. The opportunity to correct regional balance is a future strength for the company. Acquiring new stores, however, remains an organic constraint reflecting limited flexibility caused by the traditionally conservative Sainsbury's approach to property. Tesco and Asda appear better placed.

Historically, Sainsbury's results have been exceptional on all measures – net margins, returns, most notably on sales densities. Since 1993 this has changed and Sainsbury's has had to be content with poor growth, and profits that Adriano calls 'broadly in line with the industry'. As equal best in the industry they do retain a superb platform for expansion and in late 1998 the *Financial Times* was quick to note approvingly that 'JS is guarding against the complacency that so damaged the company in the past'. Sales densities are an example of maintained potential – even in a trough, they remain industry leader with only Tesco in range, meaning that investment in cost-efficiencies, technology and systems have been immensely effective, over the longest term. If growth can be rejuvenated, the efficiency gap can then widen in Sainsbury's favour, and the fact that Sainsbury's shares until the mid-1990s traded at an ongoing 10 per cent premium to Tesco shows investors accepted this indeed ought to happen. Manufacturer relationships to address the category management opportunities that others pursue are a critical element, to use both partnerships and scale to drive costs down and innovations forward. This requires new cultural thinking at Sainsbury's, and a willingness to share information and initiatives which has not yet truly penetrated an iron-clad protective Sainsbury's ethic. Worldwide experience suggests this has to happen if Sainsbury's is to move growth and food innovation ahead again. The significance of this change cannot be underestimated.

SAINSBURY'S BRAND AND INNOVATION

Traditional Sainsbury's strengths in customer profile may be inhibiting an all-out assault on customer service advantage, where Tesco among others has now got used to scoring repeated wins. Has the new Sainsbury's team the imagination and enough marketing skill and passion to turn service into competitive advantage, and will this lead to all round penetration, notably among urban, C-class family groups? This is one battle Sainsbury's has to fight, and to create the weapons to win. For the moment the powerful customer base at Sainsbury's is not the asset which it was, and while the Sainsbury's bank is one very honourable and innovation-leading exception, heartland food supremacy is the mainstream area which Sainsbury's has always known to be its core competence, and where competition has for a decade been successfully challenging Sainsbury's leadership.

A rejuvenated Sainsbury's brand should represent its key strategic weapon. Conservative family traditions, a 'show and tell' style of customer as well as staff communication have become dated. Simultaneously, Sainsbury's brand no longer invites – it has didactic emphasis, setting out a proposition based on essential need rather than want, and of talking 'at' rather than 'to' or 'with' its consumers. ('Essentials' was at one stage an overtly functional summary communication it tried to use but quickly abandoned.) Imagination of a high order, together with research to build long-term brand strategy are needed if Sainsbury's is to restore its brand's historic reputation. While this is a demanding leadership task, it is unthinkable that it is competitive advantage Sainsbury's could cede. Marks & Spencer, to say nothing of Tesco and Waitrose are now strong brand performers, a fact not lost on Dino Adriano who observed that 'recent underperformance has been due to ... the distinctiveness and superiority of the brand being eroded, as competitors improved their performance'. The most recent evidence – when the late 1998 'Value to Shout About' campaign failed in its objectives, was considered both expensive and misdirected, and irritated both consumers and employees – does not suggest that Sainsbury's are anywhere near recapturing their once infallible market touch.

Innovation delivers brand superiority and it is innovation that Sainsbury's brand and stores have lacked perhaps for 10 years. David Sainsbury's opening words of his first annual report in 1993 proclaimed that 'Sainsbury's has always been inspired by a passion for quality and innovation', then pointing out that 'the reputation of the brand ... derives from our commitment to ... innovative new products'. The priority given to these statements shows that he knew the recent record remained deeply unimpressive. Several years on, the business still has difficulty in defining how to restore differentiation and marketing leadership. The most recent reorganization (Adriano, Bremner, and McCarten as marketing director) is intended to address this, and substituting George Bull for David Sainsbury might be said to replace finance at the top with marketing. The competition understand. 'Being first with new ideas ... is essential in driving long-term business performance,' said Lord MacLaurin recently, and his successors have pointedly been driving the argument home. In their confident adoption of banking, with Bank of Scotland as partners, Sainsbury's led the market, but who is to say banking will be heartland retailer business in the years ahead? To breathe life into a rejuvenated brand strategy, innovation power and breadth must turn the tables to Sainsbury's advantage. This is the principal task of Adriano's new team at the top, and there is no doubt it understands this and is using all its own thinking as well as qualified outside guidance to generate this. Food remains the key area where change is needed. All the marketing director's P&G learning and discipline will be called for here.

THE LEADERSHIP TASK

Retailers, like all businesses, are learning companies and it is in the Sainsbury's capacity to learn that we should assess the likelihood of long-term success. The learning process in Sainsbury's is embryonic, the results all yet to be achieved, the will and persistence of a new and untried leadership not yet assessed. Signs of radical change are few. The new Sainsbury's 'Local' stores have been put in place to challenge and hopefully outpace Tesco in the high street. The purchase of Star markets is a logical continuation of its US presence. Home shopping developments and an Internet customer programme are strongly pursued. Each of these show open-mindedness, as do reports that Sainsbury's is talking seriously to Ahold, one of Europe's (and the United States's) most serious and ambitious companies. There is certainly synergistic opportunity available for both parties. But on present performance comparisons, Sainsbury's would be eaten alive by Mr van der Hoeven and his aggressively acquisitive Dutch lieutenants.

But these are not the big issues for Sainsbury's. What matters is the establishment and execution of a strategy that convinces the market and Sainsbury's itself that it can win. The most significant component of this is an innovative and revived Sainsbury's brand, built around identifiable food quality. To achieve both, the change that is needed concerns Sainsbury's itself, the culture and the team. 'People are what make retailers great,' said one of their new board members recently. Does Sainsbury's believe this and if it does, can it make it happen? Given the heritage and history it would be sad if it could not succeed.

CHANGE AND CHALLENGE

As if these were not already intimidating enough challenges, the UK market is in its most inherently competitive phase since the advent of self-service in the 1960s. Discounters, successful in their home markets, have moved in. Weak traditional retail players are being gobbled up. There are no easy acquisition targets, and in any case it is improbable that Sainsbury's would be allowed to make a major domestic purchase. The market is increasingly mature. Home shopping is a new information-led game, with new competitive forces possibly around the corner. Tesco at speed, and a more focussed Asda are galloping, unwilling to see Sainsbury's rekindle its race-leading aspirations. The retail market may be in 'shakedown', a time when there will be more failures than successes, more acquired than acquiring companies. Meanwhile Europe beckons. Continental predators and an ambitious Wal-Mart look with under-standable interest at the UK's still handsome net margins. These are big factors for a new team at Sainsbury's to weigh up and the suggestion is it does not have much time before its room to manoeuvre may be drastically reduced.

Sainsbury's has a unique heritage, recognizable strengths, tangible and diversified resources, but a striking degree of strategic challenge. As a large public company, it must simultaneously reassure investors, suppliers, customers and its own people that after a decade of uncertain performance, it has not 'lost the plot'. Current problems on both sides of the Atlantic, in the core business and elsewhere, must be dealt with effectively and quickly. The clock is ticking. So the question 'is Sainsbury's recovering, and might it be tomorrow's hero?' is not yet answerable. Positive signs are emerging. Recent Annual Reports represent an important change in style and shows the potential of a rejuvenated Sainsbury's brand. There seems to be a genuine willingness to learn. But results, to June 1999, show no progress.

For years a dedicated family business believed success to be its own by inalienable right. Consumer change caught up with and overtook the beliefs and behaviour that were the heart and soul of the great Sainsbury's company. Like other public company managements, disturbed in long-held convictions that 'we know what we're doing round here', market change was rejected for far too long by far too many people. Operating performance, held together with skill and resolution, continued to persuade unadventurous leaders that decisive change was not really happening. Even if it was, 'well, others are a lot worse off. We set the standards round here.'

It could not and did not last and the price paid has already been enormous. 'Sainsbury's', said the *Weekend Financial Times* (6/7 February 1999), 'is like a person caught in quicksand. The more it struggles to break free the faster it sinks.' It describes the 'campaign to boost sales and tackle its market share grabbing rivals' as 'a shambles'. Its image is still 'associated with discretionary treats for open-fisted foodies ... and not a recipe for success in straitened times ... The culture still seems wrong ... it needs new blood (and) to focus ruthlessly on the performance of its UK supermarkets.' This is a harsh judgement, but given the time taken to make change work, is not at all unreasonable. The 1990s have been an appalling decade for this once-dominant company and as the decade ends there is really not much sign yet of purposeful or radical reassessment. It is clear furthermore that at an operating level there are disquieting discontinuities taking place that cannot be good for an organization seeking to regroup and to reassert itself with purpose and cohesion. In one single week, the last week of March 1999, it was clear that at operating levels the Sainsbury's board was certainly not functioning as corporate boards should – namely as a unified team, heading in one agreed and visible direction. The marketing department – having unsurprisingly withdrawn their latest 'Value to Shout About' campaign, produced by one of London's most capable advertising agencies, Abbott Mead Vickers – took the decision following this campaign's failure to move the advertising account to Saatchi. The board had meanwhile taken the decision in the same week to dispense with the services of their long-established plc board finance director, Rosemary Thorne, because it considered it needed a specialist with first-class external financial experience. Both these changes seemed to beg the essential question – that it is Sainsbury's retailing performance that had been found wanting, and that it was the core delivery of the Sainsbury's brand promise in the stores that needed restoration to its former quality and differentiated performance.

Still, change has come and this gives a new and changing team, which is redefining an ethic and seeing the market through different eyes, a hopefully better-than-even chance of finding answers to rejuvenate this magnificent company. To redefine its strategy through realistic market-place assessment, appraising the open positions, is the core task. Restoring to a new and broader generation of Sainsbury's consumers the experience of excellent service and food quality can set the Sainsbury's brand on course to differentiate it once again from competition. In the world market, Sainsbury's is now surrounded by a group, perhaps 10 or a dozen at most, of successful and ambitious international players. How it manages its future – notably in the UK but not ignoring either the United States or Europe – will be a measure of how well the new Sainsbury's company can perform in the select league of world food retailers. It does now need to throw off the shackles, make a break with its recent past, and to make a new strategy work – if it is determined enough to change, it still has the resources and the talent to survive and do well.

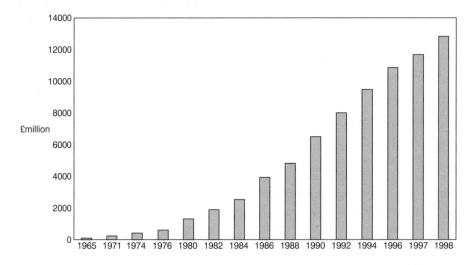

Figure 2.1 *Sainsbury's sales 1965–98*

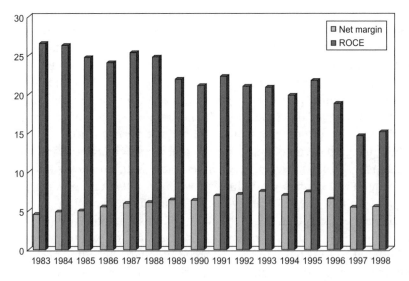

Figure 2.2 *Sainsbury's net margin and return on capital employed 1983–98*

3

The Asda story

Although its origins are earlier, Asda Stores Ltd was founded only in 1965, so it is a relative newcomer compared with Sainsbury's and Tesco. Since then, it has seen a roller-coaster ride, beginning with enormous success as a pioneer of the superstore format, then with periods of stagnation, hectic expansion and unwise diversification leading to near-bankruptcy. Since 1991, a new management team led by the young Archie Norman has carried out a textbook turnaround that has restored its finances, refocused on its traditional strengths, and built a strong, differentiated position. However, it may not have had the scale to cope on its own with the increasingly entrenched power of the leaders, Tesco and Sainsbury's. It has little international experience, and its advantage in the superstore outlet size may limit its flexibility if industry trends move away from it. Its takeover by Wal-Mart in 1999 ushers in a new chapter in its existence.

FOUNDATION: ASQUITH + DAIRIES = ASDA

The key people in the foundation and initial success of Asda were Noel (later Sir Noel) Stockdale, then Vice-Chairman of Associated Dairies, and Peter Asquith. Eric Binns, then CEO of Associated Dairies, was the third member of the team at this stage. Peter Asquith, a butcher, and his brother, a teacher ('In our family, the bright ones became teachers, the rest were butchers', says Peter) had started and sold a store in Pontefract. They then converted a cinema in Castleford, but felt that they needed help to expand beyond butchery. They had approached several multiples before contacting Associated Dairies, a large public company based on the dairy industry, but with some other interests including Farm Stores, a progressive pork butchery.

Stockdale and Asquith struck up an immediate rapport, and rapidly built up mutual trust. 'If it hadn't been for Noel, none of this would have happened', says Peter today. Asquith brought entrepreneurial flair and retailing skills to the partnership, while Associated Dairies had the capital that would be needed for the expansion that both saw as attractive. The company, starting with what Sir Noel terms two-and-a-half stores, was named ASDA Stores Ltd, from *A*squith and dairies.

DISCOVERING DISCOUNTING

In the early 1960s, resale price maintenance still operated; manufacturers controlled the prices at which retailers could sell their goods to the public. Tesco's answer to this was Green Shield Stamps, but others would have preferred more direct means of lowering prices.

The Asquiths discovered the attractions of discounting to housewives almost accidentally, while running their Pontefract shop. Crosse and Blackwell ran a consumer offer of 6d (2.5p) for the return of a coupon on the label. Fred Asquith ('A very shrewd man', according to his brother) saw an opportunity, and got the buyer, Jack Hewitt, to order 1,000 cases. The two then cut the coupons off the 24,000 cans, and sent them back. They split the savings with customers, and offered the product at a discounted price. The huge success of this offer opened their eyes to the potential of discounting. It was only with the abolition of resale price maintenance by the Heath government in 1965 that this potential could be realized.

GEM AND THE SUPERSTORE FORMAT

The early Asda stores, though undoubtedly successful, were of the then standard supermarket size – the largest was 10,000 sq ft, but most were only 4,500 sq ft. It took the recognition of another chance opportunity to show Asda the way forward to larger stores. In 1965, Peter Asquith heard that the UK premises of a US company, Gem International, were on the market. Gem had two stores in England, at Nottingham and Leeds. Stockdale, Asquith and Binns went to look at them. The Nottingham store was a purpose-built superstore of 70,000 sq ft selling space. Gem did not retail anything themselves, but franchised the space out to a variety of retailers – food, hardware, chemists, ladies' fashions; everything.

The results were not a success. When the Asda trio visited the store, they saw 'at least as many staff as customers'. Grocery takings were a measly £6,000 a week. Stockdale asked Asquith his opinion.

'I think we can make a go of this', he replied.

'How much could you take in a week, then?'

'£25,000.'

Asda started negotiations, despite not really wanting the Leeds store, which was on two storeys. The team got on very well with the Chairman of Gem, Bob Wolfson ('a good chap, with some very natty ideas', says Sir Noel today). Gem had accumulated £320,000 in losses, and Wolfson offered to sell the stores for 20 per cent of whatever Asda could recoup from the Inland Revenue as tax losses. Asda got the whole amount, and thus gained the two premises for nothing. As the rent was 10 shillings (50p) a square foot on a 21-year lease with no rent reviews, this must go down as one of the bargains of the grocery industry. With Asda's retailing skills applied, Asquith's estimate of £25,000 proved conservative, and the Nottingham store took £30,000 in its first week, and grew from there. Even the Leeds store made profits, from the ground floor only.

This was the turning point for Asda. Without the Gem opportunity, 'this tremendous leap', it would have continued to expand, but in much smaller increments, from 4,000 sq ft to 6,000, to 8,000. From now on, it would look only for premises that offered a minimum of 30,000 sq ft of selling space, parking for 300 cars and space for petrol if possible (Gem had a petrol station).

Asda knew nothing about the non-food side of the business, and therefore had to continue with the franchising for the time being. The team saw the logic of it, however, and built up its own expertise until Asda could take it over itself (it was helped in this by the fact that all the franchisees were on short-term tenancies). This took time, but Asda was looking three to four years ahead.

EARLY SUCCESS

The basic offer was set. Asda recognized that what housewives wanted was quality groceries (mainly branded at this stage) at a low price. 'Nothing we sell will be at full, normally expected prices. Our aim is to sell as much as possible at a smaller profit margin, rather than a little bit at a large profit. That is to the mutual benefit of the housewives and ourselves' (company records). Asda also aimed to offer, in the very large spaces that it was now acquiring, a broad range of products as well as food, including clothing, other non-food, and petrol in the adjoining car parks.

The success was phenomenal: on one occasion, Fred Asquith had to hold back the crowds at the door, allowing only some people in at a time. While a few others were attempting to discount, no one was going for the Asda format (Ken Morrison was the first imitator, but did not have the capital to expand as fast as Asda). The company saw that the more it sold, the more it could reduce prices.

It pursued sites aggressively, taking on all sorts: old mills, former work-shops, the classic cinemas – anything that met the size and access criteria. Planners and rivals often did not see what Asda was up to, as the concept was still new. As Sir Noel put it, 'The motor car was no longer a luxury, it was a social necessity.' People were prepared – even eager – to drive a few miles to a store in which they could get quality goods at keen prices.

WHY WAS ASDA SO SUCCESSFUL?

Others recognized the chances that Asda made the most of, but none was as successful (at this time) as it was. The reasons are many:

- Asda recognized the opportunity offered by the Gem stores. No one else was doing anything like it, and it was a huge jump from what it already knew. But it was confident enough in its retailing flair to think it could make it work.
- When it did work, Asda had capital (from its parent Associated Dairies) to expand aggressively.
- Associated Dairies also brought its own control systems, essential in retailing and particularly during rapid expansion.
- Asda strengthened its management team early on by bringing in Peter Firmston-Williams from Key Markets. 'He was brought in to control me', says Peter Asquith only half jokingly. Firmston-Williams was a tower of strength as a manager.
- Rivals such as Tesco were tied in to leases of existing high-street shops, and to forward planning pipelines also based on the high street or new shopping centres. In addition, new sites such as Asda's would cannibalize their existing stores' business.
- 'We had seven years' start', states Sir Noel now. Even when rivals saw what was happening, they could respond only slowly. (Jack Cohen actually offered

to buy Asda, and when it refused, threatened that he 'would run them out of the country'. He didn't, though Asda itself was to hit problems later.)

- Asda also revolutionized buying, using its increasing power in buying centrally to demand ever better terms from suppliers. This strategy was led by their head buyer, Jack Hewitt. Described even by his chairman as 'hard as nails', Hewitt terrified suppliers, in an approach that manufacturers would come to know well from retailers in the years to come. Hewitt even de-listed the mighty Procter & Gamble at one point, not something they were used to.

THE FURNITURE BUSINESSES

From its earliest years, Asda always had – and added to – some furniture stores too. Allied, Wades, and Ukay were a somewhat ramshackle collection, generally of poor quality. The strategic reason for expanding in furniture was that the large supermarket sites were becoming increasingly hard to find, and planning permission was getting harder. Over the coming years, management was to blow hot and cold over furniture, leading to periods of expansion and contraction. With hindsight, furniture was a distraction, taking the board's eye off the target of superstore retailing.

THE FLETCHER EXPERIENCE

With Peter Firmston-Williams due to retire as managing director, the Asda board began to look for a successor. After a thorough search, they chose John Fletcher, who had gone to Harvard after a career at Warburton, a famous bakery manufacturer. He was a bright and personable man, who continued the store expansion programme. Results continued to reflect the fundamental rightness of this strategy.

On the other hand, the second key decision was less happy. John Fletcher appeared a big character in food retailing, although his experience had not been mainly in the sector. For some reason, he set his face against own-label branding. This was a crucial error. Fletcher saw Asda as offering a wide range of manufacturers' brands at keen prices, and thought this was enough.

For a time, he seemed to be right. In 1980, Asda was rated more highly by the stock market than Sainsbury's, difficult to believe in the light of later events. Turnover and profits continued to increase, reaching almost £2 billion and £112 thousand by 1985. Return on capital employed (ROCE) in that year was an impressive 32 per cent, and the margin over 6 per cent. The figures for its main rivals were:

Table 3.1   *ROCE of Asda's rivals, 1985*

	ROCE	Margin
Sainsbury's	25%	4.98%
Tesco	21%	2.72%

Although the ROCE was to reach the even dizzier height of 41 per cent the following year, in fact the seeds of future problems had been sown. Asda was starting to struggle against competitors, and was beginning to see less response to its efforts. Its huge ROCE reflected low costs, compared with, say, Sainsbury's. But Sainsbury's was investing in the up-front development costs of own-label, and increasingly the battle for customers was being fought on quality – led by a strong own-label offer. Asda was undercapitalized (a negative gearing in 1985), and had so far stayed mainly in the north of England.

A more important difficulty was that Fletcher began to make unfortunate decisions. For example, he unilaterally cancelled the proposed purchase of two sites; the board reinstated the purchases later, but had to pay an extra £1.5 million. Worse, Fletcher started the process of moving away from the low-price positioning.

Stockdale, though happy at the stellar results being shown (a 45 per cent increase in profits), was curious as to the exact source, and asked Fletcher where the increase in gross margin was coming from. Fletcher replied that the margins on in-store bakery and on non-foods were mainly responsible. Sir Noel, sceptical, asked his finance director to dig a little deeper. The investigation revealed that Fletcher, without consulting or telling the board, had raised food prices. Although it took consumers 12 months to realize what was happening, it was clear to senior Associated Dairies management that Asda had become uncompetitive with Tesco and Sainsbury's. Fletcher, never a team player, was fired in 1984. By then, new influences were at work.

THE MFI MERGER

MFI was a previous stock market darling which seemed for a time to have found a magic formula selling cheap, knock-down furniture. By the mid-1980s, it was running aground. The City brought MFI to Asda's attention. Asda already had some furniture stores, as we saw. There was no real synergy, but MFI had had a good track record, was also a discounter, and had large out-of-town sites. The two sought solace in each other, merging in 1985. Described by one analyst as 'the merger of the challenged' (Fowler, 1997), it had little real industrial synergy, and was another triumph of investment banking rather than a brilliant strategic move. In the years that followed, it can only have been a drain on scarce management resources, producing no return.

THE HARDMAN ERA – BOOM OR BUST

John Hardman was brought in by Fletcher in 1981 as Finance Director, and had been running Asda Stores since 1983. Hardman realized that the super-stores had lost their way, and that urgent action was needed. In 1985, he announced a 'series of measures to refocus the superstore business':

- an accelerated programme of store openings;
- increased emphasis on the south of England;
- a major improvement in size and quality of ranges offered;
- the introduction of an own-label range;
- a dramatic improvement in the style, design and layout of stores;
- improved training;
- the development of a centralized distribution system.

Some of this at least was achieved. The number of stores rose from 101 in 1985 to 204 by 1991. The policy of large spaces was maintained, and the total selling space more than doubled in that period, from 3,680,000 to 7,978,000 sq ft. This included the purchase of 60 stores from Gateway in 1989 at what many thought an astronomical price – £700 million.

That price points up the looming problem. Hardman was trying to achieve 10 years' change in a much shorter time, and that necessarily involved huge outlays – for buying more expensive southern stores, in developing own-label, and in setting up the badly needed but costly, centralized distribution system. All these were laudable goals, but the rewards did not appear immediately and, in the meantime, strains started to appear. The large acquisitions put enormous pressure on an already weak marketing team, and it could not cope (Tony Campbell, who is still a senior member of the Asda team, was the only one against the Gateway purchase). Hardman's strategy, it could be argued, was right; but too much, too late.

Turnover rose, but sales per square foot were going up only slowly, from £495 in 1985 to £519 in 1991. Profit was increasing, too (see Figure 3.2) but not fast enough. Margins fell from the extraordinary high of over 9 per cent in 1989 to 3.77 per cent by 1991. The earlier, healthy figures may also have been inflated by capitalizing the central distribution expenditure and amortizing it over 10 years. Net interest, at £90 million by 1991, reflected the huge borrowings. ROCE fell dramatically to 13 per cent.

Management had, however, become top-heavy. The culture was hierarchical, with little flair shown (or allowed) at the retail level. From the front-line staff in a store, there were no less than eight layers up to the CEO of the Asda Stores board:

- staff member;
- supervisor;
- department manager;
- general store manager;
- regional operations controller;
- division director;
- operations director;
- joint managing director (retail);
- chief executive.

The hierarchy was formal, with superiors addressed as 'Mr', and innovation was stifled by bureaucracy. Entrepreneurial people at store level were discouraged, and many left. Top executives were in a separate part of the headquarters building from their operating colleagues; many subordinates felt that the executives were more concerned with their perks than with facing up to the real issues. Hardman himself set the style. Symptomatic was the company aircraft, which previously had been a valuable management tool, enabling directors to visit the far-flung stores efficiently; use was carefully controlled. Under Hardman, the main use of the aircraft seemed to be to take parties on golf trips to Spain. The management style was top-down, and communication between stores and head office was one-way.

In 1991, the Trading Department, and its relationship with the stores, was a microcosm of the problems at Asda. The department was run by a Managing Director (who was also responsible for marketing) located on a separate floor from the rest of the department. Reporting to the Managing Director were three Directors who were described as 'long tenure employees acting like power barons through whom it was difficult to get any information about what was happening; they were an impenetrable stone wall.' Below these three Directors was layer after layer of management: 'senior buyers, buyers, junior buyers, trainee buyers, assistant trainee buyers, and so on'. As was true throughout Asda, the department had become fearful during the business slowdown and there was little innovation or risk-taking.

(Harvard Business School, 1998)

The top team lost its focus on the Asda brand promise of lower prices, and had not yet made up the competitive ground in fresh food and own label. Asda stores simply became less attractive than their major competitors. The Asda offer, previously clear, became confused as prices rose, ranges changed and stores were refurbished. The stores were simply not competing with the leaders, Sainsbury's and Tesco, but had lost the price appeal. As marketing men, we would say that Asda committed the mortal sin of losing touch with its customers. Typical customer comments were: 'Asda has lost the imagination and they've lost the competitiveness'; 'I think they've got to go back a few years and do it like they did before.'

A financial explanation is that Asda pursued EPS (earnings per share) at the expense of ROCE. It had, as we noted, been rated higher than Sainsbury's in the early 1980s, and its ROCE was then higher too. But Asda's ROCE tumbled to 13 per cent by 1991, whereas Sainsbury's, although it had slipped from the previous peak of 26 per cent, had always stayed above 20 per cent (as had Tesco). If this was an attempt to retain the City's favour, it was a singularly short-sighted and wrong-headed strategy.

More importantly, Asda had been steadily losing its position as the low-price supermarket. Its largely working-class customers, who were looking for value, began deserting it, and new, more affluent buyers were not attracted away from competitors. From 1985, the average number of visitors per store per week began an inexorable decline.

Two major, correct decisions were taken in this period. Firstly, Asda started a partnership with George Davies, the man who had run the Next chain so brilliantly. The 'George' range of clothing was to become one of the great successes of superstore range expansion. Secondly, Hardman bit the bullet, and looked for a buyer for MFI. Despite brave claims, and even the purchase of a further group of furniture stores under the Maples name, MFI was going nowhere. The Asda management buyout in 1987 completed the divorce.

Neither of these was enough to stem the tide. The enormous capital expenditures and the plummeting profits told their own story. The sale of some of the crown jewels – freeholds – was evidence of the panic of a thinly stretched management. It was apparent to observers that the company had slid into a downward spiral. By 1991, it was clear that Asda's chickens were coming home to roost. The hugely expensive effort to expand into the south, to open new stores and refurbish others, and to build a centralized distribution system, had been financed mainly by borrowing. Press criticism began to single out poor management for Asda's dire condition.

Early in 1991 it became apparent that there was a real danger that the company would default on some of its debt covenants, and would need to be recapitalized – but the City was hostile to the idea as long as the current management was in charge. After a series of profit warnings, there was a shareholder revolt, and the top team paid the price. Hardman and Graham Stow – who had been Chief Executive of Asda Stores since 1989 – resigned. What was their legacy?

- A portfolio of 204 stores with an average of 40,000 sq ft of selling area. Though many were in a poor state, and few could be called state of the retail art, this estate is a priceless asset at a time when new large stores would become increasingly hard to acquire. The large spaces provide the opportunity to offer a wide range of fresh and packaged food, and a significant range of non-foods. Neither opportunity had been fully taken up, but the basis for growth is there. Asda had, perceptively or through luck, pioneered the one-stop shopping destination that was becoming the dominant model in Britain.
- The George range has been the most successful clothing product sold by a mass-market retailer outside Marks & Spencer.
- The centralized distribution system allows Asda to compete on an equal cost basis with its main rivals.

RECOVERY – THE ARCHIE NORMAN PHENOMENON

After Hardman's departure, Sir Godfrey Messervy, a non-executive director, was appointed as an interim chairman while the search for a new team took place. Patrick Gillam was appointed a director and chairman in September 1991. He was a former managing director of BP, and was Deputy Chairman of Standard Chartered PLC, chairman designate of Booker Tate, and a non-executive director of Commercial Union. The key figures, however, would be the new chief executive and the team he could attract.

The new CEO had been identified by the autumn of 1991, and he joined in December: Archie Norman, a 37-year-old former partner at McKinseys and Group Finance Director at Kingfisher plc (the UK retail group including Woolworth, the leading DIY chain B&Q, and Comet, an electrical retailer).

ARCHIE NORMAN AND ALLAN LEIGHTON

Archie Norman is in many ways a typical figure of the contemporary establishment. Educated at Cambridge, he went to Citibank, and then on to do an MBA at Harvard in 1977 (at a time when this was still relatively uncommon in Britain). He worked for McKinsey, where he made partner, then progressed smoothly to Group Finance Director of Kingfisher plc. Still only 37, he was headhunted to lead Asda out of its near-bankruptcy.

He is credited with two major successes early on: superb management of the City, lowering their expectations initially before building them up to support new share issues; and leading the rigorous analysis, developing the strategy, then leading the implementation single-mindedly. The turnaround worked, and Norman has taken much of the public credit (with numerous awards to his name as a result). His interest in politics led him in 1997 to election as Conservative Member of Parliament for Tunbridge Wells; to prepare for that, he moved to Chairman of Asda in 1996, Allan Leighton taking over as CEO. Norman was made Vice-Chairman of the Conservative Party, with the brief of sorting out the moribund organization after a stunning general election defeat. Seen by some as a rather formal, remote figure (though not all agree), he lists his hobbies as farming, music and opera (he also lists football, and started the intra-departmental matches with Allan Leighton).

Leighton could hardly, on the face of it, be a greater contrast. A year older than Norman, he was educated at a polytechnic (a type of higher education institution in Britain, more vocational and of lower status than the 'old' universities; all of them have now been named universities). Against Norman's Conservatism, he is a lifelong Labour supporter. He built his career at Mars, starting as a direct salesman, working his way steadily through the ranks over many years; he ended as General Sales Manager of the UK Grocery Division and Business Sector Manager. Picked as Marketing Director in Norman's new team at Asda, he quickly showed himself one of the most committed, hardworking and effective members. He was named Chief Executive in 1996.

Outsiders often classify Norman as the brains, the strategic thinker, and Leighton as the people man, the motivator. Leighton insists that this is not so: that although they started out very different, they have become very similar – 'We both do everything'. It is notoriously difficult to sort out who exactly contributed what in a small team working intensely hard. Talking to Leighton, it is clear that not only is he enormously energetic and enthusiastic, fizzing with ideas, but that he does have a long-term strategic view.

Nevertheless, the impression remains that the two are different, and complementary. Leighton does, as indeed his role encourages, concentrate on making things work now, as well as thinking up new ideas. He was the first to introduce the open-plan office, and he does focus a great deal of his effort on the 'colleague' culture. The two make a great team, and a key question for Asda will be what happens if and when Norman's political career takes him away from the company. The Wal-Mart takeover makes Asda part of a huge organization, which will provide opportunities but also, perhaps, constraints. It will be interesting to see how it adapts.

Tony Campbell, Trading Director since 1987, was retained, but three other key appointments were made:

- Allan Leighton, Marketing Director, aged 39, a veteran of Mars and most recently Sales Director of Pedigree Petfoods;
- Phil Cox, Finance Director, aged 42, previously Group Chief Executive of Burns Anderson plc and Finance Director of Horne Brothers plc, a classy men's clothing retailer;
- Peter Monaghan, Retail Director, aged 44, previously Operations Director of B&Q, and with extensive food retailing experience.

The new team were taking over an almost bankrupt organization. Already low expectations were talked down by Norman from the autumn onwards in what one analyst called 'masterful' management of the City. Asda was said to be in terminal decline, and the shares fell as low as 20 pence. Massive write-offs were made, as so often when a new management takes over, to clear the decks. Over 500 managers at head office were made redundant. The new store development and store refurbishment programmes were halted, and undeveloped sites sold. Other immediate actions were designed to stop all unnecessary spending, and raise cash.

The situation was still desperate. Norman identified what he called the 'Doom Loop': trying to raise margins by increasing prices drove away customers, which eroded Asda's cost base. The financially strapped firm could not expand its way out of trouble, or invest in sharply improved quality to compete with the leaders.

McKinsey, the consultants called in to help, produced forecasts that showed a continuing downward spiral. At a meeting of the executive directors, the lead consultant presented the forecasts, and asked what the men would do if offered 35 pence a share for the company (its share price was then 26 pence). Allan Leighton, on only his second day, said, 'Wait a minute. I didn't come here to sell the business. If we are any good as managers we can turn this round. We can begin by putting colleagues and customers first.'

Campbell later remembered this as a defining moment: 'Allan launched into an inspired speech saying we have no idea what this organization is capable of. And he was right, we didn't. The rest of us agreed with him, saying let's do this. For me it was very motivational.'

REAPPRAISAL

True to his McKinsey and MBA background, Norman started with a thorough situation analysis. Aided by market research, and by teams of consultants, the team identified four key issues.

PRICE COMPETITIVENESS

Although the heritage of Asda had been good value for money, the firm had walked away from it. Costs had increased, and although some margin gains had been achieved through own-label and centralized distribution, overall price competitiveness had declined. Crucially, two thirds of stores were located in areas of average or below-average income, so this loss of value perception had led to a falling customer count.

FRESH FOOD

Although the company had made an attempt to improve its fresh food offer, it had failed to convince consumers that it could match competition

NON-FOOD

The George range was good, but other products were not yet positioned to suit supermarket shopping compared with other competition, especially the out-of-town 'sheds' in DIY, garden products and electrical goods. Ranges that fitted better with supermarket shopping needed to be developed.

NEED FOR EFFICIENCY

The whole operation had become more complex, adding higher costs, especially at head office.

The team also identified the strengths of the existing store and customer base, up-to-date distribution system, good IT and effective operating management.

RENEWAL – FROM DOOM LOOP TO VIRTUOUS CIRCLE

To take the firm forward, the team produced a 10-point plan:

- *Meet the weekly shopping needs of ordinary working people and families.*
- *Re-establish Asda's price reputation.* It follows from the identification of the target market that price is a key element, both in brands and in good-value basic lines. To support the positioning, Asda has taken on 'crusades' against high prices, particularly where these are still fixed, for example in over-the-counter medicines, books and magazines.
- *Develop new formats.* This would take two forms: the redevelopment of existing stores, concentrating on fresh foods and non-food; and a discount format under the Dales fascia.
- *Drive change through store portfolio.* Norman argued that the prices of new stores had become inflated and uneconomic, so refurbishment of existing stock would provide a better return.
- *Compete through productivity improvement.* The first step was a reduction of 1,000 jobs, followed by a wage freeze. The apparently dire position of the firm made acceptance of these harsh measures easier.
- *Pursue innovation in packaged groceries.* The main plank here was to be the continuing development of the Asda own-label range. The Asda brand was deliberately positioned as equivalent quality at 10 per cent lower price than the manufacturer's brand, thereby strengthening the Asda value proposition. Tesco and Sainsbury's, by contrast, have tended to offer equivalent quality at a slightly lower price, pushing the extra margin through to profit.
- *Exploit investment in logistics.*
- *Focus on profit generation.* DPP (direct product profitability) would be applied both strategically and tactically, and IT would be used to improve store productivity at local levels.

- *Reposition and redevelop clothing, home and leisure goods.* Although the space devoted to non-food would be reduced (to give more to food), a careful focussing on products appropriate to the weekly shopping trip would mean no loss of sales.
- *Focus on fresh foods.* Asda recognized that fresh food of high quality had become central to a supermarket's attractiveness to customers, and that its efforts so far were not good enough.

This represents a textbook approach to strategic renewal. Norman promised a virtuous circle that would rebuild the business (see Figure 3.1). We shall see later the extent to which it worked.

There is one further issue that the new team tackled: the organizational culture.

ORGANIZATIONAL CHANGE

As we noted earlier, there were problems with the Asda structure. There were too many layers of management, narrow functional attitudes preventing teamwork, and a controlling, bureaucratic head-office culture. The story is told that in his early days, Norman said in public at head office, 'Let's all go down the pub.' The fortunate hostelry was crammed to the doors, as *everyone* thought it was an order, and they had to go whether they wanted to or not.

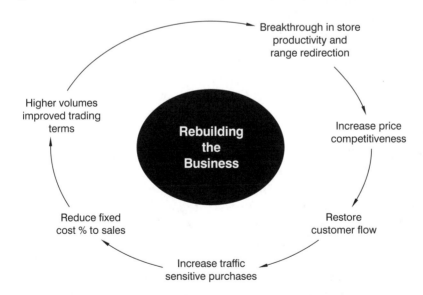

Figure 3.1 *The Asda virtuous circle*

The new strategy provided a set of common values, and a clear direction. The emphasis was to be on the stores, and on selling with personality. In a people business, the staff have to be – and feel – valued.

As we saw, 550 jobs went from head office, and the culture was encouraged to be less authoritarian, more open. A campaign was launched under the 'Ask Archie' slogan, allowing any member of staff to approach the chief executive with a question or suggestion. More communication at all levels was promoted. All the office space at headquarters was converted to open plan. The famous 'Red Hat' device allowed anyone to wear the hat for up to an hour, which meant that they could not be disturbed. Colleagues at all levels are encouraged to take initiatives, such as running an in-store promotion themselves, and are rewarded with points, badges and certificates. In an idea borrowed from Julian Richer (of Richer Sounds, well known for its highly motivated staff and customer service), branches can win the use of a company Jaguar for a month. *Asda News* ('the colleagues' newspaper') is full of staff triumphs and awards. Schemes such as the search for and appointment of a Christmas-cracker joke-writer are designed to promote the image of Asda as a fun, unstuffy place.

All this was designed to create a totally different type of retail organization. Visitors to the head office in Leeds confirm that its atmosphere is genuinely new and refreshing. How thoroughly the new culture penetrates the organization, and how it will stand up to future stress, remains to be seen. In some stores, personal visits suggest that the 'service with personality' does not always come through. Many critics think that the efficiency drive has left Asda with dangerously low staffing levels, and salaries have been held down firmly.

HAS THE STRATEGY WORKED?

The only test of a strategy, however textbook it looks, is how it works in the lumpy, unpredictable real world. For Asda, the results are impressive though not immaculate. We will look at some figures first, then take a more qualitative view. The great achievement has been to drive year-on-year sales growth at a faster rate than competitors. Like-for-like growth, or LFL, is seen as a key measure of retail competence. In generally slow-growth or stable markets such as food, natural market growth is available to all, but will be unexciting. Achieving the average LFL means staying in the game, while below-average figures suggest that the retailer is losing touch. Above-average growth in total sales by a UK grocer has usually reflected new space, from new stores or extensions. LFL growth can be achieved through quality improvement (premises, range, product quality, service) or promotion, and most competitors have shown one-year gains superior to their rivals at one time or another.

Asda's achievement has been to show the highest LFL growth *four years in a row*. And this against pretty tough competition, particularly from Tesco, which is generally seen to be motoring over this period. To some extent, Asda have been playing catch-up, and the growth reflects the fact that it has been merely bringing its performance up to the levels of the others – in sales density, for example. It must also reflect a correctly chosen strategy, tightly focussed marketing effort, and superb operational management discipline.

Increasing sales faster than costs results in higher profits, and over this period Asda has been successful in holding costs down. Sales per full-time employee (colleague, in Asda language) rose 24 per cent from 1992 to 1996, for example.

THE ASDA SHOPPER

Although all the supermarkets appeal to a broad range of people, Asda's catchment areas and their target segments suggest a bias towards younger, working-class families. Their shopper profiles show that they are hitting their target (see AGB tables in Appendix). Compared with the UK population, Asda shoppers are:

- More likely to be C2, less likely to be AB or E social class;
- More likely to be under 45, less to be over 45;
- More likely to have 3, 4 or 5+ people in the household.

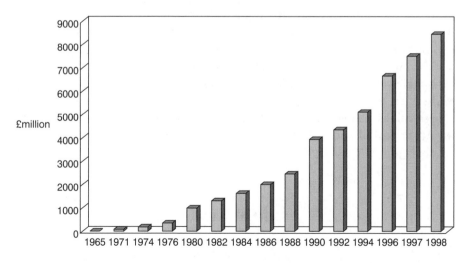

Figure 3.2 *Asda sales 1965–98*

For this group, as for all others, a good and improving standard of range, quality, freshness and availability are a given; any supermarket has to deliver these. What young, less well-off families also need is value for money: the lowest price compatible with the other benefits wanted. Asda has been single-minded in re-establishing its position as the lowest-price full-range super-market brand. Both its manufacturers' brand prices and its own label aim to give a 2–3 per cent price advantage over rivals, and shoppers clearly see and appreciate this. By 1996, record numbers – 5.6 million a week – were shopping at the stores.

THE NEXT PHASE – BREAKOUT

In 1995, the firm felt that recovery had been achieved. The next phase was named Breakout – 'the establishment of Asda as the best operator of value for money fresh food and clothing superstores in Britain'.

The key focus continues to be on value for money, but now the company is increasingly looking at how else it can position itself. Price alone would leave it vulnerable to attack in the future, either from below by the hard discounters, or from above by the big two. Low price therefore remains the message, uncomplicated by promotions or 'customer manipulative activity' (including, at this time anyway, loyalty cards). The other planks of the strategy were:

- Using the larger store size to offer a wider range;
- Building on the craft skills to develop in-store baking, butchery, and fish counters;
- The George range, which Asda aims to make the second family clothing brand in Britain (after Marks & Spencer);
- Service, 'the new battleground in food retailing' – the firm sees service as essentially people-based, and the goal is to offer 'service with personality';
- An improved and differentiated store layout, based on the 'market hall' concept.

RESULTS

Sales and profits have continued to climb (Figures 3.1 and 3.2). The margin, at 5.2 per cent in 1996, shows improvement, but is still below the main rivals, and has not yet returned to the levels achieved by Asda itself in the late 1980s. There is still some way to go.

THE WELCOME BREAK BID

Asda entered the bidding for Welcome Break, an underperforming chain of motorway service areas. The Asda management felt that they were now 'the best turnaround team in the Footsie' (the Financial Times Stock Exchange index), and that Welcome Break represented a challenge worthy of them. It was also in a related field, they argued, delivering a mass-market service.

Outsiders found it harder to see the industrial logic, and felt that it was a dangerous distraction. All the major supermarket chains have, at one time or another, taken their eye off the ball, or lost the fierce concentration on superior customer value that is so essential in this market. All have seen their performance suffer. At a time when most consumers have easy access to at least one alternative store that offers a perfectly acceptable range, no firm can afford to let its concentration slip for a moment. Perhaps it was lucky for Asda that their bid did not succeed.

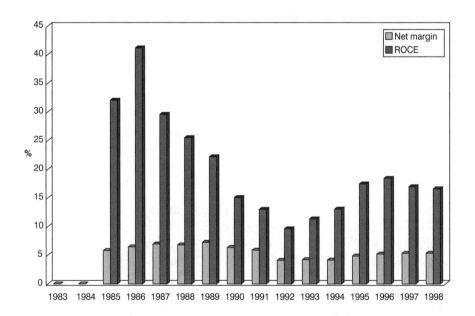

Figure 3.3 *Asda net margins and ROCE*

THE SAFEWAY TALKS – THE NEED FOR SCALE

Over the summer of 1997, the senior managers of Asda and Safeway engaged in merger talks. It was clear to both that the big two, Tesco and Sainsbury's, were likely to use their scale advantages to pull away further. A merged Asda/Safeway would leapfrog over Sainsbury's and be in a position to challenge Tesco for market leadership, so the merger (often discussed in the press over the years) would make sense.

The two firms are, of course, very different. Asda has consistently large stores and a clear value position; Safeway has a range of store sizes and locations, with a reasonable quality image but a general perception that it is slightly more expensive than its rivals (see Chapter 4, 'The Safeway story' for a discussion of this phenomenon). At this time, many observers thought that Safeway had somewhat lost its way and lacked strategic direction.

Quite how the merger would have worked is not entirely clear. If Asda had taken control, one option would have been to turn the smaller Safeway stores into high-quality shops aimed squarely at the positioning successfully adopted by Waitrose, above Sainsbury's. This would still have left the big stores of both chains, with incompatible positions. Presumably, economies of scale would have been available (figures of more than £200 million were mentioned), and increased purchasing clout, though unless the two own-label ranges were harmonized these would have been limited.

At any rate, the news of the talks leaked out while the firms were waiting for guidance from the government as to whether the deal would be referred to the Monopolies Commission. Published comments by both sides were taken amiss by the other, and the talks collapsed amid uncertainty. Both sides said publicly that the merger is no longer on the cards, though to outsiders the logic still seemed attractive.

CURRENT POSITION

Asda is, then, alone. It remains in third place in the market, and has a clearly focussed strategy; but it is not going to catch the leaders. According to Allan Leighton (Chief Executive), the key to its future is differentiation. 'Just being number two to Tesco won't work,' he says, 'Just as being number two to Sainsbury's won't work for Safeway' (Leighton, 1998). Asda therefore has to emphasize its points of difference.

The first is store size: they must accentuate the difference that the 25 per cent extra space makes. Clothing is central here, and they have two interrelated advantages. The George brand is well established, and accepted by consumers. But in addition, the brand is delivered by supply chain relationships that go back 20 years; these simply cannot be replicated by competitors. The George range now brings in £650 million, and the aim is £1 billion within a few years. Asda claims that it is the fastest-growing clothing business in Europe – 'bigger than Armani'!

Even so, non-food will always be secondary to the grocery business, and here Asda has some ground to make up. It knows that, although it wins with customers on value, its quality is seen as third behind Sainsbury's and Tesco. The drive to improve the overall quality of fresh food needs to continue, and the craft/skill-based departments should contribute to overall perceptions. The fresh bakery, discussed earlier, wins on all criteria, and as this is extended to other departments the average perception will improve. Asda's target market tends to eat less fresh food than more up-market groups, but Asda can help by driving better eating through attractive offers.

The other way of differentiating is the market hall idea, driven by the staff as active traders. The view now is that it is head office's job to get the products to the stores (at the right times, at the right prices, and so on); it is then up to the manager *as a trader* to shift it off the shelves.

This goes back to the culture change initiated by Norman and his team. 'Service with personality', delivered by motivated staff, should differentiate; currently Asda's service is rated second after Tesco:

'Asda's talking takeaway'
An example of the continuing drive for differentiation is the opening of a restaurant and takeaway in the Canterbury store. The restaurant offers a range of foods, from sandwiches to roasts and curry. A chef cooks a meal on a giant skillet in full view of customers, giving a running commentary as she cooks.
(*Financial Times*, 27 July 1998)

The other side is continuing investment in refurbishment and new stores. An Asda refurbished store, with trained management teams, can improve turnover from, say £500,000 to £850,000. New stores will be opened, at an average of 46,000 sq ft.

HOW HYPERMARKET PIRATES DRAIN THE POND

While the 40,000 sq ft superstore remains the core of Asda's strategy, it is also developing hypermarkets. They now have 20, and aim to take that to 30, each with the goal of taking £1.5 million a week as a destination store. The hypermarkets are run as a separate operation. Managers are encouraged to trade aggressively, and even fly a pirate flag to show their independence. One measure of their success is how much the rest of the chain complain.

In their catchment area, the pirates set about 'draining the pond', targeting successive categories by area. Managers go to the area in person, knock on doors, ask consumers their views, tell them about the offering, and give them a loaf of freshly baked bread. In targeting, they use data gathered from their loyalty cards (in contrast to the rest of the group). The data from cards can be used for increasingly fine focus, even down to share by factory-shift patterns. This very local use of data – 'a gold mine, not a coal mine', says Leighton – is seen to be the future for Asda. It seems unlikely that, if it really does work as well as they claim, the practice will not be extended to the superstores.

THE FORGET LIST

To maintain its single-minded concentration on its basic strategy, Asda recognizes that it cannot do everything at once. Allan Leighton says that he has a forget list – at any one time, up to 20 things he will not think about. At present, this includes loyalty cards for the chain as a whole. Experiments have been running for 2 years at 20 stores, but they will not be expanded further. They just add cost and complexity, the data set is a nightmare to analyse and, anyway, everyone else has done it.

A second major initiative that Asda refuses to take is international expansion. This would be a drain on management resources, and would be an insignificant addition. The only international operation worth the candle would be 300 superstores in the United States, competing with Wal-Mart; that is simply not feasible.

Finally, Asda will not develop financial services on its own. Instead, Lloyds TSB will operate banks within Asda stores. Such concessions can bring in very acceptable returns (£10 million in profits from concessions currently), and make more sense of the customer relationship. If Asda were the bank, they would necessarily find themselves in the position of having to say 'No' to some customers, damaging the relationship of trust they are trying to build.

FUTURE CHALLENGES

For the moment, Asda has strong management, a confident, colleague culture, and a focussed strategy. This has produced good results as it catches up lost ground, and it has further to go in equalling competitors' standards in sales per square foot, margins and ROCE. In core markets, they have not yet equalled Tesco in fresh food, or Marks & Spencer in non-food. The large store format is a differentiator and does give them opportunities – but it is inflexible. They cannot offer medium-sized local stores (as Safeway can), or city-centre small outlets like Tesco or Marks & Spencer. If the market as a whole moves away from the superstore idea, they will be stranded.

The latest results, in late 1998, suggest that the LFL growth is slowing, and that Asda are falling behind their major competitors (though some sectors, such as fresh produce and fresh meat, are doing better). This may be temporary, but is a worrying sign.

The basic problem of lack of scale remained. Without Safeway (or some other takeover or merger), they would not be able to compete with Tesco and Sainsbury's on buying power. The aborted merger with Kingfisher, and subsequent agreement to a bid from Wal-Mart (see below), showed that Asda knew that scale was still a problem.

The cost base is another issue. Although it claims that its cost base is carefully designed not only to be low, but suited to its operation, some critics feel that it is too low. Management may become overstretched, and staff may begin to find that being a colleague does not compensate for the lower-than-average wages. Some critics have suggested that the slowdown in LFL growth reflects staff shortages, leading to product-availability problems.

New initiatives continue. In June 1998 the firm announced a home delivery service, a satellite TV shopping channel, and an online store. The home delivery service will operate from a warehouse in the London area, where Asda has found it difficult to acquire sites for superstores. Leighton, who had previously insisted that home delivery from the back of a store could not work, now says that their operation will be profitable: it will break even on 500 orders of £80 a day, from a catchment area of 450,000 households without access to an Asda store.

The shopping channel will be preceded by six programmes before Christmas, and their own channel will be set up in 1999. The Internet store will offer music, videos and books, and will, according to Archie Norman, take Asda into its first international markets.

The Asda strategy therefore seemed good for a few more years, but after that they would need a major new strategic shift. What that might be was not clear, but increasing scale, either in the UK or abroad, must be part of it; management's abortive talks with prospective partners show that it recognizes this, even if it is reluctant to admit it publicly. Leighton's view is that 'It's on managing in crisis-filled times. You look around the world, there isn't a piece of good news. In a couple of places, it's really hairy. You've got to change the way you manage the business. Prune as you go. Travel light, travel fast. You must think: how can we come out of this even stronger?'

THE WAL-MART TAKEOVER

In June 1999, as this book went to press, Asda and Wal-Mart announced an agreed bid: the US giant would buy the British chain for £6.7 billion cash, trumping the previously agreed bid from Kingfisher. We had been predicting that Wal-Mart would, despite denials, be interested in expanding in Britain. It is significant that Bobby Martin, for six years head of Wal-Mart's international division, immediately resigned, suggesting that the strategy was not universally supported within the company.

As we have noted, Asda was the obvious target for Wal-Mart. It most clearly followed a similar pattern, though on a smaller scale. Asda's average store size of 40,000 sq ft put them well ahead of their British rivals, and they majored on lower prices. Indeed, much of their strategy was, consciously or unconsciously, modelled on the US leader. The scale, of course, is vastly different: Wal-Mart's supercenters in America are around 200,000 sq ft, and their grocery prices 15 per cent or more below their rivals, compared with Asda's 5 per cent.

What the takeover will mean for Asda is the subject of intense speculation. They will gain from Wal-Mart's superb IT and logistics skills (it is IBM's biggest EPOS customer). They may be able to ally that to a more efficient use of space: Wal-Mart uses fully 88 per cent of its floor space for selling, against only 55 per cent at Asda, and Asda may also have room for expansion on some of its sites. They may gain some economies of scale in buying power, although it is difficult to see this producing significant cost savings in food, at least in the short term.

The main obstacle to applying the full Wal-Mart model in Britain will, however, remain the shortage of large sites, and restrictive planning policies. Unless the Competition Commission (the re-named Monopolies and Mergers Commission) recommends a substantial relaxation of planning guidelines in order to free up competition, there is little room for Wal-Mart's gigantic stores. Even in the USA, many towns now resist the arrival of these monsters, and the climate in Britain is against further threats to healthy town centres. Even a reduced-size Wal-Mart would still be a formidable new competitor.

It seems certain that Asda's commitment to low prices will be confirmed, and strengthened. An all-out price war may not be imminent, but the pressure on prices will be downward. Asda's management team will continue to run the operations, so in the short term we expect to see evolution, not revolution.

4

The Safeway story

What we now know as the Safeway group, fourth largest of the UK's multiple food retailers, acquired the name only in 1987 (the name came from the US company, but since 1987 the British group has been completely independent of its US counterpart). Its history embraces the acquisition and disposal of some of the oldest of British grocery names going back to 1819, so it could be called the oldest as well as the newest of the current big four. It is intimately bound up with the careers of three men – James Gulliver, Alistair Grant and David Webster – who set out in the 1970s to build a business in the food industry. With hindsight, we can see four phases:

- The acquisition phase, 1978–81, in which they built up a portfolio of manufacturing, wholesaling and retailing businesses;
- The Allied stage, 1982–5, the beginning of retailing dominance;
- A stage of rationalization and concentration on retailing, 1985–7;
- The Safeway years, from 1987 to the present, leading to the emergence of a competitive supermarket chain.

For much of that period, it was third in the market, and has consistently maintained good margins. But its growth has recently been slower than that of the aggressive Tesco and Asda; Asda regained its earlier lead over Safeway in 1996. It now faces both short-term and longer-term strategic challenges, and only time will tell whether its response is good enough.

THE ACQUISITION YEARS

James Gulliver was a dynamic manager who had risen rapidly to the post of Chairman of Fine Fare (see 'The Three Musketeers' below). He had appointed Alistair Grant – originally a marketing man with Unilever – as New Business Development Director in 1968. David Webster was a merchant banker.

THE THREE MUSKETEERS

The story of what became Argyll, then Safeway, is inescapably that of the three men – all Scots – who built it. In the early period, James Gulliver was the best known, then after his retirement Alistair Grant took over leadership and public prominence; but the three men always worked as a team, and that was perhaps their distinguishing strength.

James Gulliver was the early driving force, and was happy to use press exposure to further his business aims. Garfield Weston recognized his early promise as a manager, and promoted him in his early thirties to Managing Director and later Chairman of Fine Fare (a subsidiary of Associated British Foods). Gulliver transformed Fine Fare from a barely profitable group of small stores – with poor management and no consumer franchise – into a strong national chain, highly profitable and with a group of capable managers. He achieved this with what Grant later called 'almost demonic energy, setting very tough and specific objectives for every part of it'.

At the age of 42, Gulliver decided that the time had come to run his own business, and build his own capital (he was often quoted as saying that the pursuit of wealth is the prime, if not the only reason for being in business). He persuaded Alistair Grant, whom he had appointed as Business Development Director of Fine Fare, to join him, together with a merchant banker they knew well, David Webster. The story of the whirlwind activity the trio engaged in is told in this chapter. Gulliver led with even greater energy than before; the three worked seven-day weeks, meeting at Gulliver's home every Sunday to review events and plan new initiatives.

But Gulliver was also a man who enjoyed life to the full. To quote Grant again:

> He was fearlessly assertive, and had certain fixed ideas which he could never resist articulating. For example, he habitually told French wine waiters that the French knew nothing about wine. He despaired of ever persuading David Webster and me to wear suitable neckties – ours were always too dull – and, despite his passion for ski-ing and fast cars he was always counselling me to give up horses – boring and dangerous.
>
> (Grant, 1996)

Gulliver had the drive and energy to achieve most of his goals, and the personality and flamboyance that made him attractive to many friends, and to the press. He was happy to be a public figure, and to enjoy the fruits of his success. Despite his dedication to wealth creation, he had a wider view, and said to Grant and Webster, 'Boys, always remember that business is not the main object of life – if we fail, it will not be the end of the world.'

When he retired, exhausted and perhaps disillusioned by the Distillers affair, Alistair Grant stepped into the limelight, and led the development of Safeway as we know it. From Marketing Director of Batchelor's Foods, he learned his retailing skills under Gulliver at Fine Fare, honing them in the process of turning the collection of businesses and stores that the team gathered into a coherent and competitive national supermarket group (described in this chapter). Knighted for his services, Sir Alistair Grant became Governor of the Bank of Scotland in 1997. As David Webster commented wryly, it was ironic that he had started out as a banker, but was now a grocer, while Alistair was running a bank.

David Webster, now Chairman of Safeway, is the quiet man of the trio. It is tempting to cast him as the money man, given his background, but he was always more than that, a full member of the team. He is relatively quiet in manner, but is a deep thinker with a strategic view of the industry.

Perhaps the three musketeers is an appropriate name for this threesome who achieved so much together. Gulliver was so much the public face that it is easy to forget that it was three people, right from the beginning.

In 1972, Gulliver decided that he would set off on a new career as an entre-
preneur, and he persuaded Grant and Webster to join him. The food distribution industry in the early 1970s was turbulent and changing fast; the three
saw opportunities to build up a business, but it was at the outset an opportunistic venture.

They bought a significant minority in Oriel Foods, which had a stock market
quotation; its businesses were that of a traditional bacon and provision wholesaler and an edible-oil refiner. This was in itself not a promising start, but it
gave them the base on which to build scale: they bought another wholesaler, a
VG cash and carry business, a mid-sized wholesale cash and carry, and a
frozen food wholesaler, building a total of £55 million sales, all within the
space of ten months. In many ways this was a dry run for the subsequent build-
up of Argyll.

The team had started to practise their management skills on the collection of
food distribution and wholesaling businesses, whose scale now began to give
them buying muscle, when in late 1973 RCA Corporation, a diversified US
company, offered them two-and-a-half times what they had invested; they did
not refuse, and Oriel was bought for £11 million in cash. The team stayed on to
direct RCA's European strategy, but the driving, ambitious Gulliver still saw
huge opportunities outside. The parent was experiencing major problems
partly caused by the oil crisis, and the three offered to buy Oriel back. In the
difficult economic times, with interest rates at 17 per cent and the pound at
£1.05 to the dollar, the parties could not agree a price. Gulliver left at the end
of 1976, with an embargo on re-entering the retail grocery business within two
years; the other two left in 1977. The three set up James Gulliver Associates,
and embarked on a whirlwind of takeover activity.

In 1978, Morgan Edwards, a Shrewsbury wholesale and retail group, were
making substantial losses; their retail chain, Supavalu, had adopted a
discounting strategy, but was suffering from the price war launched by Tesco.
As the trio by now had a high reputation in the trade, Morgan Edwards asked
Grant to step in as Chairman, and he and Webster took a 30 per cent stake
through the James Gulliver Associates (JGA) subsidiary, Avonmiles. Initially,
it was fire-fighting to save the company. They put in badly needed
management controls, sold businesses, closed stores and raised retail prices.
They bought Paddys, which had 31 stores, to spread overheads, and brought
the group back into profitability.

Meanwhile JGA had bought, among other companies, Louis C Edwards and
Sons (Manchester) Ltd (LCE), a meat retail, wholesale and manufacturing
business. (The eponymous Louis Edwards will be known to some as the long-
time chairman of Manchester United football club; his son, Martin, is still
Chairman.) LCE became the vehicle for the food interests of the three men,

and Webster was installed as Chairman. They closed the loss-making canning, wholesale catering and frozen meat manufacturing businesses, leaving only retailing. With the reputation of the troika firmly established in the City, they used the strong share price to buy Yorkshire Biscuits and Furniss, a Cornwall-based maker of quality biscuits.

With Gulliver now released from his covenant, the three began looking for further expansion, mainly in the north-west (the LCE base). In November 1979 they bought Cordon Bleu Freezer Food Centres, and later 38 Dalgety Freezer Centres.

As there was now a possible conflict of interest between LCE and Morgan Edwards, LCE acquired Morgan Edwards in1980 for £4.3 million. The new group was christened Argyll Foods in March 1980, with Gulliver as Chairman. At this stage, the group consisted of two biscuit manufacturers, 12 butchers plus 48 concessions in Woolworth's, freezer centres, 50 retail grocery stores, and a Spar wholesaler. The grocery stores averaged 3,500 sq ft, with a range of 2,000–10,000; they were mainly in suburban or rural locations, and operated as soft discounters.

The acquisitions continued with the purchase of 66 Freezer Fare units from Vestey in October 1980, after their third rights issue in 18 months. Five Bonimart freezer centres were added, so Cordon Bleu now had 180 stores (second after Bejam, the market leader).

In December 1980 Argyll, in a turn of the wheel, bought Oriel Foods from RCA, which had decided on a different strategy. The three men were obviously familiar with the business, as they had largely created it. The price of £19.5 million represented 80 per cent of Argyll's capitalization – but it was a good deal. The senior management team included their former colleague, Charles Lawrie, who had built up Lo-Cost discount stores (58 shops in the Midlands and Wales). Oriel also embraced Mojo cash and carry, the Snowking frozen food wholesaler, Liverpool Central Oil (edible oils), and Gold Crown Foods (blender and packer of teas and coffee). The deal was partially self-financing, and Argyll was now one of the top ten food groups, with a turnover of £250 million.

Lo-Cost was complementary to Supavalu, but more effectively managed, so all the stores were integrated as Lo-Cost. In 1982 the group bought 67 Pricerite shops from BAT – with aggregate sales £100 million, they brought additional economies of scale. Rationalization, the imposition of management controls, and tight cash management led to rising profits.

Between 1978 and 1982 sales went from £20 million to £230 million; profit from a loss of £300,000 to a profit of £7.1 million; earnings per share from negative to 7.9p; market capitalization from £0.5 million to £42.5 million.

All this gave the team a stellar reputation – but a setback was waiting. In 1981 Argyll bought a 20 per cent stake in Linfood (later Gateway), and bid for the balance; the deal would have been worth £91 million, at a time when Argyll was valued at £46 million. Alec Monk (CEO of Linfood) fought back, but Argyll's victory seemed assured when, in November 1981, the bid was referred to the Monopolies and Mergers Commission (MMC). The Argyll bid lapsed – probably the first setback the three had experienced.

THE ALLIED SUPPLIERS DEAL

In 1982 Sir James Goldsmith asked for offers for Allied Suppliers (see 'The Allied Story' below). Having assembled the group, Goldsmith wanted to concentrate elsewhere. Despite the fact that this was a much bigger business than Linfood, the deal was not referred to the MMC. Argyll bought Allied for £101 million, issuing 95 million shares to raise £81 million, the rest being paid in cash. Goldsmith had a formidable reputation as deal-maker, and many critics wondered whether Argyll had overpaid; later, the logic of the deal was justified by events, and the price seemed reasonable. Argyll's gearing was now 100 per cent.

THE ALLIED STORY

Allied Suppliers was formed by the 1929 merger of several long-established grocery chains. These included many famous names, such as Home and Colonial (see Introduction), Lipton's, and Maypole Dairies (which had originally been founded in 1819). Allied acquired Galbraith and Templeton in Scotland, and continued to grow up to the early 1980s, when it bought Cater's from Debenhams. By 1982, Allied had 923 stores, and was the fourth biggest food multiple, with sales of £847 million. Of the stores, 128 operated under the Presto fascia, and 795 as Lipton's, Templeton or Galbraith. The national market share stood at 4.6 per cent, but in areas of regional strength was higher – 17 per cent in Scotland and 9 per cent in Tyne Tees. Presto had two million sq ft of selling space, and accounted for 52 per cent of Allied sales; the stores averaged 15,000 sq ft. Liptons were mainly in small, minor towns, but had a good reputation for fresh food.

DIVERSIFYING INTO DRINKS

To understand the components of the Argyll Group public company that emerged, and the subsequent events, we need to go back several years to James Gulliver Associates (JGA). In the frantic early years of acquisitions, JGA had bought a substantial minority in and assumed effective management control of Alpine Holdings (a home improvement firm) and Amalgamated Distilled Products (ADP), both listed companies. Alpine was sold in 1982 for a large gain, but ADP was retained, and will play a part in later developments. JGA was merged into Argyll, and was renamed Argyll Group plc in 1983.

Alongside the retail grocery business, Gulliver pursued a strategy of complementary diversification. The idea was to use the cash surplus forecast from retailing. A distribution network was in place, and created opportunities for brand development and international expansion. ADP was a Scotch distiller with £13.7 million sales and £113,000 profits when acquired. In 1981 George Morton (rum) was bought for £3.2 million, and North West Vintners (the Liquorsave chain) for £4.7 million. In 1982 the team bought Barton Brands – a Chicago producer of bourbon, gin and rum, and distributor of imported beers – for £24.6 million.

Ever ambitious, at the end of 1985 Argyll launched a hostile £1.9 billion offer for Distillers Company; the Argyll market capitalization at the time was £0.6 billion. The opportunity, as Argyll saw it, was to create an international drinks business, based in Scotland, and with an enviable but under-exploited brand. What happened then is notorious. Guinness intervened, using what were later shown to be illegal and improper methods. Chaos and confusion reigned, the Argyll offer lapsed, costing £55 million, and Guinness won the battle. At the time, and ironically in the light of subsequent events, Saunders and his colleagues at Guinness were seen in the City as establishment figures, and the Argyll team as upstarts (many of the Guinness team were prosecuted, and Saunders himself spent time in jail). That Guinness then proceeded to show that the Argyll trio had been right, and that Distillers was indeed a poorly managed business with bright prospects, was little consolation. It was, in effect, the end of the drinks diversification. Gulliver decided that, without major international brands, he could not build a world-class drinks business. In 1987, Argyll sold the drinks interests and the remaining food manufacturing firms to concentrate wholly on retailing.

The rationale for synergies between an international drinks business and a UK supermarket chain is not cast-iron, and the two halves would almost certainly have had to be run as separate businesses, stretching management time and effort. Indeed, it is likely that, had the bid succeeded, Argyll Foods

105

would have been divested, and part of the history of UK food retailing would have turned out differently. So traumatic was the Distillers affair that many considered Gulliver a spent man afterwards; he left Argyll in 1987.

TACKLING THE RETAIL ISSUES

The Argyll team, led in this instance by Alistair Grant, now set out on the ambitious task of creating from the collection of fascias and properties that they had assembled 'a front-rank superstore business with the scale, profitability and quality of resources required to compete successfully in the UK food retail sector' (Grant, 1996). (Grant became Chairman and Chief Executive of the Food Division in 1982, CEO of the group in 1986, and Chairman and CEO in 1988. Colin Smith became CEO in 1993, and David Webster took over as Chairman when Grant retired in 1997.)

The first step was a profit enhancement programme to raise the margin from 1.6 per cent to 3 per cent in 3 years. This entailed:

- a unified management structure;
- disposal of surplus assets;
- improvement in working capital;
- staff reduction;
- renegotiation of supplier contracts to reflect the increased buying power;
- detailed annual planning.

The results of the profit enhancement programme were impressive: by 1985 the 3 per cent margin was achieved, and £44 million operating profit. Improving cash allowed 20 large new Presto supermarkets to be built. Liverpool Central Oil was sold in 1983, and Amos Hinton & Sons plc, a northeast based grocery chain, was bought in 1984 for £23.3 million.

DEVELOPING A MODERN FOOD-RETAILING MULTIPLE

The team could see that competition in the grocery business was now marked by established retail brands, centralized distribution systems, and computerized ordering. Argyll received only 35 per cent of its goods from central warehouses. It was operating under five fascias (Presto, Liptons, Templeton,

Galbraith, Hintons), plus Lo-Cost and Cordon Bleu in the North West division. There were three own-label ranges. All this produced high costs, no benefits, and merely added complication.

They decided to focus on Presto and Lo-Cost as the two main fascias, and concentrate on retailing. Presto would include the larger Hintons, Templeton in Scotland, and the larger Lipton's supermarkets. Lo-Cost would be used for smaller stores.

Four new Presto distribution centres of 200,000 sq ft were built, and a new total systems approach to store management was introduced: integrated with distribution. 'Information technology became the central nervous system of every aspect of operations, logistics, trading and financial control' (Grant, 1996).

During 1986–87, 369 Templetons, Hintons and Lipton's stores were converted to Presto, and 73 Lipton's to Lo-Cost. The Presto trading area gained two million sq ft, to reach 4.2 million sq ft. This allowed a wider range, especially of own-label, which reached 33 per cent of sales in 1986. A more competitive pricing policy was adopted.

By 1987, therefore, Argyll had achieved its aim of developing the basis of a modern, competitive supermarket group, and was ready to take the next major step.

THE SAFEWAY PURCHASE

Safeway, a subsidiary of the US group, started in the UK in 1962 with seven supermarkets and a few smaller stores in Greater London. Its first purpose-built store was opened in Bedford in 1963. By 1975 it was operating largely autonomously from headquarters in Aylesford, Kent. By 1978 it had 69 stores and, by 1987, 133. Fully 85 per cent of products were delivered through a national distribution system.

Despite its relative autonomy, Safeway brought over to Britain many ideas from its US parent. It thus had a reputation for innovation: in-store bakeries, money-back guarantees, larger stores with wider aisles, refrigerated displays, freshness control dating, delicatessen, self-service produce – all these were pioneered in the UK by Safeway. No less than 35 per cent of sales were own label, a high proportion for the time. The breadth of range in its bigger stores also set it apart. Its Wimbledon supermarket in 1962 was one of the largest in Europe; it stocked books and magazines, housewares, greetings cards, and hosiery alongside the normal groceries. A competitor's reported comment, on visiting the shop, was: 'We are not going to be selling stockings and tampons.' He was, of course, to change his mind later.

By 1987, Safeway UK had 133 stores, covering 2 million sq ft of selling space; it was the sixth largest chain, with 3.4 per cent of the total market (though with shares of 6 per cent in London, 7 per cent in the south, and 9 per cent in Scotland). Sales had reached £1.04 billion, and profit £43.8 million.

In 1986 the Safeway parent received a hostile bid from the Dart Corporation. With the help of KKR, the legendary financiers, it engineered a successful management buyout, but as part of the deal had to sell off assets to help pay the huge debt created. It therefore asked for offers for Safeway UK.

There was a compelling logic for Argyll in the purchase: the Safeway stores were geographically compatible with Presto, Presto had superior distribution and systems, Safeway was a great brand. In February 1987, Argyll completed the deal for £681 million. The merged chain would have 102 Presto stores, all of over 10,000 sq ft, and 133 Safeway stores (again, all over 10,000 sq ft), with a total of 4.7 million sq ft. The decision was made immediately to adopt Safeway as the main brand.

With this base, Argyll set ambitious aims: to triple the Safeway area from 2 to 6 million sq ft. To achieve this, they would convert over 100 large Presto stores, and accelerate the development of new sites. They would merge the distribution and operating systems, and retrain Presto staff in Safeway practices. A Safeway store on average achieved 55 per cent better sales per square foot than a comparable Presto, and 76 per cent better operating profit. These reflected Safeway's superior product mix, especially in fresh food. The team also saw benefits and savings in buying, central services, field management, and marketing. Using the combined asset base, and the unique store-based retail skills acquired with Safeway, they set out on a three-and-a-half year programme to transform Argyll.

There would be two stages. Stage 1 was profit enhancement. The aim was to introduce best practice in every aspect of store operations and systems; every aspect was scrutinized, and absolutely nothing was sacred. Stage 2 was Presto store conversions. Farnham and Morden were taken as prototypes, and converted to the full Safeway specification. This took eight weeks, and cost £700,000 each. Safeway staff were brought in to run the stores, while the Presto staff were sent away for retraining. The results were immediate and impressive. Sales rose 55 per cent, and profits doubled within 12 months.

With further applications in other stores, it was able to re-examine store design and construction. It found that it could deliver the Safeway proposition at 20 per cent lower cost, without impairing the effectiveness of the formula.

Total costs of the refurbishments amounted to £90 million; these were charged as exceptionals, spread over three years. By May 1991, profit had reached £291 million, (three-and-a-half times the 1987 figure), and turnover had climbed from £1.1 billion to £3.5 billion, while the margin reached an outstanding 6.7 per cent.

The remaining Presto stores also gained from the improved skill base, and increased their profitability. The name was used as a second fascia in the north of England and Scotland; this accounted for 215 stores in 1991, with 1.2 million sq ft of selling space. Lo-Cost gained the smaller stores, representing 9 per cent of total sales in1991. The chain was well established in the discount sector, and was adopted as the second fascia in the southern half of England.

The team were now well on the way to their objective declared in 1987: 'To establish Argyll as a retail group of enduring quality with Safeway as one of the most successful and respected UK food retailers of the 1990s.' They had undertaken extensive consumer research in 1989 to identify the unique features of Safeway, and how they could make the offer even more attractive. Interest centred on the product range, especially fresh food and own-label, customer care and service programmes. Regional boards were set up to make the chain more responsive to local needs. Customer suggestions schemes were adopted and conferences were held to test new store concepts. The new Coventry store, opened in 1990, incorporated many of the ideas; it was 37,000 sq ft, and was seen as a prototype for the 1990s. It was set out in zones: fresh food round the perimeter, groceries in central aisles, services in the foyer and at the front. There was a food court delicatessen, fresh fish counter, bakery and meat.

Argyll had achieved a major transformation, and could be proud both of the process and the results. But competition does not stand still: how should it continue?

SAFEWAY IN THE 1990s – BUILDING THE BRAND

At this point, Safeway saw itself as the smallest of the three major retailers, and some considerable way behind the leaders – Sainsbury's and Tesco – unable to catch them up. Apparently, they did not see Asda as a major competitor, an irony in view of the fact that Asda would in fact overtake them in sales within a few years. Asda had previously been ahead of Safeway, but had run into problems (see Chapter 3); their target market was different from Safeway, too, so ignoring them may have seemed justifiable.

There were three elements in the strategy adopted by Safeway:

- Continuing store development, using rights issues (£387 million in 1991); the aim was to open 25 new stores per year;
- Continue the development of the infrastructure, recognizing the need for a major investment in the supply chain;
- Improve the customer proposition.

The problem for Safeway was that all the others were doing the same, and the two leaders had huge scale advantages. Safeway's mixed portfolio of store sizes and locations turns out not be a major benefit in this situation. Lo-Cost was operating in an unattractive sector and, after falling into loss, was sold off in stages in 1994. Eventually, it was decided, the Presto fascia would be converted to Safeway, or sold/closed, leaving the focus on the Safeway brand.

The team recognized that, as a smaller competitor, it had to be consistently innovative to stay in the fight. It has a good claim to have succeeded, and an incomplete list of innovations in the 1990s would include:

- The 'Harry' advertising campaign in 1994, which had tremendous impact and recognition – it is generally regarded in the trade as the best supermarket campaign. It was campaignable, leading to subsequent 'Molly' and 'Baby' campaigns.
- The theme, 'Lightening the load' was adopted and is still used.
- 'Safeway Savers' in 1994 offered up to 100 low-priced frequent purchases.
- 'Price Watch', also in 1994, gave guaranteed prices as low as competitors.
- Self-scanning was introduced in 1995 as a trial in Solihull (years ahead of any competitor).
- The ABC loyalty card was launched in 1995, rolled out to 103 stores, then nationally.
- The 'Make a difference' campaign, aimed at outstanding customer service, was introduced.
- The 'Savers' pledge' came into being: Safeway Savers would save at least 50 per cent on most popular alternatives.
- In 1996 the idea of cutting out unnecessary shopper time was taken further with a test of unassisted payment (the shopper checks his or her own shopping out at a special till).
- A joint venture with BP was launched; a network of 100 food and fuel sites has been developed; the food offer aims to cover a near superstore range, and at superstore prices.
- Safeway and Abbey National launched a joint venture ABC Bonus Account in 1997.
- A personalized home-shopping service was introduced.
- A baby discount scheme for new families started.
- New intelligent scanners, which greet customers and give them personalized messages, appeared in some stores.

All this suggests that Safeway could justifiably feel that it had been doing a good job, and indeed, its results back that up – but only up to a point. The 1990s saw increasing sales and share, but Safeway did not grow as fast as competitors, especially Tesco and Asda. It was overtaken by Asda in 1996 (see Figure 0.5, Introduction).

There were two major problems: store size, and perceived price. The mixed store portfolio offers some advantages, and they have some very good sites, including superstores; but most shops are smaller and less profitable. Crucially, they missed out on superstore build-up that all the main competitors were engaged in. It is not clear why this was so: whether it was a deliberate strategic decision, or merely a failure of concentration. At any rate, this must be seen as a missed opportunity; one which has left Safeway at a strategic disadvantage, and which it has been working hard to put right.

The second problem is that the Safeway offer has been perceived by customers to be higher priced than the major rivals. This was true at one time, the firm admits, but claims that it is so no longer; but shoppers' perceptions are very slow to change. Probably as a result of this perception, it attracts a lower proportion of main shop customers than the other majors, with a consequent reduction of average spend (see AGB charts, Appendix).

Its strategic problems were aggravated by tactical difficulties in 1997. It suffered from two technical problems, the effects of which illustrate the brutal nature of the competitive battle; no one can afford to falter for a step. Safeway use satellite communication to their stores (another first), but they lost 150 stores for three days. In a separate incident, a memory card failed, and the mainframe was down for seven hours. The problem was not so much the technical failures themselves, but the fact that the business did not have sufficiently developed fall-back procedures to enable them to recover rapidly. With 20,000 stock-keeping units (SKUs) and 500 stores, an enormously complex system has little room for error.

The effect: inaccurate orders, product not available, empty shelves; availability had already been a problem, and the incidents exacerbated it. Although there is a temporary lull in such circumstances, customers soon notice, and sales dropped sharply. The difficulties also affected perceptions of value, which the firm had been trying so hard to correct.

Management took several actions to remedy the situation:

- More resilience was built into the system (including an automated fall-back procedure).
- More cost was deliberately put back into the stores: higher stock levels (and wastage), more labour, and customer incentives.
- They decided to use the ABC loyalty card to target heavy buyers: the offer was tiered rewards for higher spending (triple points for spending £240 per month). This is targeted at their main customer group, and is difficult for competitors to follow.

- The 'Price Protected' scheme offers double the price back if customers can find the product cheaper elsewhere.

The aim of the promotions is to encourage trial, by both lapsed and new customers. Early results were encouraging, but of course much would depend on competitor reaction. Availability, for example, which had declined to below 90 per cent in August 1997 (against the average 95 per cent of competitors), recovered to over 95 per cent. Safeway has developed its own statistical model, which measures stock shortages (eg 10 baskets go through with no bananas; this suggests that bananas may be out of stock, since a high proportion of baskets normally contain the item). The firm thinks that this real-time system may become a differentiator – it is hard to maintain over 95 per cent availability without extra cost. Using the model leads to continuous ordering, and wave deliveries through the day. Other initiatives include Internet access for suppliers to the stock system; this is already offered to preferred suppliers now, and will spread.

CURRENT STRATEGY

As Safeway's Chairman, David Webster, points out, it is important to recognize the overall structure of the market in which Safeway has to compete. Although we frequently talk (as do the City) of the big four, there are in reality a big two of Tesco and Sainsbury's, followed at some distance by the second division of Asda and Safeway, with sales about half those of their bigger rivals. The Co-op and Somerfield/Kwik Save have sales similar to Asda and Safeway, but are not seen as direct competition (poor quality stores and/or offer). Morrison forms a powerful third division, while Waitrose, Iceland and Budgen are niche players. The European discounters (Aldi, Netto, Lidl) have built up over 400 stores, and may offer a powerful threat at that end of the market.

Superstores are the dominant format in the UK, and only the top four plus Morrison own them. Scale is hugely important, and on this measure Asda and Safeway are closer to the top two, with 8 million and 9.5 million sq ft respectively, compared with Tesco's 14.6 million and Sainsbury's 12 million. However, Safeway in particular falls down on sales intensity, achieving only about three-quarters the level of their competitors.

Sales offer scale advantages in buying, but also in other key areas. For example, if Safeway spends 1 per cent of sales on IT, that is half what Tesco can afford. It is more sensible for Safeway to spend on TV advertising in Scotland, where it has 20 per cent share (and market leadership) than in the south-east, where it has only 8 per cent against Tesco and Sainsbury's 30 per cent or more each. Capital expenditure had to be funnelled into store development, at prices higher than in other countries because of the scarcity of land, and because planners insist on higher building standards than for other types of store (such as the DIY sheds, or indeed the hypermarkets built elsewhere in Europe). Safeway's strategy was therefore constrained, and must be seen in its context. For example, although it developed superstores where it could, it also targeted market towns hitherto neglected by the majors, where it could site a store big enough to take most of the available trade, and deter other new entrants.

Starting almost from scratch, Safeway managed to build 248 superstores by 1998, with an average of 26,000 sq ft. This gives it a total of 9.5 million sq ft, two-thirds of it in superstores and three-quarters in stores of over 20,000 sq ft.

In sales density, however, it is still some way behind. Both Tesco and Sainsbury's achieve (in 1998) almost £21 per square foot; the difference between them is that, although Sainsbury's was for many years the clear leader, Tesco has increased its sales density by more than 40 per cent over four years, while Sainsbury's has remained almost static. Asda has also increased by 40 per cent (to just over £17), while Safeway has managed only 18 per cent gain, to some £15. This was Safeway's target, but it leaves it chasing the leaders: it is under-performing Asda by £2.30 per square foot per week, or £1.2 billion per year; and Tesco and Sainsbury's by £5.75 per week, or £2.8 billion per year. This can be seen as a problem, but also as a huge opportunity if the gap can be filled. Like-for-like growth will be the measure of its retailing skills, and we saw how in 1997 technical problems caused a sales shortfall, and early 1998 saw little recovery. Its central difficulty is the comparatively low share of main shoppers, to which the stubborn perception of relatively high prices must be a main contributor. Its target is now to attract more main shoppers, thereby raising sales density to £17 and beyond – while its rivals are also straining to widen the gap.

The current strategy has five main planks:

- category management;
- product availability;
- value for money;
- customer service;
- store quality.

In its targeting, Safeway is trying to be more family-oriented than its competitors. Using an accelerated category management roll-out, it is reviewing all its ranges. In bakery, for example, this led to the introduction of 100 new lines, mainly aimed at children, and continuous baking. In 1998 alone, 50 new meat counters, with traditional butchers, were installed. Produce is also a focus, again bringing traditional craft skills back into the stores (compare the similar Asda effort: Safeway claim now to have overtaken Asda's fresh produce volume). Customer profiles from the ABC-card database help in this drive to sharpen focus and perceived quality.

The new availability programme (under the title 'Fill That Gap') is proving robust, and availability is now at 95–96 per cent. Other services aimed at the same target are:

- crèches, of which there will be 100 by the end of 1998. These are phenomenally successful, to the extent that some customers can't get in at weekends. The company claims that they are not a loss-maker.
- The Shop & Go, Easy Pay, and Collect & Go services. Customers who use these are, say Safeway, fiercely loyal. The aim is to lock in the big spenders.
- A Customer Care Performance Share Option Plan rewards good service, measured by weekly mystery-shopper measures.

In non-food, it is also trying to target the family shopper, though Safeway admits that lack of space will inhibit its efforts. This shows again how a missed step continues to hamper strategic development. The ABC card, however, which is the pivot of many of these initiatives, is still a strategic advantage if used effectively.

The company will continue to spend heavily on refurbishment and extensions (£140 million in 1998), and have developed a 'Tardis' format for medium stores. (For non-British readers, the Tardis was the spaceship of Dr Who, the hero of an enormously popular television series. The Tardis appeared from the outside to be a telephone box, but inside was vast.) The format delivers 85 per cent of the typical superstore offer in a medium-sized store. In the Slough site, this produced an increase of 15 per cent in sales.

Safeway has linked with BP to develop petrol station convenience stores; it currently has seven trial sites, and national roll-out of over 100 is planned. The trial stores are achieving over £22 a week sales density (excluding petrol).

Safeway will not go international, except perhaps through joint ventures or alliances. Its existing alliances are of limited value: the partners have different motives, so real co-operation is difficult. Bilateral schemes work best.

In summary, Safeway now has a strategy, and is implementing it – but will it work? In late 1998 and early 1999, results were encouraging: LFL increases of 5 per cent, then 3 per cent, significantly better than Sainsbury's. In the medium term, there are real challenges. Asda also aims squarely at the family shopper, it is extremely consistent, and is cheaper (which ought to appeal to the family above all). Safeway also risks alienating other shoppers by its focus (dropping other lines that non-family shoppers like). They claim that sophisticated use of the database allows them to square this particular circle, but only time will tell if they are right. It cannot compete with Tesco's volume and clout; it cannot imitate the total Sainsbury's offer. It is, in Michael Porter's phrase, 'stuck in the middle', and vulnerable. The aborted talks with Asda showed that the company appreciates the need for scale, but it is not at all clear where this may come from. A European alliance (or takeover) may offer the only way out.

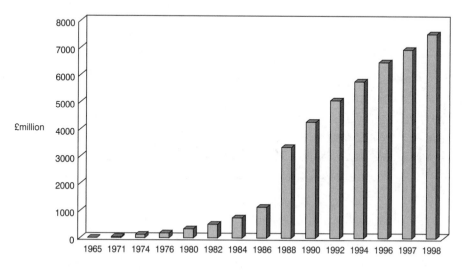

Figure 4.1   *Safeway sales 1965–98*

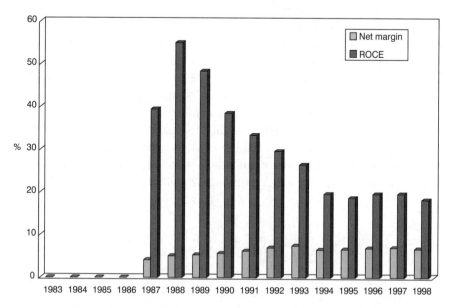

Figure 4.2   *Argyll/Safeway net margin and ROCE 1983–98*

5

The Marks & Spencer story

The rise of Marks & Spencer from market stalls to become one of the world's most respected retailers is well known. Moreover, they are not grocers – so why include them? It is true that Marks & Spencer have only a small share of the total grocery market (around 3 per cent); but their share of some segments is much higher (they claim to be the UK's biggest butcher, greengrocer and fishmonger). Most important, their influence on the rest of the trade has been out of all proportion to their modest share. As relentless innovators, they have led many new developments in food retailing, especially chilled prepared foods. Principles of partnership with their suppliers, and supply chain management, learned in their clothing business, have been applied to food with revolutionary effect. Only in internationalizing have they seemed fallible, but they are now operating successfully in 32 countries round the world.

'DON'T ASK THE PRICE, IT'S A PENNY'

Michael Marks, like many others in the 1880s, was a penniless Russian/Polish Jew looking for a better life through emigration. Although the facts are uncertain, it seems that he landed in London, intending to join his elder brother, Barnett;

unfortunately, Barnett had already set sail without warning for the New World.

It is certain that, speaking not a word of English, Michael was wandering through the garment district of Leeds (an important industrial city in the north of England), hoping to find work as a tailor. Isaac Dewhirst, an established local businessman, was standing outside his warehouse with his manager, Charles Backhouse. Backhouse, seeing that Marks looked lost, and speaking a little Yiddish, offered help with directions. After hearing Michael's story, Dewhirst lent him five pounds' worth of goods, saying that he could pay when he had sold them. Michael hawked the goods (small haberdashery items) round the villages of the surrounding villages. Seldom can a single act of personal philanthropy have had such far-reaching consequences. The Dewhirst firm still exists, and indeed is a supplier to Marks & Spencer, but it was long ago dwarfed by its godchild.

Building on his modest start, Michael began to expand, with his first stall in Leeds Market in 1884. Given the spending power of his customers, he sold only items on which he could make a profit at the price of one penny (an old penny, of which there were 240 to a pound). It is said that he coined the famous slogan, 'Don't ask the price, it's a penny' because of his poor English: if so, it was one of the more inspired ways of adapting to a limitation.

Soon, he went into partnership with Tom Spencer, the chief clerk of Dewhirst. Tom's savings allowed them to expand faster, and they built up a chain of market stalls, later to be known as 'penny bazaars'.

One of the keys to Marks & Spencer's later success stemmed from the people in charge. Michael's son Simon joined the board in 1911, and Israel Sieff, his brother-in-law, in 1915. If Michael Marks and Tom Spencer built up the successful chain of market stalls that was the foundation, Simon developed the shops that became what we know today; he formed the culture and set up many of the trading principles that still guide Marks & Spencer. Simon was chairman for 48 years; Israel Sieff took over, and retired only in 1984. His son, Marcus, followed him. Members of two intermarried families thus guided the company through its first 80 years. The shared culture and beliefs of these men must be counted a powerful influence on bringing the firm from its market stalls to a company which first made over £1 billion profit in 1997. Although Michael Rayner was the first non-family chairman, he was a Marks & Spencer man through and through, as was his successor, the present chairman, Sir Richard Greenbury. Some critics would see such in-breeding as a weakness, and City analysts in particular seem to welcome new blood at the top of mature companies. For many years Marks & Spencer avoided the complacency that afflicts so many successful firms. Commitment to continuous improvement, which we think of as a peculiarly Japanese trait, has been part of the Marks & Spencer culture from the beginning, and this turns management continuity into a strength for a time at least. As we shall see, that time seems to have run out.

SIMON MARKS – A PASSION FOR QUALITY!

When Simon Marks was born, in 1888, neither his father nor his mother could yet read or write in English; his birth certificate is marked by Hannah, his mother, with a cross. Nevertheless, Michael Marks had graduated from itinerant pedlar to a stall in Leeds Market. Working hard, and relying on providing quality goods, he soon expanded to stalls in five other towns in the surrounding area. A second child was born in 1890, and the family moved from Leeds to the safer town of Wigan in Lancashire. When a third child arrived in 1892, it was Michael's turn to mark the birth certificate with a cross.

The number of stalls continued to grow, but around this time, Michael made a crucial decision. After a spell of viciously cold weather, one of his young assistants, working on an open stall, caught pneumonia and died. Michael decided from then on to operate only from covered market halls, arcades or high-street shops.

The family soon moved to Manchester, the major city of the north-west, and young Simon grew up there. He attended the Manchester Jews School, and then the prestigious Manchester Grammar School. He had befriended Israel Sieff, and soon, as the two families lived close to each other the boys became inseparable. The Sieffs were already wealthy, and the Marks rapidly becoming so as Michael, with his partner Tom Spencer, expanded the business. Later, Simon and Israel would become doubly brothers-in-law, as they each married the other's sister.

While Israel was to go on to university, however, Simon took a different path. His parents saw that his future was in the family firm, and that knowledge of the language and culture of European countries would be invaluable to him. He was therefore sent to live first in Nuremberg in Germany, and then in Paris. After three years, he returned, to a traumatic period.

Marks & Spencer had become a limited company in 1903, to gain access to further funding. Tom Spencer died in 1905, and Michael took as a new partner William Chapman, chairman of a local hand-kerchief manufacturer. To keep pace with the continuing rapid expansion, Michael was working seven days a week. Interestingly for us, he received a takeover bid from Maypole Dairies, and met John Sainsbury at the opening of the Croydon Penny Bazaar ('I like your son, Mr Marks,' said Sainsbury, 'He will go far.') Michael was adding food products to his range; 'People must eat', he would say. After a particularly stressful period at the end of 1907, soon after Simon's return, he collapsed and died.

Because of the shareholding pattern in the limited company, the Marks family temporarily lost control of what they saw as 'their' firm, and Chapman took the reins. It would be several difficult years before Simon would regain power. Meanwhile, he took responsibility for much of the buying, and for prospecting for sites, but his character was not made for lieutenancy.

He was 'quick, outspoken, frequently explosive', said his close friend Israel; he 'was not naturally affectionate, forbearing, tolerant and full of the milk of human kindness; he had it in him to be aggressive, ambitious and even ruthless'. These qualities remained central to Simon's character, and were remarked on by colleagues and employees throughout his career. They served the company well, as they were focussed intensely on building the Marks & Spencer business, and on the other interest he and Israel shared, Zionism (they were friends and supporters of Chaim Weizmann, then in Manchester and soon to take a leading position in the movement and later become the first president of the newly founded country of Israel).

It was only in 1917, after a long struggle, that Simon won his battle with Chapman, and was elected chairman of the company. Shortly afterwards, he was called up for military duty, but this was to be short. Weizmann, now leading negotiations with the British government, asked military intelligence for the release of six men vital to his efforts, including Simon and Israel – both were immediately allowed to return to civilian life. From now on, Simon could devote himself full-time to his two preoccupations.

The company moved its headquarters to London after the war, and went on growing profitably. By 1921, however, Simon realized that, compared with the fast-expanding US-owned Woolworth chain, Marks & Spencer had 'no direction, no leadership, no thought'. Marks & Spencer were seen – accurately – as somewhat down-at-heel emporia selling the cheapest goods. It was reported that a Woolworth director had visited a Marks & Spencer store, picked up some articles, and referred to them as 'lemons'. 'They are right!' said Simon, 'They *are* lemons!' He knew a fresh start was needed, and set off for America to look for inspiration.

He found US businessmen welcoming, open and helpful. He learned many lessons, especially about the value of large premises, of checking lists for stock control, of new accounting machines, of the need for every foot of counter space to earn its keep, of the need to study what customers wanted, and of the need for staff training. The foundations for a modern retailing business would be laid on what he brought back from this first trip, backed up by frequent subsequent visits (although Israel always maintained that Simon had in fact already formulated the principles for himself, and just needed the reassurance of seeing others practise them).

The flowering of Marks & Spencer into a national institution and leading retailer, whose practices would be imitated by rivals everywhere, has been well described elsewhere. It was Simon, the 'retail revolutionary', the 'retailing genius', who drove that success, always backed up by his loyal friend and brother-in-law Israel. He developed the principles of quality first, and of long-term partnerships with suppliers, that his father had started. Prompted by Weizmann (a scientist), he introduced the application of science and technology to their product specification.

Following his father's lead again, he insisted on good conditions for the staff. In a less serious repeat of his father's experience, he happened to find out that a sales assistant would be having no lunch; he asked her why, and was shocked to be told that she couldn't afford it. Shortly afterwards, a dinner guest, Flora Solomon, attacked him for the poor staff conditions. 'It's firms like Marks & Spencer that give Jews a bad name', she exclaimed. She was appointed to take charge of staff welfare.

Throughout his career, Simon continued to take an obsessive interest in the details of his merchandise, and in particular in its quality. He would visit stores every week, and quiz assistants closely. He would personally examine products, and pick up anything he considered sub-standard; the offending articles would be produced at the Monday meeting of directors and executives, and criticized mercilessly. If in a bad mood, he would throw the garment to the floor and accuse the people responsible of trying to ruin his business. Ernest Jones, manager of the Slough branch (which was on the 'royal route' visited by Simon), described the education he received from the inspections as 'better than a university, but more frightening'. As Simon's great-nephew David Sieff put it, Simon was 'not ruthless in the search for power, but to improve the business'.

The interest in quality also found an expression in fanatical devotion to hygiene. Although Simon was not particularly interested in the food side, he insisted that if it was done, it had to be done properly. The company's manual, *Hygienic Food Handling*, was widely adopted outside; the catering officer of a large hospital wrote to say that he had never seen a fly in a Marks & Spencer store, and what was the secret as he 'had not yet succeeded in that battle'.

Simon was also a devoted servant of the Zionist movement, and a generous philanthropist in a range of causes. He enjoyed tennis, the company of film stars, and the opera. He was made a peer in 1961.

At his final AGM in 1964, he was able to report sales of over £200 million and profits of over £25 million. Since he had taken over the chair, sales had increased 500 times, and profit by almost 1,000 times. He had turned a small chain of bazaars into one of the most admired businesses in Britain, and his legacy can still be seen today.

In December 1964, Simon inspected some items in the ladies tailoring department. As usual, he found reasons for complaint, hurled garments to the floor, and complained that they were ruining his business. He returned to the first floor, suffered a massive heart attack, and died. He would have wanted no other end.

Sources: Bookbinder, 1993 and Sieff, 1986

'DIVINE DISCONTENT' AND OTHER INGREDIENTS OF SUCCESS

Readers unfamiliar with Britain will not know how central Marks & Spencer is to its shopping experience. With very few others, perhaps only W H Smith and Boots the Chemist, Marks & Spencer is an established, trusted presence in every major high street. While it is famously said that everyone buys their underwear and socks there, it must also be true that very few households contain no other items of Marks & Spencer clothing. Their men's suits (made by Dewhirst) are worn by people at all levels. Their range of clothing, for women, men and children, is now of a quality and style that often the only reason for not buying something there is that, for recognizable items, everyone will know where it comes from.

Clothing has been the driving force, and remains the major part of the business, but Marks & Spencer have expanded into home furnishings, food, and even financial services, such is the relationship of trust between the brand and its customers.

The foundations of this success are:

- quality;
- value;
- innovation;
- supplier partnerships;
- commitment to all stakeholders – customers, shareholders, suppliers, staff.

QUALITY AND VALUE

Marks & Spencer are known, above all, for offering excellent quality at a fair price, delivering value that is difficult to match elsewhere. The passion for quality shown by Simon Marks persists throughout the organization. This is tinged with commercial reality, of course, but all products must represent *value*, whatever their price.

The attention to detail of Marks & Spencer people – merchandisers (buyers), selectors (product development) and technical – is legendary. They will work with suppliers, right back to the original components, specifying their requirements in minute particulars. 'Divine discontent' ensures that even if they are satisfied with this year's product, they will still look for further improvement.

INNOVATION

Marks & Spencer have consistently moved into new areas, and introduced new products. One example was their work with Dupont and suppliers to use Lycra more widely in clothing (it is now incorporated in three-quarters of the range), and even in furniture covers.

SUPPLIER PARTNERSHIPS

We have seen that one supplier – Dewhirst – has been with Marks & Spencer since their very beginning over 100 years ago. Many other relationships go back 50 years or more, and Marks & Spencer had been actively operating the partnership principle and supply chain management decades before they were promoted by management gurus in the 1990s.

They are known as extremely demanding, even tough, partners. They specify in minute detail and bargain hard on price – but they also realize that it is in everyone's interest that the supplier makes a decent return, and stays in business. They expect – demand – that the supplier innovates, but they work with them, putting their considerable scientific and technological expertise into the partnership, as well as the purely commercial *nous*. They also expect their partners to invest, sometimes large sums, in the latest equipment.

The advantage for a supplier in working with Marks & Spencer is not that it is an easy relationship, or that they make fat margins – neither is true. They do get high levels of production, and orders that are less volatile than some others, since Marks & Spencer is less susceptible to recession than other retailers. They also know that, as long as they meet the demanding standards imposed on them, Marks & Spencer will stand by them even in difficult times.

A telling reflection on the nature of Marks & Spencer's relations with suppliers is that the idea for its brand name, St Michael, actually came from one of them. Corah, a long-term supplier, had registered many well-known saints' names, using St Margaret for their own. Given their relationship, Marks & Spencer asked Corah permission to use the name 'St Michael', which they had chosen to 'canonize' their founder. Corah willingly agreed; they remain a supplier, now as part of Coats Viyella.

COMMITMENT TO ALL STAKEHOLDERS

That Marks & Spencer are committed to customers is clear from the quality/value offering. For many years, they were the only major retailer giving a no-quibble money-back guarantee, demonstrating not only their confidence in their products, but their willingness to provide the total service that customers want. (This commitment is always tempered with a shrewd sense of business: they still do not accept credit cards, refusing to dilute their margins.)

We have seen their commitment to suppliers as partners. They have always recognized the part played by staff, and were enlightened employers from very early on. Their policies on staff recruitment, training, and promotion have been at the leading edge of contemporary practice.

In dedication to shareholders, Marks & Spencer have had their detractors. Some critics in the City have complained, particularly in recent years, of an unadventurous approach, and of low earnings growth. On the other hand, theirs was one of the bluest of blue chip shares. Their stock has been rated consistently highly – at least until the disappointments of late 1998 (see below). On a balanced scorecard, Marks & Spencer would rate highly.

Any company that survives and prospers for over a century has a soul as well as its operations. Marks & Spencer has a very strong culture, not perhaps to everyone's taste, but one which has been consistent and successful. As Peter Doyle, a leading British professor of marketing, has commented: 'If I had to pick one company in the world that exemplified consistent long-term growth, profitability and customer satisfaction, it would be Marks & Spencer … In terms of performance no British company can match them. It is very hard not to admire them' (Simms, 1998).

FOOD – THE BEGINNINGS

Marks & Spencer has always been, and still is, predominantly a textiles company. This does not mean that it never sold anything else. In its early days, it was a trader, and sold what people would buy. The penny bazaars at the turn of the century sold some confectionery, biscuits and flour. In the 1920s, loose confectionery and ice cream were added.

In the 1930s we can see the real start of food as a category; slab cake and canned goods were stocked from 1933, and provisions and cooked meats from 1934. In 1935, coffee bars selling beverages were started, building up to 100 by 1946. During and after the war, Marks & Spencer, like other retailers, would sell whatever they could get, but all this time food was very much a sideline.

In 1948, for the first time, they began to get serious. A food development department was set up, and started to develop strict rules and regulations to guide production. Applying the principles that had served them so well in clothing, they were extremely thorough, examining everything from pest control to the provenance of raw materials. At the time, this was a completely new thing to do. It was complex, as the supply chain was fragmented: 300 local bakers produced their cakes, for example.

Typically, they wanted to build relationships with suppliers, and visited factories tirelessly. Also typically, they talked of 'enforcing' the rules they drew up. It was here that we see the origins of two defining characteristics of Marks & Spencer as a food retailer: their huge scientific and analytical capability, and their long-term relationships with suppliers.

CHOOSING A NICHE

In the 1950s, as Marks & Spencer were developing their food business, the supermarket multiples were beginning to grow, either out of the grocery chains that we saw had been operating for decades, or from upstarts such as Tesco. For Marks & Spencer, the situation presented two challenges: profitability, and quality.

At this period, many supermarkets were earning margins of only 1 to 1.5 per cent; 3 per cent or above was good. Marks & Spencer do not disclose their margins, but an informed guess would suggest that they were used to reasonable margins on clothing, with an average perhaps approaching 20 per cent. They clearly were not going to become a supermarket chain, as their high-street stores did not have the space (or, as car-borne shopping became common, the parking). They would therefore have to choose a relatively narrow range, on which they could make margins of around 8 per cent.

The other issue was quality, on which their reputation rested. British food in the 1950s (and later), at least the mass-produced varieties, was generally of poor quality. Many will remember the chickens that seemed to taste of fish (not surprising, as they were fed on fishmeal). Frozen chickens seemed soggy (again, not surprising, as they were wet chilled, which made them absorb water). Bacon also tasted odd, and gave off frothy water when cooked. Britain, unlike France, had no tradition and culture dedicated to good food, and therefore neither the skills to supply, nor the mass market to demand, quality.

With hindsight, the situation was tailor-made for Marks & Spencer to enter with a small, specialist range of high-quality foods that would command a premium price. They expanded from their ambient range of provisions (cake, biscuits, tea and marmalade) to frozen and fresh foods. They applied their proven methods of very detailed specifications, right back to breeding and cultivation, through preparation to packing, transport and distribution. For example, they insisted on air-dried chickens, bred and raised in conditions that were not only more humane than some battery farms, but also produced better flavour. From very early in the 1960s, they air-freighted tomatoes.

Food was, of course, still a small part of the business – only 28 per cent by 1968. Fortunately, Marcus Sieff (Chairman from 1972–84) was a great champion, as was Derek Rayner after him.

THE BREAKTHROUGH – CHILLED PREPARED FOOD

Through the 1960s and into the 1970s, British society, like others, was changing. Prosperity was rising, and spreading through the population; Simon Marks thought that the shape was moving from a triangle (a few rich at the apex, many poor at the base) to a diamond, with a large middle group (the middle majority, in US usage). With rising incomes came a greater interest in food, helped by wider travel abroad, and the spread of writing on food in newspapers, magazines and books, even television programmes (the authors, as young bachelors in the early 1960s, learned to cook from Philip Harben's television show and book).

A major change, and a real opportunity, was the increase in working wives. 'Feminism owes an enormous amount to Marks & Spencer, and vice versa,' says Clinton Silver, who led the food division from 1975 to 1987 (1997).

There were many 'convenience' foods already, tinned or frozen. Many of these were of poor quality: 'TV dinner slop', in Silver's words. In Britain, there was simply no tradition of the French *traiteurs* and *pâtissiers*, who would produce prepared dishes that a housewife would be happy to buy on the day and serve to her demanding family or guests. The answer was to provide for Britain good quality prepared or semi-prepared ingredients and dishes.

The introduction of 'recipe dishes' is one of the great food innovations of the last 30 years, and has been widely copied in Britain (the situation in other countries varies, as we shall see, but where conditions are appropriate, it will spread). Success has a thousand fathers, and no one seems quite sure who had the original idea. Marks & Spencer themselves, Chris Haskins of Northern Foods, and Cavenham (another long-term supply partner) all played a part. Clearly, it was once again the result of close co-operation between retailer and supplier. It grew naturally out of existing products, and from the insistent demand, 'How can we do better?' Meat pies were a staple product, and a defining moment may have been during a tasting session on meat and vegetable pies; someone said, 'Why can't we use fresh carrots instead of tinned?' and from then on it seemed that any ingredient not only *could* be fresh, but should be.

The innovation caused a big upheaval – in manufacturing, distribution, and in-store. One part of the chain was already in place, as since the early 1970s Marks & Spencer had been working with BOC on the cold chain to improve the quality, freshness and flavour of produce. The BOC Cold Shield integrated chilled distribution system is now dedicated to Marks & Spencer. In-store chilled cabinets had to be installed to accommodate the new products, and the manufacturers had to develop new methods of mass-producing craft cooking processes.

The very first non-pie product was cauliflower cheese, and is a good example of what the range could do. It was a well-known dish, but frozen versions were unacceptable. At home, it took some time and skill to prepare, so a quality product that needed only to be heated would be very welcome. The range was extended with classic British dishes such as pies, chicken and casseroles; meat and poultry were the staples, since fish was more difficult (it would be introduced later, when the problems of safety and flavour were solved).

As British tastes developed, so Marks & Spencer offered Italian dishes, starting with lasagne; Chinese and Indian ranges followed. Derek Rayner, who was closely involved, was passionate about quality, like his predecessors. He and his senior colleagues were widely travelled, and knew good food. The benchmark for a product became the most authentic restaurant dish that could be produced at an acceptable cost, and Marks & Spencer staff would (and do) travel to sample for themselves the standard they are aiming at.

It is, of course, possible to be too authentic. The British passion for curry is catered for almost entirely by Sylhetis from a relatively small area of

Bangladesh; the menu of a typical 'Indian' restaurant represents what British consumers are familiar with, and like. Marks & Spencer, after a careful development process, offered a really authentic Indian dish, but customers simply did not recognize it as 'Indian', and it failed.

NATE GOLDENBERG, THE SCIENCE OF QUALITY

Nathan Goldenberg was yet another of those Jewish refugees from Eastern Europe who have so enriched British life. As a child, he had survived the post-revolutionary civil war between White and Red Russian armies, and local pogroms. With his mother, he escaped from Russia through Poland and Germany, arriving eventually in London in 1921 on 'Nansen' passports (named after the Norwegian who developed the scheme to help the millions of stateless people left after the First World War).

Despite being an excellent student, the young Nathan was disqualified from receiving a scholarship to university, as he had been born abroad and his father was not naturalized. He therefore got a job in the J Lyons and Company laboratories (Lyons was then a leading food supplier as well as running the famous tea houses). He studied part-time at Birkbeck College, in the University of London, working five evenings a week for five years for his first degree. He performed well enough to win scholarships to pay his fees for two years, but by his third year, there were no more available. In desperation, he asked the principal ('a dour Scotsman'!) if he could pay the 12-guinea fee (£12.60) in instalments. 'Yes, of course, laddie; I have been in the same boat myself', came the smiling reply. He continued to study for an MSc, and then at Battersea Polytechnic. His academic success is a tribute to his commitment and energy, but also to the strong British tradition of part-time higher education that gave opportunities to the many who in those years missed out on traditional full-time university study.

Goldenberg joined Marks & Spencer in 1948 as Chief Chemist to the Food Division. Simon Marks had great respect for science, mainly as a result of his friendship with Chaim Weizmann. Many senior managers in the food division were hostile, but the support of Marks, and the Sieffs (father and son), enabled Goldenberg to survive criticism. The scientific approach yielded results in two main areas: hygiene and quality.

The Marks & Spencer approach to product quality and supplier relationships, developed in textiles, was now applied to food. In bakery, the very large number of suppliers was gradually reduced, and the firm began to work in partnership with those who were prepared to co-operate. Typically, Marks & Spencer would develop a superior product in its labs, using better-quality ingredients and improved methods. They would then take the result to suppliers and ask them to adopt it. Some resented this role reversal and refused, despite the evidence of higher sales; they were dropped. The department also tested suppliers' products on a routine basis, using scientific methods to analyse contents and maintain quality. The success of the department's work on cakes led to the adoption of the St Michael label, previously reserved for textiles, instead of the Welbeck name. Food had arrived. Goldenberg considered that at this point, Marks & Spencer had a 10-year lead over other food retailers in cake quality, and they would go on to apply the methodology to other foods.

One story that sums up the unique Goldenberg/Marks & Spencer approach is that of the stones in sultanas. Marks & Spencer had, after exhaustive testing and comparison, adopted Greek and Turkish sultanas in preference to those from the United States, Australia and elsewhere; suppliers often used the latter because they were cheaper. The problem with the Greek and Turkish sultanas was they often contained foreign bodies, such as stones, pieces of wood, glass, stalks and so on. The first attempt to solve the problem involved finding an improved washing machine; Huntley & Palmer (a leading biscuit manufacturer) had one, and allowed others to copy the design. This was not enough and complaints continued. Goldenberg suggested that he visit Greece and Turkey, but Lord Marks 'turned it down flat, saying that the Greeks and Turks were not to be relied on!' (Goldenberg, 1989). It was only after Lord Marks' grandson had broken a tooth on a piece of cake at his grandfather's house that permission for the visit was given.

Goldenberg soon identified the source of the problem: the grapes were dried on the ground, on wooden trays, pieces of sacking, or just on hardened earth. Foreign bodies would be blown on to the drying fruit, and stones picked up from the ground. Other practices included using sacks that for the rest of the year were used for manure, leaving products in the street exposed to contamination from dogs and horses, and hopeless washing and grading processes. A long process of negotiation with growers, merchants, machinery suppliers and the relevant governments led finally to enormous improvements. Agreed standards included:

- all sultanas and currants to be shade-dried off the ground on racks, nets or concrete bases;
- the speed of fruit through the washing machine to be reduced and the fruit more thinly spread;
- the picking operatives to have their eyes tested to make sure they could see and pick out the foreign bodies.

Typical of the thoroughness of the operation was that the Marks & Spencer team personally visited the cardboard factory to explain the need for stronger cartons, and that they persuaded the Turkish government to grant a small subsidy to small, poor farmers to encourage them to lay the new, concrete drying beds.

The Goldenberg approach was eventually extended throughout the food range, often against entrenched opposition from within the firm as well as from suppliers. Even one of his admirers and supporters, Lord Rayner (Chairman for much of his career), would say of him that 'he was not an easy man, and was never afraid to stand his ground on matters of principle'. His contribution, not only to Marks & Spencer but to the food industry as a whole, was enormous, and recognized by the award of many honours, including the OBE.

Source: Goldenberg, 1989 and Sieff, 1986

SANDWICHES – AND FLOWERS

The second great leap forward was the humble sandwich. All the old coffee bars had been closed by 1961, but in 1980 a few were reopened as an experiment. Someone had the idea of offering the sandwiches produced for staff in the canteen for general sale. There was a trend towards snacking and eating 'on the hoof', and Marks & Spencer wanted to capture some of this developing market. In the first hour, they sold 2 sandwiches, in the second hour 12, but by the end of lunchtime they had all gone. Marks & Spencer now sell 1.75 million per week, and the Marks & Spencer sandwich is now an icon, representing freshness, quality and flavour (a welcome replacement for the previous cliché of the tired old British Rail sandwich).

The operation was typical of the Marks & Spencer approach. It started from the thought, 'There is a demand, we have a product or could develop one, why don't we try?' They began with what Hugh Walker (director of prepared foods in the 1990s) calls 'a bucket and spade' production process: the sandwiches already produced were wrapped in film, and put on the shelves. Then they worked closely with suppliers to transfer that to a mass scale. Today, the almost 2 million per week production comes from only four suppliers in England, giving both the economies of scale (and thence value), and close control that Marks & Spencer demand.

A third major leap, and similar in its creation, was horticulture. In the mid-1970s, Marks & Spencer could see that there was a large and growing market for flowers, but that the existing provision was often of poor quality. Using their expertise, they thought they could do better, and introduced pot plants, then cut flowers. Other major categories such as wines were added in the early 1970s, always on the basis that Marks & Spencer are a specialist, and should offer a narrow but carefully selected range that would provide the quality and performance that customers expect.

THE MARKS & SPENCER TOUCH

We can illustrate the way Marks & Spencer have applied their principles to food with a few examples:

- Tomatoes on supermarket shelves have looked good, but have had no flavour, a problem recognized by consumers and by the retailers. Marks & Spencer sponsored the development of a new strain, the Melrow.
- The Aberdeen Angus breed of cattle produces excellent flavoured beef, but was almost dying out. Marks & Spencer, with its partner breeder, led the development and expansion that has increased supplies.
- Customers wanted more flavour in pork, so Marks & Spencer sponsored a special breed of pig.

These examples show the focus on quality of raw materials that has marked the Marks & Spencer approach. They also work with suppliers on the production process. More recent efforts have concentrated on reproducing the 'home-cooked' effect in mass production. Most people at home, for instance, fry off meat before putting it in a stew. This was not done in the factory, as it was thought too difficult, but Marks & Spencer's supplier has now worked out how to do it on a mass scale ('bratting'), adding that little extra touch of flavour.

The commercial side of the operation is to use value engineering to take unnecessary costs out of the process. Much of what a chef does in a kitchen may involve moving ingredients around from place to place, for example, but this does not add value; in a factory, it can be minimized.

Technological advances mean that the partners can do more and more things now that they could not do at all five years ago, or could not do safely. With food, safety is a priority; quality and flavour are, too, but safety must come first.

In all these things, Marks & Spencer has been a leader, and this explains their success and their influence in the rest of the retail trade. Competitors, of course, have been catching up.

INTERNATIONALIZATION

Like most retailers, Marks & Spencer have concentrated for most of their life on expanding and consolidating their home base. When they did venture overseas – to Canada in 1972 and Europe in 1975 – they focussed on their main strengths in textiles. Food, though, was part of the offer.

The Paris store was typical: it started with 3,000 sq ft in the basement devoted to a limited range – tea, biscuits, confectionery, bacon, Cheddar cheese. Both native and foreign customers see these as prototypically British. The idea of a British chain selling food to the French is particularly daunting, so selling what people expect is a sound start. A Brussels store was opened in the same year, with similar policies, and later, stores opened in Holland (1970), Spain (1990) and Germany (1997).

Success at home with a wider range led to a similar expansion abroad. There are particular problems with food since, despite the so-called Common Market, there are still many restrictions. Legislation on such matters as ingredients and additives have not yet been harmonized, so what we call yogurt in Britain cannot be sold as such in France, and bread made with chlorinated flour (as in the UK) is banned in much of the Continent.

A further difficulty is that the Marks & Spencer model is built on a very slick, low-cost logistics system. This needs both high volume and a developed management information system (MIS); neither existed outside Britain. From the early 1980s, however, Marks & Spencer began to build the supply base in France through its normal practice of working with a small group of suppliers. A base of 30–40 local manufacturers was built up to supply poultry, meat, fruit and vegetables, recipe dishes and sandwiches (which were also exported from the UK). The range was a mixture of what worked in Britain and what the team thought the French wanted to buy on a daily basis. It was a totally separate operation from UK food, with its own team.

In 1994 central control was reimposed, with all buying concentrated in Baker Street (though with local selling teams in each country to provide local knowledge of what customers want). Even the local sandwich supplier is controlled from London. The reason is classic Marks & Spencer. Volume gives scale economies but, more importantly, control over quality. Buying in small quantities does not give the same measure of control as buying for the company as a whole. They are now two-thirds of the way to complete centralization in Europe. Few products need to be very local, unless long distances preclude exporting (as to Spain). Products are standardized, so chicken tikka masala, for example, is the same wherever it is sold.

Despite this widening of the range, the bulk of sales are still of 'British' products. The huge success of quality convenience foods in Britain depends on certain conditions, which do not obtain everywhere. Paris has seen considerable sales of sandwiches, which interestingly the competitor, Monoprix, has been unable to emulate despite several attempts (they can sell baguettes, which are French, but not 'British' sandwiches). Chilled prepared foods, especially recipe dishes, need a segment of people who want quality and are prepared to pay for it, and who appreciate convenience. In Paris, such a segment exists, made up of yuppies and perhaps some empty-nesters.

Dutch and German shoppers are much more price-conscious; the Dutch housewife is the only one in Europe who knows the price of 15 KVIs (known value items, or staples of the family shop). Holland and Germany are not yet ready for convenience foods to take off, but the expectation is that they will later.

Food is still largely national and local, though this is changing. Food sales in Marks & Spencer stores have therefore been slow to grow in the early years. The food offer is different, and creates a buzz initially, but it takes time to establish confidence. This may be a matter of timing, since the Paris store took many years to take off, whereas in Holland it was six to seven years. Germany was the first store to open with a complete range including chilled prepared foods. Marks & Spencer feel that convergence in taste is happening, and that northern Europe at least will follow British trends in convenience products.

Expansion beyond Europe started in 1988 in Hong Kong, and there are now franchised stores in Singapore, Thailand, Indonesia, Malaysia and the Philippines (though these sell only a very limited range of foods). Teams are actively exploring China, Taiwan and the Gulf States. Often, sales start with expatriates, and with people who have travelled to Britain. Later, local middle-class shoppers with Western aspirations come to account for the bulk of purchases; in parts of Asia, Marks & Spencer products are seen as a status buy, being a European brand. The range is therefore initiated by 'British' standards, and to ambient products (since no cold chain exists); in time, these are adapted to local tastes.

Sales therefore account for a lower proportion of the total than in Britain, between 12 and 20 per cent. Food in one Hong Kong franchise represents only 12 per cent of total sales, but it has only 400 stock-keeping units (SKUs) (though Hong Kong was showing the highest turnover per square foot in the world). Food will have a higher growth rate than textiles, but will always be the junior partner; it is also showing remarkable resilience in the current difficult trading conditions. International expansion remains a major strategic aim, and in 1998, £2 billion was earmarked for investment (both at home and overseas).

RESULTS SO FAR

The results of the innovations are plain to see: sales of food, only £256 million in 1975/76, had more than doubled by 1980/81 to £629 million, and more than doubled again in the next five years (see Figure 5.1). By 1990/91 they had reached two and a half billion, and have gone on rising (though at a slower rate).

MARKS & SPENCER FOODS TODAY

In 1998, Marks & Spencer were selling over £3 billion of food, of which some £2.7 billion was in the UK. Since they are using some three million sq ft of space, their sales per square foot per week appear to be over £17, although Marks & Spencer do not publish such figures. This compares with figures of £20 and above for Tesco and Sainsbury's.

Their range is no more than 3,000 SKUs even in the largest store, compared with the 20,000 to 30,000 in a supermarket. They concentrate on products where they believe they can offer what their customers expect: the best quality of flavour and freshness, at a price that offers value for money. As customers expect something different, they need to innovate constantly, and in some ways this is becoming harder. Every year, they replace about a third of the range, but all the easy dishes have now been done.

Moreover, their main competitors, who were nowhere in the race in the early years, have learned a lot. They too work with their suppliers, and even Marks & Spencer admit some of the competitive offerings match their own. Marks & Spencer do, of course, have the enormous advantage of having worked with the same suppliers for decades, so the closeness and trust established are difficult to replicate. When Marks & Spencer are asking for very large investment – up to £30 million for a new plant – and continuous innovation, such trust is invaluable. It is also true that, although they have a low overall share of the grocery market, they still dominate some segments, so they can offer volumes that not all rivals can. They estimate that they still have 45 per cent of the prepared meals market – down from 90 per cent, but still a dominating share.

They are, then, a specialist player and happy to remain so. Compared with a Tesco shopper, Marks & Spencer customers visit the store half as often, and spend less than half per visit (see Appendix). Compared with shoppers at the supermarket chains, their customers are:

- more up-market than any but Waitrose (58 per cent ABC1);
- older (72 per cent aged over 44);
- from smaller households (64 per cent have only two or one).

Given the nature of their offering, and the constraints imposed by the size and location of their stores, this is entirely understandable. Although Marks & Spencer would claim always to have been customer-led, they now listen even more closely to their clients. They used to say that they did not believe in market research ('A piece of company cant', according to one contemporary insider), they do now use it to a limited extent. They recognize the need to check what consumers like and dislike, and they listen to and analyse complaints. On the other hand, they point out that market research would not have led them to develop the hugely successful chicken kiev, since at the time most customers would not have heard of it.

Unlike their supermarket rivals, they were slow to recognize the potential of out-of-town shopping centres, and have only 18 such stores. They admit that they could do with more large sites with level car parking, since if current trends continue, an increasing proportion of consumer spending will be in such locations. Out-of-home eating is another trend that they recognize, and

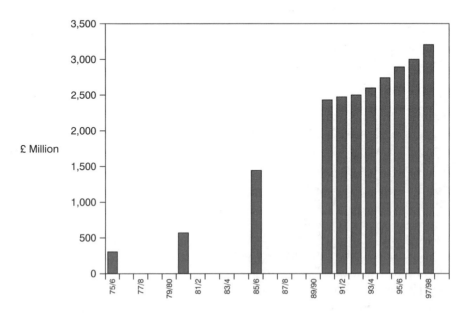

Figure 5.1 *Marks & Spencer food sales*

are trying to respond to, but again much of that could be in the huge shopping/ entertainment complexes in which they are under-represented. They argue that they are committed to the high street, where they can do their own particular job best; and that anyway there may well be a return to city-centre shopping.

They will continue to rely on the factors that have made them one of the most respected retailers in the world:

- a very strong management and staff culture;
- total commitment to quality and customer service;
- long-established relationships with supplier partners;
- an efficient supply chain, based on a superb information system;
- a database of six million store-card holders;
- innovation.

In late 1998, the strategy was called into question when they published poor figures for sales generally (mainly due to very difficult conditions in the clothing market). This led to unprecedented (for them) publicity surrounding the management succession. Keith Oates, the Finance Director, had been seen by outsiders as the probable successor to Sir Richard Greenbury. When he learned that this was in dispute; he made a semi-public bid for the promotion, and an extraordinary row followed. After much manoeuvring and argument, Sir Richard's choice, Peter Salsbury, was made Chief Executive, with Sir Richard moving to non-executive Chairman; Oates left. Salsbury is a Marks & Spencer man through and through, and a retailer; Oates was, according to Greenbury, a 'bean-counter', and anyway had been with the company 'only' 14 years.

Salsbury started to make changes: the sacking of three executive directors (including the man in charge of US operations) and a further 31 divisional and senior directors; the restructuring of the company into three major businesses; and the setting up of a new central marketing group. Marks & Spencer's problems centred mainly around misjudgements in clothing, but the real fear is that even they had succumbed to the deadly spiral of self-confidence – arrogance – complacency – failure. According to surveys, shoppers thought the stores were cavernous and uninviting, the décor dated, and the goods dull and lacking in flair. Foods were, and are, not central to the problem but, as we have seen, the danger is that competitors can now match them.

The financial slow-down will necessarily affect the pace of expansion abroad; what the longer-term effects of the management problems will be remains to be seen. The challenge will be to stay ahead of competitors who have already learned a lot; innovation, and successful international expansion, will be the keys to continuing profitable growth.

6

The second tier in Britain

What we may call the second tier of companies is not in any real sense a homogeneous group. With the top four companies accounting for more than 50 per cent of total retail business, the 'also-rans' group is itself highly segmented. These are companies that vary in present importance, some lively and likely to grow in significance. Others are making little impact and may be dwindling in size or even disappearing from view. The four entirely discrete groups which make up the second tier of UK companies can be described as:

- failing heritages – independents and the co-operative movement;
- huddling together for warmth – Somerfield/Kwik Save;
- cheap if not yet cheerful – Aldi, Lidl, Netto (the hard discounters) and Iceland;
- strong regional niche players – Morrison, Waitrose.

FAILING HERITAGES

THE INDEPENDENT GROCER

In its Victorian beginnings, the independent grocer was the primary force creating movement and change in grocery retailing. These 'men of the trade' regarded themselves as skilled craftsmen, and saw their occupations as engaged at least as much in product manufacturing as in retailing or even selling. Experience and patience were their distinguishing characteristics. Their success depended primarily on word-of-mouth reputation, created by building inherent levels of customer confidence rather than on any discrete price or value advantage. Certainly, such progressive notions as 'push' marketing or product promotion were well outside their ken. Working in the new, fixed, shop locations that were gradually replacing the local community markets, and living in cramped and dimly lit interiors, they won customer approval often simply by making available reliable, unadulterated foodstuffs – what we might regard as the green or organic products of the first environmental movement.

At the same time, they introduced a steady succession of manufactured novelties, products new in their time – such as, in 1867, the first margarine, and in later years, a veritable host of exotic 19th-century delicacies, such as jellies, jams, canned foods, pickles, sauces and many more. They created Britain's first genuine retail-led modern food revolution, in scale and true distinctiveness quite as important as the widespread innovations their supermarket successors were to produce over the last three decades for a more recent generation of consumers.

It is hard to recognize today's grocery trade and practice from these very different early antecedents. John Ruskin's resolutely wrong-headed refusal 'to compete with my neighbouring tradesmen in either gas or rhetoric', and the consequent collapse of his tea shop was noted in the Introduction. The craftsmanship approach to retailing, the calling or commitment which these early shop owners or food suppliers believed they might be following, was inevitably to be replaced by a set of commercial practices in the years before the First World War, which arrived to the intense chagrin of the professional class of early shopkeepers. 'The small trader is more and more being relegated to the back streets there to eke out a living as best he can in a poor class of trade', a Manchester history of the shop assistant written in 1910 lamented. It was much the same elsewhere across the country.

Having said this, portents of imminent and total demise were often exaggerated. At the turn of the century, the proportion of grocery sales undertaken by the new independents was still estimated at 80 per cent, through myriad small-scale local stores. As a new and more hard-nosed employee commercial manager was making his appearance on the trading scene, the reality remained that individual shop owners still owned and managed most stores. Then came the first looming signs of competition from larger enterprises, especially in the north. In 1902 *The Times* of London joined the prophets of doom, forecasting that 'the single shop grocer as his fellow traders term him is between the upper and the nether millstone, and attrition is proceeding at such a rate that he will soon disappear' (Jeffreys, 1954).

The early years of the 20th century witnessed a continuation of the decline of the independents – from 80 per cent of the trade available, they had dropped to around one half by the 1950s. The resilience of the better operators naturally remained a feature while, overall, new strong multiple competitors and a seemingly unstoppable post-war co-operative movement gained enormous ground. Independent retailing could still remain a way of life for many. Their survival would depend on their ability to sustain some kind of advantage, and there was still unique competitive advantage to be had – flexibility was one obvious example. Confronted by the complex pressures of trade, the shop owner had the options to move both home and shop, work longer hours, or even to contemplate offering extra and better service. Where labour was his principal cost he had the elementary control options available – take no pay till next week, or for as long as it might take to balance his books – and very often this is exactly what many of them did.

A key element in the survival of this group in numbers had been the authority of resale price maintenance (RPM) legislation, and its maintenance of the pricing of all branded goods. Neither the manufacturing companies nor the independent traders could see that there were any losers from its operation, and its disappearance was beyond contemplation for most of them. RPM protected everyone's margins until, in the end, its unexpectedly swift disappearance in the 1960s. The practice of brand manufacturers in seeking universal distribution of brands meant that the highest cost retailers – the independents – were encouraged to make a good margin, come what may. This constituted perceived competitive advantage just at the time when advertised brands, now becoming big spenders on the new independent commercial television channel, were starting to command mass consumer loyalty. So that writing in the early 1950s, Jeffreys believed that all was not yet lost, and he concluded, one senses, a shade wistfully and rather more in hope than in expectation, that the independent's decline 'had not yet become a rout'.

But collapse was now imminent and the key agent of change was to be the emergence of the new self-service multiples. In retrospect, it is easy to say that the independents had not done enough to merit continuing survival. The author remembers selling Hudson and Knight's then famous 'Omo' brand in rural Cambridgeshire in the 1960s. A revolutionary new stock-turn partnership philosophy had been conceived, a harbinger of future category management initiatives perhaps, to unite salesman and shopkeeper trading objectives for the first time. The salesman's goal had hitherto been to ensure that if, as was often the case, Omo occupied most of the shopkeeper's stockroom, then overflow quantities – promoted on a 'buy now, I promise you'll never see this price again' presentation – could find a legitimate temporary resting-place in the corner of the shopkeeper's family kitchen or, at a pinch, even on occasions under the marital bed. Stock pressure selling had succeeded but to nobody's advantage. The demise of RPM removed a key brick from the wall. In fact it sounded the independent's death knell, his coffin pulled enthusiastically along by aggressive new supermarket owners, and watched passively by a local consumer community that saw no particular virtue in prolonging the life of some increasingly irrelevant and outdated shopping traditions.

Some effort was made by the voluntary chains and groups (such as Spar, Mace and VG) to provide compensating advantages of scale. To some degree this worked. Thus buying range and power, marketing and merchandising and even elements of price competitiveness were offered as brave new disciplines to a disbelieving sector, without which its demise would have been quicker. Even today, numerically three-quarters of stores are still formally termed 'small independents', some 21,000 in total. A quarter or more remain members of a symbol group. Their catchment areas are skewed to the fringes of rural Britain, and feature in what are regarded as (commercially) the least privileged communities. In remote Scots border and highland villages, in deepest Yorkshire or the far south-west and Welsh interior, they still occupy their traditional and preciously guarded community role. On relative price, however, the whole world knows they are incapable of competing. Elsewhere, their role in emergency or 'top-up shopping' has diminished, as Sunday opening and extended shopping hours have become the latest universal competitive weapon for ambitious multiples. Is even the tiny 10 per cent market share independents still hold vulnerable?

Probably it is. After a century of decline, it is difficult to imagine this rudimentary, polyglot and ill-equipped army having the expertise or even the will to survive in hardening conditions. Share losses if anything accelerate. Academic studies reveal that the latest generation of independent shop owners are now very often new British Asians, deeply anxious to play a significant role, but surprised to have the responsibility, and uncertain how to discharge it. There may indeed be bright new opportunity in the high streets, but the human, capital and marketing skills to succeed are rarely present among today's independents, and they are being replaced by a group of high-street multiples, who are taking the best sites and have the systems and knowledge to make them work harder. Encouraged by some late-in-the-day hardening of national planning policies seeking to constrain the growth of out-of-town sites, and perhaps by a dawning recognition that the motor car's role must finally be circumscribed, the neighbourhood store could be due for post-millennium resurgence. Around the world, there seems to be a new awareness of the convenience and the specialty store, catering to a growing group of aspirational but time-starved urban shoppers, some of whom clearly prefer this kind of shopping to the mainstream supermarket visit. However, one has the feeling that it won't be many of today's private shopkeepers who cater to them.

The multiples have led the charge – Marks & Spencer the first, but Tesco moving positively and quickly with its new Metro and then Express stores, based on petrol station forecourts, and others following. The oil companies have been hard hit by price competition, a loss of petrol volume, and by weakening margins, and Shell Select, and the BP/Safeway alliance are an attempt to shift the battles ahead on to the away pitch – the food retailers' own ground. As one door closes, another opens. Successful multiple convenience store operators – such as Alldays and Dillons – are making good progress, and use the new learning of scale and expertise to fund expansion, showing a degree of purpose the independents could never and seemingly cannot generate for themselves.

It is not yet clear how far high-street renewal may take us. In the long term, it may depend on home shopping's advance, and whether there remains a worthwhile role for local distribution. Short term, there seems little question that high streets need vitality, breadth of activity and regular customer visits, providing the price premium is not too daunting. It will be the local convenience store's ability to offer excitement and relevant focus – through excellent meal solutions, or a restoration of truly personal services – that will make recovery a reality. Sadly it is hard to see many of today's independent food shops playing much part in the process.

THE CO-OPERATIVE MOVEMENT

If sadness clouds the decline of the independents, then the lack of progress of the co-operative movement represents a half century of unalloyed tragedy. From 19th-century visionary beginnings and effectively managed local business growth that produced both national leadership and ethical trading distinction, the Co-op has dropped to sixth place overall and seems today to have nowhere to go but further downwards. Even to suggest that the co-operative societies are an entity is an exaggeration – they are a fragmentary collection of societies, with two principal contenders for movement leadership, the CRS and CWS, apparently intent on pursuing separate and conflicting directions. An undeniable death wish attaches itself to this once great enterprise.

It was not always so. The Rochdale pioneers who established the co-operative mission are renowned in retailing history. Their persistent idealism as well as practical business ideas were to provide for a working family's everyday needs at minimum cost, and return any profits to their customers in the form of the famous Co-op dividend. The Co-op built a reputation for clear and fair pricing and, importantly, for honest trading. They eliminated credit that had been the scourge of the 19th-century working-class. They set out to fix decent food quality standards, avoiding adulteration, and used their extensive reach and size to keep consumer prices down. Ironically in the 1870s the movement was itself boycotted for using unreasonable amounts of muscle against the independent grocer. What goes around, comes around – later the multiples were to work an identical tactic on a confused and fragmenting co-operative movement – a real case of the biter bit.

But growth through the late 19th century was immensely strong. By 1900 they had 15 per cent of the market, by 1920 it had risen to 18 per cent-more of a market share than anyone in Britain has today. Twenty-five years ahead of the first multiples they had succeeded in creating strong foods growth while faithfully clinging on to their democratic co-operative processes. Not for nothing did the earliest socialist Parliamentarians owe their allegiance to the 'labour and co-operative' movement. The movement's appeal, most powerful in Scotland and the north where economic conditions were harshest, was exclusively working-class, and the business which the Webbs and G D H Cole described so lovingly, was closely linked in these years to the credibility of the Labour Party. Branding and advertising were always anathema to their ideals, and as competition began to use marketing approaches, the co-operative movement's rigid and uncommercial approaches were found wanting.

Membership blossomed, however, bolstered by the unchanging appeal of the dividend, and by democratic ideals and a reputation for honest dealing. Two million members grew to 5 million by the 1920s and a staggering 11 million – more than today subscribe to the famous Tesco loyalty card – at its apogee by the end of the Second World War. By 1950, market share was at least 25 per cent, and on some measures the Co-op had achieved one third of the entire market, greater than all the multiples combined, and achieved effectively from 4,000 fewer shops. But the storm clouds were beginning to gather.

Jeffreys, writing in 1950, asks himself with foresight if capital constraints might at some stage inhibit the Co-op's growth (!) but notes in its favour its rapid adoption of the new techniques of self-service. Fragmentation is seen as a problem, but the unique democracy and the dividend are viewed by him as long-enduring advantages. As the large supermarket and later the out-of-town superstore arrived, the Co-op seemed frozen into inactivity and inevitable decline, with no structure capable of generating coherent decision-making, finally and inevitably losing overall market leadership but as recently as 1985. They failed, and still fail to make the one move that might have strengthened their resistance – that of unifying themselves into a single cohesive enterprise with a recognizable strategic focus.

Today there are 50 societies and the Co-op has a total share of 5 per cent, having been left trailing both by the big four and also now by Somerfield/Kwik Save. Since 1990, at constant values, sales have declined in a growing market by 15 per cent. Today's movement is an improbable combination of two still worthwhile (CWS, CRS) and many smaller, societies, all dancing to a set of individual drummers. Important regional groups still occupy the old heartlands with fair trading success, and a convenience store approach – United Norwest, Midlands, Anglia. Of the Co-op's 2,000 stores, 300 are major superstores and they still have many small high-street outlets. Sales per square foot are stable but at a level around one half of the efficient retailer average figure. Of course these assets could still have real and durable value, if someone could be found to make them work properly. Looking at the co-operative stores around Europe, in Italy, in Scandinavia and in the highly affluent towns and villages of Switzerland, one can see that there was no need for this once great enterprise so continuously to fall upon its own sword.

Is there, at this eleventh hour, a solution in sight? It seems unlikely. Criticized for operating economies of scale to the detriment of smaller competitors in the past, the Co-op cannot itself now get anywhere close to market costs. There are divergent current strategies. CWS – with a high-street, convenience-store belief – seems likely to sell its superstore franchises, while at the CRS a new team apparently still wants to go flat out and challenge the mainstream operators. Divided policies, for so long the Achilles heel of the movement, appear destined to haunt it to the bitter end. Meanwhile there has been a well-publicized return to idealism – to such policies as ethical trading, environmental sensitivity and more consumer disclosure, eg on labelling. The dividend has been revived, with a high consumer payback (5 per cent), but only on Co-op merchandise – actions that are eminently sensible but far too late and, therefore, on their own insufficient to ensure profitability or survival.

In 1997, a venture capitalist (Andrew Regan's Lanica Trust) moved against the Co-op, intending to take a radical stance to underutilized CWS assets to improve efficiencies and returns. The movement resisted wholeheartedly, and saw Regan off, showing a unanimity that all too rarely it applied to its market and trading strategy. Sadly, the problems – no capital, no strategy, no store profile, in essence no co-operation – persist. Graham Melmoth, the Chief

Early Tesco store fronts (1930s)

Jack Cohen: Tesco founder

Tesco, Havant, 1999

Tesco Metro, Dundee, 1999

The first Sainsbury store, 1869

John James
b1844 d1928
founder of Sainsbury's 1869
company service 1869–1928
chairman and governing director 1922

Mary Ann
b1849 (née Staples) d1927
founder of Sainsbury's 1869
company service 1869–70s

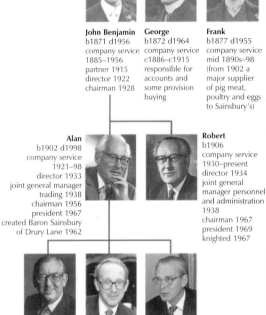

John Benjamin
b1871 d1956
company service
1885–1956
partner 1915
director 1922
chairman 1928

George
b1872 d1964
company service
c1886–c1915
responsible for
accounts and
some provision
buying

Frank
b1877 d1955
company service
mid 1890s–98
(from 1902 a
major supplier
of pig meat,
poultry and eggs
to Sainsbury's)

Arthur
b1880 d1962
company service
late 1890s–1929
director 1922
responsible for
provision buying
and supervision
of factory

Alfred
b1884 d1965
company service
1906–41
director 1922
responsible for
grocery and
canned
goods buying

Paul
b1890 d1982
company service
1921–38
responsible for
building
development

Alan
b1902 d1998
company service
1921–98
director 1933
joint general manager
trading 1938
chairman 1956
president 1967
created Baron Sainsbury
of Drury Lane 1962

Robert
b1906
company service
1930–present
director 1934
joint general
manager personnel
and administration
1938
chairman 1967
president 1969
knighted 1967

James
b1909 d1984
company service
1926–74
director 1941
awarded CBE 1960
responsible for
establishment of 1936
factory, and for setting
up Haverhill Meat
Products 1958
(later known as
NewMarket Foods)

John D
b1927
company service
1950–present
director 1958
vice chairman 1967
chairman and
chief executive 1969
knighted 1980
created Baron
Sainsbury of Preston
Candover 1989
created Knight of
the Garter 1992

Simon
b1930
company service
1956–79
director, financial
policy and
personnel 1959
deputy chairman
1969

Timothy
b1932
company service 1956–83
and 1995–present
director, estates, architects
and
engineers 1962
MP for Hove 1973–97
held various government posts
1983–94, including
Minister for Trade and
Minister for Industry
knighted 1995
non-executive director 1995

David
b1940
company service
1963–98
director 1966
director and financial
controller 1971
finance director 1973–90
deputy chairman 1988
chairman 1992
created Baron Sainsbury of
Turville 1997

Sainsbury Family Tree

Sainsbury family directors at the Chelsea branch at the time of the company's centenary in 1969. Left to right: Alan Sainsbury (Lord Sainsbury of Drury Lane); Sir Robert Sainsbury; John D Sainsbury (Lord Sainsbury of Preston Candover KG); Mr James Sainsbury; Mr Simon Sainsbury; Sir Timothy Sainsbury; David Sainsbury (Lord Sainsbury of Turville).

Asda Checkout Champions Award Winners

Asda Colleague Share Option Scheme

Safeway shop front of the 1990s

Safeway ABC (loyalty) card

Safeway 'Handiscan'

Marks & Spencer 1912

Marks & Spencer 1990s

Marks & Spencer product proliferation

Le Shuttle takes Marks & Spencer to Europe

Wal-Mart: Santa Fe, New Mexico, USA

Wal-Mart employee: Tucson, Arizona, USA

Wal-Mart's founder: Sam Walton

Executive, is realistic. Addressing his own team he characterized the industry as having three divisions, Sainsbury's and Tesco in one, Asda and Safeway in two, and the rest in three. 'The Co-op with . . . its fragmentation and uneven patterns of investment has a battle on its hands to remain in the third division.' The only uncertainty perhaps is how long break-up will take to happen, before this once great democratic movement disappears. If it does, so will a major element of recent British history.

HUDDLING TOGETHER FOR WARMTH – SOMERFIELD/KWIK SAVE

The merger of Somerfield and Kwik Save was announced in 1998. It is now clear that it was not a merger at all but a takeover with Somerfield as the controlling partner, and an energetic pragmatist David Simons as the new company's Chief Executive. Given the profile of the two companies, and the tougher conditions that lie ahead, the merger case was a good one. The chances of long-term survival remain much in question, but the Somerfield record over five years has been surprisingly positive and well sustained. The issues for the two franchises, now being managed increasingly as a single entity, remain strategic. Given a poor opening position, can a distinctive and competitive profile be engineered and will management have the resources, time and money to make it happen? Simons's team is short neither of ideas nor the will to implement them effectively.

Neither company today has any leadership aspirations, and both have seen better days. Gateway, part of the Somerfield base, was a strong brand, notably in the west of England, and Kwik Save behaved with admirable tenacity as the low-price marker and branded-goods specialist through successive recession conditions during the 1980s. Today, their combined market share has taken them well ahead of the Co-op into fifth position and they have practically caught up with Safeway. Recent share trends for Somerfield and Kwik Save have, however, been downwards, with Kwik Save's decline the steeper. Each is primarily a high-street operator, and the combined chain owns few super-stores. 'There are lots of people who don't want to go there', Simons points out with truth on his side. The trading background is at the low-price end of the market, with Kwik Save owning a heritage that, until the hard discounters arrived, had carved out its niche and escaped virtually unchallenged on the high street. Somerfield has been raising its core appeal from the C1/C2 base while Kwik Save's is to the C2/D customer, so the merged business needs to confront the classic Asda target customer, admittedly from a different store base. Whether they can play in Asda's league, or, *a fortiori*, take on Morrison in the north is unproven.

Financially the picture is not a pretty one. Operating margins are well below industry averages and even if a rationalized company can improve, it cannot begin to bridge the gap between the best performers in the 6 per cent net margin range and Somerfield/Kwik Save's at around half this level. Similarly, sales densities are at half the best benchmark level, well below Asda and Morrison. The result, in terms of operating profit per square foot, shows Somerfield at half of Asda and one-third of Sainsbury's/Tesco. Kwik Save is a whole lot worse. The conclusion is obvious. While Somerfield offers Kwik Save a chance of survival it could not have achieved alone, it will not be enough to use cost synergies to raise Kwik Save to the standards of Somerfield's best stores – a lot more is required. The new business intends to drive the two companies into a rejuvenated Somerfield brand, which seems the best strategic choice – but it risks isolating the core of Kwik Save's remaining loyal customers, still a worthwhile number. Somerfield has a lot on its plate and if market conditions worsen, they are one of the market's weakest players. Fainter hearts would have given up already.

The strongest contra argument is David Simons's excellent operating record since taking over Somerfield. While the brand is certainly not yet strong, his achievement has been considerable. Formed from the rump of Alec Monk's Dee Corporation, Somerfield emerged to take over the post-Isoceles company, the Somerfield fascia then being then a minor element of this very mixed and heavily indebted business. Temporarily ring-fencing the Isoceles debt until flotation in 1996, Simons rationalized rapidly, revitalizing the Somerfield brand and restoring price credibility with the Price Check campaign. Fresh foods importance was recognized and raised dramatically.

Juggling three franchises (Food Giant discounters and Gateway alongside Somerfield) Simons raised Somerfield's profile, recognizing a measure of return to local convenience shopping and feeling his company well placed to move with this trend. With partner Elf, he entered the petrol market, and further European partners enhanced a modest but apparently successful buying consortium. Argos catalogues filled the loyalty bonus role for Somerfield and alongside Price Check, he experimented with flexible local pricing. Home shopping began with a belief that in Somerfield's case, as opposed to the out-of-town superstores, the growth could genuinely be regarded as incremental. Cost management – without doubt a strength the hands-on Simons possesses in spades – was driven forward enthusiastically. Simons is not short of chutzpah and has not allowed innovation to pass his struggling businesses by. He has tried and will try most things.

By contrast, Kwik Save is now a shadow of its former self. Formed in 1959 as Britain's first serious limited-range discounter, Kwik Save featured the manufacturer's brand in its profile, and received enormous reciprocal support principally because they had shied away from any interest in own-label. Tactical approaches to keeping costs down worked well, including allocating concessions to partner franchises on the premises – a move that eventually caused the company problems of control and service. Kwik Save's low-price strategy was regarded as acceptable by all the majors who were prepared to give the company space to hold its desired price position in the market. The company acquired a large number of neighbourhood stores, in which disused cinemas featured prominently, and delivered a strong low-price message to poorer customers, particularly successfully in recessions. Based in North Wales, Kwik Save did especially well in the north-west, the West Midlands and in Wales – well differentiated regional strengths.

As the mid-1980s recession ended, Dairy Farm from Hong Kong took a 30 per cent interest, providing a succession of Antipodean CEOs at the no-nonsense but very distant Prestatyn headquarters – Graham Seabrook, and Graeme Bowler. The ending of the early 1990s recession was to become Kwik Save's undoing. Committed hard discounters were now presenting themselves at very low prices, a key new factor in everyone's calculations, most of all at Prestatyn. Consequently, and in addition, the big four reacted sharply both to the recession and the discounters' arrival, and their stronger own-label promotion exposed the Kwik Save flank further. A once-clear strategy for differentiation was comprehensively threatened and, given Kwik Save's sheer physical inability to change either policies or prices quickly, it was clear their approach was now fundamentally flawed.

Neither an anti-discounter 'no frills' rock-bottom price range nor some enormously expensive strategic Andersen consultancy advice were to provide the answers either. Andersen set out to recommend some obvious changes for the 'New Generation' Kwik Save, getting a proper own-label range, moving away from discounter competition to challenge the mainstream operators, and eliminating non-performing stores. But this did not give Kwik Save anything substantial in which to believe and it was not enough to stem their fast haemorrhaging margins, slowing sales densities or the declining volume there had been since 1993. Strategically '2nd cheapest place to shop in town' is, as Simons pointed out to me, not much as a potentially winning ticket but neither the consultants nor the company itself were able to find a way out of this dilemma. The writing was on the wall and takeover became inevitable. It is difficult today to know how many of Kwik Save's numerous 850 stores will survive – perhaps no more than 200 – under the Somerfield banner.

Can the merger produce the needed improvement for the merged companies? Somerfield's Houdini-like five-year record in moving profitability ahead is a positive argument. So is improving service and good like-for-like sales movement in the Somerfield business. There is a coherent if reactive strategy. It will not confront the out-of-town superstores but will work to the positive dynamics of the customer group that want to shop in smaller stores, in the high streets, many of whom are either frail, older or simply time-poor. Simons can point to his own team's track record which makes such stores work. With little of the arrogance associated with some of his bigger competitors, and a modest desire to promote and learn from effective supplier relationships, he is perfectly happy to copy others' successes. He has a range of methods – organic, semi-organic and acquisition-driven – to maintain growth. His lower profile – not being one of the big four – is probably a help. He appears to believe the company capable of significant growth, certainly of their ability to pass Safeway in size, and even to get to 10 per cent of the market. These are ambitious statements but Somerfield have not in the past been guilty of overclaim and, in the end, it is probably their street-fighting abilities that might see them survive when others would well have been persuaded to throw in their cards.

CHEAP IF NOT YET CHEERFUL – ALDI, LIDL, NETTO (THE HARD DISCOUNTERS) AND ICELAND

THE DISCOUNTER PHENOMENON

Halfway down London's Old Kent Road, in one of the poorest parts of the urban south-east, is a large, singularly unattractive, windowless brick warehouse with the blue sign that tells you that one of Europe's largest and most drivingly successful retailers is inside. Yet in Britain, Aldi, the German market leader, remains a mere parvenu, still not 10 years old, with a national share less than 1 per cent of the UK market. Some three miles further south, by the two Tiger's Head pubs in modest suburban Lee Green, there was until recently a smaller, even dingier shed which housed French-based colossus Carrefour's most recent foray into the UK grocery business, the 'Ed' chain of hard discounters. This has now failed, and been sold to Netto, a subsidiary of Dansk Supermarkets. Two miles east is a big and highly visible new site in a worthwhile, possibly slowly reviving inner-city Deptford location with considerable presence – one of the bright new Lidl discounter stores. Each is representative of a well-known discounter company, a recipe that has succeeded in many countries. Despite its present insignificance in the UK, it may well be set for long-term growth, and whatever the result, the movement looks to have committed itself for the duration, to create an impact on the British market. They have arrived rather late and have a long way to go.

One of the first casualties of the discounters' arrival was the forced abandonment of Kwik Save's 'cheapest family shop in Britain' position. Kwik Save
did not have the ammunition to compete with the stripped-down simplicity
which this new breed of hard discounter could offer to truly focussed price-
conscious customers. Aldi offers incontrovertibly lowest prices on a slim
range – only 600-odd lines are stocked – usually of their own or tertiary (ie
branded but insignificant) lines. The process is an easy one to understand and
in Germany, where Theo and Karl Albrecht learned their trade as one visible
element in the post-war *wirtschaftswunder*, the stores have become a saga in
their own right, like a genuine German Coronation Street, a continuingly
popular part of the national culture. BMW and Mercedes owners happily
throng the stores, and widely bruited price-awareness of their promoted lines
ranks with the major news stories.

Manufacturers of brands justifiably trod warily where the discounter
phenomenon was concerned, feeling there might be no long-term gains to be
made, and seeing from Europe the effect on brand franchise as well as
margins. In Germany, the strongest brands learned from bitter experience to
stay away from the seductive appeal of Aldi's prestigious volume-moving
power – it's fine when you're friends but when arguments break out, the
sudden change of heart can be both vicious and painful. Brand companies
moved overnight from strong profit positions to barely covering their overheads – so great were the volumes which Aldi could generate. So you won't
find brand leaders in the Aldi assortment. Nor – with a few exceptions tactically stocked by Netto, which may be token sales, under strictly controlled
buying terms from manufacturers anxious not to be charged with policies of
being unwilling to supply to the new discounter operations – will you find
them anywhere else in this class of trade. To this extent, brand owners and the
key major retailers seem to have been able to club together and recognize a
distinct continuing common interest.

But times are changing and so too may the willingness of manufacturers to
trade with the new entrants. For the moment, Aldi & Co can be dismissed as 'a
pinprick', as one of their major competitors described them to me. But capital
resources are very large, and their strategies are both proven worldwide and
clear to consumers. The stores themselves may be chillingly crude and stark –
a far cry from the modern retail temple, built with care and affection (a
provocative comparison would be Safeway on the outskirts of Edinburgh). But
their structure and simplicity is compelling. This is a place where each
assistant knows by heart the prices of an entire product range. There is a visible
desire to provide a measurable value-driven proposition for the poorest
consumers seeking lowest everyday prices. True the queues are longer, the
space limited, the wire baskets nastier and the whole experience a whole lot

shorter on aspiration than British consumers have been used to – but there will be a segment, and it may grow, who are prepared to settle for lower aspirations providing perceived value remains greater. Can British consumers choose to be immune?

Aldi and their imitators have spotted a market gap in the UK which is latent and growing. Our retail margins have been some of the highest in the world, and offer measurable incentive to provide other ways of getting everyday staple requirements into the hands of needy consumers. The surprising thing was that it took so long for these European powerhouses to enter the UK market. In delaying as long as they did, two things happened which makes their opportunity now a smaller one. Firstly, it became even more difficult, post-1993, without acquisition, to get good sites in tight urban environments. Second, they gave the British companies more years – most of two decades in fact – to establish the big-range out-of-town superstore as the universal routine (and to claim 'there is no better') form of food shopping for the market. Once rooted, it is more difficult to change especially when it involves such an obvious retreat from the better presentation and appearance of the out-of- town stores. This suggests that if they do want to become a force in the UK, the existing discounters will have to change their approach, which after five years has brought them such limited success. Perhaps it also suggests that it may take a company with the global confidence and truly innovative record of US Wal-Mart to make genuine food discounting work for the first time in Britain. That day may not be far away.

ICELAND

Iceland is a modest-size high-street supplier of frozen foods, formed in 1970. It has, through time and of necessity, broadened its offer to include chilled foods, other packaged goods, and latterly food service and appliances have played a part in Iceland's range. Times have been hard for this enterprising young company, and the 1990s have seen its leaders under heavy pressure as bigger competitors have taken more interest in the high-street opportunity.

There has been a pattern of recent losses in volume and margin. As a company it has been prone to experiment and, since its successful takeover of Bejam in 1988, has tried a range of different deals to build distinctiveness and expertise. Few have worked. The fact remains that today it has around 750 stores and a grocery share approaching 2 per cent, so it is about equal in size to Waitrose. However, there the similarity ends.

Margins have been a cause for concern. From an operation generating an amazing 7 per cent in 1990, it has dropped to little over 4 per cent today as price-cutting strategies ('Pricewatch') failed to work with a customer base that had already convinced itself that Iceland offers were cheap enough anyway. Its sales densities are a further major anxiety, at half the retailer average, perhaps unsurprising from small stores with a limited assortment. Diversification moves – such as the trial partnership with Littlewoods – have brought no advantage.

It is tempting to regard Iceland's early and highly publicized venture into home shopping, where it has sought and gained – for the moment at least – a leadership position, as an innovation born of desperation, a last throw of the dice. It is difficult to see where advantage can come from such a move. For the moment the considerable costs of the move are not covered, although the company is running experiments intended to make sure consumer contribution to delivery can cover their own investment. Home shopping as an issue is covered elsewhere in this book. Iceland has shown the commitment of true innovators – as Carrefour's Daniel Bernard would say, 'Above all, be first' – and the inherent quality in its approach is admirable. It would certainly gain high levels of incremental volume if it could make home shopping work for it. Meanwhile too, Iceland is an early retail adopter of employee empowerment, and the enthusiasm of its store staff for the experiment is noticeable. Despite these factors it is unlikely that the market is really ready for home shopping on the Iceland model to happen, and equally unlikely that when it does, Iceland will be an important beneficiary of the change. In this case, *pace* Daniel Bernard, first-movers may not in this instance get the advantage. However, one has to concede early in 1999 that Iceland are getting good levels of like-for-like growth.

Home shopping is a catch-22 for Iceland management. Its intention has been to build a new customer base, and it is unclear whether this is working. It needs to cover the significant costs of home delivery and so far would not seem to have done this. If and when either of these approaches do achieve their ends, we can be sure that major players, all carrying out their own experiments, and watching the US developments, will need to participate. They may by then be ready through better, more cost-effective propositions, to make a broader-based market appeal than Iceland can offer. If this happens, Iceland or some of its stores themselves would become an attractive takeover target.

STRONG REGIONAL NICHE PLAYERS – MORRISON, WAITROSE

MORRISON

Morrison is the sole survivor of a number of regional Yorkshire retail chains. It celebrates the centenary of its foundation in 1999, and since 1962 this

Bradford-based business has rejoiced in having the redoubtable pilot Ken Morrison at its helm. With 40 per cent of the shareholding under family control, the business is under no pressure to sell and, given its market capitalization, it has every prospect of retaining its independence for as long as it wants, and of extracting a big premium were it ever to capitulate gracefully to its predators. With just under 3 per cent of the market and a concentration of stores in the north-east, it should still be considered a niche player. However, this underestimates the formidable local power of a consistent, well-managed company, and the confidence to expand to the south which it has already shown.

HUMBLE BEGINNINGS – KEN MORRISON

While doing his national service in Germany in 1950, and a very long way from his Yorkshire home, Bradford boy Ken Morrison took what was to be an important phone call from his mother. 'Did 18-year-old Ken want to keep the family market stall in Bradford that had been theirs for many years?' His father had become too ill to continue. Ken thought it over for a few days and then decided he would have a go. It was a choice that would provide significant on-the-job learning for a young man, and his days in Bradford Market taught Ken things about trading and customers that he never forgot.

In 1962, with the retail world changing around him, another significant decision came his way. New stores were replacing the market stalls, and a novelty called self-service was the way in which they were attracting customers in droves. Ken knew the local area well, and had come across a disused cinema in Thornton Road, and thought be could convert it to be his first Morrison store. To his disappointment, and not unnaturally in a cinema, he found its floor sloped badly from back to front, and that he needed £1,000 to level it. 'I've got no money, but get it done, and properly', Morrison told his architect, who not only delivered, but then found Ken a bigger site on the other side of Bradford's ring road, at Bolton junction. This second one had come on the market because the builder had gone bankrupt, and would cost £3,000 to purchase. It was an opportunity, of course, but where was the money to buy it to be found? Worse still – Morrison had calculated he might need £100,000 just to get the stores up and running and to manage his working-capital needs and his cash. It was an unheard of sum of money in those days, especially for a market-stall trader.

So Morrison turned to his Bradford bank, the local Midland branch, across whose threshold he had never previously walked. The market stall transactions took place at a downtown branch. Morrison asked to see the branch manager. 'I know what you're here for,' said the manager to a surprised Ken. 'You want to know if these Provident Clothing shares are worth buying.'

'No,' said Morrison. 'I'd like you to lend me £70,000 for my new stores.' He simply couldn't bring himself to ask for £100,000.

'That'll be all right,' was the unexpected reply. Nothing had been, or indeed ever was written down. No business plan of any kind had been presented. Walking out, in amazement, Morrison realized he didn't even know what interest rate he might be paying, and as it happened, he didn't ever use the facility, so he never did find out what it might have been. But this was how Morrison got started.

Ken Morrison now takes on the mantle of the industry's Grand Old Man – although he'd never accept the title. His style has not changed though Morrison has almost 100 superstores, and close to £3 billion in sales. When I asked him what he might have done differently, he said he felt he was overcautious, and described himself as 'not a risk taker'. Disclaiming any intellectual pretensions, he goes on to credit himself with few original ideas. He still keeps the business on a tight rein, borrows very little, and regards the City with some disfavour, as 'obsessed with short-term growth', a viewpoint with which others might agree. His austere head office, still on an unprepossessing part of the Hillmore Road in Bradford, must constitute the least pretentious corporate headquarters from which any major retail company does its business. Simplicity wherever you go in Morrison is the watchword.

Morrison's own philosophy exudes simplicity. 'Know what you want to do and then make sure to do it well.' He treats both his competitors – who he likes to talk about – and his customers with interest and respect. 'Everyone deserves a bit of dignity' is the way Ken, in his quiet Yorkshire tones, puts it. Sometimes it is the simple ideas framed in humble beginnings that work best in the long run.

Behind only the four majors in superstore penetration, Morrison owns fewer than 100 stores, but these are large – usually 40,000 sq ft of selling space – and impressive. Morrison has enjoyed faster recent percentage growth than any significant competitor having more than doubled business over a decade.

Profits performance has also been compelling – over the same period, profits doubled and then proceeded to double again inside 10 years. Margins at around 6 per cent on sales are as good as any in the industry, surely a surprise for a company that is less than a quarter of the leader's size, and which sells at low prices. At 20 per cent, return on capital beats most competitors, and Morrison's gearing is negligible. Sales densities, while under pressure, are at the leading edge. This company has the fundamentals right and has the operating profile of competitors three and four times its size.

Morrison has been able to match the best in the industry. Ken Morrison attributes this to an intelligent appreciation of what consumers require in terms of value for money. He views his approach as 'democratic' – shades of a once dominant, and also northern-based co-operative movement – and believes, as the Co-op did too, that political as well as economic choices matter. Financially prudent Morrison has avoided onerous leases and set out to own its trading land. It also owns its distribution systems and a significant percentage of its own packing of fruit and vegetables, cheese and bacon, believing this has given it better cost and quality control. Relationships with the brand manufacturers have been personally and consistently managed – suppliers rarely found it difficult to get in to see the Morrison chairman. Finally, Morrison is a people business, and it is no surprise to see the chain's wage rates, located in the not usually overpaid north, at a level higher than most national competitors.

A clear business strategy is reflected in the deceptively simple 'low prices mean best value' proposition. The Morrison formula eschews corporate bureaucracy and avoids what it sees as trading gimmicks. Thus it has stayed away both from trading stamps and now, bravely but coherently, from loyalty cards, preferring to compete strongly on KVI (known value item) pricing, and using its distinctive yellow-and-black own-brand to drive its price message home. Innovations, once proven, are persisted with, but Morrison's philosophy of trading is not a new one, nor is it over-intellectualized – 'I'd rather you tripped up over a pile of cheap cream crackers than give you a loyalty card' is the way Ken himself puts it. There is distinctive marketing in the lively and colourful 'market square' trading format. Increasing concentration behind service counters – with some real people behind them – and heavy emphasis on fresh foods compare with the best superstore offerings. Finally, Morrison himself now seems confident enough to bring the proven mixture south, and stores have been opening in the environs of London – Banbury, Chingford and Erith – for example. There is every sign that these are succeeding. It would be wrong any longer to treat Morrison as a regional concern. The recipe now seems to work anywhere.

In the industry there is regular speculation that Ken Morrison, now in his late sixties and without an heir, might be persuaded to sell. He told me, with a mischievous twinkle in his eye, that his own outlook on the apparent choice depended on 'how he felt that morning'. He has absolutely no need, nor does he exhibit any inclination to leave his powerfully managed company. A rock-solid share price reflects a premium that takes account of this. No doubt Tesco and Sainsbury's are reflecting on promising modes of successful courtship, and his franchise would represent a perfect foothold for an overseas investor, an Ahold, or even a Wal-Mart. There are similarities in style between the Morrison way of doing business and Wal-Mart's. Of course it is conceivable that economies of scale may begin to bite against Morrison at the finest levels of aggregation, but he has avoided this for 35 years and there are precious few signs of this today. As rationalization at a European level happens, Morrison's size may well be a handicap, but again this constraint is some way off.

In the meantime with a confidence of spirit that is tangible, and a growth record second to none, Ken Morrison is well placed to move his operations to a national platform. His is one of the simplest and most impressive long-term stories in British grocery retailing.

WAITROSE

Different in every respect, but no less impressive is the John Lewis Partnership's grocery chain – Waitrose – named at the turn of the century after two of its founders: Messrs Waite and Rose. All the employees of John Lewis Partnership have owned the company for 60 years, and at times in their lives together it has seemed an uncomfortable and even unwilling marriage, with the grocery chain not always capable of embracing fully the ethic and practices of its studied and appreciated department store parent. 'Never knowingly undersold' has never been a concept Waitrose could espouse in grocery, and as an acknowledged high-price operator in the field, nothing could be further removed from its current business strategy. There are certainly a number of trade-offs visible in looking at relationships between 'parent' and 'subsidiary' and there was even a time in the 1960s and 1970s when one questioned whether the (parent) Partners wanted to be present at all in the hurly-burly of the grocery supermarket business where its Waitrose (subsidiary) had found itself. However, the two companies have learned to live together, time generating mutual respect and cementing confidence, and today's market signals show a level of joint and individual certainty that is backed by sound strategy, a brand with the clearest differentiation, and increasingly good results.

Waitrose remains a pretty surprising grocer. Some years ago, when Sainsbury's led the market, Waitrose could have been likened to a small but high-priced home counties Sainsbury's. No longer. They have sales of £2 billion and a market share around 2 per cent, a wide range of store sizes from

15,000 sq ft to the biggest, with, however, very few superstores. Interestingly, high-street or near-high-street locations predominate and with limited non-food diversification ('petrol and food simply don't fit together') they might go unnoticed in a market where size and visibility are the prerequisites. This would ignore the dedicated and planned individualism of this business, determined first by an all-pervading partnership ethic that has for many years avoided aggressive marketing techniques, and kept in their place such atrocities as extended hours and Sunday trading – at a considerable cost to their volume it must be said. ('Trading on Sunday was illegal', management pointed out to me accurately, and the improbable thought that the partners might ever be seen collectively to break the law did seem to me quite a powerful argument.) It would also miss Waitrose's brand strength built in a finicky and affluent south-eastern heartland, where along with Marks & Spencer it can claim first-level ownership of the high-quality shopper franchise. This is still a place where Madam is seen to shop, and where two-or-more-car families predominate.

Brand strength owes a lot to product innovation, measurably better service delivery, and high commitment to real and fresh foods and to meal solutions – and Waitrose like to record that it was first with organics, for example. Finally, it would not recognize Waitrose's sculptured shopping experience, consistently rated by customers eg in a recent Consumers' Association survey, at levels markedly above the best. The survey showed that 72 per cent of Waitrose shoppers judged their shopping experience as excellent while the four majors jostled each other anonymously around the 60 per cent level.

Waitrose can now see the distant peaks, and are climbing fast, but they have wallowed in the troughs, which reflected a stuttering lack of progress at earlier times. Change at Waitrose is rarely violent, and evolution is planned and preferable. The management approach is calm, studied and analytical. Value means best quality and accepts that Waitrose does have higher prices, and they still focus on their AB target catchment group, although now 'not so severely' according to Chairman David Feldwick. With limited scale from its 120 stores, margins modestly lag the majors, as you might expect, but sales densities are up with the best and accelerating – indeed only Sainsbury's and Tesco are ahead.

Innovations are a key part of its future strategy. Home shopping at a cost of £3 per order, store scanning and office ordering are all under current test, and in moves to bring the Waitrose offer more into the mainstream, there is greater willingness to offer promotions, rather than the 'everyday low – well actually usually high – prices' that had been their historic practice. However, Waitrose's shopping ethic is different, well expressed by Feldwick's statement about the effects of recession on trading: 'When this happens, the competitors cut, we nurture.' Carefulness, adhering to store procedures, knowing that information matters, and a real concern with the quality and especially the taste of good food are some of the hallmarks. Waitrose can talk with real passion about what good food means, and where it will be found – sometimes it is ready to admit on retail shelves outside the UK. Of course learning and training of staff is critical, and not surprisingly its wage costs are measurably the highest in the industry. Fair pay for a good day's work is how they describe their policy, but partnership staffing is a reality that – while others emulate it – is a difference of cultural significance. It is a thoroughly coherent pattern of business with long-term focus which has catered to their unique if still limited consumer profile.

Still Waitrose has future issues with which to deal. It cannot expect to grow quickly, and while independence from the financial markets helps, one senses that the grocery leadership would sometimes like the freedom to raise its own equity. It has just a few major superstores, and little of the capital funding needed to build or acquire new ones, but at the same time it must be conceded that those it has are superlatively well-structured offerings – Beckenham, for example. Some of their neighbourhood stores, and there are too many of them, lack the distinctiveness and pulling power of their best sites. Logistic systems is an area where Waitrose must seek to match best practice, but as with promotions and marketing, there are indications it is playing rapid catch-up in these areas. There is a hardness of purpose in Waitrose that was not present in its more bureaucratic civil service past – although on the day I visited Feldwick in the Victoria Street Partnership headquarters, I was encouraged to see two managers working on the *Telegraph* crossword in the lift. It is still prone to over-deliver and under-claim, but one senses that it now has honest aspirations to be the best food retailer, and to raise its head above the parapet not just in this regard but also in respect of pricing. 'We are not as expensive as you think' may be the message of the future.

Meanwhile, it is difficult to quarrel with Waitrose's results. Profit margins from a low 1994 ebb have doubled and are now respectable. Return on capital has also more than doubled in three years and, given a limited number of new sites, is at 27 per cent the best in the industry. Its competition, with the exception of Marks & Spencer, seems in style and purpose strategically remote, and even Marks & Spencer cannot claim, as can Waitrose, to be an over 20,000 item full-line grocer. It should therefore be well placed to cock a snook at future market rationalization. Shortage of capital may remain the crucial constraint.

Looked at, as it must be, as a long-term market player, Waitrose is distinctive, psychologically confident and an increasingly competitive performer. It feels well equipped to take on the best, now certainly including

Marks & Spencer, and its marked cultural differences – based on a search for real quality, better customer service and a trading style that exudes honesty and reliability – should fit it well for future generations, particularly in positive economic conditions. Together with the John Lewis Partnership its future in its respective markets looks both unique and secure.

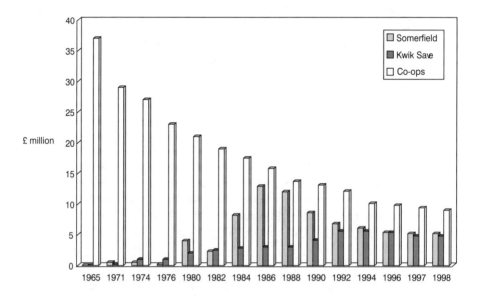

Figure 6.1 *Somerfield, Kwik Save and the Co-op sales 1965–98*

7

The market in Europe

EUROPEAN MARKETS – RETAILERS LOOKING OUTWARDS

There has been a degree of vibrancy and fluidity in the European grocery retailing scene that compared to other developed markets has been continuous and compelling. Over the years since the Second World War ended, and particularly over the past two decades, the changes have been rapid, dynamic and increasingly international in scope. Powerful new businesses have arisen across a range of northern European countries, many of them confident enough or constrained by the stagnation on their domestic horizons to extend their operations across national boundaries and indeed in many instances into new continents. Once assured they could penetrate the contiguous markets in Europe, several European retailers set themselves stretching global ambitions and expanded into the Americas, south as well as north, and into Asia, building themselves a strong future foothold there. Others, taking a positive view of the reviving central European opportunities, extended eastwards to their erstwhile European heartlands.

The extent to which key mainland European players have broken out of their domestic markets is striking. Restrictive planning controls in France and

Germany, and the smallness and maturity of the domestic markets notably in the Low Countries but progressively in the whole of western Europe have been factors driving the need for transnational expansion. The predominant pattern in the UK and – with the exception of Wal-Mart – emphatically in the United States has differed and stay-at-home/grow-at-home has been the accepted modus operandi. This assumption is now under tighter examination, but the leading European world players have established a solid platform of advantage in terms of time and operating experience on foreign fields which should stand them in good stead as the market becomes steadily a more global entity. The differences from the UK and the US markets are illuminating. But here too, change is happening very rapidly.

THE NEED FOR AND THE PACE OF CHANGE

It is worth making a preliminary point about the case for change. In the mass of European acquisitions, mergers, cross-border forays and joint ventures it is noteworthy that until recently Britain barely figures, the reasons for which will be reviewed later. They are not simply a reflection of the politics of exclusion, or the strategic incompetence that successive British governments displayed in their dealings with the growing entity of Europe (on which point see Hugo Young's splendid analysis in *This Blessed Plot*, 1998). Britain's anything-but-splendid isolation needs explanation since it is now clear that a significant market-growth opportunity has been substantially ignored. By comparison with continental Europe, the UK business environment in which retailing has grown through the self-service years has been both more adventurous and less restricted, which has meant that learning and experiment has been faster here, and domestic UK profits on the whole, and for the handful of public company winners, that much greater. The principal participants in the European market who became established in the years of post-war rebuilding appear much more inured to change, and have profited through their ability to develop across boundaries through the lively post-war years, as Europe itself has restructured its institutions. Norman Davies describes how widespread and essentially integrated economic development has been, and how the major countries have vied with each other for post-war success:

> West Germany's Wirtschaftswunder lay at the heart of Western Europe's resurgence … contrary to popular misconceptions … [Germany] did not however exceed the performance of all its rivals. Italy's Miracolo was hardly less spec-

tacular and ... Erhardt spurned the kind of government planning preferred in France ... Germany did not generate the Continent's highest standard of living.

(Davies, 1996: 1082)

It was in this outward-looking competitive climate that the leading food retailers grew and consolidated, notably in France and in Germany but also in the smaller countries, notably the Low Countries, Switzerland and Scandinavia. The indications ahead are that the rate of European change is set to accelerate significantly as opportunities not only in big and fast growing Mediterranean countries but now in Central and East Europe open up simultaneously. Retailers now appreciate that the global positions now being taken, in Europe both west and east, in the United States and in Asia will determine the shape of future world leadership, and the European leaders are certain to use their current platforms and experience to play an important part in occupying some of these key global positions. European companies with an established record for technology, innovation and customer service should be well placed to build new sources of long-term growth, providing that the processes of organizational and strategic change to compete globally are implemented quickly. There are visible signs that this change process has started but not before time. There are also emerging signs that some of the more ambitious European world players are moving very much faster than their counterparts.

NATIONAL FRAMEWORKS IN EUROPE

Grocery retailing in Europe over three decades has nurtured diverse successful formats that have satisfied customers in national markets, while quite early on the most successful strategies were exported smoothly across national frontiers, making the protagonists inherently confident about their capacity to compete more widely. Virtually all the major European companies have been looking to create strength outside their homelands. One notable exception has been the unique French-based franchising concern Enterprises Leclerc, for reasons connected no doubt to the surprisingly democratic and disaggregated structure that the formidable crusader called Edouard Leclerc and his equally committed successors have put together, which has taken them in their own right in France to a key position in the European league table. Few companies have defined their retailing ambitions in quite the same radical, socially advanced and strikingly French nationalistic way that Leclerc has done, however.

The two primary national market growth engines have been located in France and, in a very different retailing climate, West Germany. These have stimulated growth elsewhere, by expanding principally from France to the south, and to the east from West Germany and then deciding to spread even further afield. Practically no other nation's retailers have participated in this powerful *Drang nach Osten/Suden* movement. Holland is an adventurous retail market and Ahold and Makro corporations have played modest European roles, as have important Belgian corporations, but it has been growth driven from either side of the Rhine that has been the formative influence. Ahold, whose international development has been among the most rapid in the last five years, has concentrated almost exclusively on generating major equity finance to grow in the United States. British retailing appears to have been operating in a different world, scarcely penetrating the European market itself, but priding itself on its seeming invulnerability to attack from these aggressive Europeans when they have tried to penetrate. There have been forays from Carrefour, and attempts to establish new formats from Makro, but German Aldi and their fellow discounters – Lidl, Netto and Ed – are now significant elements on the UK landscape, perhaps the first ominous exceptions to the invulnerability rule.

Today the European market is an entity that will integrate more rapidly in the years ahead, and it is so viewed by the key players. For more than 30 years now the normal pattern of development has been through the *hypermarché*, driven principally from a developing French model, which Carrefour is credited with initiating, but imitated widely elsewhere and over time. There are similarities in Germany but there the major players have been much more individual in behaviour. There has been a much greater tendency to rely on and communicate low-price strategies – inevitably so, as a stricken German economy recovered, so much more successfully than Weimar did 30 years earlier, from the painful post-war years. The strength of the discounting format in Germany was one obvious direct consequence which is now rooted in the very core of German grocery trading. Aldi was a distinctive and genuine pioneer from the day the two Albrecht brothers started to create their powerful empire as early as 1948. Metro, Europe's largest single retailing entity, has competed in a bewilderingly complex array of market sectors, formats and fascias. The less well-known but significant Rewe is another large and diverse trading group and, at an integrated level, has been Europe's second largest player. It is a set of interlocking co-operative retail and wholesale developments but once again with no single or dominant pattern. The building of strategies that are becoming recognizable over the long term and the need for flexibility, particularly with regard to the importance of the discounting appeal, can now be observed as key factors. A further important development may now be the growing importance of the neighbourhood convenience stores.

THE EUROPEAN COMPANIES

Germany's Metro is easily the biggest overall, but it has achieved its position, it must be said, without any obvious definition of retail strategy. After Metro, and in the top 10, there are a range of players – many of them one-time family businesses with considerable stakes in their home markets and traditional heritages built over many years – who are not very different from each other in size and power. All the way down to Leclerc at no. 10, they have sales well in excess of 20 billion euros – which compares very favourably with the biggest British retailers. Tesco and Sainsbury's approach them in size but it is in the markets of heartland western Europe where the fastest growth has been. The market has exhibited recognizably similar patterns as it has grown, and there have been distinct signs of 'follow my leader' and 'after you, Claude' in the imitative nature of the strategies pursued and the timing of the moves that followed. However, competition is now very tight, reflected in the slim net trading margins, and an increasingly hell-for-leather drive for the new markets that are opening. A shake-out now looks to be on the cards which will leave perhaps only half a dozen surviving European food-retailing companies at the end of the day. The better Europeans have not been able to achieve much more than around half the net margin that the average UK supermarket operator produced over the same period and, whether as a cause or a consequence, there is a naked simplicity, a stripped down operating and service climate detectable in the European hypermarket or discounter that is far removed from the well-engineered calm, service cohesion and carefully manipulated elegance of their British equivalents.

FORMAT DEVELOPMENT IN EUROPE

The European hypermarket format is now going through a phase of experiencing severe problems. Particularly in France and Spain where the format has been most dominant, the major financial indicators are now all pointing downwards. Both discounters and supermarkets have greater current consumer appeal, and the 'convenience handicap' of the hypermarket – too much driving time and even *too much* choice when I get there – has apparently not been overcome. Legislation, based on a thesis of consumer protection, limiting the rates of expansion and preventing goods being sold at a loss, has contributed substantially to the lack of scale advantage that hypermarkets can continue to generate. The hypermarkets' reaction – to expand their non-food assortments – has probably not helped, and there are signs that in the key food markets their consumer appeal is now weakening. Strategies with more precision, focus and clear areas of advantage –

including a distinctive and topical profile for development of fresh food and quality grocery shopping – are now their crucial requirement.

Franchising has played a large part in European store development and has been a contributor to keeping down both capital investment and running costs. The best European companies have raised their net margins to around 2.5 per cent in recent years, usually through major moves in scale, accompanied by an increase in non-foods assortment and turnover. However, the 1–1.5 per cent range has been by no means uncommon for large and highly successful companies – eg Promodes in France and Tengelmann in Germany – and shows just how tough life now is for some of these formidable and well-established operators.

The obsessive secrecy of many competitors means it is not always possible to determine what margins and profitability are really being taken – a far cry from the visibility of performance, and simultaneous detailed financial analysis attaching on a quarterly basis to the results of British or US operators. What is clear is that their returns are nearer the US model than the UK's, and following recent US consolidation, most of the big Europeans do not begin to match in scale the biggest US groups (one of whom is of course now owned by Holland's Royal Ahold concern).

Innovation, technology and scale as they have moved across Europe have delivered big efficiencies, but it is doubtful whether there is now a great deal more to go for. Hence the drive for new geography and virgin or emergent self-service markets. The growth of the discounter and its appeal in some of Europe's poorer markets to the south and east, with the global retail market now arriving at pace, suggest that margins may, however, be set to contract rather than rise. Europe's biggest, highly diversified competitor (Metro) seems to recognize this and is putting enormous pressure on consolidation, behind four focussed fascias and resultant efficiencies. There will be inevitable shake-out among the second-rank players and of course, well within range now, there lurks the imminent threat of Wal-Mart, the world's largest retailer, on the way to building a world as well as European food retailing presence. The strongest UK food-retail boardrooms are now casting anxious eyes across the channel and further south at the cost and pace of developments. 'Get a permanent seat at the top table or prepare for the starvation years' is the message they have been getting and this has been in its own right a powerful catalyst.

THE IMPORTANCE OF THE FAMILY

The increasingly ruthless nature of today's market is a novel and unpleasant experience for many of these companies, who have proud and stable histories, some going back as much as a century. A roster of famous ruling families has played a major role in this industry's development. Tengelmann, more than a century after its German beginnings, still responds to the leadership of the great-grandson of their founder. It has become master at dealing with major interference, regrouping and re-establishing its core activities twice this century already, following its disappearance through confiscation at the end of two world wars. It has not diminished its resolve to recapture lost ground, eg in East Germany, and it has established a unique vertically integrated German foods business, while getting worthwhile footholds in the United States (with the purchase of A&P) and later in Italy with Superal.

In France, the Fournier, Mulliez and Leclerc triumvirate of families played the crucial central roles in building the big and omnipresent French brand names of Carrefour, Auchan and Leclerc. There are more than embryonic signs now that they are, with the utmost reluctance, beginning to relinquish a powerful family grip on the reins of power. Carrefour, a widely spread company with apparent world ambitions, recognizes it must put in place strategic structures to manage its future, and that family voting rights must rapidly be reduced. It is likely that Auchan will be persuaded that it needs to follow.

In Germany, Otto Beisheim was until 1994 sole owner of Metro, astonishingly for such an enormous concern, still a private company with a single owner. This is a 180-company conglomerate, where it is truly impossible to fathom the labyrinthine controls and systems that obtain in what is Europe's biggest retailer. At Aldi, the 'twins' Theo and Karl Albrecht have played a well-choreographed but also highly secretive part in the successful growth of their Aldi company, now well represented both in Europe and the United States. There is a suggestion in Germany that the dual leader approach (north and south separate and competing) has been a deliberate ploy to maintain the tightest control of staff costs and conditions – on the grounds that it is easier for two leaders to say 'No' to wage increases than just one!

The importance of these European dynastic families cannot be overestimated. Their survival in power has been a force for process consistency and the pursuit and acceptance of long-term strategies – the century-long hegemony of the Sainsbury family in Britain was entirely comparable in style at least until John Sainsbury began to take the company public. In Europe it is, however, now set to change – Carrefour have been heard to speak explicitly of an apparent need for patterns of Anglo-Saxon governance. In this regard the change in Britain has preceded Europe's current re-examination – Sainsbury's floated the company in 1973, non-family board members have been in the majority for years, and there is a professional chief executive and now the first non-family chairman. Tesco's last family chairman stood down, albeit with considerable unwillingness, in 1970. Elsewhere in the UK, professional managers rule the roost – as indeed they do in Holland, where the expansion of Ahold in the United States has accelerated mightily under Cees van den Hoeven's determined personal leadership since 1993.

There is a feeling that it has been the ethos of the individual companies themselves and influentially the families in the shadows behind them pulling on the strings that have determined the essential nature of these continental European markets. Transparency has not normally been a characteristic. While it worked admirably when each ruling family knew and essentially respected the areas of potential dominance to which their competitors aspired in growth markets, whether these same companies can now change their behaviour, accept more visiblity and accountability, and take on world competition is quite another matter. On the record, however, big market shares have been built in important new markets – Spain, Brazil, East and Central Europe are all examples. At the same time, there have been notable and expensive failures – an innovative and expansive Carrefour throwing in the US towel being one. As the need for capital intensifies, and as shareholders begin to make more insistent demands, and want proper and regular performance information, the rate of change will accelerate and many more visible mistakes will be made. Such unsuccessful acquisitions as Casino and Cora in France and the poor post-acquisition performance of Euromarche for Carrefour (who forced out the CEO as a consequence) and of Catteau for Tesco (who knew they were hugely lucky to find a quick buyer) are cases of recent errors. We can be sure there will be more, as hostile acquisitions play a significant part in the market's consolidation and growth.

GOVERNMENTS AND LEGISLATION

A further important difference between the Anglo-Saxon and continental markets has been the attitude of national governments and the role of legislative constraint on the big retail companies. In France through the *Loi Royer* there has been considerable restriction on development of hyper-markets, usually exercised through the imposition of absolute limitations on new site developments. The motivation has been to protect the centres of French towns and villages, and thereby the livings of small shopkeepers. In this regard the policy can be said to have achieved its objectives. Comparing French and British high streets today is illuminating, and shows the extent in Britain to which decades of laissez-faire government planning and inconsistent local policy have created a threadbare high street and communities deprived of many former local shops. French high streets and communities have in this respect fared better.

Elsewhere in Europe restrictions have also been considerably more demanding than in the UK. In Germany there are legislative constraints on outlets above 1,200 sq m in size, called the *Baunutzungsverordnungen*, not dissimilar to France's *Loi Royer*. Restraint in Germany has operated as much through the limitations of price and cost as overt government controls, but the resulting position is not very different from France. A stronger local community has been preserved and while Britain, post-1993, was forced into a process of learning from previous mistakes, it has on the whole been Europe's good fortune to have been influenced by a series of more interventionist social policies and therefore to have been able to avoid most of the problems of the disintegration of local communities in the first place.

Relationships between retailers and governments have sometimes been openly hostile, nowhere more so perhaps than reflected in the unpredictable activities of the militant grocer, Edouard Leclerc, who founded his discount hypermarket buying group in 1949. Now France's second biggest retailer, Leclerc has more than 300 hypermarkets, and nearly 200 large supermarkets. Leclerc was quick to spot the consumer appeal of the hypermarket and began to change his formats early in the 1970s, since when his stores have delivered exceptional levels of French growth. However, it is Leclerc's vision, his policies and, notably, his uncompromising hostility to standard French commercial practice that distinguishes Leclerc not only from French competition but from food retailers everywhere. Leclerc was determined to do battle against what he saw as the strong supplier monopolies, and at the same time to build a reputation for offering lowest prices. He has uncomplicatedly pursued these two focussed policies. The other differentiation of Leclerc's business is its franchise-based structure. Operating rules are very strict, nobody can own more than two subsidiaries, and controls are designed to keep costs down and eliminate both excessive personal and commercial profit. Leclerc has triumphed in circumventing France's tough *Loi Royer* (1973), while successfully defeating competitive monopolies in such areas as fish, books and petrol. His has been an improbable career, particularly in dirigiste France, but in its effects have been highly instructive and healthy for the development of the market as a whole.

BUILDING BRANDS

There has been little genuine brand-building in most European retail operations. Companies have been content on the whole to behave as holding companies behind a veil of secrecy and to create new store fascias or brand portfolios where they were needed operationally. There are large aggregations of market sectors and operations grouped under a single holding company name, with food usually predominating. Albert Heijn was originally a tiny family business, founded 100 years ago in Ootzaan by the side of a Dutch canal. Ahold have shown a capability of building a strong consumer brand in Holland where the Albert Heijn chain of stores is highly innovative, and experiments widely with technologies such as scanning in store and home sales. Heijn is the gold standard in Holland with a firm stranglehold on the Dutch consumer psyche, and a share three times its nearest rival. Ahold now has footholds in 16 separate world markets, yet on a European scale it is relatively insignificant and remains under represented vis-à-vis major competitors. The signs now are that its board is aware that this approach must change, recognizing, according to their chairman, that 'the introduction of the euro and other measures are setting Europe in the direction of becoming a truly common market' (van der Hoeven, 1998).

Meanwhile, Ahold has established a truly excellent position in the large east coast US markets, describing itself today with some real justification as the Dutch-American retailer. Ahold has moved with speed and purpose, acquiring the New England Stop 'n Shop supermarket stores in 1996, gaining control of Washington's Giant Foods, from under Sainsbury's nose, and most recently (1999) taking over the New York Pathmark company. With further good east coast franchises (Bi-Lo, First National, Mayfair and Edwards) Ahold is evidently capable, ultimately, of rebranding these fascias and by this means creating a well-integrated and powerful US-based concern. It has left formidable larger competitors a long way behind in getting this excellent foothold, and Ahold's consumer marketing can be ranked with the best. It might feel it needs a major alliance or acquisition to gain European credibility, and will be casting covetous eyes towards the vulnerable French majors, perhaps Promodes or Auchan, or conceivably at any one of the British big four or five. Its US achievement has been impressive and has not been achieved at the expense of results at home – Ahold's operating margins are some of the best in continental Europe. Cees van der Hoeven has set a target of doubling sales within five years and repeatedly confirms Ahold's intention of becoming the world's number one food retailer, and at the same time of creating the world's strongest food brand. On the record so far he might well do it.

Just about as unlike Ahold as it is possible to be, Aldi's brand is predictably positioned and confidently operated. Aldi is uncomplicated, down to earth, and where price is the paramount requirement, its determination both in Germany and elsewhere – it took more than 10 years for it to make Denmark profitable, for example – speaks for itself. However, Aldi branding lacks any element of emotional aspiration, and it must be questioned whether it has the skills or the speed to reproduce German success in developed markets (eg the United States, where 10 per cent of its sales, from its Trader Joe's stores, is now generated). It is not going to stop trying and strategic commitment shows in its willingness to wait patiently for success. Fifty years of terrific consistency and tradition in Germany cannot be ignored. 'The rich want to come here and the poor have to' has been the Albrecht brothers' persuasively simple claim. East Europe should provide rich pickings for Aldi, and little change to its brand or store recipe will be needed to create success there. Albrecht has not been afraid to move Aldi into neighbouring markets – it is present in Austria, The Netherlands, France and the UK, as well as in Australia and the United States. Given the obsessive secrecy about its plans, but its acknowledged ability to measure retail performance with exactness, Albrecht may now know a lot more about strategic market dynamics than it is given credit for. Its standardized brand is already travelling successfully into places far removed from the poverty of 1948 Germany, and many markets exist where Aldi's coherent brand, ability to focus and clear value appeal will be a strong proposition.

THE GERMANS

Where Aldi's strategy has been clear and integrated, the same cannot be said for the two leading German retailers – Metro and Rewe. Metro grew rapidly but haphazardly for 30 years from its establishment in 1964. Following Beisheim's retirement in 1994, Metro has embarked on a long-overdue process of consolidation and simplification of its retail empire which embraces a huge range, sold through every conceivable retail format from hypermarket to cash and carry. As an international business, Metro is still underperforming internationally – under 20 per cent of sales is outside the home market – although its stated strategy is now to concentrate on focussed foreign growth, and specifically and interestingly on Turkey, Poland and China, alongside its plans for domestic consolidation. Having acquired full ownership of the Makro business, Metro's European site position is inherently its strongest asset, and it has attractive property flexibility options – retain, develop to retail, or sell – with its extensive property portfolio. Its German-based operations, including wholesale, give it an excellent East European platform from which to expand.

Metro holds some very big cards – whether it is yet capable of deploying them to advantage at the highest level is at the moment unproven. Metro is big and powerful, with the highest range of developed formats. Scale and diversity are its advantages. Its disadvantages are its enormous range of operations and concomitantly the execution of a growth strategy. With Wal-Mart now competing in its home market, time is not on Metro's side. However, if it can deliver the strategy it espouses, it will remain difficult to dislodge. To date, there are few signs of strategy delivering results, and fewer indications that it will deliver strong growth in shareholder value in the future.

Metro is one-third bigger than its next biggest European and German competitor, the equally complex Rewe group. This very large German business is domestically powerful, but has grown rapidly being represented in the East and West German markets, and now is present in many of the Central European markets. With 80 per cent of sales in food it is, by sector at least, well focussed, as is Metro. Originally a buying group, or collective with 6,500 retailer members, Rewe has progressively converted to direct retailing on an opportunistic basis as possibilities opened up in its home market. There is considerable happenstance in Rewe's approach to the conversion process but policies were not unsuccessful in generating growth from both the wholesale and retail arms of its business. Apart from hypermarkets, Rewe have concentrated on developing its Penny Market discounter brand, and have begun to enter more foreign markets. While it failed with the joint operation with Budgen in the UK, it did a lot better in Austria with a subsidiary that was wholly owned. Apart from the moves to the east, they have now reached a partnership agreement with Esselunga, a significant northern Italian operator. Rewe is another conservative company that has grown quickly through pragmatic evolution but now faces a host of new changes – formats, geography, competition – so that it is difficult to forecast Rewe's prospects in the more global market.

Finally, in Germany there is Tengelmann, perhaps, over the longest term, the most impressive of German-based competitors, although they are smaller than Metro and Rewe and equivalent in size to the bigger French companies. Founded by the Schmitz family in 1867, it is distinctive for its pursuit of vertical integration policies, enabling it to concentrate on high-quality own-label production. Tengelmann has moved progressively from a luxury approach to create a more mainstream profile and 75 per cent of its volume is now in foods. Rapid German growth through the post-war years rebuilt the business that Tengelmann twice created and lost through confiscation after the world wars. Acquisition in Germany of the Kaffeegeschaft chain and of significant Co-op stores fuelled growth, as did the development of their PLUS (*Prima Leben und Sparen*) discounter operation. With what could be called a sense of adventure, Tengelmann bought the failing but once great American A&P chain, with 1,100 stores and a big but notoriously low margin-revenue stream. Tengelmann too has an Italian business (Superal) and is increasingly becoming better represented in the main western European markets including France, Spain and The Netherlands. It has developed retailing skills, good technologies, a sound innovation record, and enough confidence to enter the biggest world markets. How these competences and its ability to survive on tight margins support it in the years ahead against bigger but hitherto less-focussed German competition will be a key issue for it. It can also expect East European competition from many sources, an inevitable clash with French and German companies in Italy, and challenges in Europe and the United States from Wal-Mart. Tengelmann's stretched profile suggests the need for rapid success or focus and rationalization in the immediate future.

THE FRENCH

French retailers behave by inclination as committed European exporters, driven by restrictive legislation at home and economic stagnation in post-Mitterand France. In overall scale, Promodes ranks as the biggest although there is very little volume difference between it, Carrefour and Auchan. In terms of results, profitability and its capacity to set ambitious objectives in a world of retailing changes, Carrefour must be seen as clear leader. Founded in 1959 by Badin Defforey and the Fournier family, Carrefour is credited with inventing the hypermarket format, and it now has more than 100 in France itself. The largest French retail multiple (as opposed to buying group), it has used non-food to build new growth and margins simultaneously, and has been alert to the opportunity for new discounter formats alongside its main Carrefour brand.

Very much more willing than its competitors to experiment, Carrefour is not at all afraid of entering joint ventures – including one with Metro AG. New markets – savings, banking, insurance, telephone services – have all been tackled, and the Carrefour strategy is by no means risk averse, but on the record sound and on the whole productive. While the hypermarket has been the main engine of Carrefour growth, it is building new growth from discount operations, admittedly per se unlikely to hold or raise margins. But it is as a foreign investor that Carrefour has beaten an individual business path. In Spain, Brazil and Argentina, Carrefour has strong subsidiaries, and the Pryca (Spain) and Brepa (Brazil) operations are key to current performance. Carrefour has built a strong level of brand awareness, is a noted retail merchandiser, and has an aggressively driven own-label franchise. With the exception of its damaging US failure, it has an improving operational record, is generating strong French cash flows and at the same time is working in a wide range of markets outside France, now deriving less than 50 per cent of world profits from its French company.

Italy, where Carrefour uses its own fascia to build organic growth, is the next crucial expansion market and will test its resources. In France itself growth has been choppy. While it succeeded in taking over Euromarche, it cost them a chief executive. It then failed to acquire all of Cora, encouraging Fournier to complain wearily about the perils of *cannibalisme*, an evocative Gallic equivalent of consolidation that is now adversely affecting the French market. Its latest acquisition has been Comptoirs Modernes. There remains, however, a directness and an urgency about Carrefour. Deliberately recognizing a world market including Asia and Latin America, it is moving to a professional organization and board to handle tomorrow's developments – the maxim 'think global, act local' and a consequent reduction in family control being obvious corollaries.

CARREFOUR'S INNOVATOR – DANIEL IN A DEN OF LIONS

Daniel Bernard has been Carrefour's chairman since 1992 when a round of painful arguments among members of the Fournier family about acquisition opportunity (see attitudes to *cannibalisme* and consolidation) created an unexpected opening at the top. Bernard, who had been expected to get the top job at European Metro, came home as happily as most Frenchmen do to France to take over this important company in a situation where Carrefour's aggressive pace of global expansion appeared to be slowing and its decision-making faltering. He was to find a company with severe problems.

Within a year, a badly bruised Carrefour had shelved its previous US expansion plan, closing down US stores with a crippling loss of US$ 35 million in its wake. It seemed as if this highly internationally-minded business simply did not have the necessary clout to succeed in the lion's den that is the competitive US market, where locally driven promotion and price-cutting, opposition from trade unions and local communities, and consumer dissatisfaction with Carrefour's brand and poor product range had all contributed to a very expensive and highly visible international failure.

Daniels found among the lions do not sit on their hands. The signs are that Bernard's capacity to create strategies with global perspective may be turning Carrefour round. He has played many strong cards simultaneously, but all within the most overt and clearest global context. In recognizing the need to tackle a global future, Bernard is capitalizing on what always was Carrefour's defining difference. It was the earliest food retailer to export formats and brand franchises across borders effectively, taking the successful French *hypermarché* format to Spain as early as 1973, and venturing to South America thereafter. This experience should enable Carrefour to start with big inbuilt global advantage – such was his reasoning.

But Bernard appreciates that geographic presence will not be enough. Carrefour has been willing to expand across the full range of grocery formats – with supermarkets (in France purchasing Comptoirs Modernes to achieve this), hard discounters and huge supercenters all making worthwhile contributions. Innovation to create new product field opportunities has been a vital element – with a recent move into cheap telecoms services, backing its loyalty card, the most provoking. Carrefour is recognizing the importance of information technologies and the know-how and learning that goes with it. Finally, Bernard is an overt disciple of global retailing through brave measures of empowerment carried out on an international scale. Carrefour's open-minded philosophy is anything but top-down, and delegates a great deal to a highly trained complement of store managers. It understands that there are acute cultural differences between markets and, included in this, between the countries in Europe itself – even between such similar and physically proximate markets as, say, France, Spain and Italy.

So it is with his uncompromising enthusiasm for global retailing that Bernard is most strongly identified. 'There is a race and a lot of companies are qualified', he said (Bernard, 1998). 'To go global you need to be early enough. Generally in new countries you need to be first in, for the first win. If you arrive at number three or four, it's too late.' Three reasons prompt Bernard's 'global or nothing' policies – mature demanding consumers, investment in capital, and effective management of international suppliers. It is a coherent and passionate doctrine and its philosophical roots are being dug deep into all Carrefour's operating processes.

While the innovative Bernard is not alone in expressing his global views (van der Hoeven at Ahold and Glass at Wal-Mart certainly share them), he is driving ahead as fast as he can go to make them happen first at Carrefour. On the record he can point to things working. Operating profits in 1998 were up nearly 20 per cent and Bernard forecasts the same increase in 1999, in spite of Carrefour's pronounced exposure to recently rocky and emergent Latin American economies such as Brazil and Argentina. Time alone will tell whether these *coeur de lion* policies are right, and if it is best to be in first wherever you can.

Carrefour's French rival, Auchan, is difficult to assess if only because of the familiar secrecy that once again permeates its policies and operations. Until recently, the Mulliez family owned 80 per cent of Auchan, which opened its first hypermarket in 1967. Auchan has from its earliest days banked on size – the Asda of France – some of its aptly named Mammouth stores being well over 40,000 sq ft. Unlike Carrefour and Promodes, Auchan has concentrated on building a domestic French business, and has diversified into shopping centres, restaurants, sporting goods and clothes to circumvent the known grocery constraints. Its principal foreign company is Alcampo in Spain, and it is represented in Italy, Portugal and the United States at a limited level. Auchan is noticeably vague when the topic of future strategy comes up. A hostile bid for Docks de France, a bolt from the blue, succeeded. More likely, renewed concentration on the core business, some divestment and a key emerging relationship with Rinascente in Italy may represent useful pointers to the approach to future strategies at Auchan. Whatever happens, a developing Italian self-service market is already identifiable as an excitingly over-populated retail cockpit for European supermarket competition. Deregulation there could hugely increase its potential but competition for brand presence and share will be fierce.

Finally we come to Promodes, the youngest, biggest and most vulnerable of the three. Founded as a wholesaler in France in the 1960s, Promodes has experienced explosive growth, sales having tripled since 1985. Margins are very narrow and its operations depend heavily on the financial flexibility created from franchising. It has created two strong brand names – Continent in hypermarkets and Champion in supermarkets – and has exported its brands to the Mediterranean and, with particular success, to Continente in Spain. Promodes has remained faithful to its food heritage and knowledge and has the most focussed position.

Recognizing that it cannot stand still, Promodes has been chasing growth by other means. It failed expensively and visibly to acquire its rival Casino, which bitterly divided the Guichard family Casino board members, another signal of the imminent collapse of family hegemonies in European retailing. It then acquired Belgian GB and Catteau from Tesco, and claims that the majority of its sales are now non-domestic. Not to be left out, through a share of GB in Italy it too has put down its own powerful Italian marker. Promodes has recognized the need to compete in the discount sector and, using the brand Dia from their Spanish company, is well positioned to do this. These ventures are in line with a stated 'foods focus + international expansion' strategy, and have created scale and at the very least bought management some time. Profitability remains a key issue for its professional team. It will need to run hard to stay ahead of the impending European consolidation that everyone now anticipates.

SUMMARY – THE EUROPEAN STRENGTHS AND WEAKNESSES

It is now possible to summarize the European market, and the strengths and weaknesses that exist. Firstly the strengths. There are a group of powerful competitors, with substantial operating experience not only in home markets, but in cross-border situations. Many are genuinely international in outlook as well as in business performance, and those that are not either will learn internationalism quickly, or will subside into less effective national units, ultimately falling victim to purchase by one of the international groups. Alongside a continuing spate of alliances and joint ventures, hostile acquisitions are becoming a little more customary in today's competitive market, and companies know they must grow internationally or disappear – those that live by the sword will die by it. Successful expansion – worldwide by Carrefour; to the south, by the French and some others; westwards ie to the United States by Ahold (with most success), Aldi and Tengelmann; and forcefully to the east by the German principal players – have all created the prospect of a few major international trading groups. Size and international expansion can be supplemented by a widening array of formats, flexibility and efficiency. Most competitors have had to respond to national legislation controlling their growth prospects and even their prices, and to the usual stop-start European level of economic performance. They have lived through, at best, sluggish and difficult home markets, managing to create a range of retail formats, including strong discount operations, and to survive in a highly competitive world with – for most companies, most of the time – the thinnest of net margins. Continental European retailers could reasonably claim to have had an open and world-directed view of the market for many years. Their competitors for the world market – US, UK, and Asian companies – have only discovered this recently, if indeed they are yet persuaded the market will be global. The rewards for vision and for identifying and taking the risk to expand have been perceived, and there are now companies with strong track records.

There have been and there certainly remain significant weaknesses. First and foremost must rank the obsessive secrecy surrounding the strategies and results of most competitors – Ahold and Carrefour being exceptions – but the unfortunate climate persists. The family structures that have sheltered behind the facades of these major companies have controlled strategies in ways that are now surprising in the free democratic cultures where they trade. The question 'who needs shareholders anyway and what can they tell me about running my business?' has never been very far away in the continental European retail markets. An atmosphere of secrecy and shadowy behind-the-scenes family control raises the question 'how well placed are the main players and the industry to face the best of professional free-market competition?' The cultural and leadership changes required and the speed with which strategic and management adjustments must be made to face global competition are daunting.

On the other hand, two companies can claim they are properly positioned to compete. The first is Holland's Ahold – still, however, as Europeans quite small and with a small country base. Carrefour is the other – after some failures they can point to strong and distant expansion in Brazil, Argentina, Spain and even Asia. Both Carrefour and Ahold are innovative companies with new ideas. Behind them, Aldi's stripped down discount format may yet have continuing appeal and relevance in emergent world markets. The others have scale, potential and aspiration, but little concrete evidence of a capability of competing against best world standards.

A COMPARISON OF CONTINENTAL EUROPE WITH THE UK

The comparison of the European market and the domestic market in the UK remains fascinating. As so often when comparing UK and European processes, it is unfathomable how these markets have developed in such different ways. The causes determining divergence and the wide gulf now separating retail practices make suggestions of future implications delicate. There may be three primary sources of difference that account for divergent developments over the past half-century. They are:

- the nature of the industry and the companies that make it up;
- factors concerned with government, and the communities where the developments have been located;
- consumers themselves, their experiences and their attitude to the role of food in their lives and specifically to food buying.

NATURE OF FOOD RETAILING

Firstly the industries and the companies themselves. The importance of family-controlled concerns in Europe needs to be acknowledged, whereas in Britain only Sainsbury's exerted comparable dynastic influence and this is now exhausted. Enormous secrecy about European plans and performance is countered in Britain by constantly debated strategies, and records of performance catering to an investor community where little or no news is very bad news. Greater visibility for the innovations and the results of retailing development, and the impact of competition in the UK has not occurred elsewhere in Europe, where news is spasmodic and controlled, and financial performance, rather than retailing strategies and competences, is the focus of interest.

Radically different investment policies have obtained in the two markets. Continental European retailers, from as early as the 1970s, began rapid expansion out of their home markets. In the UK, only Sainsbury's atypical and isolated Connecticut venture was significant. US influence on the market in Britain – Sainsbury's and Safeway are both key examples – was greater than in mainland Europe, where indigenous models, particularly hypermarkets, grew up and extended from France and Germany south and east across the continent. In summary, two fundamentally divergent models now co-exist, each successful in its own right but so far owing only little to the other.

There are now some early signs that this difference may now be becoming more limited. Tesco – in the process of extending its reach through East Europe and, recently, further afield – in its chairman's words admitted that 'everyone was talking to everyone' in the world supermarket industry. The comment was sparked by the £19 billion merger/takeover of Asda stores by Kingfisher in April 1999. Kingfisher's European aspirations through its earlier acquisitions of Castorama and Darty are well attested and it deserves the title of the UK's most outward-looking general retailer. There is little evidence that the proposed merger will make any difference to the penetration of the Asda brand or its store profile in food retailing in Europe, however, and the conclusion has been that the move is essentially defensive, and that Kingfisher's primary motivation had been to use the Asda cash flows for its existing extension plans. As we went to press it was not clear that the Kingfisher/Asda deal was final and the possibility that Wal-Mart itself, Carrefour or Ahold might be persuaded to make a higher offer was being actively canvassed.

THE IMPACT OF GOVERNMENTS

Societal and governmental impact on development and performance in grocery retailing is next. No UK companies will concede they have had an easy reception from national or local planners, and since 1993 the UK's own version of environmental restrictions has begun to bite more seriously. But restraints have been imposed late in the day and at a stage where retailers have stakes irrevocably rooted in out-of-town locations. Locking the British stable door long after the horses have bolted is the classic European view of British public policies. Restrictive legislation and a concept of hostility to the big national self-service food company, and especially to its most gargantuan demonstration – the hypermarket – has been an ongoing feature of retailing's existence in mainland Europe as it was, interestingly, for many years, under the aegis of Robinson-Patman, in the federation that still is the *United* States. This has taken the form of tight limitation to the physical expansion of selling space, and constraints such as preventing predatory pricing in visible market sectors. Fighting the restrictions neither diverted the intent nor limited the efficacy of the planning processes put in hand.

The UK, described – ironically, many years ago by a famous Frenchman – as a nation of shopkeepers, adopted the 'free-market' model, notably through the crucial decade of the 1980s when literally hundreds of out-of-town superstores began to dot the landscape, and a new-style 100 per cent car-based shopping behaviour became dominant. The European model – at its zenith in France but copied elsewhere – was a profoundly philosophical attempt to retain the essence of town and village high streets and existing shopping configurations with their plethora of small specialist food suppliers. This offers immeasurably greater protection to a whole gamut of small shop-keepers. The policy has on a relative basis succeeded, the differences being there today for anyone who cares to see. To my knowledge, there are more greengrocers, butchers, bakers, fish and cheese shops supplying the daily needs of the 2,500 inhabitants of the rural French tile-making village of Salernes in the Var than survive in another 'village', metropolitan Blackheath in south-east London, where the population is at least a dozen times the greater, coincidentally considerably more affluent and, one might even have assumed, a lot more demanding.

Whether as a cause or a consequence, the UK legitimized car-borne shopping earlier and to a greater degree than mainland Europe did, and apparently this was a difference deliberately created. A further important difference is that UK supermarket leaders have traditionally exercised more public policy-making influence than their counterparts have been able to do in Europe. The several successive Lords Sainsbury, Lord MacLaurin, Sir Alistair Grant – their titles speak for themselves – are prestigious establishment figures with high levels of public awareness, whose public statements and opinions carry real weight. Grocery retailing has come of age and is formative in British life in a way that must now surprise French and German retailers. This has enabled a visible and soundly managed industry to play a part in setting for themselves the free-market conditions where they operated, to ensure acceptance of codes of behaviour, and equally importantly in some instances the preservation of the status quo. In most of Europe this was less possible. Public interest was normally defined differently and by a different consultation process.

CONSUMER INFLUENCES

Finally we turn to the influence and predilections of consumers. Post-war reconstruction was a gentler, more evolutionary process in Britain, which had after all not been invaded. The country where the Albrechts started trading was a tougher environment than post-war Britain, and the same was initially true of France. Viewing the market as a continuum with high quality/high cost at one extreme and low prices/standard quality at the other, it is now clear that the markets elected to behave differently. In Germany and in France low prices and the role of the discounter in supplying them in a simple, uncomplicated store environment has been a more prominent feature than it has ever become in the UK.

The birth of and consumer appeal exercised by the giant European hypermarkets where superior economics – that is to say a much bigger range and, apparently at least, much lower prices were pragmatically an indisputable winning formula – were a natural extension of the discounter phenomenon. Consequently, affected by the headlong expansion of UK superstores in the 1980s and the capital investment requirements for new stores, trading margins in the UK have been markedly higher than in Europe – currently, they are on average three times higher than in France, for example. But UK consumers have been prepared to pay for the difference, and the quality of the shopping experience in the best UK superstores compares very favourably with its equivalent European hypermarket, and is certainly superior to any discount store. Hence, perhaps, the failure of the hard discounters in the UK to date.

The final issue is the role of food, the importance of quality in food purchasing and its acceptance by consumers in their respective societies. That there has been an element of late renaissance in aspirations to and provision of British food quality nobody would contest, but at the same time few would claim that the UK consumer achieves a higher standard of food awareness or provision than in France certainly, in Italy probably, or even perhaps in modern Germany. What has happened is that British retail multiples play a larger role in providing the market's response than do their French or

European equivalents. Retaining main-street, town and village shops with the high-quality, small, specialist food shops that still exist in French and many European towns and even small villages means that consumers can find and rely on quality and variety at a price, when and where they want it. In Britain, high streets are now usually the home of building societies, estate agents and restaurants. It is now uniquely and specifically more often the supermarket's responsibility to provide the right balance of quality and variety and at the right price, and usually the location will be out of town.

So two very different social equations have been reached, and in each case, superficially at least, the two societies seem content that it should be so. It will be interesting to see what elements of future convergence may in due course start to happen. Particularly in Britain where high-street decline went to an extreme, the return of serious investment to the high street and a resurgence in the range and quality of local and speciality stores may be the start of a new trend. Ironically, perhaps inevitably, it is these same superstore operators, to some degree for defensive reasons, who are now keen and ready to provide new choices themselves, thereby keeping their hands firmly on the food quality/range/price equations which consumers are offered.

THE OUTLOOK

Will the European companies penetrate Britain more than they have in the past? Will the strongest British retailers, now facing a prospect of lower growth and slimmer margins, look to Europe for serious growth? The answer to both questions seems inevitably 'Yes'. There will be purchase opportunities in the UK market, and major European companies will be encouraged to buy on signs of performance weakness, and where they see good site development and business potential. The UK candidates seem pretty obvious. Tesco has begun its entry into Europe, now in Hungary and Poland. It is late into this competition game, but the decision must be sensible and it has learned since the purchase and subsequent sale of French Catteau (another case of family constraints). Sainsbury's too will be reflecting on the wisdom of a solely US-based external strategy. Marks & Spencer have a European toehold, and must, one assumes, in time begin to expand their food interests. Other alliances will be on the cards. But the pace now needs to accelerate – British retailers cannot expect to be allowed to remain dominant in their island fastnesses for much longer.

$bn (last reported sales)

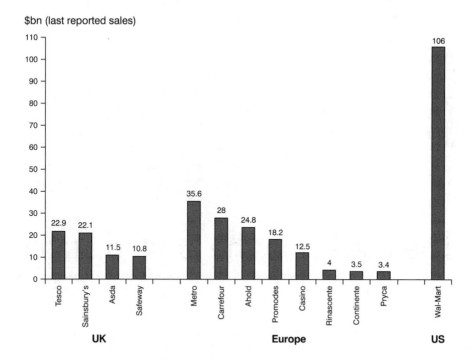

Figure 7.1 *Global-scale players*

8

The market in the United States

'Americans will eat garbage if you sprinkle it liberally with ketchup.'
(Henry Miller)

Miller's unkind view may once have been widely shared but not any more – the US grocery and foods market continues to be a Mecca for the world's retailers. Not just store owners, but developers, commentators and policy-makers beat a path to New York, to Los Angeles, to San Antonio, Texas, and now even to Bentonville, Arkansas, the better to understand US companies, stores, innovation, best practice and the presentation of food in all its aspects. Indeed *pace* Miller, the belief still holds that US is biggest and best. Biggest it certainly is and likely to stay that way, given the rate at which the vast new supercenters are now being built. The United States can certainly claim to have been at the leading edge of food marketing and retailing. Twenty-five years ago a leading commentator could say 'the important American experience on which Europeans can draw is the effect that intense competition between stores can have on store strategy and the viability of different retail forms in the future.'

Today consumers ask for and get astonishing levels of choice. New retail formats diversify, multiply and disappear. The market's appetite for experiment in food retailing is apparently insatiable, and as befits a young society with self-belief, the United States has become a model for food retailing, ever since the first conversions from Mom and Pop stores to self-service happened. But the course of development has been staccato rather than smooth – periods of calm where it seemed very little was happening and other periods when big changes took place incessantly. The latter is the pattern today. But for countless years, essentially local, fragmented markets with virtually no overlap existed. Strategic, cross-regional development was limited. Reappraisal began in the 1980s as legislative constraints were reinterpreted. This accelerated over the next decade as a potentially global industry gave free rein to new players, retail formats, and a distinct change in the historic power balance between manufacturer and retailer. Simultaneously, the major players themselves then consolidated rapidly, a process that is causing rapid and exciting transformation in this hitherto stable industry.

A THOUSAND FLOWERS BLOOM – POST-WAR FRAGMENTATION

Today change is rife and indeed change was inevitable in an industry at once so fragmented and undifferentiated. The changes that began in the late 1980s, and have accelerated through the 1990s, are by no means complete but it is already clear they will result in an industry which bears only remote resemblance to the undifferentiated US model that existed for most of half a century. Many of the visible differences between the US and European industries are disappearing, and a discernibly uniform global model is starting to appear. Why were they so different in the first place? Why – when change and consolidation was happening in Europe, and particularly in Britain – did the US industry remain in a key commentator's words so 'stubbornly unconsolidated?'

One big difference is of course the size and geographic spread of markets but probably the real answer lies in the economic regulation under which the grocery industry operated. Americans were the first to experience the revolution to large self-service stores, and no doubt this encouraged them at a level of governance to monitor the development with care. Some important influences were embedded in the culture of the society, where local areas differed very much one from another, and in the Jeffersonian spirit of the pioneering fathers, competition was encouraged to flourish everywhere, locally as well as nationally and, as time passed, this was nowhere more true than in the most basic of markets – the supply of food. The development of collections of heavily capitalized retail enterprises, and the concentration of market power and share in the hands of a small number of companies operating on a national or at least a multi-regional basis in the US market was a trend the United States chose deliberately to constrain.

From the earliest beginnings – Saunders' Piggly Wiggly Memphis supermarket in 1916, through the raucous King Kullen in Queens, New York, in the early 1930s, and certainly including the potentially dominating Great Atlantic and Pacific Tea Company shortly afterwards – Americans were deeply worried about the power these enterprises might exert across their country; they were frightened of their potential and national power. A key element in their consumer defence therefore was the Robinson Patman Act (1936) that inhibited price discrimination, seeking to prevent the elimination of the smaller, independent trader and the established regional and local markets. A possibly unlooked-for consequence is that Robinson Patman was thereby instrumental in maintaining, at least until recently, a substantially more powerful position for the US foods manufacturer than obtains in the UK or Europe. Brands have, of course, always exercised great importance and play a major part in the development of America's markets for consumer goods. Another important regulation was the 1950 Kefauver Act, regularly employed to prevent creeping, cross-border extension into new regions by dominant local retailers. In each case the legislation caused a distinct and different pattern of supermarket development than that which has occurred in Europe.

Keith de Vault, Customer Service Vice-President at Lever, speaking to me in the midst of today's apparently frantic pace of national consolidation, wisely remarked that the US market 'continues to be a decentralized, fragmented arena substantially still operating on a local market-by-market basis – these differences continue to be very pronounced and are underestimated by many commentators'. Wrigley, quoting a chairman of A&P stores – one-time holders of an amazing 13 per cent market share of the national market – comparing the evolution of the US and British markets said, 'in the post-war years … the US market place, because of Robinson Patman, moved to a regional structure and the old large chains lost out … but the UK, without this disadvantage moved to the consolidation route with the advantages of purchasing leverage driving the success of a few national chains' (1998b) He was right. In 1990 the market share of the top 20 firms was roughly the same as that of the top 20 in 1950. Nor had many names changed. Compared to the big European markets or Britain, where less than half a dozen competitors dominate each national market, traditional US models have been different.

Sheer scale, albeit applied regionally, together with the recognized US penchant for imaginative and determined solutions has ensured that innovation was strongly pursued – and not just by the biggest players. Across the United States the local supermarkets strongly reflect the conditions in the area. Thus urban Chicago differs strongly from San Francisco or Los

Angeles. The redeveloping markets of the old south (Atlanta or Charlotte, for example), and huge new sunbelt cities like Phoenix and Tucson have excitingly modern and different shopping structures and patterns. The west is quite unlike the urban east, and New York is *sui generis*, with a character all its own – as indeed it had when we first lived there in the 1960s and saw the Manhattan grid of streets and avenues covered with the classic architectural brickwork of the Great Atlantic and Pacific Tea Company stores. Diversity of local markets produced a constant flow of new food ideas and presentations, some quite unique, and simply irreproducible anywhere else. (Thankfully, some Europeans said!) The most bizarre has been Stew Leonard's hilarious but highly effective retail dairy in Norwalk, Connecticut.

LEONARD – IN A STEW

Forty miles north of New York City, in a middle-ranking New England seaside town called Norwalk is the country's, maybe even the world's most astonishing grocery store. It has an excellent food-product range – so what? you might say. It retains many attractive elements from the one-time dairy it was. But it has created a host of new features that would be wildly improbable in grocery stores anywhere else in the world. Stew Leonard's dairy 'shattered for ever the tedium of grocery shopping' said the business pages of no less an organ than the *New York Times*. The good ladies of Fairfield County, Connecticut – one of the east's wealthiest districts – seem to like it hugely and its fame brings in shoppers from miles around. From this one single store, sales can amount to as much as US\$ 175 million in a year. Following its success, Stew Leonard has now opened two more Leonard dairies not far away.

Entertainment pure and very simple is another thing the Leonard dairy offers. It can be likened to an edible Disneyland, and much of the humour is indeed breathtakingly infantile. Milk cartons dance, celery stalks sway and sing, hidden banjos play in displays of fruit, and there is a small zoo for live geese and goats. The staff happily dress themselves up as farm animals, and engage in appropriate welcoming farmyard noises. Robot dogs amiably bark out the day's special offers. The proprietor himself sports a cow suit and sings out special greetings – 'good mooorning' being the accepted standard – to customers. Free balloons and ice cream cones are given to the youngest customers. What's all this to do with food? you might well be asking.

But of course behind the fun there is serious business to be done, and strict commercial rules apply. 'Rule no. 1' it proclaims on a huge stone sign as customers enter – 'The Customer is always Right.' 'Rule no. 2' it says underneath – 'If in doubt read rule no. 1.' And each week 200,000 customers push Leonard's oversize carts round 20 ft wide aisles running up unimaginably big grocery bills.

The fame of Connecticut's very own big butter-and-egg man soon spread far and wide. Tom Peters appraised Leonard's own approach to retailing excellence, and Wal-Mart senior associates have been observed studying the dairy as apparently serious competition. President Ronald Reagan, always a fan of small businesses, gave Stew his own special award. But nemesis lay in waiting. It transpired that, in a unique, brilliantly written and expertly concealed computer programme, Stew had been skimming large amounts of cash from the daily till rolls, and shipping the surplus to his own private bolt-hole in the Caribbean. A private informant, probably a disgruntled employee, was unkind enough to pass on details of the scheme to the Inland Revenue Service. In the largest criminal tax case in Connecticut's history, Leonard was convicted of 10 years of carefully engineered tax evasion and the court heartlessly handed him a 52-month jail sentence.

Stew in turn handed management of the stores over to sons Stew Jr and Tom, readily conceding that 'I've made a mistake, I'm very sorry and I'm prepared to take the consequences'. Was it the end of an era for the dairy? 'No sirree! It was business as usual,' they said. 'We are packed … our customers are very supportive.' While it wasn't clear who had taken over Stew's crucial 'moootivating' role, Fairfield County shoppers were still turning up in droves at Norwalk's dairy. Subsequently, son Stew Jr, in five later and quite separate offences, appeared on his very own set of tax evasion charges in the same Connecticut courts. Yes down at the dairy, as they said, it remained indeed, business as usual.

But in truth the United States is rich in individual and successful operations, many more orthodox that Leonard's dairy and firmly established, with a style and a strength of customer base all their own. Minnesota's stunningly attractive (Fleming) Cub Stores, a range of lively and successful Californian chains including the doyen Safeway, Pathmark in New York, New England's standard-setting Stop 'n Shop and Hannaford chains, the highly innovative

Wegmans stores, a polished series of attractive winning formulas across the sunbelt states, Florida's Publix markets benchmarking customer service standards, and hosts of recognized innovative names like Byerly, Food Lion, and Ukrops ... the list is endless. Most impressive of all perhaps, the H E Butt company – expanding from San Antonio, Texas, and now itself in the league of top 10 grocery retailers – has set market-leading standards both for customer service, pricing and cost-efficiency. There are many others – without even remarking the biggest factor now and in the future – Wal-Mart – a retailing phenomenon that merits consideration all on its own.

By any standards, US supermarkets have been exciting, vibrant and well-presented environments in which to shop. Market by market, tough competition ensured net margins were held tight – so tight indeed that at 1 per cent or less on sales, some great names have been able to hold on only with difficulty – the once great A&P, now owned by Europeans, comes to mind. Strong economic belief has fuelled rapid growth and product development. Characteristically the US cobbler has stuck to his last, concentrating on what he knew best – providing a constantly changing and improving weekly food shopping basket at prices that moved at levels of increase below general inflation.

Outsiders' views of the pre-eminence of America's food culture may differ. At home, where it has mattered, consumers have perceived quality as good, and Americans young and old, rich and poor, with big families or none at all, responding to enormous choice, have been ready to vote their approval.

THE US CONSUMER – BURGEONING OPPORTUNITIES

Consumer optimism in US society is inherently high and concern about economic issues has been stable for some years, even if it may now – given some turmoil in world markets – be set to rise. The consumer makes an average of 2.2 visits to the supermarket weekly, including 1.7 visits to the 'primary store'. The number of these visits has been pretty constant and indeed may now be starting to decline as alternative one-stop formats multiply, competing with the supermarket. More than half of US consumers visit the convenience or multiple stores, and paradoxically today in the age of the new supercenter, this behaviour is still on the increase. Loyalty cards are now used by one in five shoppers and will become a crucial weapon as supermarkets learn to tap their potential.

Satisfaction with the primary supermarket remains high among all sectors of the community – more than eight in ten rate the offering as 'very good' or 'excellent'. Supermarkets have played an inclusive role in the communities and local areas that they served – realistically they may be said to be more 'owned' by the locality than can be said of their equivalents in Britain and most parts of developed Europe. Strikingly, therefore, it is some of the poorest (those with an income up to US$ 15,000 per year), the elderly, the least educated and the non-fully employed who score their supermarket performance the highest. 1998 indeed saw a significant rise in the highest level of consumer approval ratings (FMI Trends). Market maturity in food self-service retailing is a factor. There is just the faintest suggestion that concern with rising prices is increasing, and the size of the average weekly shopping basket may be modestly turning downwards. The decline is most observable in the east, where the market for food may be at its most mature, whereas in the south and west and in non-urban and suburban communities, grocery expenses are still rising. The richer (over US$ 75,000 per year income) and younger (under 39) consumers unsurprisingly show the clearest propensity to switch primary shopping stores; location and pricing being the reasons cited for doing so. But disaffection as a whole seems a long way off.

In terms of range, fresh food and delicatessen are showing the most pronounced rise. Nutrition and health information are becoming more important to US consumers but it is in the field of meal solutions that the changes are most visible and are happening fastest. Meals eaten away from home are now much less often purchased at fast-food or normal restaurants, and are frequently bought at supermarkets, the incidence having doubled over ten years. Meanwhile, the range of specific and highly polished 'food on the move' stores is becoming a common feature of city and town centres and some are expanding their specialty ranges with some élan. The difference they all seek to promote is freshness. Men, the young and the elderly, small households and lower-income groups are most willing to purchase meals at their supermarket and it is ready-to-eat vegetables and freshly prepared salads that are proving the most attractive items. Consumers are serving more ready-made foods whether they are frozen, refrigerated or ready to eat. FMI Trends data indicates that time matters crucially – eight out of ten consumers consider preparation ease and time key elements in making this decision. Ultimately supermarkets are now competing in a service industry for meal provision, and it is quality of life – product quality, freshness and service quality – at an affordable cost that will determine success or failure in these new market sectors.

Given the space and availability of good locations one cannot help being struck by US high-street retailing innovation and the quality of its presen-tation. One Harvard Business School retail commentator recently described the Marks & Spencer range in the UK as 'terrific' and indicated that most US chains would not yet match this level of quality. He may be right and the data suggests that US supermarkets have a long way to go in satisfying the most discriminating food-buying consumers, and especially the users of meal solutions so that they can compete effectively against specialty stores and restaurants and indeed against best world standards in what is an increasingly international market. But today the fresh food choices are there for all to see and supermarkets will have to match these new standards.

Widening choice, alternative distribution channels, and of course education are making the US consumer more critical about brand claims. Multi-brand acceptability or repertoire shopping is replacing the fierce brand loyalties of the past. Own-label penetration – while a long way below UK or European levels – is growing and has crossed the 20 per cent of purchases threshold for the first time. It has been estimated that the US consumer has 12 seconds to make a brand choice in each category and again, as UK research indicates, while actual prices across the category are not usually known, relative prices between the 'competing realities' are more easily appraised. The effect on brand communication is obvious. Merchandising, store pricing and promotion are alongside channel diversification, playing an increasing part in determining brand choice.

While there has been some shift away from 'high-low' pricing, and frequent consumer promotions, influenced by the everyday low-pricing initiatives of the most strategic of the brand marketing companies (notably P&G and Campbells) and retailers (notably H E Butt and Wal-Mart), it is not entirely clear that EDLP (everyday low pricing) has yet gained any absolute or permanent advantage. P&G have been able to derive both short- and long-term gains from their innovative approaches to EDLP, which they have now been operating for more than five years. What is equally clear is that all branded manufacturers have heard the wake-up call regarding loss of control in a more competitive retailing world, and are using new initiatives to maintain strong brand franchises, co-operating with retailers through a wide range of category partnership programmes. The market as a whole is set to gain from these category initiatives, which are capable of taking substantial cost out of infrastructure. New retail formats – and the strongest competition for providing meal solutions increases choice substantially for shoppers – make the outcome another win–win for a lucky US consumer.

THE INDUSTRY IN THE 1980s – DEREGULATION UNDER REAGAN

The significance of antitrust regulation in the development of a fragmented US industry has been noted. Through the 1980s, change took place as the regulatory constraints – under which businesses, including grocery retailers, operated – were abandoned. Government agencies were encouraged to look the other way in Reagan's United States, and explicit decisions not to enforce antitrust laws became common practice. When the takeover of Dillons by Kroger and the merger of American Stores with Jewel in Chicago were both happily waved through, it was clear that a new, more flexible wind was blowing which was to have dramatic long-term consequences. Simultaneously, and because of post-oil-crisis anxiety about US macroeconomic performance and overall competitiveness, a search for new kinds of more flexible financial instruments began, from which high-yield financing (now associated with Milliken and junk bonds) was used to facilitate hostile takeover attempts.

Firms – particularly those that were cash-rich and could point to stable continuing demand – were able to reorganize their costs by embarking on leveraged recapitalization and buyouts (LBOs). Quintessentially many grocery retailers matched the required profile, and between 1985 and 1988, 19 of the 50 largest food retailers – accounting for 25 per cent of total sales – undertook some form of LBO or recapitalization. The technique was to borrow against projected cash flow, thereby building the financial base through heavily increased debt. Included were US volume market leaders Safeway and Kroger, as well as some of the most efficiently operated chains eg New England's Stop 'n Shop. Wrigley points out that within four years debt rocketed by as much as 50 per cent among the major retailers sampled, producing divestiture ie enforced asset sales and rationalization among key competitors. This in turn created opportunity for others – new market entry, geographic expansion and purchasing opportunities for less encumbered market players, and fleet-of-foot new entrants in the years ahead.

Asset sales and the 'core focus' strategies that resulted created a market where firms sought, above all else, to protect core leadership positions in those markets where local dominance enabled them to hold or lead margins and profitability upwards. Peripheral markets were sacrificed and what commentators have described as the 'geography of avoidance' or policies of competitive 'forbearance' were practised. 'The amount of intra-market competition between the leading firms is ... remarkably limited' concludes Wrigley. Overlapping geographic areas between the three major competitors were heavily circumscribed. Only in 6 out of 54 Grocery Manufacturers of America (GMA) areas did the 3 major players (Kroger, Safeway and American Stores) choose to compete with each other – hence the description ' forbearance'.

The second key factor was the reduction in capital expenditures instituted once again by the major players including Safeway and Kroger, and inevitably emulated by many others. Severe constraints on investment and declining service performance were the obvious consequence – Acme and Pathmark in the Philadelphia market, both aggressively managed growth concerns, are frequently cited examples. But the phenomenon was widespread and created, as surely as night was to follow day, an open window of opportunity from which acquisition and merger in the 1990s could drive retailing forward into a more efficient world.

Up to the late 1980s, consolidation had in fact remained noticeably absent. American Stores from the mid-west had bought west-coast Lucky, temporarily securing market leadership, and anticipating a wave of trans-regional mergers to come. The top 20 firms in 1990 were still holding a share no greater than they had held in 1980. Furthermore, many highly leveraged and undercapitalized chains had become trapped in a downward performance spiral from which they could not escape. Some were forced into liquidation, or fell victim to the wave of strategic, often foreign-influenced acquisition that followed. Then came the Drexel Burnham Lambert heavy 'fine' and this seemed to mark a watershed after which junk bonds declined in importance. A combination of the rejection of high-yield financing as an instrument and worsening individual business performance took their toll of many supermarket chains. The stage was set for a dramatic and reciprocal set of changes to the US supermarket industry.

CONSOLIDATION AND SCALE IN THE 1990s – THE WHEEL TURNS FULL CIRCLE

The 1990s have seen roller-coaster change which is still continuing and which has transformed the US market. The key players could already see by 1990 that their market was experiencing new competitive forces outside the localities within which they had operated, and had learned the lesson through the financially engineered years of the late 1980s that ruthless cost management was a necessity and that bold new measures were required to survive. Initially it was in the areas of union-negotiated wage rates and in a tougher approach to supplier costs and manufacturers' terms that solace was most immediately sought. More comprehensive and organic reviews of their own systems and costs were scheduled to follow, particularly as scale offered scope for rationalization, and the aggressive new market entrants forced the pace on efficiency. The asset-reducing, high-yield years were over as the industry retreated from its highly leveraged positions. Debt as a proportion of total capitalization reduced steadily through the 1990–95 years, a trend that was to accelerate thereafter. By 1996 it was one-third lower than it had been at its peak and there was a whole new game (survival of the fittest) on.

Inevitably competitive advantage began to shift to the firms that possessed clear growth strategies, critical scale, and the capital resources and management aspirations to stake out a strong, long-term position in an increasingly national industry. From now on advantage was on the side of the big battalions, and a pattern of development in the US market, much more akin to that in western Europe, over two decades became recognizable. A wave of important acquisitions and mergers took place as retailers realized the advantages of scale, simultaneously appreciating that continued concentration on the historic approach to exclusively local market dominance could not any longer guarantee survival. The major players were all involved, and the pattern of forbearance – where east never crossed swords with west, and neither competed in the central/mid west – was broken once and for all. The other key change involved the European entrants – interlopers themselves scheduled to play a major part in the consolidation process. Lurking on the wings there was the amazingly aggressive yet seemingly counter-cyclical Wal-Mart, born in its southern and mid-western rural fastnesses but cognizant of the national food and general merchandise retailing opportunity and with a development record, and a rooted cultural attitude to cost management that could propel it to market leadership.

Pincer movements were soon quick to begin from east and west. Albertson's – a major local force from the Pacific north-west – became overnight a major buyer, sweeping up a series of smaller north-west operations, and temporarily taking national market leadership with its acquisition of Chicago's American Stores. (American, ironically, had been an earlier national US market leader when it had bought Jewel in Chicago. This was 'dog eat dog' and with a vengeance.) Safeway, long-time holders of a major national share deriving from its strong position notably in California, kept pace, acquiring their Californian neighbours Vons and more recently Dominicks in Chicago. A strong west/south-western retail conglomerate emerged with the Yucaipa group which moved to take over Fred Meyer and then Smittys, Smiths, Ralphs, Food for Less, Quality Food Centres and Hughes. Further to the east, pathfinder moves were made by Holland's spirited Royal Ahold which, starting from scratch in an enormously adventurous three-year buying spree, bought a host of strong positions right across the United State's eastern seaboard – Stop 'n Shop, Giant, Tops, Finast, Edwards and Bi-Lo, and most recently the New York chain Pathmark. 'Pathmark is a well run company but under-invested because of a highly leveraged balance sheet' its new owner, Cees van der Hoeven was to remark. His aggressive purchases had en passant served to outflank Britain's Sainsbury's in the process, and suddenly catapulted the Dutch concern to a top-four position in the US league table as well as to unchallenged east coast leadership. Food Lion, owned by Belgium's Delhaize, acquired Kash 'N Karry in a further European incursion in the east. Europe was playing a distinct consolidating role in these key US markets.

Finally, in the position reached by the end of 1998, came the move many had expected – a major acquisition by Kroger of the Fred Meyer (Yucaipa) group, which gave the new company a double-figures market share, a position of real power across the west and mid-west and, currently at least, market leadership. Not surprisingly, acquisition multiples on the US exchange had gone up by one third in this process. It was clear that a rapid hunt for scale and supremacy was on. Regional barriers to entry were collapsing but the US frontiers themselves had been breached with a vengeance. It was also true that the US market remained, from the shopper's viewpoint, recognizably a series of local markets, with the specific fascias and brands often persisting after the merger had taken place.

The effects of these moves on market structure have been significant. The additional fact that the US market has – by virtue of its regional and, to some extent, protected development – also become 'over stored' means that the impact of consolidation will be greater, and the shake-out effects further exacerbated by the elimination of significant numbers of redundant stores. By the year 2000, concentration of power will have doubled and, from being one of the most fragmented in the world, the US market will in a period of brief but widespread change have taken on an appearance more akin to the other developed grocery markets eg north-west Europe. The biggest winners have been the new Kroger/Meyer company with a share of around 10 per cent; Albertson's, now firmly established as a major player with 7 per cent of the market; Ahold and Safeway. Publix, Winn-Dixie, Food Lion and now H E Butt have maintained positions in the top ten, holding momentum but some way behind the big four. Simultaneously, that once great bastion, A&P, now owned by Germany's Tengelmann, has drifted downwards in share, continuing a process of sustained losses over half a century.

It is self-evident that consolidation has some way still to go, and that market competition will be greater during the shake-out than during the 1980s and 1990s, as major companies seek secure long-term positions in the rapidly consolidating mature market. What will be particularly interesting is to see which of the (predominantly) west or mid-west enterprises will acquire a strong east-coast base, whether Ahold can themselves expand further west – and indeed whether either of these moves can inhibit Wal-Mart from its unstoppable drive towards food-market leadership.

THE INVADERS – EUROPE MOVES IN WITH VARYING FORTUNES

In retrospect it is ironic that resulting from a period of ill-judged short-term financial re-engineering through the LBO period, and subsequent undercapitalization and indifferent performance, the United State's powerful home-grown retail industry laid itself wide open to foreign market entry. The specific acquisitions have already been noted but it is worth considering the very different approaches adopted by Britain's Sainsbury's and Holland's Ahold in putting down their respective footholds.

Sainsbury's was first in the field and in an early development (1983) the British company bought a major, non-controlling holding in the New England Shaw's company. The stake was subsequently increased to full ownership, and 10 years later Sainsbury's moved to establish part-ownership of the Washington-based Giant foods chain. The two Sainsbury's ventures were not particularly successful, whether regarded as the first stages of a US entry strategy, or as a partner to the (then) UK market-leading chain. There are no signs that Sainsbury's was able to use its first-mover position in the US to get ahead of the game in the UK or elsewhere and, during the period at the end of the 1980s when acquisition opportunities opened up, it was unable to make much more happen. Indeed the US perspective is that Sainsbury's rigorous outside controls contributed to its own poor results. A leading sales vice-president, observing from close hand both Sainsbury's and Ahold simultaneously, said, 'The Sainsbury failure is traceable to their taking control of operations in consumer visible ways that turned consumers off in a big way.' In the shorter term Sainsbury's have been beset by operating problems both in Shaw's, and its former Giant investment, and since these occurred during a period when it was also ceding domestic leadership to Tesco, the disappointing US strategy and results have been of concern both to the company and to investors in Britain. Labour disputes, ill-judged expansion north to Philadelphia, and below par operating results prevented Sainsbury's from pushing forward with its investment in Giant.

So it was Ahold, not Sainsbury's, who in a remarkably well-timed move at a price of US$ 2.6 million acquired full control of Giant. At an earlier date, when Ahold had acquired the Boston Stop 'n Shop concern for US$ 4.1 million from KKR, as the latter set out to simplify its portfolio, Sainsbury's were given the chance to buy the Connecticut Stop 'n Shop stores because of overlap with Ahold's existing Edwards positions. Sadly the Connecticut stores, now branded Shaw's, have also not to date been a happy experience for Sainsbury's. Questions persist about the viability of Sainsbury's US strategy, if indeed there is one at all. Sainsbury's and Ahold have been toe-to-toe competitors in New England, and emphatically it is the latter who are calling the shots. David Bremner, Sainsbury's Vice-Chairman, who has responsibility for US planning, has emphasized these elements in the Sainsbury's strategy – to become a strong no. 2 in Connecticut, to improve margins and to make effective Return on Net Assets (RONA) returns. The task of establishing a differentiated brand and retail offering and widening the customer base still eludes Sainsbury's. In the meantime their experiences, coupled with the inertia of other British chains, lead commentators to remark that international expansion remains the Achilles heel of UK retailers.

Ahold, on the other hand, sail adventurously ahead in the US mainstream, powered by a strong following wind, and a gung-ho Dutch captain (Cees van der Hoeven) hungry to acquire yet more territories. Royal Dutch Ahold, Holland's biggest company, with global sales of US$ 36 billion and 3,600 stores in 17 countries, see their opportunity as one challenging Wal-Mart or Carrefour for the position as the world's leading grocery business. Already dug in to both Asia (Tops) and Latin America (Disco and Bompreco), Ahold is using its dominance as a hugely strong private company in The Netherlands and attractive home margins (approaching 4 per cent) to fund purchases of a rapidly expanding US series of chains. What has been distinctive about the Ahold stance in the United States has been its marketing open-mindedness, confronted by the highly localized set of markets that constitute US retail. Ahold has made no attempt to rebrand acquired fascias – not that its own name or Albert Heijn would have struck emotionally friendly chords in main-street United States. They have been more willing that Sainsbury's to keep consumer service and operations in the hands of US operators with very favourable results in terms of service and quality perceptions. Local brands, store profiles and consumer franchises have been kept intact, while economies in technical systems, purchasing and manufacturer relationships have been pursued aggressively. The scale from its position as no. 4 US retailer, and its ownership of a benchmark professional chain like Stop 'n Shop – a long-term systems and marketing leader – has given this harmonization renewed impetus. Policies are working, and already the US operations are generating cash and profits available for further US or world entry. In March 1999 Ahold announced a profits increase of 29 per cent to US$ 620 million, from a 15 per cent increase in worldwide revenues where its US operations are playing an increasingly significant part. Van der Hoeven's roller-coaster ride is very dependent on his private company's ability to generate funds when it needs to, and there are suggestions that his dependence on Dutch equity, where Ahold is no. 1 in the guilder-issuing league, is bound sooner or later to slow his meteoric growth. But there are no signs of this constraint so far.

For the moment indeed it is Ahold who are making the US pace in terms of growth, scale and synergistic policy. It was always possible that a strong European company would be able to emphasize long-time experience and knowledge of own-brand development, systems evolution, manufacturer relationships and management of working capital to set new standards for a consolidating US retail market, and Ahold's managers have certainly grasped this opportunity with both hands. Might there be a case for Ahold and Sainsbury's joining forces? Given the proximity of the two operations, side by side in New England, and their very similar aspirations, it seems pretty likely over the period ahead that they may consider some form of partnership, with Ahold, however, likely to be the major partner. This consideration may stick in the longer-established (in the UK as well as in the United States) British chain's throat, and may slow co-operation, but given the US patterns, it would seem perhaps to be in the interest of both companies' US strategies, were it to happen. There would be big wins for both enterprises – in the US through further scale and synergies, providing it were allowed to happen. It would give Ahold a UK, and Sainsbury's a European entry. We must wait and see if what seems a powerful logic can be made to work.

A MATURING INDUSTRY – EFFICIENT CONSUMER RESPONSE

Because of conservatism, and fragmented geographic structure, US retailers were initially slow to adopt systematic approaches to removing costs and adding value. They were not helped by the US food manufacturers who for years held the whip hand in relationships. The power of the manufacturer's national brands backed by heavyweight advertising represented the key consumer weapon. Backing the brands, manufacturers deployed equally large funds for trade dealing and promotions, on which retailers were uniformly dependent. No single competitor could break what was often an unproductive loop. Massive purchasing volumes were achieved during the manufacturers' promotion specials, but little or nothing was sold in between – a process inimical to the effective management of working capital. This phase in the United States has sometimes been described as 'the dark age of procurement' as promotions and price deals moved enormous brand volumes. A large sub-industry grew up in its shadow making additional profit by 'diverting' low-price promoted goods to new unintended destinations, ie from over-supplied to under-supplied markets.

Similar inefficiencies existed through the practices of the largest US retail chains. Stock holdings were suboptimized. In a typical product range assortment of 25,000 items, 8,000 would, according to Management Horizons at least, represent less than 10 per cent of the aggregate volume. These were often the heavily promoted 'dog' brands, which did not justify a presence in any assortment. Horror stories could happen in many big-volume categories. In soft drinks for example, the number of SKUs (individual sizes from one product line) normally held in stock by the average supermarket had moved over 10 years from 100 to 500, with little increase in either sales or margin. All chains stocked an amazing range of packaged detergents, many with shares of 1 or 2 per cent of the market. The power of Procter and Gamble (P&G), Lever and Colgate sales teams and their marketing dollars gave them, so they argued, no alternative. The retail 'division of power' between locally-based chains with modest national market shares and profitable manufacturers who were dictating store feature and pricing through their brand budgets destroyed any semblance of meaningful cost control. Yet nobody wanted to make the first move, fearing it might upset a mutually owned and lucrative apple-cart. Reform was inevitable, and was driven both by manufacturers intent on working to a vision of more sensible brand strategies, and by retailers determined to use increasing scale to cut costs and provide better margins.

Widest awake of the manufacturers was Cincinatti-based Procter and Gamble whose worldwide trade experience could envisage an era where bigger, more effective retailers would ultimately be better placed to influence consumer purchase decisions. With a string of US consumer goods as market leaders in its brand portfolio, P&G had more to gain and less to lose from the elimination of inefficient promotion practices such as high-low pricing and the resulting stock peaks. P&G sales managers had been to the best school of learning they could find – in Bentonville, Arkansas, home of value leader Wal-Mart, where they had set up a series of business-building and category-management 'experiments' with Sam Walton's company. These had been led by enterprising Sales Director Lou Pritchett, who worked hard both in the offices and on carefully planned fishing trips to persuade Walton to co-operate. Over five years, huge growth took place in P&G's Wal-Mart business, and reductions in cost for an already formidably cost-conscious Wal-Mart (and for P&G) accompanied the growth. P&G had leapt ahead of their competitors with Wal-Mart and in the 1990s they sought to extend this advantage to the rest of the US trade. For P&G it was a long-term winner. It strengthened their brand franchises, established P&G as category leaders, later called 'captains' with key retailers, cut back the need for or potential of own label, and delivered substantial cost advantage for both sides.

Admittedly, retail enthusiasm for P&G's everyday low-pricing policies had been initially muted. Traditional promotion using standard accounting systems still produced big dollar pay-outs which retailers were not keen to forego. It was when industry studies showed that new retail players (clubs and discounters) were deploying the new approach against the supermarkets to their own cost advantage – sometimes by as much as 25 per cent on key items – that interest in building on EDLP to do the same or more for supermarket chains themselves grew sharply. Efficient consumer response, long overdue, was the answer. It was simply a partnership between brand manufacturers and supermarket chains designed to restore competitiveness to the traditional supermarket, and inhibit momentum of the newer retail formats, who were dependent on cost and price advantage to grow. Efficient assortment, replenishment, promotion and new product introduction were all key elements, and it quickly gained widespread adoption through the US trade. FMI Reports confirm that the levels of cost reduction that can be expected, with little delay, from the adoption of efficient consumer response (ECR), in these four key areas are likely to be more than 10 per cent of base cost. Not unexpectedly, therefore, 1998 Reports confirm that nine out of ten supermarket operators now use category partnership with brand suppliers in their businesses. The implications have been fundamental – concentration on net rather than gross margins, the overhaul of incentive and reward systems among retailers and suppliers, and root and branch redirection of organization systems to concentrate decisions at the manufacturer/retailer interface.

The effects have been considerable. Management Horizons conclude that brand shares will change – in favour of stronger brand equities. Manufacturers can expect to gain operationally in the short term and as more effective product developers in the longer term, but not always. The big winners are retailers, who can gain significantly from category management ECR development. Savings of US\$ 20–50 per SKU (stock keeping unit) per store are confidently predicted. Management Horizons report that best-practice models differ from traditional practice in three ways conceptually: context, data and process. The ECR best-practice model recommends that assortment is reviewed in the most openly defined category management context; that it considers three data streams – retail, market and consumer; and finally that process formally integrates contextual and data material. While ECR models have materially helped US retailers drive efficiencies up and costs down, the supermarket sector started the process relatively late in the day, and is in the midst of a consolidation wave that is destined to go further. Not just supermarkets have gained from ECR. Wal-Mart, with extensive P&G help, was the industry pioneer, and the discounter section have made substantial ECR gains underscoring pricing advantage. A battle between US trade sectors continues and shake-out is the one forecast that can confidently be made. Among the losers will be traditional supermarkets which have neither service nor cost advantage – sadly still a numerous group – but there are winners as well, formidable innovators of which H E Butt is one of the most noteworthy.

MULTIPLYING TRADING FORMATS – A RICH VARIETY

All indicators point to a sustained period of trench warfare where winners and losers quickly emerge. In most places, US consumers have wide choices of shopping format. A sizeable wholesaling sector still operates between manufacturers and some retailers. Supermarkets, warehouse clubs, convenience stores, vast new supercenters and traditional discounters all compete for grocery business. Innovative new formats, sometimes called 'hot niches', selling specialty food items, with enormous portfolios, are growing apace, catering for 'food on the run' consumers. Home and Internet shopping is happening, and 'its impact will be a lot more ubiquitous than people think', according to Gary Hamel, author of *Competing for the Future*. This is no market for the faint-hearted, the inflexible or the unimaginative.

If the primary weekly shop is the criterion of progress, however, then the outlook for the supermarket is not so good. Less than 60 per cent of shoppers now claim to do their weekly shop at supermarkets, compared to 76 per cent five years ago. With clubs and warehouse stores under pressure, the winners look like first of all discounters, still growing (33–36 per cent), then convenience stores showing surprising resilience (24–31 per cent), but critically the new supercenters, small in number but growing fast (5–10 per cent) and firmly committed to being tomorrow's big winners. One-stop shopping is still a growing consumer appeal, practised by half of US consumers, who now can find practically all their household requirements under one roof in the new supercenters. Paradoxically of course there is the compensating trend to increase the limited item top-up shop, and to purchase food for immediate consumption and often in small quantities. Traditional grocery shopping patterns are breaking up under these pressures, their demise unmourned. Consumer choice is increasing, and contentment growing – 79 per cent express full satisfaction with their chosen store (cf. 70 per cent). Innovators feel and are rewarded.

Discount department stores have shown steady growth over 10 years and this is a trend forecast to continue. However, if supercenters are excluded, then specific discounter growth is slowing down. A process of simultaneous transformation to supercenters and rampant market consolidation is taking place. Expanded food offerings are a key element in discounters' strategies, and the food space available (say 80,000 sq ft) in supercenters encourages wholehearted exploitation. The theory is that as supercenters gain food-market share, they expose shoppers to higher-margin general merchandise more frequently, and generate sales across the store. The three big discounters are Wal-Mart, K-mart and Target who together account for 80 per cent of sales. Wal-Mart are moving food sales fastest, opening more than 100 supercenters every year, and now experimenting with growing food sales through conventional and their new and smaller 'Neighbourhood Stores'. K-mart's new stores have focussed on 'The Pantry', ie food and household items alongside children and home decor, but their recent improving cash flow has encouraged K-Mart to recommit to full supercenter development based on their classic discount store heritage. Now no. 3, Target is extending food range in some locations. In every sense, however – scale, range, innovation and pricing – Wal-Mart is simply streets ahead and the gap is visibly widening.

Convenience stores have bounced back, exploiting evolving shopper needs and new market gaps and reversing a sales decline in the early 1990s with revenue growth since 1992. Younger shoppers from all income groups predominate. Meal solutions are increasingly emphasized as key areas for growth and convenience stores are well placed by style and location to drive this trend forward. Bigger operators are forging partnerships with the fast-foods companies. Others, including leader Southland (7/11 stores) have developed proprietary food presentations. Gasoline purchases are the single largest item bought, and oil companies are all expanding their convenience store offerings, eg Mobil's 'On the Run' and Exxon's 'Tiger Express'. The convenience store's profitability has improved markedly as Southland, easily the biggest force in the sector, improved the efficiencies of its chain, albeit with lower total revenues, down 20 per cent over five years.

'Clubs may now be yesterday's US news and are rationalized to three players: Price/Costco, Sam's (Wal-Mart), and BJ's. Sales have matured and the number of outlets is now in decline, with productivity driving industry results. Price/Costco the innovator and early leader is now confronted by Sam's, blatantly imitating its approach, but Price/Costco sales per store remain well ahead of Sam's. Wal-Mart has not found it easy to position the clubs' offering within their range, and constant top-management change suggests that it has yet to find the answers to making this format work. Low prices and margins – the clubs' gross margin is half the food-industry median – make new entrants unlikely. It seems the two principals will be left to fight it out in a battlefield of limited future potential but once again it seems ultimately to be Sam's rather than Price/Costco that is more likely to emerge as winner.

Limited potential also applies to food wholesaling which is a mature sector with slowing sales and relevance. Two operators – Fleming, based in Oklahoma, and Minnesota's Supervalu – have achieved national presence. The advent of sensible purchasing policies by retailers following EDLP further constrain the wholesaling opportunity, and a combination of systems efficiencies, married to vertical integration (Supervalu owns Cub Stores, for example) into direct retailing are strategies wholesalers need to employ to survive. The arrival of the new Wal-Mart Neighborhood Stores, targetted to replace the independent operators supplied by these wholesalers, adds to their business problems.

Finally the supercenter – *the* phenomenon in today's US market. Growth in new units is multiplying, and doubled in the five years to 1996. The stores appeal to younger and family shoppers, their value perceptions and delivery attracting both-poorer and price-sensitive shoppers, incidentally the heaviest users of own label. Convenience is a key objective for this group, a criterion the 'any time/any product' supercenter is brilliantly placed to satisfy. The supercenter is regarded as appropriate for the major family shop, less appropriate for fill-in trips, with food- and general-merchandise-buying being evenly balanced. These mammoth structures have pitched their appeal coherently – price leaders in the market , own-label strength, one-stop shopping and round-the-clock opening. They deliver their promise – hence their explosive growth which is forecast to continue. Supermarket owners beware, is their message. The supercenter is here to stay.

Multiplicity of formats is, with consolidation in traditional sectors, an influence with far-reaching effects. Overnight, to nurture the brand has become complex – not just because of tightening costs and prices, own-label growth, and discounter penetration, but through new relationships emanating from a changing power balance between marketer and retailer. Private label increases share, fewer consumers rate brands 'worth the extra cost' and in two years, consumers who said they 'had one brand they preferred to buy all the time' dropped by more than 10 per cent. (Management Horizons). New formats and consolidation mean shake-out among weaker retailers and spells speedy elimination for weak brands.

SUPERMARKETS – WHO WILL SURVIVE?

US Supermarkets are used to living in a mature market, with no price inflation, new format competition and a consuming public that no longer cares as much as once they did for their stores. The plethora of ready-made food ideas and notably meal solutions from a host of new locations are today's news. The number of supermarkets continues to shrink as consolidation drives forward with fewer, stronger national players. Sales per store – through eliminating the weak tail of shops – and store-operating efficiencies are moving upward again. Dedicated attention is paid to the holy grail of category management. New techniques – such as shopper loyalty cards – actively promoting own-label and experimenting with delivery and electronic shopping are the new experimental routes to competitive advantage. Meanwhile through frenetic acquisition and merger, leaders jockey for the surviving positions at the top table for the new century.

Three kinds of competitor can be recognized in the United States as consolidation gathers pace. Merger and acquisition have much further to go before they are exhausted. There are significant buying opportunities, and there are acquiring companies with leadership aspirations and still, today, only the new Kroger/Meyer has a 10 per cent market share. The three groups are:

- the four multi-regional leaders, strengthened through acquisition;
- a clutch of companies operating with dominance in localities;
- extra-industry competitors – Wal-Mart but with more to come.

The *soi-disant* 'new elite of US food retailing' are now a big-four group, two originally western (Albertson's, Safeway); one Dutch but with an east-coast base (Ahold); and one with a long-time central power base (Kroger), now boosted with strong western and south-western positions (Meyer). Kroger has emerged from its recent Meyer takeover as the single largest player and temporarily has put clear water between itself and the following group. Prior to the Kroger move, the Meyer/Yucaipa group had acquired a group of six western companies, in a buoyant expanding set of markets in the south-west of the United States, under the Fred Meyer banner, and had established a share of more than 3 per cent and fifth position overall in its own right. The new Kroger/Meyer company has sales of around US$ 50 billion, and it now seems that only Wal-Mart, or a merger between Safeway and one of the other big four – inherently unlikely to happen perhaps – could match Kroger in size.

Albertson's – originally from Boise Idaho, and since acquiring American Stores, with sales of US$ 36 billion and a market share of around 7 per cent – was perhaps the first genuinely national company in US retail grocery. Its strategy has been to move with speed, strengthening its western/mountain base through the Californian Lucky stores which came with the American acquisition, and becoming leader in the key mid-western market (Chicago) via America itself. This augments existing leadership positions in the east through Acme in Philadelphia and in Chicago with Jewel. Safeway, with strong western roots, acquired Vons in California in 1997, has recently taken over Dominicks in Chicago, and is expanding east. It is now in third place, and given recent moves is somewhat isolated, but future acquisition moves by it look probable.

The most enterprising performers have been privately-owned Dutch Ahold (see above), the United States' leading foreign grocery company, who have employed acquisition aggressively to come from nowhere to fourth place in the market overall. Ahold's share is now approaching 5 per cent and its leading east-coast presence generates sales of more than US$ 20 billion from a clutch of stores each with its original and retained fascia. This group of four should now pull away from the remainder of the top ten. Some notably strong performers with good growth records exist in the latter group, and with local dominance in their markets, they cannot be discounted.

Inherently strongest may be one of the smallest, joining the top 10 division in 1998 – San Antonio's H E Butt. Butt has a magnificent growth record, setting benchmark standards in key respects in US retailing and, for many, ranking with Wal-Mart as an accomplished innovator. Naturally, given its Texas base, it has been the first US chain to make a major push into Mexico, and is planning to open 60 stores south of the border. Winn-Dixie and Publix have individually-strong franchises in the southern and south-eastern states. Each has seen solid growth in business and share in the past five years. Winn-Dixie is bigger, while Publix sets customer-service standards for the nation. Neither can be disregarded as a future force, nor can Food Lion which has grown handsomely, and is marginally smaller but no less innovative. Of the 1998 top ten retailers, only A&P looks now as if it is emphatically beyond redemption.

In aggregate therefore, the top 10 market shares in the United States have risen markedly, from 26 per cent in 1991 to more than 40 per cent by the time of writing. Estimates are that by 2002, the aggregate share of the top 10 will be around 50 per cent, and if Wal-Mart is included nearer 60 per cent. This is quantum change and will transform market and competitor behaviour. We must now consider the company with the largest capacity to create change, probably worldwide, certainly in the United States.

WAL-MART – THE RELENTLESS RISE OF A POWER RETAILER

The growth of Wal-Mart is formidable. Sam Walton opened his first variety store in Newport, Arkansas, in 1945 as a franchisee. In 1962 he began his own rural discounting chain, concentrating on small south-western towns, noting 'if we offered better prices … people would shop at home'. Taking his company public in 1970, sales mushroomed. He achieved his first US$ 1 billion after 17 years – the next 17 saw sales rise to US$ 100 billion. By 1985,

Walton was the richest man in America, operating 859 Discount City stores with an average size of 57,000 sq ft and having five distribution centres in the central, mid- and south-west. The company's straightforward message in the rural and small-town locations it by tradition preferred was emblazoned on store facades: 'We Sell for Less.' That they did, in part driven by an emerging 'everyday low prices' philosophy that Wal-Mart pioneered. Another key difference was Walton's people philosophy. 'We care about our People' was and still is the message on store manager's lapels, and the 1985 annual report highlighted this – 'our people make the difference' being still today its straightforward claim.

With 30 years of staggering success under his belt, Sam Walton stepped down, handing the role of President and CEO to David Glass in 1988. It might have been a poisoned chalice and many thought it was. The new team had an awesome job on their hands simply to keep the momentum going from what Sam Walton had created.

THE PARADOX THAT WAS SAM

The record speaks for itself. A revolution in retailing, 33 per cent continuous return on capital and compound annual sales growth of 35 per cent over 20 years. Juggernaut results from the fastest growing retailer. Yet Sam Walton's deliberately counter-cyclical strategy had been simply to 'put good-size stores into little one-horse towns which everybody else was ignoring'. In 1992, when he died, he was not just no. 1 retailer in the world, but he had covered the whole of the United States with an enormous range of intrinsically different Wal-Mart stores. And en route this uncomplicated man who hated to display visible signs of his not inconsiderable fortune had made himself the richest man in America. He was in truth a living paradox.

The small-town rural beginnings in Arkansas, Oklahoma and Missouri grew to blanket coverage of the United States and store penetration in every state. ('Little Vermont' tried unsuccessfully to resist for a time.) The business has never moved its headquarters away from Bentonville, the insignificant Arkansas town renowned only for the presence of the United States's sixth largest company. Walton of course was the classic over-achiever, with immense reserves of energy and personal charisma. When setting the key target for 1990 as US$ 100 billion sales, he asked his associates, as he called his staff, 'Can we do it? Can we be that good? – I have an unbelievable feeling about the future that we have more opportunity than ever.' Nobody doubted him. He revelled in looking upwards and outwards. Yet this same man who managed 'by walking and flying about' was a stickler for the most mundane forms of cost-cutting, worried everyone about personal expenses, drove an old pick-up truck, borrowed money for phone calls, shared rooms in hotels, and told all his colleagues to do the same. Frugality was a religion with Sam Walton.

Walton asked for and received immense commitment from the associates. Every morning they perpetuate the Wal-Mart chant – a ritualistic, one might say Japanese-style approach to the serious business of the day's work. Yet in 1983, after losing a bet to Chief Executive David Glass about the level of profits for the year, he nonchalantly agreed to dance down 5th Avenue, New York City, in a grass skirt. 'Wacky' was not a word he would have rejected being applied to his personal behaviour. Conflicts in style were irreconcilable, yet they went unquestioned in Wal-Mart's 'anything goes' freewheeling culture.

Innovation was another paradox of Sam's policy. He was the entrepreneur nonpareil. His business has driven more successful innovation in US retailing than anyone else has ever aspired to. Thirty-five years of successful discounting, the growth of super-centers, the move to foods, leadership after late entry in warehouse clubs, neighbourhood markets, you name it – Wal-Mart have been there and done it. But nobody better demonstrates the truth that innovation is perspiration, dedicated pursuit of the daily details of customer service that grind out winning strategic advantage. Walton believed value was everything, that 'people enjoyed going to shop' and personally questioned whether electronic shopping would ever carve out a substantial share of retail business. But you could be sure if it happened Sam's Wal-Mart would be there to make it work for them.

The Harvard Business School has written compellingly about the quality of the business that this very simple man founded. Sam was given the United States's highest award, the Presidential Freedom medal, the citation recognizing that he was 'an American original. He embodies the entrepreneurial spirit and epitomizes the American dream.' Perhaps it's the originals who thrive on paradox and then achieve so much.

Walton's achievement had been epic, flying directly in the face of many well-established US retailing practices. The achievement of his successors, led by Glass, has been equally astonishing. They took Sam's traditional approach, retained those elements of cultural significance to the company he founded and for which, by the time of his death in 1992, he was an icon, but transformed the business, broadening its remit out of recognition in the last decade. Wal-Mart is now a force without equal in US retailing. It has shown an intention to do worldwide what it has succeeded in doing at home – taking on the best competition and beating it at its own game. Today's company has moved into new formats and, learning quickly how to make them work, has set benchmark performance others could not match. The combination of scale and muscle and faithful adherence to the discounter's low-cost/low-prices belief makes Wal-Mart a difficult company to challenge.

Walton's heirs moved the company from a general-merchandise platform into food, where it is well placed (already in the top five or six) in the US market. Explosive organic growth through new store formats has built share rapidly through the 1990s. There is no sign that the bandwagon is slowing down – quite the reverse. The latest profit statement showed after-tax profits growing by more than 26 per cent on total annual worldwide sales heading for US\$ 140 billion. Wal-Mart's shares closed up nearly 5 per cent, a staggering four times the level they had been in January 1997, a mere two years earlier.

A major engine of Wal-Mart's recent growth has been the enormous (150,000–200,000 sq ft) supercenters which Wal-Mart is building at a rate of more than 100 each year. These huge modern conglomerates do sell slightly less food than general merchandise. In 1998 food sales reached US\$ 32 billion and by 2002 they are estimated to achieve US\$ 75 billion by which stage Wal-Mart will probably be no. 3 in the US food market. While its stated objective is to 'grow and to be the best in food', Wal-Mart's relentless march to US food leadership looks unstoppable. Already, and by some margin, the world's largest retailer, it has complete national representation in 50 US states to help it achieve this. The recent introduction of a further new development known as Neighbourhood Centres, operating on reduced scale (around 40,000 sq ft) to the vast supercenters, will further enhance Wal-Mart's coverage and is an indication that despite rapid consolidation in the supermarkets, Wal-Mart is determined to increase its own pace of growth.

The company's progress has been marked by substantial risk-taking and rapid learning from experience. No longer a rural/small town concern, it has repeatedly sought to identify best existing practice, locate close to it, and then learn from, emulate and beat it. (This point is well confirmed in the two excellent Harvard Business School studies on the company 1986, 1998.) An early example was positioning the first Wal-Mart centres close to H E Butt major stores, to learn both from sensitive consumer pricing policies and their presentation of fresh produce. Wal-Mart did exactly the same with the attractive Cub Stores in Minneapolis, and more recently with Ukrops, which had built a unique Home Meal Replacement business in Richmond, Virginia. In other respects, Walton's earliest policies have more than stood the test of time: steady, everyday low prices; the use of relentless cost-cutting to feed into still lower prices; systematic cutting-edge retail technology to cut working capital and again lower costs; clear and striking consumer messages. The vision is simple and consistent, as easy to understand for Wal-Mart's customers as it is for their 675,000 employees or 'associates'.

Perhaps because of its small-town origins, and a Bentonville, Arkansas, headquarters, and doubtless underlined by a continuously strong family shareholding, leviathan Wal-Mart rarely loses the local touch, happily conforming to a conceptual view of the United States as a series of local market places. Each new store-opening funds a local student scholarship. Local fund-raising by Wal-Mart associates is actively promoted. In 1995, as mammoth store openings swept the country, Wal-Mart established a Home Town stores division, a conscious return to its small-town variety store heritage, the objective to re-create the community around the local store. Walton's famous counter-cyclicalism had found yet another new outlet. Wal-Mart is apparently entirely undaunted by having demanding and complex strategic growth objectives at one and the same time. Simultaneously, Glass was pushing the international business forward into a host of new countries. A recovery in the warehouse clubs sector was being achieved with Sam's clubs. The potential of both the Internet and home shopping was being welcomed – 'we expect this to be a significant contribution to our growth.' In Wal-Mart paradoxes abound, but the mission is simple, and accelerating complexity is managed with apparent sang-froid.

Why is Wal-Mart different? What makes it unique? An innovative founding father set it on its feet, but subsequent progress has not flickered. The consumer franchise remains strikingly clear and well presented. Reaching its mid-30s there is not the remotest suggestion of mid-life crisis. It has to be Wal-Mart's internal clarity of purpose, a strategic vision owned by committed people, that creates the difference. Associates feel special, their goals inspirational, and both factors have long been underpinned by favourable stock-ownership arrangements. Experiment is encouraged and the group believe it is a winner. This is a company with a decisive competitive edge. Deep down it knows this and has the record to keep it going.

THE US FUTURE

In a period of continuing change to market forces and behaviour it is difficult to forecast trends in the US market. It may be easier to forecast where channel growth will occur and who will be among the likely winners.

The world retail grocery market is becoming global and at speed. Surprisingly in food retailing, the US has only one competitor of true world stature and that is Wal-Mart. Wal-Mart's commitment to lead the world market is clear, and the company is moving quickly to establish positions in Europe, Asia and Latin America. Rich in scale and resources Wal-Mart has profound depth of experience, given its emphasis on delivering value, cost-effectiveness and appropriate retail formats. Its people-management skills are industry-leading. Wal-Mart should continue to be the world's number one retailer. They will seek and may obtain US and subsequent global leadership in food retailing. Not to downplay Wal-Mart's domestic rivals, Europeans Carrefour and Ahold look the only serious competitors.

The role of food delivery through retailers is changing substantially in the US, and meal solutions represents a tremendous new opportunity. There are opportunities for specialists (hot niches) to grow rapidly, for convenience stores to take a share through partnerships, and for traditional supermarkets and supercenters to increase their competencies in this market. While there are great new innovators around now, there still seems – against best world standards – some distance for the United States to go to offer consistently good and innovative taste experiences in much prepared-food and meal solutions – although the ever-improving 'value' proposition leads the world. It is possible that increased bought-in meals at home will, in the end, take most business from fast-food and mainstream restaurants themselves. The key consideration will be achieving quality and freshness at prices consumers are prepared to pay, and delivery at an affordable cost, given the conflict between freshness and the costs of shrinkage/disposal. Success in the area of meal solutions will be an overall discriminator.

The process of consolidation among the US supermarket chains will continue. Ten chains should take a two-thirds market share with Wal-Mart as one of the ten, quickly. Thereafter a further wave of consolidation will continue and mergers among the current top ten will occur. Within ten years we can expect to see two or three leaders in the United States with market shares well into double digits. Wal-Mart will be one, and Kroger, Albertson's, Safeway and Ahold should be represented among the rest. It is very difficult to see either a new entrant or one of the other current competitors getting into the top group. The Internet and home shopping may be the catalysts that can create discontinuous change.

The progressive move to one-stop shopping with a combination of food, general merchandise and other regularly purchased services under one roof will continue and take a growing share of food retailing. Wal-Mart will lead the way, but the best supermarket and supercenter operators will be present. Market share, having doubled in the past five years, should double again in the next five. Discounted prices and low costs will be key appeals as will convenience and round-the-clock shopping. Brands will remain under pressure and will lose share. We can expect continued own-label gains in US food retailing. Well-positioned brands will remain strong, but will need effective participation from category management programmes.

It is difficult to see growth for convenience stores, despite their resurgence, increased efficiencies and service delivery. Their best hope of profitability is probably through effective management of the gasoline opportunity, and partnerships of an innovative nature with specialty food providers. However, genuine food-quality advantage – such as Marks & Spencer achieved in a step function in the UK – could represent an opportunity if it can be grasped ahead of bigger competitors. This could take significant business from current fast-food providers. Similarly, it is hard to see recovery for the club or warehouse stores. In tomorrow's cost-driven market, wholesalers will defend a narrowing opportunity.

As consumers appraise an increasing series of shopping opportunities – from the one-stop shop at supercenters to the specialty-meal solution round the block – the dominant share of traditional supermarkets will be threatened and rationalization will continue. Fewer competitors, fewer stores and a struggle to maintain sales per store will mean a reducing share of the food-shopping budget going to supermarkets in the years ahead. Nevertheless, supermarkets are working hard to ensure that they retain the majority of the weekly food shop, and this they ought to be able to do – at least for 10 years.

Finally home shopping and electronic commerce will make their mark. A consortium of leading US manufacturers, wholesalers and retailers studied consumer direct marketing and delivery from dedicated fulfilment centres in 1996. Already significant companies make online grocery shopping work. NetGrocer partners with FedEx to deliver non-perishables nationwide. Streamline offers 'lifestyle', ie more than groceries, providing home-storage units when no one is there to take delivery in the home. Peapod, who made one of the earliest entries, has extended across a range of US regions, teaming with some of the very strongest established retailers. This selection confirms a widespread view of the opportunity that meets a consumer need for convenience and flexibility. How far it will grow in the next 10 years it is hard to forecast. Equally uncertain is who the new leaders will be. Gary Hamel, who thinks the change will be fast, says that leaders in one paradigm rarely lead in the next – 'It is unlikely that the winners in ... shopping centres will be winners online.' What seems certain is that US experimentation and practice will lead the world so its penetration will go farther and faster in

Britain than anywhere else. Online shopping patterns will come from the United States. And so to end where we began, it is likely that the study trips to New York and Los Angeles will not diminish in frequency or importance in the years ahead!

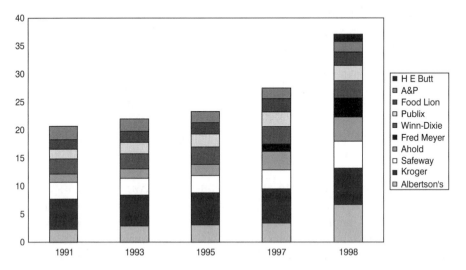

Figure 8.1 *Top ten US shares 1991–98*

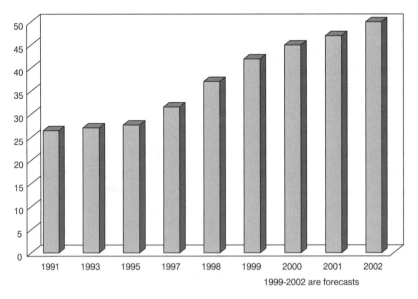

Figure 8.2 *Share of top ten food retailers 1991–2002*

9

The lessons learned

SUPERMARKETS HAVE PLAYED A CRUCIAL ROLE IN ALL OUR LIVES

Supermarkets across the developed world have been a key feature of the second half of the twentieth century, and the UK supermarket in its own right has, in a world context, been both important and distinctive. Its activities have affected all our lives and changed them as substantially as probably any other single influence. Supermarkets are universal, their customers drawn from all elements in society, from richest to poorest. It has been calculated that today the average British citizen will spend two years of their life – or 3 per cent of a normal waking life – inside the doors of a supermarket (Cable and Wireless Research, 1999). Perhaps only the workplace, the school and the motor car will match this whole-life allocation of time for most citizens. Supermarkets are also highly visible. Few days pass without their activities being featured in news affecting our own lives and communities, and physically there are virtually no communities in Britain that they have not penetrated. Their product, delivery of service and innovation, their prices and value are examined and re-examined every day, and now for much of the night as well, by unending streams of critical customers. Reputations can evolve quickly, at least on a local basis, as consumers consider their weekly, sometimes daily purchases.

Market positions can and on the record do change. We can point confidently to areas of retailing performance where UK retailers have been able to lead the world – their approach to own-label development emphatically is one, and the use of IT to drive both cost advantage and now customer service direction is probably a second – and there have been others. De facto the continuous intensity of capital investment to create a now saturated out-of-town super-store environment may be a third. So by any measure, supermarkets are of prime significance in British society. We can try to understand the lessons for the industry as an entity, and then consider them from the standpoint of the individual companies participating. Through time the nature of the market changes and with it the forces that determine success. The modern models of retailing development have evolved from those that held sway through the 1960s and 1970s, itself a period of high change. Today's model in turn may itself now be set to give way to even more radical change as global and infor-mation opportunities turn historic retailing practice on its head. Certainly, the urgency with which ambitious companies (Wal-Mart, Ahold, Carrefour, and in the UK at least Tesco and Marks & Spencer) are driving themselves to develop their strategies and global portfolios suggests that key players do not feel time to be on their side in reappraising and restructuring their presence. Let us look at lessons for the UK industry.

FOLLOW THE LEADERS AND MOVE AT SPEED

The UK industry quickly spotted the important trend to self-service in the years following the Second World War. The United States had established the trend in the first place, not unnaturally given their wealth, size and immediate freedom from internal conflict, and of course the US willingness to experiment and their inherent sense of adventure must have played its part. But the UK learned quickly and followed fast. A common language and intrinsically strong links between the UK and its closest ally encouraged British retailers to study US innovations and practice while much of the rest of the world had other economic priorities.

In 1949 the experienced Alan Sainsbury launched his business on the road to self-service following one of the more important of these voyages of discovery to the New World. Sainsbury's can be counted the real pioneers of self-service – its moves being a source of considerable surprise to many of its established customers, seemingly a far cry from the traditional marble-top counters, dignified shop assistants and staid conservative shopping milieux which it had made its preserve. The Sainsbury's lessons were provided by a dramatically successful new store in Croydon and where it led, others followed fast.

These followers were a motley crew – Asda's first Pontefract store, Ken Morrison's restructured Bradford cinema, Jack Cohen's harum-scarum store conversions – and they behaved in a more pragmatic and notably less analytical manner than Sainsbury's had done. British retailers, amazingly when we reflect that their customers, emerging from an era of acute food scarcity, were still content to be carrying post-war food ration books, set out on a journey of customer innovation that everyone – even an unadventurous and pathologically uncommercial co-operative movement – was ready and keen to adopt. The consuming public took no time at all to demonstrate that they thought the changes were very much an improvement on what had gone before and it was not difficult to see why. For the first time, the reality of increasing food choice was put squarely on the consumer's daily agenda. Simultaneously, consumers themselves were given the freedom to exercise the choices in the way they wanted, and at a time and place of their own choosing. There was an atypical and free-market kicking open of attractive new doors in a restructured post-war Britain, where many of the changes that were simultaneously improving consumers' lives were slower, could be costly, and needed government policy adoption to force them through (education, health and housing, for example).

It was a massive psychological change which seemed to remove, at one blow, a host of historic behaviour constraints that had shackled countless previous generations of food shoppers. Crispin Tweddell, the most analytical of commentators, told me:

> self-service took off because it answered customer needs for popular approachability and convenience. It communicated the proposition in a way that everyone understood with the store format as the medium. So brilliance of message and medium hit the spot for the consumer just as Frank Winfield Woolworth did with his 5 and 10c stores … overall it seems to me that retailers take off when they answer *real* popular needs and communicate in devastatingly simple ways. We should never forget it. (1997)

Wise words. Sometimes, alas, their more modern successors still manage to forget.

These new retail pioneers uninihibitedly exploited the enormous room for manoeuvre they encountered to drive their changes forward. The UK model of food retailing through an entire half-century is characterized by flexibility and open-mindedness, unquestionably when compared with continental European practice, but even more surprisingly often also in relation to the United States, where antitrust and pricing legislation restrained and cocooned nationwide development and radical change practice for many years. While in Britain there was constant bickering, and sometimes trench warfare with local planners to establish the in-town and later the fringe and out-of-town superstore sites, the protagonists entered upon these negotiations with controlled passion and a sense of strategic purpose. As usual in Britain the debate was nearly always conducted in a thoroughly civilized manner, and the developers' point of view was adequately heard. Nearly always there was more than one company keen to win control of the new site, which gave astute local authorities the chance to drive what they could rationalize as community enriching bargains.

But the onward march to bigger and better sites continued unabated – and despite tougher national regulatory constraints, remains alive and well today. As time passed it was not just freedom of location that mattered. Opening hours were progressively extended (it is interesting to compare German or Swiss practice over the same period), and in due course went on to embrace the controversial matter of Sunday opening. Initially many supermarkets simply ignored the existing laws, as a host of the small independents had been doing for years, but the effect was to make round-the-clock shopping become a omnipresent reality. With the many big new sites, and vast increase in shopping hours, came a series of competitive moves to widen the supermarket's product range – first of all in foods, and then in related non-food areas. Ultimately, wherever the independent shops had established a franchise – the butcher, the baker, the greengrocer, the pharmacist, the newsagent, the bookstore, the sports store, the off-licence and now the bank – was regarded, perfectly legitimately in the eyes of the new competitors, as an opportunity for self-service development. Taking advantage of free-market conditions and the legislative and trading freedoms that have always been prevalent in Britain was and is a hallmark of the UK industry. For this reason Britain's retailing developments have moved faster and often on the whole more innovatively than in the equivalent continental European markets, and the differences that existed between the UK and continental Europe 30 years ago, in many cases persist today.

VOLUME AND PROFITS – A SUCCESSFUL RECIPE

The self-service operators could see with their own eyes a huge volume opportunity staring them in the face and became strongly committed to volume growth. They were able to register consistent market share advances year on year from the 1950s onwards. The decline of the independents and the co-operative stores was matched by patterns of virtually indiscriminate growth for the self-service multiples – or so it seemed. In the early years the market was really a free-for-all. While the companies that did best were those with a sense of strategy, and a heritage in retailing (Sainsbury's scored on both counts), or dedication and experience to store and size focus (Asda and Morrison featured on these criteria) the retail bandwagon was now rolling and a host of cavalier and disorganized players (included in this group were such improbable bedfellows as Tesco and the co-operative movement,) jumped merrily on board. Improvements in convenience, service and lower prices 'went with the territory' so that weaker independents, invariably supplied by local whole-salers, found themselves in the last resort incapable of competing on all these critical dimensions. The rise of voluntary chains and groups might even the balance but the economic realities prevailed and they were powerless to arrest an accelerating trend.

What is noticeable is that – even as self-service growth accelerated, and perhaps because of its helter-skelter momentum – few strategies were single-mindedly based on low prices as the core promise. Gubay, an early entre-preneur who was associated with the Kwik Save idea, might have been a well-known exception, but even he was apt to remind his devotees, 'I don't sell cheap goods, I sell goods cheaply.' Prices could not but be lower, financed by bulk-buying and high store volumes, and equally importantly they were seen to be lower – most consumers came to believe – on virtually everything and almost all of the time. But the fact was there was no need to build business on an overt low-price promise – as the discounters had done in France and Germany or as Wal-Mart was first to do in the United States and then farther afield.

The phenomenon that was to endure for decades in the UK, through several important changes of market leadership, was that volume and market-share growth were the prerequisites but there was no need for the obverse side of the coin to be a consequent decline in margin. Quite the reverse – the inde-pendents, now losing share hand over fist, were the first to be heard protesting that their own margins needed to improve to enable them to survive at all and many manufacturers were listening to them. An unwieldy co-operative movement could agree on precious little, but it too needed margin stability both to pay for its crucial dividend and for endemically wasteful fragmentation in activities. Such defensive postures played firmly into the supermarkets' hands. Volume and margin could be manipulated like juggling balls. A growing portfolio of new products appeared from grateful manufacturers (and gradually from retailers themselves) to fill the big new areas of available shelf space. It was above all the era of the fast-moving consumer goods brand, and manufacturers too were in their heyday. The brands were strongly promoted with growing scale efficiencies, and there was universal agreement these were better competitive tools both for the long- and the short-term than costly and damaging price wars. They were good for the brands, good for the big new stores and – most important of all – customers in this best of all possible worlds could see a wind of change blowing for the better all around them. This appealing economic outcome generated few losers – and none that generated much sympathy.

PROFITABILITY

It is a commonplace that British supermarket groups are much more profitable than their counterparts elsewhere in Europe or the United States – isn't it? The companies themselves do not agree, and claims and counter-claims fly around like confetti. The field becomes a playground for those whose toys are lies, damned lies and statistics. Critics used emotive phrases – 'obscenely profitable', 'margins two or three times those elsewhere'. Supporters sound like lawyers, pleading that, firstly their clients are not guilty, and secondly if they are guilty, it is for very good reasons.

We must recognize that each side is trying to make a case, using whatever form of evidence best fits. Several factors make comparisons inherently difficult. One factor is that the UK groups are all publicly owned, while many of the continental firms are still private. Definitions of profit, and the motivation to declare a higher or lower figure, are different. If you want to please the stock exchange, you tend to declare high profits; if you and your family will be paying income tax on the sum, you may want to minimize it.

Another factor is that accounting conventions vary, in particular in relation to the treatment of goodwill, and amortization of property costs. Sums arising from the purchase of goodwill are amortized against the profit and loss account over 20 years in France; in the UK, they will usually be written off immediately to reserves. In France, store assets (land and buildings) are depreciated over a 20-year period, while in the UK this has not until recently been true. The argument in Britain was that because of the high quality of the buildings, they would not decline very quickly in value over time, and the residual asset would have a high resale value. This was clearly not true after the collapse of the property market in the early 1990s, and increasing criticism from analysts eventually led some retailers to acknowledge the validity of the argument. First Morrison and Asda, then later all the others, agreed from the mid-1990s to depreciate their freehold and long-lease buildings. This reduced profits in the first few years (see Wrigley, 1994). We shall see the effect of this on profitability comparisons later.

With these preliminaries, we can look at some actual figures. There are (at least) two ways of analysing profitability: margin on sales, and return on capital employed (ROCE). It turns out that they produce different patterns. We will start with margin on sales, as critics most often quote this. At this level, it is clear that the UK supermarkets appear to have an advantage. The profit margins on sales in Britain generally rose steadily over the decades until the early 1990s, and have consistently been above those for Continental and US operators. Over the period 1988–93, the average operating margin for six French supermarket groups was 2 per cent. For six British groups, the average was over 6 per cent (Burt and Sparks, 1997). Adjustment of the British figures to take account of the differences in accounting treatment mentioned above (and certain other factors), will bring the UK figures down but there will still be a gap. On this basis, the UK figures will be around 4 to 5 per cent, but the French figures will still be significantly lower at 1–2 percent. Almost all US supermarket chains have been nearer the French than the British levels (though in general, US and European margins have been rising through the 1990s, while UK rates have been falling).

These comparisons have aroused most attacks from critics. They claim that the UK margins are the result of massive buying power exerted by the groups, and the use of oligopoly power to impose on consumers a higher-than-normal price level. We have seen elsewhere that it is virtually impossible to compare price levels across countries, and it is also the case that there are large and powerful buying groups in many other countries. The British firms tend to be more centralized than some continental competitors, and to use a single fascia; this should help in reducing buying costs. It may also be that the British supermarkets are more skilful in using their power to extract better terms from their suppliers, but this is an area shrouded in commercial secrecy, and we cannot reach any firm conclusions.

Other possible explanations for higher British margins flow from lower costs:

- We have referred elsewhere to the British companies' lead in applying IT to logistics. Their distribution systems are centralized, with deliveries to a small number of company warehouses. Such efficiencies are reflected, for example, in fewer days' stockholding: an average of 20 days in the period 1988–93 for British firms, compared with 35 for French (Burt and Sparks, 1997).
- Labour costs are lower in the UK, both because of lower social costs borne by employers, and because in Britain the proportion of part-time labour in supermarkets is higher than elsewhere.
- The significantly higher level of own-label penetration in British supermarkets means that the average cost of goods sold is lower than in the rest of Europe, and the gross margin higher.

On the other hand, as the UK operators are keen to point out, the costs of buying sites and building superstores are considerably higher in Britain than in other countries; not all cost comparisons favour the British.

To summarize the margin debate, then, British supermarket groups do make higher margins than their rivals in Europe and the United States. Part of this is due to the nature of competition in the different markets, which we discuss elsewhere: price plays a much more important role in both the United States and continental Europe than in Britain, for whatever reason. Part of it is due to the centralized management structure and single-fascia strategy adopted in Britain, and part due to associated efficiencies achieved by superior management.

When we turn to ROCE, we see a different picture. Which figures one chooses, from which year, alter the detail, but the overall pattern is clear. A study of the years 1988–93 showed an average ROCE for six French companies of 19 per cent, and for six British (the big four, Morrison and Kwik Save) of 21 per cent (Burt and Sparks,1997). A later analysis (Deutsche Morgan Grenfell, 1998) compared store groups in Britain, France, Belgium and the United States. The results from 1991–97 were consistent, and 1997 showed:

ROCE per cent	
Six British companies	16
Nine US companies	21
Eight French companies	20
Three Belgian companies	24

The inclusion of Kwik Save in the British group will have lowered the average, but any comparison of ROCE across countries shows that even the best British supermarket groups are similar to their rivals – better than some, worse than others – but certainly not more profitable overall. The higher capital investment in Britain (see 'A Note on Capital Intensity' on page 226) needs servicing by higher margins, but the result in ROCE is the same as that produced by the different structures overseas. How long the British can sustain their model is another question, to which we return in the final chapter.

To answer the original question, then: 'Are British supermarkets more profitable than European and US rivals?' Yes and no, depending on what you measure! All measures of profitability are subject to doubts and cautions, and international comparisons are particularly fraught. On the least-bad criterion of return on capital employed, British firms are not unusually profitable.

SUPPLIER AND COMMUNITY RELATIONSHIPS – THE CHAINS DOMINATE

A further distinguishing feature of the UK market has been the relationships that retailers came to enjoy with their suppliers. As retailer shares consolidated in a free-trade and fast-growth environment, it was not long before the balance of power began to shift, and shift decisively. The ensuing game was a novel experience and entirely different from that which had been played out between the manufacturer and traditional stores, where expertise and investment had always been loaded firmly on the manufacturer's side of the equation. After all, as the well-qualified corporate marketing managers would remind themselves, 'We have the brand, and you can't do without it, can you?' However, removing resale price maintenance was a nail in many independents' coffin, and made supermarkets, overnight, into a more formidable phenomenon.

Crucial interactions were with the suppliers of fresh foods – meat, vegetables and bakery. They could be large- or small-scale producers, who were offered attractive volume contracts but with limited security, and as the market became more competitive, they had to absorb and act upon endless requirements not merely to keep quality standards up, but at the same time to improve efficiencies and lower costs. The supermarkets were in a uniquely strong position to exploit volume strength. Gradually, but with equal resolve, the retailers were able to shift power in their favour with the manufacturers, eventually even with those owning the biggest brands. While manufacturers with strong marketing and logistic teams could participate in these negotiations and produce counter arguments, the pressures became irresistible. Today, in the UK, the retailer has been the dominant force for more than 10 years. A big manufacturer, classically, may find 10 per cent or 15 per cent of his brand selling through a single retailer buying point, which will take a mere 1 per cent of its purchases from this same manufacturer. The retailer's conclusion is obvious – 'You help me, or I help myself. In the short term, I can buy from your competitor. Of course I'll develop my own-label brand and if I do it well I should make more net margin doing it.' Few brand owners (notable exceptions were P&G, Kellogg, Mars and Lever) have been able to resist the seductive short-term financial gains from supplying this very same own-label themselves. They managed to ignore the strategic realities of what they were conceding in doing this, without much resistance. In the longer term, the brand owners were simply putting their heads in an ever-tightening noose. It is not now difficult to see where the cards are held. The ongoing turf wars over retailers' 'look-alike' imitation brands are one further obvious indication of the amount of ground the brands have lost to own-label in modern food markets, and this phenomenon has been more significant in the UK than elsewhere in the world.

Relationships with suppliers have been pursued in a world of some growing public unease, the manufacturers for the most part content to keep their heads down, but with ultimately only one winner. In their ability to manage relationships in local communities, retailers have been increasingly adept, given the apparent difficulty of the opening positions in which they found themselves. Negotiating with planners was never easy, but at the end of the day, most planning authorities have bowed to a combination of consumer apathy – or even tacit support for the new supermarket sites – and the ability of the retailers to 'sweeten the pill' on their arrival in a new locality. Programmes of support for local activities and projects were funded by the new community superstore owners. They were replacing long-established local industries, which through the 1970s and 1980s disappeared from the scene, as a part of the UK's swift and entirely unplanned transformation from a manufacturing to a service economy. Consumers and local communities for the most part have concluded that there was nothing much for them to lose. First the handsome new superstore with attractive, ultra-convenient one-stop shopping and lower prices arrived. Key local aspirations that had seemed too expensive to fulfil – cleaning up derelict areas, building sports fields and social centres were favourites – gained crucial new support. Hundreds of new jobs were immediately created. The only losers were the collections of locally-owned high-street stores which had for years been fighting a losing battle for custom, with prices that were perceived to be too high, parking that was inadequate and service that appeared and indeed often was both slow and old-fashioned. Furthermore, it was usually months or even years after the new superstore's arrival that the downside consequences became apparent.

One has to admire the skill with which the retailer chains played their hands in one community after another. Whether locally or nationally, the British model showed the new arrivals leading the way suffused in the kindliest of lights. New store openings were like large-scale day-long parties, bizarre but eagerly anticipated local events attended by huge hoop-la, and graced with figures of national importance or even notoriety. Meanwhile the biggest national benefactors have themselves been food retailers. Efficient Sainsbury's altruistically bale out an incompetent and mendicant Opera House and build the imposing new eponymous wing for the National Gallery. Go-ahead Tesco help to rescue a confused and under-resourced Millennium Dome, and give valuable computers for underfunded schools to help out the education budget. Managing national and local interfaces with sensitivity but determination has been a noticeable ongoing feature of the success of British operators, more so than in surrounding countries where, in a more clandestine trading environment, the big European retail dynasties lacked the imagination or the acumen to do the same. Ultimately they found growth and margins more limited and the application of resources much more constrained.

TWO CONCLUSIONS – AT HOME, AND IN THE WORLD

Has it worked? In the end, for any industry, this is what really matters. In crucial respects, as we will show later, British food retailers can realistically claim to have led the world. The inherent style, quality and variety of the British supermarket is the equal of anything the rest of the world can offer. It offers a much more diverse range than the United States, which has had longer to learn, has many more stores and is five times our size. The UK is today often seen as the world's most innovative retail market. Presentation and range, including adventurous new chilled food and meal solutions are product fields that the rest of the world is still discovering, where it is difficult to fault UK sourcing energies or innovative drive. Next there is own-label playing an increasingly important and developmental role in this respect. Efficiency, the ability to manage systems and logistics effectively, and to extract costs from operations is a third area where long-term progress has been immensely impressive, albeit in an environment where it could be argued that the dice have for a decade been loaded in the store operators' favour and where the store operation's cost-reduction has spelt endemic weakness for many brands and demise for small suppliers. Developments of the same IT tools that have driven cost efficiency for many years are now beginning to influence the components of individual customer service advantage and store loyalty. Again the brands and their owners will be playing at best an auxiliary role in this process.

INFORMATION TECHNOLOGY

Like most firms, the food retailers have adopted IT over the last decades. Unlike some, they have done so spectacularly well, becoming world leaders in their field. The different groups moved at varying paces, with sometimes one leading, then another; but such has been the competitive importance of success in IT that all have kept at least in touch with the leading edge.

Like most users, they started with simple financial systems, and at first moved only slowly to more sophisticated applications. The early developments were in warehouse management, and store-level inventory. In the warehouse, early progress was on productivity, optimizing layout, making picking more efficient. Vehicle-scheduling was another area where early gains could be made using hard data and automated models. The first half of the 1980s saw major progress in these areas. The approach varied: Argyll developed its own systems, while Sainsbury's and Tesco bought systems and modified them. Asda started centralized, as did Sainsbury's, Tesco started decentralized but moved to centralization.

The big step forward came in the mid-1980s with bar codes and EPOS (electronic point of sale). Bar codes and scanning are now commonplace, but they were a revolutionary change for retailers. Now they have, potentially at least, an enormously rich source of vital data. They can measure – in real time if they wish – exactly what is being sold, where. Focus moved from store- to product-level, and real efficiencies could be made, for example in space allocation. In the late 1980s and early 1990s, the chains moved to sales-based ordering, led by Tesco and Safeway. Given that the retailers had taken over control of most of the supply chain by now (with their own distribution centres mainly replacing wholesalers and direct store deliveries from manufacturers), they could squeeze costs out of the chain. They were applying the principles of just-in-time delivery, but since they could measure and control so much of the process, they could do it remarkably effectively. Goods spend less time in depots, and arrive fresher. Developments such as cross-docking – in which goods arrive at a distribution centre in one lorry, and are picked directly into other vehicles for onward delivery to stores – reduced costs even further.

> It is widely accepted that, in terms of integrated logistics and supply chain management, the major UK food retailers were significantly ahead (perhaps as much as ten years) of the North American equivalents at this time, and also in advance of their major continental European rivals.
>
> (Wrigley, 1998c)

Current logistics systems are so sophisticated that, whereas a one-hour delay in a delivery used to be a problem, now a 10-minute delay appears in an exception report to the IT Director of Tesco. Fork-lift trucks in warehouses are fitted with a computer terminal, and if the terminal is not working, the truck cannot work. In the most modern warehouse, a machine can be programmed to sort products so that each cage is automatically loaded with the heaviest goods at the bottom, and with all products for a certain part of the destination store in the same cage. Deliveries are scheduled throughout the day and night, so goods spend the minimum time in the stores (leading to the reduction of back-of-store inventory, thereby freeing up space to be converted to selling area). Current developments include movements from electronic data exchange (EDI) (see 'Into the Acronym Jungle' on page 21) to extranets, where preferred suppliers at least can access the retailer's system directly.

The sophistication of these systems has two implications: investment and robustness. All the major retailers have had to invest very large sums in IT, not only in hardware and software, but in staff and training. While IT costs are small relative to total store development programmes, they are nevertheless significant, running into hundreds of millions of pounds. The second implication is that the business can, quite literally, not run without IT. As we saw in Chapter 4 on Safeway, even a short downtime can have serious effects if reliable back-up procedures are not in place.

The other side of the coin is customers. The 1990s has become the decade of the customer, and supermarkets have unrivalled knowledge of customer behaviour. Early uses of IT were such things as multi-buys, where a three-for-two offer can be implemented even though the products go through the till scattered through the basket. These, and similar developments such as linksave (a special price for strawberries and cream, for example), lend themselves to promotion, and to exact measurement of the effectiveness of that promotion.

This led to the next major step change – the introduction of loyalty cards by Safeway and Tesco (Safeway was the first to trial its ABC card, but Tesco launched its own card nationally first). As is now well known, when all or most of the competitors offer a similar card (Sainsbury's followed, apparently reluctantly), then no one gains a permanent advantage in attracting or keeping customers. On the other hand, loyalty cards bring scanning data to individual purchase level: the retailer can now tell not only what it is selling, but who is buying what. This is a huge step forward, potentially allowing very sophisticated analysis and targetting.

It is perhaps as well to stress *potentially*, as the volumes of data produced are also huge, and the task of reducing them to manageable proportions is significant. There is much talk of data warehousing, data mining and neural network techniques to produce sophisticated and surprising results. The only one always quoted is the supposed placing of beer next to disposable nappies (diapers), on the grounds that data analysis showed that the two items were often purchased in the same basket (the new parent, unable to go out for the night, gets in all the necessary supplies). There may be other striking examples, but such results, if useful to the retailer, are commercially sensitive and very unlikely to be publicized.

We do know that the major chains are using card data to derive finer and finer customer segments, and are moving towards that elusive goal of one-to-one marketing.

For their first letter to card holders, Tesco sent out six different versions. In late 1998, they sent a mailing with 60,000 different versions. They aim eventually to delight each customer with an individually tailored letter. All the groups are experimenting with methods of analysis and application of loyalty data. They can now segment within a customer base, by store, moving back from the total standardization that centralization previously meant. Those who master this area quickest will gain real competitive advantage.

Consumers will nearly always say, whether spontaneously or prompted, that they are happy with the choice offered, regretting neither the absence of competitively-priced local shops carrying a decent range, nor the recognizable quality of a more deeply-rooted national food culture, with outstanding local produce and food advice such as is offered in say, France, or Italy at their best. The eight leading UK retailers are a heterogeneous group but they have battled bravely, and mostly successfully, to retain the initiative against the efforts of would-be invaders. Neither Carrefour blazing its adventurous world trail, discounters with the hardest European track records (Aldi, Netto, Ed and Lidl), strong German and Dutch concerns (eg Makro), nor the best of the US warehouse clubs (CostCo) have made any significant inroads for any length of time. Fortress Britain had remained inviolate and alone of developed markets until, that is, June 1999 when, in spite of Wal-Mart's Chairman, David Glass, dismissing such talk as speculation, an agreed takeover bid was announced with Asda.

In the bright new era of the 1990s where category partnerships are the order of the day, it is the retailers who hold the whip hand within these consortia. They can generate cost savings and innovative opportunity from the partnership to fuel their volume and margin growth, compensating for the decline in the importance of food in the family budget. It is not clear that brand manufacturers can expect similar gains to be made. The conclusion is that that the British grocery retailing model works for British consumers, and may become a pattern for deregulated markets elsewhere when similar economic and trading conditions exist.

There has been one major downside. The continuing dominance of a few key chains seems to have made UK companies complacent about the global opportunity, and leaden-footed when it comes to exploiting their skills outside the UK. Sallies abroad have been modestly conceived and too often operationally ineffective. Sainsbury's has held a significant US presence for 15 years and were one of the first foreign companies to put down a US marker, but despite recent acquisitions, it is now viewed as a bystander while consolidation sweeps at furious pace across the United States. Tesco, which started later, preferred to build a European base, initially failing dismally. Its recent moves into Ireland, central Europe and Thailand have been more purposefully managed, but Tesco itself would accept that it remains a pawn in today's world market. Asda's domestic acquisition policies have been random and opaque, and during the 1980s, simply wrong-headed. Its statements suggest that it is now prepared to accept the role of a respectable national player. It may doubt its ability to survive as the market shakes out in the years ahead, and world predators decide to tackle the British market. If so, similar dark premonitions will be exercising the leaders' minds in the Safeway and Somerfield board-rooms. The Waitrose partnership, Morrison and Marks & Spencer can, for contrasting reasons, treat such disturbing trends with relative sang-froid.

The abiding lesson is that control and dominance, exercised through satisfying domestic consumer needs, is a defensible strategy at least while markets are isolated. Once conditions change, it is harder for even the strong domestic companies to move outside their borders than it is for those operating in tighter, more regulated markets, where they have had to become international or stagnate. In the long run, this may be Ahold's, Carrefour's and even Wal-Mart's most powerful asset.

WHAT HAS DRIVEN UK RETAILER STRATEGIES?

The UK industry has pursued a course of development that is radically different from Europe's and indeed until recently from the United States's. Why have strategies been so different in economies and societies that in other respects have so much in common? As long as a company is privately owned, its strategy is defined by its owner/manager. Its objectives, profitability and rate of growth will depend on their ambitions, drive or interests. As soon as the company becomes public, different constraints appear. One of the striking differences between the French and UK markets has been the extent to which French supermarkets have remained family controlled. In the UK, and unlike their predecessors (independents and co-operative stores), all major groups have been publicly owned for more than two decades and although, in some cases, family influence has been influential, the power of the UK stock-market culture has meant that even family-controlled managements have had to deliver what the stock market wants. It is interesting to contrast the margins earned by Sainsbury's, for example, when it was private (1–2 per cent) with its subsequent drive to the 'normal' market leader margins of 6 or 7 per cent or even higher.

On the Anglo-Saxon model, investors buy and sell shares in public companies on the basis of expected future total returns from dividends and capital growth. As capital growth is itself driven by expected future profits (apart from any speculative bid premium) then we can simplify by saying that the company has to deliver constantly growing sales and profits. This UK supermarkets have done, with consistency – hence their rating as excellent defensive stocks at a time of market downturn – and sometimes spectacularly, as with Sainsbury's in the 1980s.

If they are aiming for a national presence and for substantial market share, food stores cannot segment the market the way a manufacturer's brand can. It is simply too expensive not to aim to serve the majority of shoppers in their location, providing them with the majority of their shopping needs. Failing to do this limits economies of scale that underpin the current supermarket model. Thus in the UK attempts by the leaders to run separate fascias have usually not lasted. France and Germany seem to be different partly because of different ownership and capital structures, but perhaps because they have not yet realized they could make more money by sacrificing historical fascia loyalty for greatly improved efficiencies. Equally, however, the discounter history from the beginnings in both Germany and France has been substantial and very different to the UK's.

Supermarket sales are produced by total selling area times sales density and much of the successful chains' growth has been fuelled by increasing selling space. Once the superstore model was established as the one that was universally successful in the UK, the race was on to acquire as many sites as possible. The rate at which they did so reflects several factors:

1. The historic store portfolios (so Asda, with no history, could concentrate single-mindedly on large sites from the outset, while Sainsbury's and Tesco with extensive holdings could change only at more measured pace.)
2. Management's recognition of the opportunity (again Asda to its enormous credit were the first to grasp the superstore model with only Yorkshire-neighbour Morrison following quickly). Safeway, inheriting a very mixed bag of shops to lick into manageable shape, were hampered in their aspirations to join the big-store race.
3. There is the inherent attitude to risk – Sainsbury's being notably risk-averse through its history, and therefore in the 1980s expanding its big store sites more slowly than other market leaders might have done, and very much more slowly than Tesco did.
4. Availability of capital (Asda's problems under Hardman were that his ambitions outran the ability of his company to fund them. The Norman/Leighton position, that they were not looking for rapid expansion of new sites, was more likely a de facto recognition that they simply did not have the cash.) See 'A Note on Capital Intensity' on page 226.

A NOTE ON CAPITAL INTENSITY

A peculiar feature of the UK supermarket industry has been that it is far more capital intensive than that in other countries. This stems, firstly, from certain aspects of the UK property scene. Britain is a small country, and land for development is scarce and therefore expensive. During a long period of generally rising prosperity and therefore demand, it has become more scarce (as Mark Twain noted, 'They've stopped making it'). In these circumstances, leases always contain regular, upward-only rent reviews. Ownership of commercial sites is concentrated among institutional investors, who are interested only in their capital gains and revenue streams. British leasehold law allows the lessor to recover all rent due from the head lessee, even though the lease may have been assigned, often many times. The original lessee may thus find that – when the latest tenant has defaulted, and even if the premises are shuttered – the owner will pursue him for all rent owing. British supermarkets have therefore concentrated almost entirely on freehold properties.

Further, the planning authorities have insisted on high building standards, so the cheap, large sheds typical of continental or US hypermarkets are not an option for the UK grocers. One estimate suggests that a US supermarket can be built for half the cost of its UK equivalent.

High investment has also been needed for the IT systems on which a modern retail chain depends. It would be impossible to run a group of several hundred stores, each with 20,000 or more SKUs, without a formidably effective IT system (or, at least, it is theoretically possible to imagine such an operation, but the sheer cost and inefficiency that would have to be built in beggar belief). Such sophisticated systems do not come cheap, and all the UK chains have invested hundreds of millions of pounds over the years in IT.

Finally, compared with France at least, UK retailers have to fund more of their own working capital. In France, the large food retailers take at least 90 days credit from their suppliers; in Britain, the figure is nearer 30 days. UK manufacturers may feel that they are supplying their retail customers with much of their working capital, along with their products, but the situation is much worse elsewhere.

High capital investment has thus been forced on the UK chains, and has dictated much of their strategy; they *have* to achieve high margins.

Their drive for efficiency has led them inexorably to the superstore format (seemingly unique to Britain, because of the size and population density), and to take over much of the distribution chain themselves. Return on capital, the ultimate measure of profitability, shows that they achieve similar results to their competitors elsewhere – higher margins, but much higher investment to service (see 'Profitability' on page 214).

CAPITAL INVESTMENT

Apart from sheer number of sites the skill lies in finding the best locations and the optimal size for that location. While planning policies looked on benignly, and the stock market was content to fund expansion, the main supermarkets have been good at this. Lately, as planning has tightened, and fewer sites have become available, they have adapted by looking at inner-city (Tesco Metro) or market-town, medium-size stores – three of the four majors and indeed Somerfield all have working models. Location is the single most important factor in the shopper's store choice, so all the companies would like to be represented in the majority of catchment areas of the country – but there is a limit to the number of shops and superstores that an area can support. Quite apart from public-policy constraints, saturation has now been reached in most parts of the country. On this basis the PPG6 regulations can be regarded as nothing more than a late-in-the-day bowing to the inevitable.

The other part of the equation – sales density – is where pure retailing skills come to the fore. The fact that Sainsbury's has led the field for most of the period, until recently by a significant margin, underlines their reputation. We cannot ignore the effect of location of course but it is hard to separate the major competitors on that score, certainly not Tesco and Sainsbury's, so what other factors account for the differences? We need to recognize how the answer to this question has changed over our lifetime, what the present position is, and how it may evolve again into the future. Before answering the question let us consider the illustrative case of Sainsbury's.

SAINSBURY'S – CRUCIAL FACTORS IN TWO IMPREGNABLE DECADES

Only one company has ever dominated the market for a significant length of time and that was Sainsbury's. (The co-operative movement had a dominating share for many years but the seeds of its demise were present as soon as self-service took over. Tesco have built a lead now but four or so years is a short time to be ahead.) Sainsbury's manifestation of strength through the two decades of the 1970s and 1980's can be attributed to three factors – a winning brand strategy, effective implementation at store level, and powerful unyielding leadership. We can examine these factors in turn.

THE STRENGTH OF BRAND STRATEGY

The Sainsbury's strategy derived from brilliant, century-long development, but it was equally effective as a management tool in driving forward policies and actions for the future. The twin notions of improving food range and quality, coupled with a presentation that 'good food costs less' at Sainsbury's were strongly-positioned cornerstones. Building from its unique dairy heritage, Sainsbury's created and nurtured a perception of company and brand pre-eminence, a reputation founded in fresh and dairy foods which, through meticulously faithful attention wherever it might matter, became a virtue consumers were prepared to attribute to an entire food portfolio. Even in the highest performance categories, Sainsbury's own-label was always a benchmark that had to be taken with the utmost seriousness. In most sectors it represented the most serious challenge to the performance of the brand leaders and in some cases it could reckon to leave the manufacturer brand performance behind. It invariably set the best retailer brands standards – wine was an early and surprising example in a market where the depth of specialist British knowledge had existed for centuries.

Sainsbury's caught up within a decade and other retailers have now followed and matched them, changing the supply patterns – most would say for the better – in the most traditional of markets. The Sainsbury's brand in all its markets was backed by a carefully engineered, typically clinical presentation, consistent across the entire store range. High volume growth and entrenched operating efficiencies then made the company cost- and margin-leader by a distance. This wheel of commercial virtue enabled Sainsbury's continuously to raise its own standards, and reinvest in food range and quality as well as diversifying into new stores (Homebase, Savacentre, US Shaw's Giant and

Star were all examples). Its polished and powerful community ethic shone brightly, locally and nationally. Sainsbury's kept a close watch on the pulse of opinion leaders, who could occasionally find themselves shopping in competitors' stores, but deep down knowing reliable Sainsbury's to be the gold standard, they felt slightly ashamed of being temporarily led astray. The strategy was crystal-clear, and it was effective. Sainsbury's employees and managers alike understood its implications – or else!

COST-EFFECTIVE EFFICIENT IMPLEMENTATION AT STORE LEVEL

For many years, if they were honest, Tesco management just wanted to get within shooting distance of Sainsbury's performance levels. Nor indeed was there anything wrong with the notion. For Sainsbury's second crucial advantage was effective store-level implementation. 'Retail is detail' is a favourite saying of aficionados and Sainsbury's at all levels was visible testimony to this enduring truth. Store management and planning, distribution, supply systems, the management of fixed and working capital cost, and net return on assets were the specific measures where Sainsbury's led comprehensively. Store expansion never overreached itself and was handled at a sensible pace that kept returns consistently high, and store traffic at its maximum. Rarely did Sainsbury's contract for more space than it could plan ahead it would soon need. Delivery of best value across the food range was spontaneously associated with the company.

Although consumers knew that Sainsbury's was rarely cheapest, or even in any absolute sense either cheap or low-priced, they were persuaded that its track record of food-quality control had no value rival on the high street. Sainsbury's in turn watched competitors and their innovations, as it did its own suppliers and theirs like hawks. It took the responsibility to lead in and enforce market discipline, both in terms of standards, where it set a hurdle others might aspire to but not cross, and in pricing, where it knew exactly how much room for manoeuvre it would give competitors. 'Not much' was the customary answer, other than when dealing with an iconoclastic and unrepresentative Kwik Save whose customers would not be attracted to Sainsbury's stores anyway. It was regarded as an acceptable national low-price point-marker, a position Sainsbury's never intended itself to be found occupying, so entirely different from the Sainsbury's kind of store as to be *sui generis*, and therefore permitted, in catering for hard-up shoppers patronizing poor stores, to behave differently. The rest of the market was invited to fit themselves somewhere in between the two poles, and not surprisingly they usually did just this.

Manufacturers and suppliers were accorded the famous Stamford Street glacial courtesy, preparing themselves in advance, rather like for a bad day at the dentist's, to be hauled over the coals as soon as anything went wrong, and often indeed well before this happened. Sharing of worthwhile market information was philosophically discouraged, on the grounds that one doesn't normally show the tradesmen where the family silver is kept, and negotiations were invariably protracted and tough. One major manufacturer who had 'must stock' brands that provided Sainsbury's with margins regarded as inadequate through the late 1980s was invited arbitrarily by the Sainsbury's operations director to cut his brand distribution list in half – with the additional incentive to 'choose which half – if you don't, I will!' By 1990, Sainsbury's were cock-of-the-walk, masters of the ultimate virtuous circle – leading scale efficiencies, lowest costs, best systems, and possessors of a uniquely well-rated brand reputation with which only Marks & Spencer in their own niche could compete. To go with a winning brand strategy, it was unquestioned implementation leader. How could this ever change?

THE CHARACTER OF THE LEADER

A third factor played a significant part in Sainsbury's dominance. That was the nature of the leadership exercised as it had been from their very beginnings by a succession of family chairmen, firmly from the top. The company had been private and family-owned for a century when it floated in 1973. Through a succession of overlapping family directors, and persistent adherence to long-term goals, a powerful autocratic leadership culture developed and was recognized and even admired inside and outside the company. Senior appointments were thought about years before they happened, canvassed with care and managed seamlessly over a lengthy time period. One has the clearest impressions of the style of leadership that was exercised – determined, clear-thinking, risk-averse, Calvinist and thoroughly steeped in managing for results at each and every level.

This ethos reached its culmination and had its most masterly exponent with John (later Lord Sainsbury of Preston Candover) in the quarter-century from 1968 onwards. Particularly towards the end of his tenure as chairman, it seems that achievement of the most crucial public results (profits and EPS growth especially) had become the uniquely important yardstick. The business was a wonderfully predictable colossus and it knew how to respond to a trusted leader's call. Today we might describe it as a dependency culture. 'We know best' can certainly be applied to Sainsbury's plc as the 1990s dawned. It was impregnable, a well-oiled money-making machine, gliding smoothly forward on all cylinders, regarded by friend and foe alike as incapable of being caught.

HOW COULD IT CHANGE?

But caught it was, and the change can be attributed to all three elements that created unique UK-industry dominance for it. At a strategic level, Sainsbury's brand had merely been 'going through the innovative motions', no longer intent on distancing its rivals. Marks & Spencer had with unexpected rudeness elbowed Sainsbury's out of the driving seat. Suddenly, overnight, everyone seemed to be talking with a sense of wonder about the food revolution their new meals were creating. Professional metropolitan dinner parties, attended by those same opinion leaders who Sainsbury's had courted so assiduously were found to be buying and even relying on them, creating a kind of social revolution in its own right.

Waitrose in London had growing aspirations, and Sainsbury's gap against other majors, Tesco included, had narrowed to invisibility. Consistency of presentation was still there but uniformity had become boring when others were changing style, recognizing that novelty and entertainment needed to engage customers and play a more important role. The core notion 'good food costs less' had lost all salience, and literally *meant less* to consumers, if indeed it had ever meant anything very much in recent years. Not surprisingly, Sainsbury's then abandoned it, for a range of other hastily adopted and equally rapidly jettisoned advertising claims. Results remained good, but an increasingly confident Tesco was catching up, applying the tactics of the fast follower and using many of the weapons that Sainsbury's had itself adopted to gain leadership – better information systems and relationships playing key parts. Some of the Sainsbury's diversifications, notably Shaw's and then Giant Foods in the United States were not producing the expected results and diluted overall company performance without carrying any compensating benefit in terms of added reputation or globally applicable competitive learning advantage.

The gap in implementation took longer for others to bridge. However, by the 1990s the combination of Tesco's value lines with specific customer service developments and a focussed relaunch of Asda on a clear promise of lower prices and better value was chipping away at Sainsbury's market-leading position from two different vantage points. It was an unpleasant pincer movement to which Sainsbury's was uncertain how to react. Along with pricing and value, and the challenge to its status as a food-quality leader, almost unthinkably, at this very time, Sainsbury's confronted exceptional problems with the availability of product on its store shelves, deriving apparently from hasty and premature adoption of new SBO (sales-based reordering) procedures. Competition was still monitored closely, but it was no longer Sainsbury's alone who was in a position to exert leadership in standards or pricing. The mailed fist that governed suppliers' contracts was still the formidable and widely resented

Sainsbury's tool. Alert competitors were stealing a march by committing with their competitors to the category-management approach, thus strengthening manufacturer and retailer relationships at key interfaces, and leaving Sainsbury's isolated and frozen into its own individual but mechanistic supplier approaches. To summarize – Sainsbury's virtuous circle of efficiency and leadership had been forfeited as market aspirations moved in some new directions.

Then came the biggest change of all. As everyone in Sainsbury's had expected for years, but timed for the moment when strategy was wearing thinnest, and implementation efficiency being forfeited, leadership changed – David taking over from cousin John at the top. They may have had the same name but they were like chalk and cheese (see 'Chalk and Cheese' on page 62) with divergent and deeply conflicting views of the management task. It was always inevitable that the big changes needed to develop a rejuvenated firm would be perilously delicate to steer. The supremely confident approach, directed by a succession of dynastic family chairmen, would be much less appropriate to a dynamic new competitive situation where the company was no longer automatically stationed in pole position on the grid. What Sainsbury's needed was a new phalanx of quick-thinking retailing pioneers, change agents and creators of a learning company, and it needed innovation, driven from all levels, not just from the top as had been for long its accepted if unwritten convention. David quickly perceived that it needed quickly a new and more inclusive business culture within Sainsbury's, as befitted the best of corporate business which he had studied at Columbia in his formative years. Strategy to create new sources of functional advantage was required, and life and relevance to be infused into a trusted but dull and anonymous brand. Diversification policies required root and branch reappraisal, just as new global opportunity and new worldwide competitors were making their presence felt. This combination of fundamental challenges was, and remains today, a very tall order indeed and it is not yet clear that Sainsbury's has found leaders who understand or have the ability and persistence to respond to them.

WHAT IS COMPETITIVE ADVANTAGE FOR THE MODERN RETAILER?

The Sainsbury's example illustrates how competitive advantage can be gained and lost. The dominant reputation that Sainsbury's created was derived from a combination of factors, and its loss was caused by complex change and an absence of appropriate reactions. One can draw conclusions about what constitutes sustainable advantage for modern UK retailers. They have secured a position where turnover, profitability, employment levels and market power place them right at the forefront of UK corporate life. How did they reach this position, what is sustaining it today, and what might happen in the future? The three answers are different.

Competitive advantage has been broad-ranging, and while winners and losers have existed, the major players – certainly the big four – have all been able to exercise the criteria we note below within their individual competencies. Hitherto they have grown with the buoyancy of their market and in tandem. In reaching today's position, *location* – the creation of large stores on highly accessible sites with significant dedicated same-level free parking and easy commercial vehicle access – has been crucial. Limited competition in the catchment area from similar stores, has been the concomitant 'location' driver of the volume and profits growth which the key players have succeeded in managing simultaneously.

Size has been the next key determinant of success. From the days in which the ability to hold ranges of stock that the smaller independent stores could not match to today's platform where the 40,000 sq ft superstore creates enormous potential, size and the lure of convenient one-stop shopping has been a key driver that attracts increasing numbers of time-poor shoppers. Size can accommodate range, and the numbers of SKU's stocked by the biggest stores has risen steadily and seems certain to go on rising. Targetting range as specific advantage has been a weapon that Asda uses confidently, and Safeway seeks to emulate. One-stop shopping is the core advantage, and as consumers find more things to do with their lives, is the pattern which seems to have taken the firmest of roots, certainly in the UK and the United States (hence the over 100 all-product supercenters with 200,000 sq ft of space that Wal-Mart is building annually). It will be difficult to accommodate Wal-Mart's space requirements in many situations in the UK, but the principle remains the same – space gives flexibility, and flexibility means more capacity both for product innovation and effective asset management. Those who are weak on this dimension – Somerfield for instance – point out that not everyone votes for the mammoth superstore experience, but even David Simons admits that its attractiveness for the majority outweighs the problems that minorities experience.

Size advantage is greater when the superstore is able to create potential for further specialist stores to set up on the same site – in effect creating a new shopping community in its entirety. With size goes scale efficiency. Scale creates efficiencies at the chain level, nationally and locally at store level. Size provides economies – eg in logistics, merchandising and own-label development – and confirms competitive strength in purchasing, negotiating with suppliers, planners, employees even whole communities. Size also enables the chain to manage its portfolio of stock-keeping units effectively, generating margin growth while maintaining price reputation – it provides necessary room for constant tactical pricing manoeuvre, yet still retaining an overall reputation for offering value.

Price is itself a component of advantage. Shoppers in the UK, and indeed across the developed world, will spontaneously claim it as the primary requirement, recognizing in their reply that responsible homemakers ought to know what the prices they pay are. Alas, they don't. Most have only the vaguest awareness of the overall price differences between stores, or indeed of the prices of most of the same items stocked by different stores. Nonetheless, while no mainstream full-range retailer can allow the price gap between themselves and the market 'floor' price to become significant, none can ever – on UK market evidence to date – hope to make price their abiding differential advantage. Wal-Mart may in time decide to challenge this premise and may have the best chance to become an exception to the rule.

Successful retailers have succeeded in managing their price reputation or image and recognize that it is a balancing act which requires consistent quality, range, service and price management that promotes a reputation for fair dealing and constantly stimulates consumer confidence. Sainsbury's achieved this for many years with the 'good food costs less' signature. Today Morrison succeeds with its value statement. Tesco, in a series of linked initiatives, is intent on furthering its reputation today. Safeway have over time been associated with higher price and (cf. Carrefour vs. Leclerc in France, in a fine example quoted by Corstjens, 1995) find this damaging perception, once established, tremendously difficult to eliminate. Asda traditionally maintained a small but distinct real shopping basket reduction in its favour, and in days when Kwik Save were a low-price dynamic, priced itself just below the remaining majors, but clearly above Kwik Save. While neither rigidly adopted nor, obviously, ever written down, it was a well understood framework for the participants, but the accepted Kwik Save floor has now disappeared which makes the process for those who remain more volatile and, in a sense, rudderless.

Shopping experience has been a further area where competitors have looked for differentiation. For many years Sainsbury's perceived brand quality and consistent presentation set a standard that the market flirted with but could not, through any length of time, aspire to or deliver. However, others have caught up and consumer evidence suggests that there is little if any difference between the four majors in this regard. The smaller companies have taken important initiatives. The Consumers' Association records that Waitrose achieves objectively much higher response rates for service satisfaction. Morrison has created an individual framework and makes splendid use of innovative design and layout as differentiation. Marks & Spencer, on a limited range, have a reputation lead and for the time being have replaced Sainsbury's as the food-quality bell-wether. But the fact is that advantage generated in this area is short-lived. It is necessary to achieve improvements, which consumers will often notice and appreciate, but they will be insufficient to create any permanent sustainable advantage.

The brand is probably the crucial strategic area of differentiation to consider. Manufacturers created brands to establish lasting consumer relationships directly rather than through unwanted middlemen. Today retailers, wresting power back, have created their own brands, the impetus for which was, ironically, the especially poorer margins stores made on big and aggressively marketed manufacturers' brands, often priced by all the major retailers from time to time as virtual loss leaders. Yesterday's manufacturer brand scale advantage has become today's insoluble problem – the best brands created a powerful stick with which the best retailers now take pleasure in beating them. Own-label brands have been a key element in helping the retailer to control the manufacturer, but have so far had a more limited role in differentiating individual retailers one from another. The early own-labels, which were low quality and often generics, threatened the weak, unadvertised manufacturer brands most, and initially leading brands believed they had 'seen them off', using their proprietary R&D and better consumer marketing.

Increasingly, however, the potential for high-quality own-label is being recognized, and in important product fields, say chilled foods for example, own-label now leads innovation and has the lion's share of sales. Sainsbury's saw the potential long before anyone else, but it is now Marks & Spencer (100 per cent own-label), followed by Waitrose, and indeed the whole range of Sainsbury's major competitors who can see the benefits of upgrading own-label to create sustainable advantage. Who will emerge as the leader of the movement to use own-label or the retailer brand for discriminating advantage is not yet clear, but the potential is widely understood and everyone will be trying.

It is here that *information development* and focus play an important role. For some years massive focus has existed among all the supermarket operators to put in place information systems directed towards increasing efficiencies from all parts of the supply chain. The industry as a whole became expert in producing year-on-year cost improvements from the myriad aspects of better purchasing, stock and distribution planning, and all elements of business systems and logistics that created cost in the retail supply chain. While the biggest gains were usually made by the largest companies, (Sainsbury's but later Tesco have led the way), everyone had no choice but to participate to stay in touch with a fast-improving set of industry benchmarks. Naturally much of the efficiency and cost reductions were attributable to more efficient supplier networks, and the pressure to deliver was felt by suppliers across the board. The chains were perfectly able to insist on efficiency savings as a condition of stocking and supporting supplier brands and initiatives. Through time the process became more comprehensive and disciplined, and it was at this stage that genuinely strategic systems improvement as well as cost-effectiveness programmes were mounted in specific market sectors, under the overall heading of category management initiatives. By this means, partnerships were put together to exert a more synergistic (win–win) pressure on efficiencies, and use shared activities to produce even greater savings. Category leaders and captains have been the owners of these programmes which are now widely adopted by all the key companies.

However, it is from the later application of specific new data-based information in the consumer service and marketing area that even greater and more individual advantage will be obtained. Loyalty schemes are the public face of this movement (see 'The Pursuit of Loyalty' on page 39) and they are becoming an omnipresent element in retailer marketing programmes. While the expertise to use the data generated effectively and imaginatively at disaggregated levels is still in its infancy, there is little doubt that, at the individual level, using this data for individual customer advantage will have enormous potency for specific retailer advantage. The best of the brand manufacturers have also invested very heavily in developing and understanding these individual data banks, and the promotion programmes that they can deliver – Coca-Cola, Campbells, and Unilever have made big progress, but the first major investor in the field was P&G, both in the US as well as the UK, and they now have a time advantage against the rest of the market. This subject, so crucial to future retail leadership, is dealt with again in the final section of this chapter – 'Where Britain leads the world'.

Cultural and human factors have been key determinants of success. The retailing winners have been lucky or clever enough to attract and retain *strong leaders*, able to marry strategy to extracting improving operating results. Sainsbury's had an astonishing series of outstanding family leaders for a century. The 20 years when MacLaurin with Malpas and the rest of the team moved Tesco ahead, then read the signals and accomplished a smooth handover to Leahy, ranks as the most effective leadership continuity over two decades. Safeway rationalized a portfolio with a wise and practical troika of managers – led by Grant and latterly by Webster, who has a formidable task on his hands. Asda veered uneasily between brilliance and waywardness, eventually creating a platform for turn-around treatment from a strategic analyst (Norman) and a consumer marketing man (Leighton). Holding to and then evolving a winning strategy is very demanding. Morrison has had the paterfamilias directing growth for 30 years, his determination a visible measure of success. Simons has come up with the goods, keeping his head well above water, with only Somerfield's odd collection of assets.

The impression is that the human component, and specifically the quality of consistent leadership has been a discriminator, par excellence, and this industry has been lucky to have had more than its share of performers able to marry strategic vision for the longer term with delivery of operating results satisfying increasingly demanding shareholders. Most of them, typically, have had many years in the chairman's or chief executive's office – stability has been the norm.

Staying with the human factors, the ability to *focus* (for differentiated advantage) and the possession of *humility* in the organization's culture have played a major part in long-term retail success. There is a suggestion with the most significant companies that there may be a model that exists to describe the behaviour of the leaders, which they must understand and ultimately avoid before it becomes self-destructive. Business success is achieved and through time and constant repetition becomes an expected norm of the organization. Arrogance follows – Sainsbury's fell prey to this but perhaps briefly Tesco too was beginning to fall into a similar trap in 1993. With arrogance comes complacency, and inevitably as a consequence poor performance and failure follow. Sainsbury's triumphed because of intense focus on doing what it did best, following maxims first instilled in the company by the founder. Alongside this dedication a genuine sense of business humility, a desire for constant product and store improvement played its part in Sainsbury's progress, a factor that began to diminish in the years after the business became both a public company and a dominant market force.

Tesco moved in the opposite direction – from Cohen's incoherent braggadocio to a dawning recognition that it needed established priorities just to survive. There remains an anxiety to be measured as a high-level performer today at Tesco – there is no strain of detectable arrogance in this market leader's make-up. A willingness to stay simple and stick to delivering attainable goals is present in both Morrison and Waitrose. The outstanding example of cultural coherence has probably been Marks & Spencer, where the vision was driven by the concept of divine discontent, that knows it can do a better job, and will not rest until it has delivered it. In foods Marks & Spencer's leadership has accomplished this once, but needs now to create an encore to retain its reputation as a leading innovator. Today their entire business is in turmoil and it is difficult to see foods innovation being able to rescue them.

JOCKEYING FOR POSITION – WHERE KEY COMPETITORS SCORE

Strikingly, over half a century few periods of outright dominance exist. The industry points to this as a sign of mature and healthy competition, and there is truth in this. Since 1980 there have been four potentially leading companies, but realistically two leaders – Sainsbury's and Tesco. Asda has exercised influence at different stages in the market's evolution. The single-minded drive to build genuinely big stores, its northern strength and simplicity, and the heartland 'Asda price/better value' reputation have been principal assets. Inability to use these assets consistently has constrained earlier leadership aspirations. It is now too far behind in a maturing market to challenge without an alliance. Hence its own interest in merging with Safeway, denied at a national level and apparently on monopolistic arguments. Actually the gap between a merged Asda/Safeway and Tesco would be smaller than the gap that separates either from Sainsbury's and Tesco now. Asda may now be on the horns of a dilemma, needing continuing cost reductions to justify the Asda price strategy, but those very cost requirements are what is threatening availability and quality.

Safeway has sustained volume and profits growth, and built cohesion from indifferent sites and a weird initial assortment of regional franchises. Instilling order into this array has been Safeway's achievement, and it has committed to a high-quality Safeway fascia and created a recognizable brand with coherence from nothing – other than its US progenitor. Safeway's marketing strategy – steadily to slipstream Sainsbury's growth and presence while making Safeway more individual and welcoming – was capable of working for many years, but the strong performance of Tesco (whose 'every little helps' marched arrogantly through Safeway brand territory), coupled with Asda's resurgence in the 1990s seems to have stunted the approach, minimizing Safeway's points of difference. There has been anxiety about Safeway's price competitiveness and as Sainsbury's fell back, so, given its imitative approach, has Safeway.

Kwik Save's distinctive low price worked brilliantly for a time. The proposition was highly individualistic, widely accessible and uncomplicated, but it became a casualty of the arrival of the foreign discounters, who departed clutching most of Kwik Save's low-price clothes. Cost- and systems-effectiveness of better-resourced competitors exacted a further dose of pain, and unsurprisingly it then succumbed tamely to Somerfield advances. The original Kwik Save idea will be hard to resurrect, even if discounting takes off the UK. At its zenith Kwik Save held nearly 8 per cent of the market, above what the merged Somerfield/Kwik Save holds today. Somerfield itself is well managed and making progress but its deeply unimpressive store base makes it unlikely to be anything other than a reasonably profitable follower.

Morrison's consistent strategy worked in the north and it may from a distinctive base be ready to do the same further south. What happens when the redoubtable Ken Morrison gives up his baton is anyone's guess. Waitrose is even more differentiated. Privately owned, it too is small but it has ideas about service and quality difference, and its results are impressive. Marks & Spencer have been the phenomenon, the single radical innovator in terms of food delivery to consumers. Their prepared-foods offer is world class, effecting significant change to a UK industry which appreciated the requirement to raise standards overnight. They have difficult options to face in expanding their base.

All three of these distinctive companies are of insuffient size to grow to leadership. Whether they survive as independent retailers as global players with major investment move in, is itself a question. Hard discounters have made very limited progress, but Aldi is a formidable competitor, with a powerful European base. It would be a significant departure in the UK if Aldi were to make share gains, a sign that limited range and low price were becoming an attraction for a worthwhile consumer segment. A Wal-Mart investment may be just the catalyst this movement needs. This is the major anxiety, a vulnerability shared by one and all among the current industry participants.

Today's market confirms there is no potentially dominant player. Tesco's high energy and ambitions have given it a lead and management is both hungry and suitably anxious. It recognizes that a handful of years is a very short time to be top of the slippery pole. Its achievement is nonetheless remarkable. Tesco has married increasingly attractive consumer service with aggressive innovation. Without an upheaval or a major external acquisition its wide-awake team should not easily be caught.

WHERE BRITAIN LEADS THE WORLD

There are specifically three areas where British retailing performance has led world standards. Firstly the ability to attract high levels of capital investment over more than 30 years has, in a deregulated environment, built a position of virtual impregnability for the major superstore operators. The level of market saturation now achieved means that an aspiring entrant will be forced to acquire or merge with one of the existing major companies if it is to make significant market impact. The inability of the discounters, the clubs and foreign entrants to build strength from organic growth over several decades is evidence for this. While entry via purchase remains a strong possibility, the entry price will be high and a demanding investment market will require continuingly good results.

Secondly, British retailing companies have set a standard for own-label products, now legitimately called retailer brands, that has created world benchmarks. Only Migros has had a comparable element of influence and then within the tight boundaries of Switzerland. The reasons for this achievement and the peculiarity of the UK dynamics have been noted. What is undeniable is the determination that the best UK companies have shown in grasping the opportunity. Sainsbury's was the rate-determining step for many years. More than 10 years ago, half Sainsbury's business was already done in its own-label brand. High competence and an unwillingness to accept second-best standards created the brand's reputation, which was then fuelled by an ever-increasing range of categories where the Sainsbury's brand was seen to be the most innovative. Sainsbury's has now been caught by competitors who, while not yet seeking to emulate the high percentage of business that Sainsbury's achieve, do now match its standards both for quality and range. Meanwhile, as we have seen, the Marks & Spencer arrival in food, and particularly in prepared meals, sets a new UK and seemingly a world benchmark that has changed the market parameters. Americans willingly concede pre-eminence to Marks & Spencer, and it is worth noting, at a general level, that retailer brand penetration in the United States is still at a level less than half the UK average.

The third area where UK retail performance leads world standards is in its early adoption and performance of information-driven systems advantage and cost-effective operations. The potential came from rapid consolidation of an industry where a few scale operators compete on the same operating platforms and in close proximity. Systems advantage across the whole range of supply-chain activities thus became a major source of operating advantage, and it was simply impossible for any major player to afford to be left out. While Sainsbury's was the recognized leader in this set of disciplines, its leadership was not a permanent feature, and as new sources of information potential opened up, others were in a position to take their own initiatives. Tesco, from a zero base, made enormous progress through the 1980s in driving forward systems advantage in purchasing, distribution and logistics, and created a board function to handle this specifically. The role of the brand manufacturer became an important one since the ability to manage the supply chain as a shared activity opened up new areas for effective cost-management. At this stage, therefore, all the major operators are capable of creating further levels of information-driven advantage to which, through category management programmes, manufacturers are contributing and from which, in due course, the best will benefit most.

But it is in customer marketing that information will have most influence. The sources of data-driven advantage which retailers now possess to analyse and direct the purchasing behaviour of their loyal and occasional customers will be a key future weapon. The most significant manifestation has been in the adoption of loyalty cards and the ability that exists for retailers to use the purchasing records these provide to generate cost-effective growth. While Safeway was the earliest experimenter and made good progress in the field, it is Tesco who seems to have moved the activity forward with most determination, and who looks most likely to gain most from it. As we go to press it has announced a relaunch for its card in the summer. There are players who are prepared to sit the loyalty card development out (Asda, Morrison), but significantly they do not include Sainsbury's who is now participating. This is an area of information-driven leadership where UK developments now lead world performance, with only Wal-Mart's formidable array of skills and a limited number of other US companies such as H E Butt operating in the same league. UK companies have a major lead over continental Europeans in this area. The critical factor in successful exploitation will be the calibre and direction of the teams of people that companies can assemble to create measurable advantage from this source.

HOW COMPETITIVE ADVANTAGE IS NOW SET TO CHANGE

THE CONCLUSIONS

Four key competencies are most likely to determine competitor advantage in the UK market in the years ahead. They are:

- brand performance;
- customer-systems ingenuity;
- people and learning;
- mastery of global strategy.

A comment on why each is critical follows. There are of course many other elements of competence that have been able to drive retailer business success, which will remain important in the future but they are unlikely to generate differentiated strategic advantage per se. They include:

1. Pricing. Evidence suggests it is difficult to create leadership using price alone. Triers (Kwik Save, the discounters) have not succeeded. Nonetheless, Wal-Mart or a big European could make a play. The incumbents would react decisively to kill this at birth – if they could.
2. New formats. These are now par for the course in the United States and the UK as they have been for longer in Europe. There are no indications that more rapid format development improves margins or creates scale effectiveness. But the leaders have no choice and will be multi-format.
3. Fresh food. This is unquestionably a consumer discriminator, the area of the shopping basket that consumers care about and on which they can discriminate. Unfortunately, everyone has spotted it and is equally determined to deliver.

4. Meal solutions. This is the sexiest element of modern food shopping. The segment will continue to grow. It is unlikely that anyone will create the degree of advantage Marks & Spencer achieved, but everyone will probably have to try. This sector is individualistic enough to create space for new entrants and alliances. The sector is moving fast now in the United States.

5. Store service and appearance. No area has been worked over more exhaustively, and no doubt investments here will continue at a high level. This criterion is an important sub-set of retail branding, and the long-term winners will be the companies with strategies and brands. Service initiatives and fascia or store upgrading are visible and matchable.

We can turn now to the four future discriminating criteria. Here, it is suggested, the real winners will probably be found. They are:

1. The *brand*. Dominance requires brand leadership, and few companies are capable of operating on the strategic plane that fixes this as a priority objective. But some have succeeded, and the best can seek brand primacy through function (innovation) and emotional brand-building. Skill, time, great people and dedication are required, ie this is not easy!

2. *Consumer-systems ingenuity*. Embryonic work to develop user/trier/non-user databases to accommodate individual targetting and promotion exists. With technology and expertise available, committed first-mover experience and dedicated experiment may create a single company winner. Few of the present leading companies seem convinced they can be this. They may be missing a very big trick if this is the case.

3. *People* and *culture*. This has enormous potential but weak delivery. Asda ('shopping with personality') has tried. Consumers may begin to see the people in retail service as crucial, and companies in turn may recognize that the implementation of business learning for their whole team would offer massive long-term differentiation. There would be a big cost and it would take time, but both might be worth paying for.

4. *Global awareness*. This is a competence UK companies have wantonly ignored – it signifies strategic weakness. Understanding and developing experience outside the UK and a search for appropriate global learning and alliances have the potential to create new future winners in the UK market. Failure would be extremely bad news for British companies. They could conceivably all then go under. But there's no earthly reason this should happen, given their collective business record, and it would be a pity and a surprise if it did.

10

New ways of shopping, the Internet and all that jazz

It is always wise to look ahead, but difficult to look further than you can see.

(Winston Churchill)

Airplanes are interesting toys, but of no military value.
(Maréchal Foch)

I think there is a world market for about five computers.
(Thomas Watson, Chairman of IBM)

It is a brave – indeed foolhardy – person who would venture firm forecasts of how the applications and uses of technology will develop over the coming decades. If one believed all the hype, our world is about to be totally transformed by the convergence of IT and communications, by multimedia and by the Internet. Children are using computers from the age of five or younger; our televisions will be multimedia centres, digital and interactive; current ways of doing business will be blown away in the tornado of change already upon us. Computer power will be pervasive: it will be everywhere, in appliances as much as – indeed more than – in computers as such. Devices such as hand-held organizers and mobile phones will be able to access the World Wide Web, send and receive messages, and generally carry out all the functions that PCs now perform, and more. Computing and communication power will be built in to refrigerators and microwaves. In such a world, say some, shopping will be completely different. At the other extreme, a leading European food retailer has said that he does not believe that home shopping for groceries will be a big thing in his lifetime.

Gary Hamel, one of today's leading business-strategy gurus, is one of those predicting a 'convulsive development' in retailing. He argues that easy cost comparisons – 'frictionless capitalism', as Bill Gates calls it – made possible by the Internet will drive down retail prices. 'Money comes from knowing people won't comparison shop', says Hamel; 'People make enormous amounts of money out of friction' (*Financial Times*, 1998c). However, we should be cautious. The theory of comparison shopping on the Web is that intelligent software agents, or 'bots', scour the Web for the best prices, making it easy to find bargains. But one journalist concluded, after testing three of the latest bots, that this is 'another case where the hype is outrunning reality'. Searching for a range of consumer durables, he found that, 'Not one of the shopping services came close to turning up all the items I sought. And none offered the best prices' (Wildstrom, 1998).

What makes this particular future so hard to predict is the interaction of the variables. We can confidently say that computer power will continue to increase and its cost decrease, so that huge processing power and memory will be common and cheap. Digital television is already with us, offering hundreds of channels and potential interactivity. With Web TV, you can check your e-mail while watching TV, go direct from an e-mail message to a Web site, explore a virtual shop, and (at least in theory), buy goods – all from your armchair. We can also say that there are clear barriers to the rapid expansion of such home shopping.

PC PENETRATION AND INTERNET ACCESS

Although some 50 per cent of US households have a PC, the figure in the UK is currently only half that, and is similar in other European countries. Internet connection is even lower, but is growing fast. By the end of 1998, estimates put the number of adults (aged 16 and over) with access at some 80 million in the United States, 38 per cent of the population; about 11 million people use the Internet in Britain, or 18 per cent of the population. According to one study, 10,900 new users a day were logging on in the UK (compared with 9,900 new users per day in Germany and 2,700 in France). The spurt in Britain is probably due to the launch of free Internet services, led by Dixon's Freeserve (in Britain and most of Europe, users have to pay for the cost of the telephone calls). Dixon's have been followed by Tesco and W H Smith (a national high-street chain based on stationery), and even by tabloid newspapers. When the *Sun* and *Daily Mirror* start offering and promoting free Internet access and cheap computers, usage may indeed be about to take off in Britain. About 60 per cent of users in Britain access the World Wide Web from home. These figures (from www.nua.ie) will be out of date by the time you read this, of course, but they show impressive growth. The real increase will come when new devices – particularly mobile phones and combined wireless phone/organizers – are available cheaply.

DIGITAL TELEVISION

Digital TV was launched in Britain only in late 1998 (Sky and OnDigital), and at first offers only extended choice of television channels. Interactivity will come later.

INTERACTIVITY AND COUCH POTATOES

Several trials of interactive TV have been run in both Europe and the States. The operators have been up-beat in public about the results, but tight-lipped about actual details. Most observers think that the trials showed that most people are happy to reschedule their television viewing to suit themselves, but evinced little interest in using any other interactive facilities.

PAYING FOR TV

British consumers have shown a marked reluctance to pay for extra television channels: only a quarter do so (10 per cent cable, 15 per cent satellite) even after many years of availability. No digital, interactive channel will be free-to-air, except possibly BBC, and even that may be by subscription.

BANDWIDTH

Most households have only a copper-wire telephone connection into the home. Anyone who has used such a connection for the Internet will appreciate why, even with a 56Kbits per second modem (the fastest currently available), the Web is known as the World Wide Wait. ASDL, cable modems and so on will offer speeds hundreds of times faster, but they are still in the future as far as the real world is concerned. The full potential of interactivity will not be realized until speeds increase dramatically.

ECONOMICS

Although many of the experiments now being run are store-based, many think that the economics of this look impossible. Apart from ordering costs, a human has to physically pick each order and assemble it; even allowing for greater expertise, this will never be cheap.

PRACTICALITY OR, HOW DO YOU GET A FROZEN CHICKEN THROUGH THE LETTER-BOX?

Although home delivery is not essential, as we shall see, it is usually seen as an important component of convenience. Traffic delays aside, the costs of delivering to a scattering of homes at times suitable to all customers will also be significant.

Technophiles will argue, correctly, that many of these problems will be overcome in time. What we have difficulty forecasting is the exact outcome of the complex interaction between technology, economics and consumers that will determine what actually happens. To help think our way through the maze, let us now look at closely at what 'new ways of shopping' really involves, before coming to any conclusions about the most likely outcomes.

WHY SHOULD NEW WAYS OF SHOPPING BE NEEDED?

We know that new technology – or rather the entrepreneurs involved in and surrounding it – look for problems to solve. Sometimes they succeed, as with recorded CDs and players; at other times, as with digital audio cassettes, they fail. In the end, it is the market that decides; in other words, consumers are convinced that the new product offers them real benefits, in a form they like and at a price they are ready to pay. What forces suggest that there is a need for new ways of food shopping?

The major study carried out for the Coca-Cola Retailing Research Group by Coopers and Lybrand in 1996 suggested eight drivers:

1. *Underlying consumer problems with the existing food shopping process*: much food shopping is a chore, frustrating and unenjoyable.
2. *The emergence of realistic new modes of shopping*: this chapter will examine how realistic the new models are.
3. *Heightened external competition for foodstores*: eating out is taking a growing share of stomach.
4. *Intensification of internal competition within the existing system*: the main competitors in the UK and many European countries are reaching domestic saturation, and looking to each other's territories for expansion.
5. *The long-term erosion of mass-marketing and its replacement by mass-customization*: customers may get to like and expect individual treatment.
6. *The certainty that established and foreseeable consumer trends will make the food-retailing environment more challenging*: the next chapter will examine how divisions between haves and have-nots, and the ageing population, are bringing new threats to the superstores' legitimacy.
7. *The possibility of more radical socio-economic fracture lines opening up*: extreme consumer militancy or environmental disaster are possible scenarios.
8. *The challenging regulatory and political environment*: planning policies in many countries, packaging regulations in some, and increasing public criticism, are examples of constraints on the current model.

Many of these are dealt with, explicitly or implicitly, elsewhere in this book. Some, such as the doomsday scenarios, are beyond our scope. In this chapter we will concentrate on the interaction between One and Two: are there serious enough problems with existing food shopping that emerging technology can offer solutions to?

We know that some social groups already have serious problems with food shopping – especially those in deprived areas, and the old; more generally, those without cars, and living in the wrong place – a problem of access. Most of us, from experience and anecdote, would agree that there are other problems: time, traffic, parking, queuing, wobbly wheels on shopping trolleys, screaming children (other people's, or our own), and so on. The retailers are tackling many of these, but there are residual issues around the fact that much supermarket shopping is repetitive and unrewarding. As people's lives become more crowded, alternatives that will save time, or effort, may be attractive.

WHAT DO WE MEAN BY 'NEW WAYS OF SHOPPING'?

As the Internet is sexy at the moment, discussion of home shopping often focuses on that to the exclusion of other modes. We need to break the process down, and look at all the possibilities. We can see that many possible combinations are possible, some of them quite simple (and already adopted or planned by retailers). The situation can be elaborated, as Figure 10.1 shows. The basic variables are six:

- product and service range;
- pricing;
- fulfilment;
- service provider;
- interface between customer and service provider;
- point of order.

From these flow almost 40 possible solutions. Some of these are simple, and can be implemented now. A shopping list, produced from loyalty-card data,

| | Receive at: | | Fixed or Mobile Order/ | |
	Home	Office, Friends, Home, etc.	Collection Point	Food Store or Service Centre
Order from:				
Home	✓	✓	✓	✓
Office, Friends, Home, etc.	✓	✓	✓	✓
Kiosk	✓	✓	✓	✓
Fixed or Mobile Order/ Collection Point	✓	✓	✓	✓
Food Store or Service Centre	✓	✓	✓	✓

Figure 10.1 *New mode possibilities*

could be produced by swiping the card when the shopper enters the store; store staff could pick the routine, packaged items while the customer spends time on the more enjoyable tasks of choosing fresh produce and wine, or has a snack, or indeed goes somewhere else (if there is anywhere else to go within reach). Safeway's Shop and Go, with self-scanning and autonomous checkouts, shows what is being offered. Other experiments (see below) use telephone, fax or Internet ordering, while some offer home delivery. In fact, we should separate the two main aspects – order capture and physical delivery – as they are quite distinct, and can be tackled separately.

WHAT DO CONSUMERS WANT?

'The issue is not remote shopping but how to service customers', says Roderick Angwin of Safeway. We cannot generalize about customers as if they were all the same. We know that they are very different, with different needs, preferences and resources.

It seems certain that there will be a segment that will welcome Internet shopping. They will mostly be young, 'time-poor, cash-rich', computer-literate, with fast access to the World Wide Web at work or at home, and willing to pay for a service that gives them value. The ability to order from their desk appeals to them, as it saves time and avoids the unpleasant aspects of shopping (crowds, queues, traffic). They are confident in their ability to choose the right products, and not particularly interested in browsing (around supermarket shelves, that is).

Equally, however, it seems certain that many people currently do not want to shop in that way. Even though the service may not be PC-based, as many now argue, it will still need input. Pervasive computing, digital TV, voice recognition, and other technologies that we still do not know about will make the whole process much more user-friendly. This may draw in a new segment of people who basically do not like shopping: provided the technology is available to them, in an accessible form, they may be interested.

What we cannot know is how big these 'non-shopping shopper' segments will be. We may speculate about what exactly retailers can offer them out of the total shopping experience, and what they cannot. We know that offering shopping lists, reminders, linked purchases and tailored promotions is straightforward. Although the first trial by a new remote shopper may take quite a long time (perhaps even longer than a real shopping trip), after that the process should take no more than five or ten minutes.

To simulate browsing, however, is more of a problem. Most shoppers go into the store without a shopping list, so impulse purchases make up a significant proportion of the final basket. The products we buy through browsing – fresh produce, unusual or luxury items, chocolates, prepared meals, wines – are not only the more enjoyable purchases for us, they are likely to be among the higher-margin products for the retailer. So-called virtual reality cannot reproduce the shopping experience for such goods at present, and it seems very unlikely that it will be able to in the medium-term future, if ever. This limits the attractiveness of the process for consumers, and may also not be very appealing to the retailers.

Estimates of the size of the segments that will take up remote shopping vary, but are mostly between 5 and 10 per cent. Even at 1 per cent, of course, that is still a large amount of purchasing power, so every retailer will want to make sure that they are not losing it to a rival.

Beyond true remote shopping, the rest of the population will still have needs that existing systems do not meet. Some may respond to self-scanning, others to a personalized printed shopping list, others to a screen on the shopping trolley; some to the ability to collect an order previously phoned in, others to home delivery of goods personally selected in the store; and so on. Experience of other new technologies suggests that many of us do not know in advance exactly what we do want; when the reality is presented to us, we see how we like it. Most electronic cash experiments, for example (using smart cards that can be loaded with cash value and used for a variety of small purchases), have failed – but no one could have predicted that without trying it.

WHAT ARE RETAILERS OFFERING?

Remote ordering and home delivery are, of course, well established; mail order has been around for decades, and newer forms of direct marketing such as TV shopping channels are also successful. Internet commerce, though the majority is now business-to-business, has also made inroads in consumer markets such as computer hardware and software, CDs and books (though we should note in passing that the much-hyped Amazon.com does not expect to make a profit this century). When we look specifically at grocery shopping, the field is much less developed.

We should perhaps separate out home delivery as such, since in its basic form it has always existed, and still does in some parts of the market. In the United States, many smaller chains offer home delivery as part of their service, and it can be a useful competitive weapon (though the costs must help to keep margins very low). There are a few examples of specialized services else-where, such as the grocer in a part of Norway with many weekend homes in his area: 'he mail-dropped all of them and offered to deliver a pre-ordered basket of groceries ready for the weekend. Sales increased by 50 per cent' (Coopers and Lybrand, 1996). In the UK, Iceland, which is a medium-sized chain of frozen food stores, is the only firm offering home delivery nationally. Most commentators initially saw this as a final, desperate attempt to stay alive, but in 1998 Iceland showed 10 per cent sales growth, at least some of which must have been due to the new service (some was also due to its early banning of genetically modified ingredients – see Chapter 11). Generally, home delivery of groceries disappeared along with counter service, and is only now reappearing in combination with new ways of ordering.

Firstly, we can distinguish between what the grocers themselves are doing, and what new rivals offer. As so often with the application of new technologies, there are challenges from outside the traditional industry, with newcomers offering a remote ordering and delivery service for grocery products, often via the Internet. The best-known is Peapod in the United States, which employs personal shoppers to pick orders (supposedly getting round the problem of choosing fresh produce remotely). An alternative is NetGrocer, which offers a limited range of dry goods, which are delivered anywhere within two days by FedEx. Neither has made much impact, or, so far, any profit.

A similar but lower-tech service is run in London by Flanagans, offering home delivery for a charge. Their problem, as with any similar start-up, is that they have neither the buying power to obtain competitive prices, nor the brand name to give consumers confidence. In March 1999, Somerfield bought Flanagans for £3.25 million; the business, which had 10,000 customers, was thought to be losing £100,000 a month, and most of the purchase money will go to pay off loans. (Interestingly, at the same time, Nordstrom in the United States bought 30 per cent of a similar operation, Streamline, with fewer customers and higher losses, for US$ 23 million: who is right?)

It is entirely possible that some service such as this, provided it can get the logistics and the exact consumer offer right, could take a significant share of the market. A service company with the competencies in order capture, fulfilment, delivery and billing might, with sufficient investment, reach the scale required. So far, this has not happened.

The major UK retailers are all experimenting with various responses to the emerging need. Tesco, for example, currently offers home delivery from 12 stores. Of these, 11, which have been operating for over a year (as at late 1998), offer ordering by phone, fax or Internet; the twelfth offers only Internet ordering. The Tesco operation was subject to some teasing when it became known that originally an Internet order went to its computer centre, where it was printed out and rekeyed into the order system. The speed of adaptation is shown by the fact that now the Internet order goes direct to the picking trolley, in picking order; the items are then scanned and simultaneously checked against the list (helping to reduce one of the main irritations of remote ordering, wrong selection). Consumers can choose any two-hour slot for delivery, which makes for more complicated van scheduling and thus higher costs than a more rigid system ('we visit your postcode area on Tuesday afternoons', for example). The charge for the service is £5, and it is unclear whether this can ever be profitable. Tesco's view is that it has to offer the service (in case someone else does), and wants to find the best way of serving their customers. It is currently concentrating on Internet ordering and home delivery, but is aware of the range of options. It has tried delivery to offices, which Waitrose is offering; the fact that Tesco is no longer doing so implies that it did not find it viable.

Tesco is operating from existing stores, as the capital costs have already been paid. Operating from a specialized warehouse would lower current costs, but incur new capital costs. To make money from any operation will need scale, and therefore it will be interested in any devices that penetrate deeply into the consumer market: digital TV, especially if a cheap home scanner becomes available, would be attractive. Accepting that some charge will be necessary, Tesco feels that this will not confine the appeal to the rich. A couple consisting of two teachers, for instance, would be potential customers. Tesco is pragmatic about what the eventual level of remote shopping will be, but is determined that it will not miss out. 'If it's only 1 per cent, and we are not getting it, that would be serious', comments Ian O'Reilly, IT Director.

Safeway, as we saw, takes the view that its job is to find the best way of meeting different customer needs. It is taking a cautious approach, and has been piloting a phone/fax ordering service from one store; customers pick up the goods themselves. The pilot has been running for over a year, and is being maintained but not rolled out, suggesting that Safeway is not yet satisfied that it is the right package. Given its problem of a shortage of main shoppers, it sees an opportunity to target the best customers: shoppers generating a high volume and profit could receive the service free, while others paid. For the future, it is working on research projects with IBM, which it describes as at the cutting edge. It clearly sees the advent of pervasive computing, and new devices, as offering the really exciting opportunities. In early 1999, the first fruits of this approach were the launch of Easi-Order, which allows customers to use a Palm Pilot (hand-held computer, similar to the Psion organizer) adapted to incorporate a bar-code reader. Two hundred customers of the Basingstoke branch who were already using the 'Collect and Go' system were given the device free. They can use it at home to scan bar codes from items they have bought; it also stores a structured list of all the things they have bought over the past four months, and they can switch to a screen showing promotions and suggesting impulse purchases. These can be based on intelligent data-mining of the purchase patterns of customers buying similar products. Tesco has also launched a similar device, though it is charging for it. This approach, adapting a small, familiar device to new uses, shows great promise.

Asda, again reflecting its strategic position, is taking yet another tack. It has started a home delivery service from a dedicated distribution centre in London, where it has found it difficult to find sites for stores. The service has a catchment area of 450,000 homes with no Asda retail store. Customers will order from a catalogue delivered free to their homes, offering around 5,000 lines; they will phone a call centre, and pay by debit or credit card. Delivery, as with Tesco, will be within an agreed two-hour slot. If it works, this is a very neat way of extending coverage into territories that Asda could not afford to penetrate with conventional superstores. Typically, Allan Leighton has named it 'our "stealth stores" approach to the home-shopping market'. Asda is also using its position in sales of books, music and videos to offer those online; it may be that such a service, when established, could be extended to grocery as well.

All these services are relatively new. The fact that they exist, and are still operating, shows that there is some demand. The retailers are being tight-lipped about results, and it is far too early to tell whether they will be profitable.

THE FUTURE

Accepting that we cannot predict with any accuracy, what can we say about the future? The outcomes for food shopping depend on the interaction of many variables, but we will concentrate on three major influences: technology, economics and competition.

Rapid or even steady development of new ways of shopping will depend on the wide availability of technologies that offer bandwidth and ease of use: these would include interactive TV, voice recognition, smart telephones, combined personal organizers (palmtop PCs) and phones, and kiosks (and, of course, things we have not yet dreamed of). Interactive TV is already with us, as is some form of voice recognition (though few consumers will be willing to spend hours training their system by reading 467 sentences into it, as one does with a current 'leading' package). Really effective voice recognition could be a major step forward, unless of course people are so fed up with dealing with automated call centres ('For fresh produce, please press one; thank you: for meat please press two ...') that they react against any such process.

What seems likely is that the current situation will change only slowly; that is, that the most sophisticated technology will be the slowest to spread widely through the population. The time that new technology takes to be adopted is certainly falling. The telephone took almost 40 years to reach 10 per cent penetration, while VCRs took less than 10 years. However, 10 per cent penetration will not enable a mass-market grocery service, especially as the majority of people seem unready to adopt a radically new shopping experience. While new technology, especially perhaps better software, can overcome many barriers, remote shopping for food cannot replace the actual experience, both the physical experience of seeing, smelling, choosing produce, and the social experience of being with other people.

Even if the adoption of technology does allow remote grocery shopping, will it be profitable? The Coopers and Lybrand study (1996) estimated the costs for four types of operation:

Table 10.1 *Cost of operations*

	as % of sales total
Store	20.4%
Store order/store pick-up	32.5%
Remote order/home delivery	32.2%
Remote order/remote delivery	25.4%

Only the store order/store pick-up option allowed any profit margin. This may seem surprising, given that the existing store-based model contains many apparent inefficiencies. The answer is that many of the costs are currently borne by the customers themselves. Consumers make millions of individual trips to and from the stores, usually in their own transport; they find their way round a very large space, locating a small number of items (under 50, probably) from a range of 20,000 or more; they take the items off the shelves; at the checkout, they unload the goods, and reload them in the basket; they wheel them to the car and pack them; then they transport them home. In a remote shopping service, most of these have to be carried out by the service provider, and costed.

For such a model to work, one scenario would be viable. It is easy to imagine an economy produced by the continuation of the trends towards increasing inequality seen in both the United States and Britain in recent years. In such a society, there will be an ample supply of people available and willing to work for low pay in the distribution sector: women working part-time, certainly, but also former miners and factory workers, the prematurely retired, all those with little education and low skills, the over-65s with an inadequate pension. On the other side, there will be a smaller, but much richer, group, working very long hours for very high pay, and willing and eager to pay a premium to someone else to pick and deliver their groceries. This is not a political statement, but a cool interpretation of current trends.

In other scenarios, the challenge is to produce a new model, and that is where new competition may come. Gary Hamel argues that every time there has been a big change in retailing – such as the growth of out-of-town shopping or the arrival of huge 'category killers' – new arrivals have attacked the current occupants. 'With each of those shifts, never did the leaders in one paradigm become the leaders in the next. I think it is just as unlikely that the winners in out-of-town shopping centres will be winners online' (*Financial Times*, 1998b).

This is a sobering thought for the supermarket giants. They will be tempted to reject it out of hand. But this book has told the story of how they got to where they are, and it was precisely in the way Hamel describes – by seeing the new paradigm and adapting faster than the old competitors. All the well-established names of British grocery retailing – with hundreds or thousands of shops that dominated the scene until the 1950s – have disappeared or been absorbed by the new model armies. Are the new generation really any different now?

They are, to be fair, responding to the new challenges. They are all aware that they are vulnerable, and that even a small percentage of the market lost to new methods will be very significant. Estimates of what that share will be vary, though most fall within a fairly narrow range. The Coopers and Lybrand study, the most thorough published, examines seven possible growth scenarios. The most likely, in their view, is a modest take-off, leading to just over 5 per cent by 2005, and 10 per cent by 2010 (1996: 73). 'This reflects the view that the under-lying long-term consumer and competitive logic is there for new modes, but the economic, technical and consumer inertias are massive', they conclude.

We share that view. We are confident that there will be a demand for new ways of shopping – not just remote ordering or home delivery, but a variety of modes and combinations – and that the existing retailers will have to meet those demands if they are not to lose control of a significant share of their market. It seems likely that each competitor will reach a different solution, depending on their specific situation and strategy. Wholly new competitors may emerge, since a small share of the huge grocery market is well worth having, but they are likely to be targeted, perhaps specialist. The danger for the majors is that the specialists could cherry-pick the most valuable customers (those most willing to buy high-margin items, for example, and concentrated in inner-city areas that are easy to serve economically). That could have a more-than-proportional effect on the retailers' profits. It will be a fascinating battle to watch.

11

Winners and losers in the retail revolution

In every revolution, there are bound to be winners and losers. Some of the winners from the retail revolution are obvious: the shareholders, managers and employees of the successful supermarket chains. On the other side, the owners, managers and employees of the firms put out of business by the revolution – not only small independent grocers, but butchers, green-grocers, fishmongers, dairies, wholesalers and, increasingly, other trades – have lost. This, you could argue, is just the normal operation of economic forces, the 'creative destruction', as Schumpeter called it, unleashed by innovation.

But business operates within society. What of the other interested parties who are affected? Consumers and suppliers are the most closely involved stakeholders, but there are also questions of the wider environment, and of people as citizens. Do the new shopping patterns created by the out-of-centre superstores contribute to increased road traffic and pollution? Are the poor and the old disadvantaged? Have the all-powerful superstore groups helped to kill off the traditional town centre? Who bears the costs of the externalities, as economists call them, created by increased road use – by lorries carrying goods to central warehouses and to stores, and by cars travelling to and from those stores?

Critics have levelled many charges at the supermarket groups, as they have at any big and successful organization. The issues are complex and interrelated, but they are important and we need to look at them squarely. In this chapter, we will first examine the issues of consumers and society in general; we will then go on to analyse the effects of retail concentration on the industry as a whole – in particular manufacturers and other suppliers .

Firstly, society. We must recognize that, over the period that we have been discussing, there have been enormous changes in society, in Britain as elsewhere; any successful business has reacted to and profited from these changes, as have the supermarkets. The changes are well known, and we will just summarize them here:

- Wealth has increased, for everyone. Although inequality has grown during some periods, even those groups at the bottom of the pile are better off now than they were. People have more money, own far more goods, live in pleasanter housing.
- One change that is very relevant to some of the arguments in this chapter is the growth in car ownership and use. Household expenditure on motoring increased in real terms by 91 per cent between 1971 and 1995. By the early 1990s, more than 20 per cent of households had the use of two or more cars.
- Domestic technology has changed. Widespread ownership of refrigerators and freezers enables households to buy in bulk, for a week or more at a time, rather than having to shop almost daily.
- Far more women now go out to work; female employees grew from 9.4 million in 1971 to 12.3 million in 1996, while the number of working men stayed the same at 15.6 million. In the majority of couples of working age, both partners work. This gives the household more to spend, but puts greater time pressure on women (since women, sad to report, still carry out the bulk of household chores).
- Most people in the 1990s are better-off than their counterparts in the 1950s, but have less time. They welcome anything that allows them to use their car to save time and effort ; supermarkets did not create this situation, but they have certainly responded to the opportunities it has created. Car ownership and use would have increased without the growth of superstores, as would out-of-town shopping. We will examine the extent to which superstores have aggravated the problems associated with car use later in this chapter.

Now we will look at some of the specific criticisms that have been made, starting with consumers: how well are they being served?

CONSUMERS

Shoppers have gained many concrete advantages: a huge range of products, sourced from all over the world; a one-stop shop, where this range is gathered in one place, increasingly with other services such as pharmacies, dry cleaning, access to cash, post office, petrol; the sheer convenience of being able to park easily – and free – while they shop; and a choice of competing stores offering this range. They have voted with their feet – or rather their car-keys – patronising the supermarkets and superstores at the expense of other outlets. The vast, gleaming superstores – the cathedrals of Thatcher's Britain, St Tesco's on the roundabout, St Sainsbury's on the interchange, open seven days a week, some 24 hours a day – are the clearest possible evidence that consumers are getting what they want. When asked, the great majority of shoppers are pleased with the advantages of superstores (Peston and Ennew, 1998).

This does not mean that shoppers are completely happy with everything. One study (Coopers and Lybrand, 1996) identified over 150 possible problems with the total shopping experience. These range from the existential ('What do I actually need?') to the narrowly operational ('Aisles too narrow'), and many of them are already being tackled by the store operators. The 1990s have shown, rather more clearly than preceding decades, that the retailers are genuinely trying to meet consumer needs, whether in reducing queuing times, in providing more helpful labelling, or in setting up crèches. In a competitive market, they know that, to use Tesco's slogan, 'Every little helps'. From their point of view, every little improvement helps to differentiate their offer, at least for a time.

The quality of the supermarkets' offer has meant that, until very recently, they seemed immune to criticism. There have always been some critics, to be sure, but they were in a minority, and their voices were not widely heard. Broad public support for supermarkets brought political support. In 1998, however, something changed. Articles in serious newspapers and weighty television programmes appeared, charging the grocery firms with all manner of things. We will rehearse the charges levelled against the supermarkets, and the companies' replies, before reaching our own conclusions.

IS THERE REAL CHOICE?

Firstly, how real is consumers' choice? When the range of goods and the general price level are very similar across the main competitors, there is really very little to choose from, except location. More importantly, once the shopper is inside the store, the switching costs become very high for that trip. The fact that a favourite brand or variety is not in stock may be a nuisance, but most consumers will not abort the trip with the shopping half-completed, and drive to another store to go through the process again. One couple may argue about whether to shop in Sainsbury's or Tesco because one stocks Rombout's one-cup coffee filters and the other does not, but they are pretty unusual. Where the out-of-stock is a brand, there will be an own-label equivalent, which is surely just as good (an argument we will return to later). The retailers reply that of course there is ample choice, not only between the leading four, but of discounters and local independents too. Shoppers do not, they say with some justification, complain that they are starved of choice.

DO BRITISH SHOPPERS PAY TOO MUCH?

The second question is that of price. It is well known that British food retailers make margins that are significantly higher than those of their European and American rivals – around 5–7 per cent compared with around 2–4 per cent, roughly, though there is considerable argument about which exact figures to quote and what they mean; see 'Profitability' on page 214). We examine the financial arguments surrounding this gap elsewhere (see Chapter 9), but one view is that the British grocers have managed to persuade their shoppers to accept higher price levels in return for the range and quality of goods, and the *ambiance* of their more attractive stores.

Price is perhaps a surprising question to raise. After all, is price not the main selling point of supermarkets? Low prices certainly figure largely in the retailers' rhetoric, and price campaigns seem to come along frequently. It is true that the average prices paid in supermarkets have risen more slowly than the overall Retail Price Index over recent decades (between 1993 and 1998 food-price inflation averaged 1.5 per cent, compared with general inflation of 3 per cent): the supermarket chains have indeed made huge efficiency gains, and passed on some of that to customers.

We should make two comparisons: what shoppers could buy the same or similar goods for in Britain, and the price levels in other countries compared with Britain. The results of different measurements unfortunately produce confusing and sometimes conflicting results; we have to be clear what is being measured, and what shops are being compared. We discuss below the particular problems of the disadvantaged groups, who have to pay higher prices in local food shops than those available in a supermarket. In this specific context, local food shops (neighbourhood grocery/video/off-licence stores in poor areas) do charge higher prices. A basket of popular brands cost £11.75 in the supermarket, and £13.47 in the local shop; for the cheapest available product in a range of staple items, the supermarket price was £5.17 and the local shop £7.87 (Consumers' Association, 1997).

On the other hand, *Panorama* (the most prestigious of the BBC's investigative current affairs programmes) quoted price comparisons between supermarkets and high street specialist shops (1998). To heighten their overall message, they chose Grantham, famous as the birthplace of Margaret Thatcher, and the site of her father's small independent grocer's shop. Taking a bag of fruit and vegetables, they found the prices shown in Table 11.1.

Table 11.1   *Fruit and vegetable prices*

Independent greengrocer	£1.39
Asda	£2.25
Tesco	£2.35
Safeway	£2.45
Sainsbury's	£2.61

For a bag of mixed cuts of pork, they found the prices shown in Table 11.2.

Table 11.2   *Pork prices*

Independent butcher	£9.74
Asda	£10.45
Safeway	£11.96
Sainsbury's	£12.51

Note: Tesco did not have all the items in stock, so was excluded

Consumers interviewed seemed not to care too much about whether they were getting the best possible value for money: they knew what they wanted, were very busy, and so just rushed around without looking too closely at prices. Other evidence (Peston and Ennew, 1998) bears this out. Consumers know from experience that, although some individual prices may vary from week to week as between the supermarket chains, overall they are much the same. Indeed, so closely do the groups shadow each other that many prices for staples – especially KVIs or known value items – are identical: *Panorama* found ketchup at exactly 61p, bananas at 49p/lb, own-label baked beans at 23p and own-label orange juice at 69p in all the major chains. Most shoppers apparently prefer the convenience of free car-parking and one-stop shopping to searching out the best prices at different high-street shops (even though they may, in fact, walk as far around a huge superstore as along a high street).

When we come to international comparisons, we enter notoriously tricky terrain. People in different countries have different attitudes to food, they buy different things, store formats vary, tariffs and taxes complicate matters, exchange rates change, and so on. Not surprisingly, then, the studies carried out produce varying results. One study by Taylor Nelson AGB in the early 1990s (quoted in Raven and Lang, 1995) looked at 15,000 households in 13 countries and found that British prices were among the lowest, beaten only by Spain, Belgium and France, and another comparison came up with similar figures.

On the other hand, KPMG carried out an exercise in 1991 that measured the prices of a basket of 11 foods across 4 countries. Their results, shown in Table 11.3, included taxes and suggested that, even if UK retail prices were not out of line, the margins taken by retailers were higher than everywhere except Sweden.

Table 11.3 *Margins in a basket of foods in 4 countries, 1991*

£ sterling	UK	Germany	Denmark	Sweden
Manufacturers' selling price	19.17	18.96	18.08	23.11
Wholesaler margin	0	0	0	0.63
Retailer margin	7.19	4.57	6.44	7.88
Price ex tax	26.36	23.53	24.52	31.62
Tax	0	1.62	5.44	7.89
Retail price	26.36	25.15	29.66	39.51

The retailers would say that this shows that they are not out of line (and that ROCE (return on capital employed) comparisons show that some continental retailers are more profitable than some British firms). The *Panorama* programme in 1998 priced a shopping basket in four European cities, and found the results shown in Table 11.4.

Table 11.4 Panorama *shopping basket*

£ sterling	
London	73.30
Paris	70.49
Berlin	63.57
Rome	55.60

Tesco, in an attempt to counter the charges that it was ripping off its customers, asked A C Nielsen to measure the prices of a 'more representative' basket in

1998. Crucially, it included own-label products, which it claimed had been left out of other surveys. The results are shown in Table 11.5.

Table 11.5 *Tesco's shopping basket comparison*

Country	Store	Total cost of basket
UK	Tesco	£40.38
Italy	Standa	£39.33
France	Leclerc	£42.75
Belgium	Delhaize	£43.81
Netherlands	Albert Heijn	£40.40
Germany	Globus	£40.78

Source: Tesco

An OECD (Organization for Economic Cooperation and Development) study to be published in 1999 is expected to show that, while UK prices of some goods are significantly higher than in some other countries, a basket of food costing £100 in Britain would be cheaper in Portugal, but would cost £128 in France and £122 in Germany (*Financial Times*, 1999d). The case remains unproven, and perhaps unprovable. Prices of many goods vary between countries, sometimes for obvious reasons such as real cost differences, sometimes because the market will bear higher prices in some countries than others. This may be changing, a point we return to below.

Of the four majors, Asda has the clearest low-price position, and is 5–10 per cent cheaper than the others. Each has at some time run price promotions, but since the price-cutting days of the 1970s it is difficult to see fierce, continuing price competition. Each chain offers a low-price range, and promotes certain price cuts on specific products, but overall a complete shopping basket costs a remarkably similar amount in each. The discounters have made little headway, particularly in the south of England. Although Aldi, Netto and Lidl are all now operating in Britain, they have not, so far anyway, made much impact. It is true that British margins have been declining in recent years, suggesting that price competition is making an impact.

The fact remains that many observers, including distinguished ones, think that the superstores now have a case to answer. Sir John Harvey-Jones, a former chairman of ICI, and one of Britain's best-known businessmen through his *Troubleshooter* television series, commented in the 1998 *Panorama* programme that British supermarkets now charged the highest prices in Europe, far higher than in the United States; they make far higher profits, two or three times that achieved elsewhere. If customers are paying higher prices, he concluded, and the retailers are paying lower prices to suppliers (see below), then to describe this as ripping off the customer would not be too far out.

The only retailer who would appear on the programme was a spokesman for Safeway, and he pointed out that the costs of doing business are far higher in Britain, especially the costs of property and distribution (see 'A Note on Capital Intensity' on page 226). As the retailers are reluctant to release detailed figures, we can only draw our own conclusions. An investigation recently carried out by the Office of Fair Trading (OFT) did not shed much light on this murky question, and previous enquiries by the Monopolies and Mergers Commission (MMC) and the Office of Fair Trading have not been persuaded that the supermarkets are in fact abusing their power.

If the Tesco figures are representative, and the British supermarkets are price-competitive between themselves and against their counterparts in other countries, they have not managed perceptions very well. Consumers are happy, but when senior and influential figures such as Harvey-Jones clearly believe that prices are too high, the companies have a problem. The perception has even reached the United States; readers of *Business Week* were told recently that 'Britons wait on endless lines to pay high prices for everyday groceries', and that 'the media and politicians are attacking . . . obscenely profitable supermarket chains for price-gouging' (1999: 27). Allowing for journalistic licence – and a horror story is always preferred to good news – the supermarkets are beginning to have an image problem.

In this, they are not alone. Even the august *Financial Times* was moved to say, in a leader:

> Perhaps … the power of the big oligopolistic retailers to resist those [deflationary] forces is breaking down. In recent months, there has been a rising tide of public resentment in the UK against perceived over-charging. Why does meat cost so much when British farmers are going out of business? Why do cars cost so much more than everywhere in the EU? Why do travellers to New York find they pay the same dollars for clothes or food as they do pounds in London? (*Financial Times,* 1999b)

The American *Business Week* (1999) article quoted above repeated the point, mentioning specifically cars, computers and groceries. They quoted Martin Hayward, of the Henley Centre, as saying that 'British consumers are starting to flex their muscles'. If these commentators are right, the supermarkets' margins will continue to come under pressure, and many people will be watching their prices closely. Or are they powerful enough to enforce their own price level? There is some evidence that senior politicians would like to make a case: Stephen Byers, the trade and industry minister, announced a campaign against over-charging in March 1999, but the impact was somewhat dampened by the fact that another minister immediately dismissed this as 'a stunt'.

Whether as the result of political pressure or not, in March 1999 the OFT referred the food retail industry as a whole to the Monopolies and Mergers Commission (MMC). The general feeling is that the OFT *suspects* that the supermarkets are making excess profits at the expense of consumers, but cannot prove it. The commission will look at every food retailer with 10 or more supermarkets of 6,000 sq ft, and their investigation will take up to 12 months. It is unclear, to put it mildly, what the commission might recommend to cure any problems it may find.

AN OLIGOPSONY/OLIGOPOLY, OR ARE THE SUPERMARKETS MONEMPORISTS?

Economists love perfect competition, which maximizes consumer welfare, and hate monopolies, which minimize it. By extension, an oligopoly (dominance by a few sellers) is also potentially harmful. Few people question the fact that the big four supermarket groups now constitute an oligopoly, or complex monopoly, apart from the supermarket chains themselves. They refute the suggestion, pointing out the previous OFT and MMC investigations. The recent OFT study used a complex econometric model to try again to determine whether the chains are making super-normal profits. Most observers accept that oligopoly is a fair description of the current situation. In another industry, after all, Microsoft claims that it is not a monopoly, despite having 90 per cent of the market for operating systems for PCs!

The supermarkets also form an oligopsony, or complex monopsony: that is, they are dominant in the *buying* of goods from their suppliers. A monopsony or oligopsony may use its power to drive down the prices at which goods are bought, but this may in itself be good for consumers. If the price savings are passed on to consumers, their welfare is increased.

Where firms are both oligopsonists (buyer power) and oligopolists (seller power), as the supermarket chains in Britain undoubtedly are, they are called by some economists *monemporists* (Dobson, Waterson and Chu, 1998). They may use their collusive power both to buy very cheaply from suppliers and to impose higher-than-necessary prices on consumers. They gain rewarding margins for themselves, but at a cost to consumer welfare.

Oligopoly power may be resisted by *countervailing power*, as Galbraith argued. If the grocery market were really competitive, consumers could exercise their power by choosing the store that offered lower prices for equivalent quality. That store would gain sales and share, and others would have to copy the price reductions. Apart from at certain periods, this has not always happened in Britain. Investigations by the Monopolies and Mergers Commission in 1981 and the Office of Fair Trading in 1985 concluded that, on the whole, lower prices were passed on. In the late 1990s, there was some evidence of price competition, as margins declined from their peak (see Chapter 9). Over most of the last decades, however, the major firms have managed to avoid price wars, and their margins – which have risen steadily over most of the period – suggest that they were keeping some of their power-derived savings for themselves. We may conclude either that consumers' countervailing power has not been exercised (because they preferred range, quality, convenience, etc), or that the big four's oligopoly power has allowed them to fix a price level more suited to them than to consumers.

Some observers have suggested that, against most opinion, the share of the leading supermarkets is not high enough! McKinsey, in a report on British productivity generally, pointed out that, although the leaders in food retailing were very strong performers, there is a very long tail of weaker ones that drag down average productivity. 'The average would certainly be higher if the leading performers commanded a bigger share of the market' (McKinsey, 1998). It is also true that in some other countries (mainly small ones such as the Scandinavian countries and Portugal) the concentration of the grocery industry is higher than that of Britain. McKinsey's suggestion that planning restrictions should therefore be relaxed seems bizarre to most people (see below), although it is possible that the MMC enquiry will look again at whether existing planning practice is a barrier to entry, or otherwise reinforces an oligopoly.

There is, of course, an argument for economies of scale, and there is no doubt that such economies are available in modern British food retailing: 'in such a market, a relatively small number of large players may be the best outcome in terms of productivity and competition' (Coker, 1999). This is true, if the industry is competitive.

The retailers themselves, of course, indignantly deny that they are profiteering and declare categorically that there is no collusion in the industry. Other participants may agree that there is no formal collusion, but would argue that the chains act through suppliers to ensure that prices stay in line. This is not collusion, but it is a use of oligolopoly power. Given the atmosphere of fear and secrecy in these areas (see the discussion on suppliers later in this chapter), such claims and counter-claims are hard to evaluate.

Beyond these somewhat abstract arguments, consumers have a choice, the retailers would say. The fact that most of them have not consistently chosen to shop at the discounters such as Kwik Save means that they are happy with the price/value combination that we offer. We have passed on to them much of the efficiency savings we have made by good management, keeping for ourselves only as much as we need to reinvest and as the stock market demands that we make (and as Chapter 9 pointed out, the capital-intensive nature of the British industry, and the fact that the groups are all publicly owned, does place peculiar demands on them). What they omit to mention is that, in many areas, there is only one supermarket (in fact, in a third of the UK's 1,300 shopping catchment areas – *Financial Times*, 1999c).

All this is based on an implicit assumption that shoppers are a homogeneous mass – but of course they are not. In the discussion above, we ought to have used the phrase 'car-borne shopper', since the great majority of shopping trips to supermarkets and superstores are made by car (Asda shoppers are unusual in that as many as 25 per cent of them travel to the store by public transport or on foot). What of the others?

DO THE POOR PAY MORE? DIET, HEALTH AND THE PRICE OF FOOD

In both Britain and the United States, inequality of wealth has been increasing. In Britain, there has been growing evidence of increasing inequality of health: for the poorest group in society, all the health indicators are significantly worse than for the wealthiest. They have lower life expectancy, higher incidence of many diseases, lower birth weight, and generally a lower quality of life.

More recently, there has been evidence that some of these differences are due to a poor diet (eg Department of Health, 1996; Murcott, 1998). Such evidence has been available since the late 1970s, but a report in 1982 was effectively suppressed by the then government, which consistently denied that a problem existed. What is especially disturbing is that the situation of the poorest seems to have got worse since *a century* ago. In 1899, Rowntree found that 10 per cent of the people surveyed in York could not afford to buy a diet that contained the basic nutrients at the cheapest price. In 1997, researchers found that 21 per cent of the British population were living in this condition (quoted by Lang, in Walker and Walker 1997).

In 1992, the then Ministry of Agriculture, Fisheries and Food (MAFF) produced a diet that was, theoretically, nutritionally adequate and would cost no more than £10 per head per week (essential if those living on benefit [welfare] were to be able to afford it). As one of the MAFF consumer panel commented:

To follow [MAFF's low-cost diet], low-income households would have to cut out meat entirely, more than double their consumption of tinned fruit and frozen vegetables (an implicit assumption that they cannot afford enough fresh fruit and vegetables), double their consumption of breakfast cereals (in order, presumably, to achieve sufficient levels of fibre and fortified vitamins), eat five times more wholemeal bread than at present, and eat more white bread. Of the eight slices of bread to be eaten each day, only three would have even a thin spread of margarine and butter; the rest would be eaten dry. Yogurts and other dairy products are completely excluded. Expecting poor consumers to eat a totally different diet from the rest of the population is discriminatory. And as one commentator said, they had better not watch any television, especially if they have kids.

(Leather, quoted in Lang, op.cit.)

Such facts are shocking and disturbing, but supermarket executives might be forgiven for saying that they reflect deep-rooted social and political problems. What have they to do with us? Part of the answer lies in the availability of cheap food to those who need it most. Many researchers had been documenting the problems the poor and the old have in finding, let alone affording, a balanced diet. Eventually, the issue hit the front pages.

THE POOR OF BRITAIN ARE GOING HUNGRY, HEALTH CHIEF WARNS

This was the headline across the top of the front page of the *Independent*, a leading British quality newspaper, on 15 October 1998. The article, which was to lead to a campaign under the banner 'Breadline Britain', published the arguments already familiar to specialists. It quoted Sir Donald Acheson, a former government chief medical officer: '*It is now almost impossible for many of the poorest people to obtain cheap, varied food. Local shops have closed down because of the growth in out-of-town supermarkets, leading to the creation of "food deserts" in the inner cities and increasing poor nutrition, putting mothers and children at risk.*' Succeeding issues graphically illustrated what food deserts mean for the deprived, living in decaying estates with few shops. One young mother quoted prices in the local mini-market, in effect a corner shop.

> You can see that pop here is 60p, but I can get it in a supermarket for 15p. Bread is 60p – in Tesco's a loaf is only 23p. Tinned peas are 39p. I can get them for 9 pence. Sugar is 80p here. In Tesco's I pay 69p. I could get everything even cheaper if I went to Netto's. But I can't afford the cab fare back – it's £4.50. So I rely on people giving me a lift.
>
> (*Independent*, 1998b)

As the article points out, two-thirds of households in the estate do not own a car. In London as a whole, 40 per cent of households do not have access to a car (LPAC, 1994).

The following week, the *Independent* contrasted the opening of a showpiece new Tesco's in London with the threatened closure of Safeway and Tesco stores in a poor area of Edinburgh. Visitors to London will see Tesco's glass palace on the main road into town from the airport and the west. On its opening day, Sir Terence Conran was among the celebrities admiring the 'sushi and espresso bars, the antipasto and olive counters, checking out the ready-made meals of seafood paella, teriyaki beef and tagliatelle' (*Independent* 1998c).

In Edinburgh, meanwhile, Safeway had been taken to court to try to stop it closing the main supermarket on the Wester Hailes estate. Safeway wanted to close the Presto store because it was making unsustainable losses, but the court ruled that it must keep it open (Scottish law is different from that of the rest of Britain, and such a ruling would be impossible under English law). Tim Lang, Professor of Food Policy at Thames Valley University, said, 'The supermarkets have abandoned the poor. They have deliberately chased the affluent consumer. The result is a ruthless cycle. In Scotland, you need to double the amount of fresh fruit and vegetables that people are eating.' That is difficult when, as the young mother in London pointed out, the cheapest apples in the local shop were 24p a pound. 'But I could buy 4lb for 50p if I could get to the market' (*Independent*, 1998b).

The supermarkets could reject all such arguments as irrelevant. Taking the extreme Friedmanite view, they could claim that their job is to maximize returns to shareholders; if there are social problems, it is up to government to solve them, not business. A Safeway spokesman seemed to take this stance: 'If the government can sort out the problems then the retailers will follow. But we're not going to do it alone. It would be a recipe for disillusionment . . . *We have abandoned these areas, frankly,* because of the problems of crime and vandalism' (my italics, *Independent*, 1998c).

The truth, as usual, is more complex. The remark was taken out of context, in that it referred to a minority of the stores that Safeway had shut down; in those cases, the situation for staff had become intolerable. The general point that Safeway was making was that urban regeneration needs a comprehensive strategy which must be led by the government. Other retailers would agree and Tesco, for example, would point to its 200 high-street stores and the £3 million a year it spends on free bus services. All would argue that their pricing, their store location policies, their promotion of healthy eating and so on are evidence of their responsible attitude towards the whole of society.

There can be no question, however, that the supermarket groups have been pursuing a business strategy of building larger and larger stores, with car parking on the same level. This is the business model that has proved enormously successful for them. The fact is that sites for such stores cannot be found in city centres, so they have been built in edge-of-town or out-of-town locations. The point of the superstore and the hypermarket is to make people from a large catchment area travel to them. Most customers – the car-borne majority – accept and even like this. The concomitant closing of small, unprofitable shops in city centres has, however, left the poorest, most vulnerable people in society without access to decent, cheap food. The big four's use of their ever-growing buyer power has meant that their price advantage over small shops has increased, making it ever more likely that they cannot compete, and will close. (The supermarkets have started to open or reopen some town-centre small shops, but this seems to be a reaction to the drying-up of large sites. The shops are not, generally, in deprived areas.) Even those independent shops that do survive are finding it more difficult to get supplies, because wholesalers have also gone out of business in large numbers. The old local authority approach to food poverty was to bring cheap food to the people through open and covered markets, many of which opened at the turn of the century. The approach of the free market has been the opposite.

What has been allowed to happen in Britain is the spread and eventual dominance of a business model that brings huge profits to the leading supermarket chains, even if it has also led to the closure of thousands of specialist and local shops. Discounters have been kept at bay, partly by anti-competitive moves by the supermarkets themselves. An anonymous former buyer for one of the supermarket chains has said that they threatened to de-list any supplier who sold to 'a new, continental discount store'; it was common practice for all buyers to actively discourage suppliers from selling to the new discounter. 'It's very anti-competitive, but that's business', she said (*Panorama*, 1998).

No one would expect supermarket groups, any more than any business, to pursue policies that are inherently unprofitable. Major problems of poverty, deprivation and food deserts are a challenge for society as a whole. But it would be surprising if the big four supermarket chains did not want to contribute to a solution.

FOOD QUALITY AND SAFETY

The safety of food has become a topic of concern to the public since the scare of BSE, and outbreaks of serious food poisoning from listeria and *E.coli* bacteria. The *E.coli* outbreak in Scotland in 1997 killed 18 people, and was traced to infected meat from a butcher's shop. More worryingly, the *E.coli* epidemic in the United States in 1996, which also caused several deaths, was eventually traced to unpasteurized apple juice aimed at a health-conscious, preservative-free market; it turned out that the orchards had been fertilized with farm slurry, in keeping with its organic approach. An outbreak of dysentery in West Sussex in 1998 was caused by 'pick'n'mix' fruit salad in a local Sainsbury's.

Here, the supermarkets have a good story to tell: the Sainsbury's example is a rare one. Their own standards are generally high (see the Marks & Spencer example, Chapter 5), and they have often been in advance of government advice and regulation. They have been quick, for example, to remove products from shelves at the slightest suspicion of contamination.

More proactively, they have taken a lead in trying to remove genetically modified (GM) ingredients since the issue blew up in 1998 and 1999. Iceland, a modest (under £2 billion sales) frozen-food retailer, announced in early 1998 it was banning GM ingredients from its own-label products. Although this caused controversy at the time, the firm is convinced that it helped them to a 13 per cent LFL sales increase (its home-delivery service contributed too). The majors have taken similar action in 1999, when the issue hit the headlines and the general public became seriously (if unscientifically) worried. Consumers seem to have lost faith in the government's ability or willingness to enforce strict standards of food safety against the interests of agri-business, but the setting up of the Food Standards Agency should help.

The supermarkets know that they rely absolutely on their customers' confidence in the safety of the food they buy. They work hard to deserve that confidence, and their record shows that they do. Beyond that, they have also promoted healthy eating (led in this by Tesco), though it has to be said that they also sell a great deal of processed food, since that is what many of their customers want.

On the more sinister matter of deliberate contamination, there have been many incidents in many countries. In Britain, there have been well-publicized threats against Sainsbury's, and less well-known attempts to blackmail Tesco, among others. Mainly, these are part of an extortion plan, but the threat of deliberate contamination is a powerful one. In the nature of the case, the firms are not anxious to publicize their policies, but all have crisis-management plans in readiness. In those incidents that have been reported, the companies have dealt well with the threats.

THE DEATH OF THE TOWN CENTRE

The market towns of Britain used to be one of its glories. You could walk around the central square, or down the broad main street, with its harmonious collection of buildings of different periods from the mediaeval to the Victorian.

A daily or weekly market would be supplemented by a variety of local specialist shops. The town described in 'A visit to the grocers in the 1940s' in the Introduction had all the specialist shops you could wish for, pubs and an 18th-century hotel, three cinemas – a complete community for a population of 15,000. The only national chains represented were W H Smith and Woolworth's.

Today, it is a different story. Leaving aside the depredations of the planners and developers of the1960s and 1970s – which destroyed so much of beauty and replaced it with concrete – many towns now present a depressing picture. The town of 15,000 has now doubled in size, but the centre has no grocery shops and no cinemas. A new shopping centre has been built on the site of the former woollen mills, but many sites in the town centre are boarded up or occupied by temporary businesses. In most towns, the high street is taken up with national chains (but not supermarkets), building societies and estate agents ('non-shops', as some people call them). Empty premises and charity shops are common. You could stand in the high street of many towns in England, and have no idea where you were – it could be anywhere.

This is, perhaps, nostalgia for a past that never really existed – but there is a large grain of truth there too. Again, we cannot put the blame entirely on the supermarket groups, and should not forget the poor, unstrategic and often haphazard town planning of the 1960s and 1970s – but what part have they played? The most authoritative recent study was carried out by the Department of the Environment, Transport and the Regions (DETR, 1998). Their report rehearses the facts of decline in shop numbers: from 147,000 grocers in 1961 to 28,700 in 1997. It shows that the total floorspace has in fact increased – to 98 million sq ft in 1996 – and that superstores account for an increasing share of that, now some 40 per cent (accounting for 54 per cent of total trade). It quotes the Environment Select Committee report of 1997:

'small and historic market towns are, by their very nature, unlikely to be possessed of town centre sites which can accommodate a modern supermarket with associated parking facilities'.

The answer of the government during the 1980s and early 1990s was to let development take its course, with most planning applications for large edge-of-town or out-of-town superstores granted, either initially or on appeal. As we have seen, the big four made the most of their opportunities, opening as many new stores as they could finance and find sites for. Did this *cause* the subsequent (or possibly parallel) decline in town and district centres?

Perhaps surprisingly, a causal link is hard to establish. One study (BDP and OXIRM, 1994) found that it was impossible to demonstrate that 'the opening of a superstore would have severe adverse effects on the scale, structure and diversity of town centres'. Even if there would clearly be diversion of grocery shopping from the centre to the new store, that would not necessarily have a serious effect on the centre as a whole.

Nevertheless, it was clear that something was wrong. One study found that market towns were making less progress than large cities and urban centres: only 3 per cent said that their centres were vibrant, and as many as 15 per cent said that they were actually declining (DoE, 1994). By 1993, even the free-market Conservative government recognized that some change was needed. The planning guidance PPG6 was revised, and re-titled 'Town Centres and Retail Development'; for the first time, it specifically acknowledged the importance of food retailing in small towns. As other evidence and opinion accumulated, the government made a further revision to PPG6 in 1996. The main result of these moves was that local authorities, in partnership with developers, had in future to take a 'positive yet flexible approach to new retail development', and that they should use a sequential approach. The 1996 version of PPG6 says that:

> Adopting a sequential approach means that first preference should be for town centre sites, where suitable sites or buildings suitable for conversion are available, followed by edge-of-centre sites, district and local centres and only then out-of-centre sites in locations that are accessible by a choice of means of transport.

The health and vibrancy of a town centre may be affected by many things, such as changes in the local agricultural and industrial scene, population shifts, and wider regional changes. Food shopping in the centre cannot alone be responsible for its success or failure. Yet food shopping is the most common and frequent type of shopping, and a trip to a food store is often linked to other shopping. If the food store is removed, then that may contribute to a more general decline in shopping, and to the viability of the centre. Even a marginal loss of trade, say of 10 to 20 per cent, may make the difference between trading profitably and failure.

The DETR study was the most ambitious and coherent attempt to measure these effects. Apart from a thorough literature review, and a survey of all local authorities, they conducted detailed case studies of nine market towns and district centres. The results are striking. They found that the opening of large edge- and out-of-centre food stores had an impact of between 13 and 50 per cent on the market share of the principal food retailers in the centre. For convenience stores in the centre, the impact was between 21 and 75 per cent (note that the calculation is based on *share* before and after the superstore opening: thus if a central store had a share of the total grocery market of 3 per cent before, and 2 per cent after, this counts as a 33 per cent impact).

In Grantham, a typical market town, a specialist greengrocer said that he and the other high street specialists had survived the coming of a large Morrison superstore, and then a Safeway; a new Asda, the largest of all, had just opened, and he wondered how many more they could take. 'In the end, the lovely surroundings and the free car parking will win.' Alderman Thatcher's former grocery is now an aromatherapy and chiropractice clinic.

More general patterns are, however, more complicated. The expansion into new product categories made possible by the larger floor space of superstores means that a shopping trip to the out-of-town store may now include purchases of many other items that would otherwise have been bought in the town. Whereas in some towns, the decline in food shopping can be linked to declines in other (comparison) shopping, to the closure of some shops and thus to a general decline in the viability of the centre, in other towns this did not happen. Centres that have some other cause of vibrancy – strong tourist business, an active town-centre management, for example – are not adversely affected by a loss of food shopping. There may also be knock-on effects on investor and retailer confidence, and therefore a general decline in the quality of buildings, but again this is not inevitable.

The DETR study also examined other issues, including effects on employment, on transport and on clawback. On employment, superstore openings are always accompanied by announcements of large numbers of new jobs – but of course, many old jobs will be lost in existing shops. One previous piece of research had found strong evidence that new superstores have, on average, a negative net effect on retail employment; this is logical, if they are significantly more efficient than smaller competitors. The DETR study could find no conclusive evidence of either positive or negative impact on local employment.

As to transport, we might expect that a new out-of-town store, necessarily attracting mainly car-borne shoppers, would generate an increase in car travel. This does happen, but the effect is small. The report points out that, 'When people have a car available, they will almost certainly use it to undertake food shopping. This suggests that mode choice [i.e. car rather than bus or walking] influences the decision where to shop rather than the reverse'. This is an important point.

On the other hand, retailers' claims that, at this late stage of development, a new store will actually *reduce* the mileage travelled, because shoppers will transfer from a superstore further away, is not supported. Obviously, the net effect will depend on any difference in distance travelled, on any change in mode or frequency and any change in linked trips. This will vary between different towns.

The clawback argument is that a new superstore will actually benefit the centre because it will claw back traffic from a more distant store (and centre).

Again, the results are mixed. Whether any clawback occurs and the extent depends on the size and accessibility of the new store and the nature of the catchment area.

Unquestionably, then, new superstores do have effects on town centres. Food retailers in the centre suffer, though to varying degrees. Other retailers, and the centre as a whole, may or may not decline as a result. Larger centres should be better balanced, and better able to withstand the loss of food retailing – though, as we saw, there may be very serious consequences for some inner-city areas. It is striking that in many other countries – eg France, Germany and Italy – government has been far more proactive in defending small stores and town centres. Laws limiting large superstore development appeared far earlier than in Britain, and laws prohibiting the use of loss-leaders are common. The British 'free market' approach has contributed to, even connived at, the effects of unrestrained superstore development.

The question we must ask ourselves is, again, so what? The supermarket groups are running businesses. The success of the superstores shows that they are meeting the needs of shoppers (at least, the majority of them). The retailers, having discovered the right business model, recognized the opportunity; government policy let them rip. People want to use their cars, and will do so whenever possible, especially to shop for bulky, heavy goods such as a weekly food order. The supermarket chains are merely reflecting changes in society, not leading them.

If Britain as a society wants to change travel patterns, reduce pollution from cars, and lessen the cost and frustration of traffic jams, then people have to find ways of achieving that, probably through government action. In any case, the revision of PPG6 locked the stable doors after the horses had bolted. Most viable sites had already been bought, and some areas were beginning to look over-shopped. Indeed, some people believe that the big four, although protesting in public, were privately relieved that a halt was being called. They have, already developed or in the pipeline, all the sites they want (or, at least, all the sites that they can profitably develop, given the price that their rivalry had driven land to). The difficulty of obtaining new planning permissions will be another barrier to the entry of new competitors.

EXTERNALITIES

Externalities are costs caused by an activity, but not paid for by the actor. Every time we use our car, we cause a range of costs, some of which we pay for directly, and some that are borne by society as a whole. We pay for the fuel we put in the tank, for the depreciation on our capital in the vehicle, for spare parts and repairs, and so on. We do not pay directly for our contribution to air pollution and traffic congestion – in fact, we probably think of those as mainly caused by other people. In recent years, we have become increasingly aware of these external costs, and there are some attempts to allocate them – for example, in making industrial polluters pay, or in charging for road use in congested areas.

Critics claim that the modern supermarket/superstore system has increased road traffic in two main ways: in the delivery of goods to regional distribution centres, and onwards to stores, by road; and in encouraging (some would say forcing) shoppers to drive to and from edge- and out-of-centre shops. The fact that the store groups have been able to make very substantial efficiency gains in their logistics has meant that they pay only the direct costs of road transport, but pass on many more to society as a whole. They gain, in increased profits, but we lose in poorer health, traffic delays and higher road-building costs. Their answer is that, in fact, they have reduced total road traffic, because their centralized distribution systems have cut out many thousands of journeys made by all suppliers to all stores.

It is, of course, not just the supermarket multiples who use road transport, and they would argue that they are merely using the most efficient means available to them. At the time that they were building their distribution chains, the British railway system was in decline. Had it been flexible and responsive to industry demands, it is possible that groceries (and many other products) could have stayed with or converted to rail transport. The regional distribution centres, at least, could have been located at railheads, and only the local transport need have been by road. However, British Rail, as it was then, was not able to offer what the industry needed, and it now seems that the opportunity has been lost for ever. The supermarket industry alone cannot be blamed for what has been a general trend, both in Britain and elsewhere.

As to driving to the superstore, we have seen that even the DETR report recognized the ineluctable fact that, given the choice, the great majority of people *prefer* to use a car for their main shop. One effort to make them realize the externalities would be to make them pay for the car parking at the store, a suggestion that has, not surprisingly, been fiercely resisted by the supermarket groups. It is, frankly, difficult to see how we could be persuaded that we should travel by public transport for a weekly family grocery shop, or that we should go back to the old habits of shopping every day or so. Although the grocery-plus superstore undoubtedly makes a significant contribution to car use, it is only one contributor. Solving the problems caused by road traffic will need to tackle the whole system, not just one part of it.

Packaging is another issue on which the supermarkets have been accused. A major change from the old days is that now, you could buy virtually all your groceries ready wrapped, including fruit and vegetables, meat and fish. The enormous use of plastics this entails gives rise to very large external costs: the use of petrochemicals causes pollution; the collection, storage and disposal of rubbish all cost money, and have knock-on effects – for example, pollution from landfill sites. In some countries, notably Germany, there are now Draconian laws governing packaging, and this may allocate the costs more effectively. Elsewhere, including Britain, such regulation has been resisted – and British consumers are probably not yet as disciplined as Germans or Americans in their readiness to sort and deal with their rubbish. Supermarkets would argue that they are only responding to what consumers want: convenience and cleanliness. They have also made some moves to reduce packaging, mainly by trying to persuade shoppers to reuse plastic bags.

A further externality is the reduction of choice. Although within a single superstore the choice is huge, we can no longer choose from a range of small specialist shops, because they have been driven to the wall by the multiples. Increasingly, we can choose between two, three or four superstores offering an almost identical range. However hard they try to differentiate themselves, the four main chains do in fact offer more or less the same range of products, at more or less the same price. The major difference between the different stores in a catchment area is probably their relative age, the newest (or most recently refurbished) being the most attractive and the oldest the least. Any real difference, that is one that consumers like, will be quickly copied by rivals if they can. Most shoppers probably go to their nearest store, if the competitors are more or less of comparable quality and price. In smaller shopping areas, such as many towns, there is room for only one store anyway. As we saw in the Safeway chapter, they have made it a plank of their strategy to close out any future competition in such areas by building the optimum size of store to cater for all the shoppers in the town. We as consumers, therefore, have a very restricted choice, and total consumer welfare has declined. If we insist on seeking out the specialist cheese supplier or remaining fishmonger, we have to take time, almost certainly drive, and therefore increase our own direct costs, and add to externalities even further.

Other major externalities have been mentioned above, but need to be stressed. These are exclusion and community. Out-of-town shopping centres exclude the poor, the old and the infirm: this is a loss to society as a whole. The loss of community is the result of car-borne shopping to out-of-town centres, too. Town-centre shops are part of the traditional social interaction between people from the same neighbourhood; local shops are part of the local community, and without them the community decays – both in towns and in suburbs and villages. 'This is a major externality that harms even those who use out-of-town facilities. Community is a public good which everyone enjoys, but its benefits are not reflected in the prices which individual consumers pay. Note that these benefits are enjoyed even by the prosperous' (Rowthorn 1998).

We should note that the effect of the oligolopoly on the health of the local shopping community is indirect as well as direct. Direct competitors such as small grocers and specialists find it hard to compete, anyway; but as the super-market groups have taken over much of the function of wholesalers, small shops find it more difficult to obtain supplies at all, let alone at competitive prices.

CONCLUSIONS ON CONSUMERS AND SOCIETY

The supermarket groups have done extremely well for themselves, then. They provide for shoppers a broad range of products in a pleasant, safe environment. Their food is safe and hygienic, and generally thought by shoppers to give value for money. In some categories, they have led a drive against excessive manufacturer margins. They respond to, and lead, changes in taste; they help to educate consumers (eg, in wine); they try to be responsible (in offering healthy eating options). They are so trusted by consumers that, of all deposit takers (banks and other financial institutions), they are growing fastest.

On the other hand, they have reached such a level of concentration that they wield enormous power. We cannot assume that they will always use it for the common weal, rather than for their own selfish interest. They have undoubtedly driven thousands of small shops out of business, possibly increasing overall effi-ciency, but reducing choice. They do not serve the poor and the old well. They contribute to increased road traffic, with all the ills that brings.

Have they served their turn, as some critics argue? They played a valuable role in breaking down previous oligopolies, particularly where manufacturers charged higher-than-necessary prices, but now they are too big, they are them-selves an oligopoly, and they have outlived their usefulness. We may compare them with the clearing banks, which for many years enjoyed an unchallenged hold over retail financial services. Now, new competition has made people realize that they do not need banks as such: they can use telephone or Internet services, other retailers, and a whole raft of providers. The clearing banks were notoriously slow to catch on to the fact that they were there to serve their customers, rather than the other way round. The supermarkets, certainly in the late 1990s, are not making that mistake, though arguably they did in previous decades. But what will happen if the public come to believe that what they have lost may, in the end, be more than they have gained? The supermarket groups have enjoyed high levels of public and political support, because they have persuaded us that they are doing a good job; but recent publicity has suggested that that support is no longer guaranteed. The stores will have to demonstrate – continuously – that they truly have consumer interests at heart, and that they are not abusing their enormous power just to enrich themselves.

THE EFFECT ON SUPPLIERS

If consumers are the biggest group affected by what supermarkets do, suppliers are also intimately involved. For some, the decisions of a few buyers may make the difference between profit and loss – in extreme cases, the difference between survival and closure. When four buyers between them control the majority of the market – up to 60 or 80 per cent, depending on the category – then the threat of de-listing is a serious one, and the negotiating power brought to bear is enormous.

Every supermarket group has hundreds of suppliers around the world, and we cannot analyse all of them. We will look at two groups who account for a large proportion of purchases, and who have been particularly affected by the multiples' growth: manufacturers and farmers.

MANUFACTURERS

By manufacturers, we mean makers of the packaged goods that form the bulk of supermarket products – fast-moving consumer goods, or FMCG, in the jargon. Many of these are huge companies themselves – the P&Gs, Unilevers and Nestlés – and not without power. Typically, however, in any one category or even business unit, the biggest multiple will account for more of the supplier's business than vice versa. All suppliers live with the conundrum that they need distributors, and the distributors need them; but the distributor does not necessarily need *all* suppliers, whereas each supplier does need all the big four retailers. It is clear where the balance of power lies.

This shift in the balance of power, from manufacturers to retailers, is most poignant for the large FMCG companies. People in senior management today started their marketing career at a time when they, the manufacturers, held the whip hand. They had the size, the money, the management sophistication which retailers lacked. They told retailers what to do, more or less; the retailers, more or less, did it. Readers with long memories will remember supermarkets festooned with manufacturers' promotional materials, hanging from the ceilings, plastered over the windows, enlivening the shelves, cluttering the aisles. How many manufacturers' promotions do you see in-store now? Now, it is the retailers who call the tune, and they have demanded increasingly tough conditions for allowing their scarce shelf space to be used.

This was a hard change for many suppliers to accept. In the 1980s, relations between the two reached a nadir. The retailers were by now powerful enough to flex their muscles, but not yet as sophisticated as they later became. Negotiations with suppliers focussed solely on terms, and could be brutal; de-listing was threatened, and sometimes used. Some manufacturers were slow to come to terms with the fact that their world had changed, irrevocably. A few were paranoid, muttering privately of forming a cartel, or seeking government action (see Randall, 1990;1994). One buyer asked, perhaps rhetorically, 'Who needs brands? We don't, and consumers don't either.'

Gradually, sense prevailed. Both realized that they lived in a symbiotic system, depending on each other. Co-operation was better than warfare. Led by the more clear-sighted companies, with P&G in the van (in the United States anyway), manufacturers began to treat retailers as partners, not as a passive channel for their products. Retailers improved the calibre of their managers, so that the people dealing with each other from the two sides were more similar to each other; they spoke the same language, and could understand the other's point of view. Initiatives such as efficient consumer response (ECR) and category management brought all participants in the chain together to work for their mutual benefit. Partnership became the buzzword.

This does not mean that conflict has been banished. Although retailers and manufacturers have mutual interests, they will always be competing for their share of the value added through the chain. Large, powerful manufacturers can stand up for themselves, but many of the smaller firms still live in fear. The supermarkets are accused of anti-competitive practices based on their enormous power, such as demanding overriders. An overrider is a discount, based on volume sold over a period such as a year: it is demanded, and taken, by the retailer. As one supplier pointed out, the saving is not passed on to consumers in lower prices, as the goods have already been sold; it goes straight to the bottom line of the retailer. Another common practice is to 'ask' for a donation to charity, which is then passed on in the retailer's name. The charging of slotting allowances, or higher prices for special positions such as gondola ends, are also common, but seem normal business practice rather than anything more sinister.

Partnership is, however, becoming more prevalent. What suppliers and retailers have found is that working together, sharing information and seeking common goals can be more efficient than a confrontational, adversarial relationship. The shift in the balance of power matters to the suppliers, in that they feel that they have less control. There is no evidence that there has been a real transfer of profit from manufacturers as a whole to retailers (though many suppliers *feel* as if there had been). Does it matter to society that there has been a change in industrial structure?

We saw earlier that, in principle, oligopsonistic buyer power is not bad in itself: if lower prices are passed on to consumers, then their welfare is increased. There is some evidence that British retailers do not always pass on as much as those in other countries (and we discuss below what happens to lower farm prices); rising margins at certain periods suggest that counter-vailing power has not always operated, and that retailers have been able to use their dual power to increase profit. The falling margins of recent years should, on this argument, mean that the retailers' power is decreasing. We shall see; it would be a brave bet that margins will continue to fall much further.

A more insidious danger, according to manufacturers, is that the stranglehold exercised by the big four will reduce the attractiveness of markets, and therefore reduce suppliers' commitment to them. In a report to the Office of Fair Trading, economists agree, concluding that 'buyer power may be socially detrimental where it undermines the long-term viability of suppliers and their willingness to commit to new product and process investments' (Dobson, Waterson and Chu, 1998).

It is here that own-label plays a crucial part. Own-label (OL) – or private label, or distributor's own brand – has become one of the most important weapons in the retailer's armoury. From being a cheap, low-quality version of national brands, it has moved to a position where consumers perceive some OL brands as at least as good as the manufacturers'. Retailers use their OL range in their positioning, trying to differentiate themselves from competitors (if they compete on manufacturers' brands, they might have to compete solely on price, something to be avoided at all costs).

In Britain, OL has penetrated much deeper than in most other countries. In the big four, OL accounted for 40–50 per cent of sales by the mid-1990s (higher for Sainsbury's), compared with around 20 per cent for large French groups such as Carrefour, Promodes and Casino (Corstjens and Corstjens, 1995). Moreover, there is a correlation between the proportion of OL and profitability, both as between UK and French retailers, and among the British groups (Corstjens and Corstjens, 1995).

Marks & Spencer has, of course, led the field in the development and use of OL, first in clothing, and later in food. Of the big four, Sainsbury's has been the most dedicated and successful practitioner. As we saw, those who were late to recognize its importance – arguably all of Tesco, Asda and Safeway at different times – suffered from the neglect. If Marks & Spencer and Sainsbury's were the pioneers, all have now learned the skills, and British retailers lead the world in their use and the sophistication of their OL offer.

These are now brands in their own right, and some would argue that retailers have now taken over some of the manufacturers' function in innovation.

This is where the problem may lie. The major retailers' policy has been increasingly to stock, within a given category, the brand leader, possibly a strong second, and their own-label. Brands lower than no. 2 in the market, and sometimes no. 1, have been de-listed (ie effectively killed off), unless they have a strong niche appeal. Manufacturers may respond in various ways, including making OL products themselves; some concentrate purely on making OL products, and may make a perfectly satisfactory living doing so. The strongest response is, of course, to make sure that their brands are inno-vative, of high quality, and differentiated from competition. Where manufac-turers invest in their brands in this way, they can resist the OL invasion. In categories such as soaps and petfoods, OL has made little headway.

The question is, if manufacturers see that profit margins are being eroded and that some of their weaker brands may not survive, will they then cut back on investment and innovation in the category? And does it matter? It does not, if the retailers do in fact take over the innovation role, and continue to provide consumers with improving products.

The history of OL is that retailers' products have been imitations of manu-facturers' brands (with the major exception of chilled prepared foods, where retailers have led from the start). What manufacturers complain about is that they invest in the innovation and development of new products, and expect to have the opportunity to recoup this investment by a period of selling at a reasonable margin. We may compare the situation in pharmaceuticals, which is an extreme case: millions need to be invested in R&D to produce a new drug, but it is protected from imitation by patent for a period, so that the manufac-turer can earn a return large enough to repay the outlays and make profits. In grocery products, retailers have strong relationships with captive suppliers, and can imitate a new brand within a very short time. They will sell it at a significantly lower price than the brand, eating into its sales and possibly putting downward pressure on its price.

Retailers have in the past ritually professed surprise that anyone should think their OL products were imitations, but anyone walking round a super-market knows the truth. (When I pointed out to a then managing director of Sainsbury's in the late 1980s that their OL fabric-conditioner packaging was identical to that of Comfort, he expressed astonishment and, turning to his colleague, said, 'We must look into that'.) The worst cases have been the so-called look-alikes, where the 'trade dress' is a direct copy of the national brand. In notorious examples, Asda were forced to change the packaging of a 'Puffin' chocolate biscuit that was very similar to United Biscuits' 'Penguin', and Sainsbury's changed the design of their 'Classic Cola' after protests from

Coca-Cola. Both United Biscuits and Coca-Cola are powerful and confident enough to challenge (and even sue) the retailers, but in most other cases, that has not happened. Manufacturers simply cannot afford to alienate the big four by being too difficult. Legal protection in the UK is anyway rather weak, though stronger elsewhere in Europe, Australia and the United States.

There is plenty of evidence that consumers are confused, or taken in, by look-alikes. An NOP survey found that 21 per cent of consumers had purchased look-alike products expecting them to be something else, and other surveys have confirmed this. A controlled study by Kapferer found that consumers make strong connections between national brands and copycat own labels, widely assuming that the brand and its look-alike are probably made by the same manufacturer. When 100 brand managers were questioned, more than half had seen their brands closely copied by retailers, and eight out of ten of those had lost sales as a result (all quoted in Dobson, 1998b).

Retailers' OL products therefore gain a free ride on manufacturers' investment and risk-taking. Look-alikes, and OL products that are not straight copies but still borrow large elements of the brand's trade dress, are deliberate attempts to cash in on others' work. They could be justified on a societal scale if they widened consumer choice and reduced price levels. Retailers may argue that they do just that, and they might – *in the short term*. In the longer term, consumer welfare may be damaged. The argument depends on three steps:

- Manufacturer competition is healthy, as it leads to product and process innovation, improved products and wider choice.
- OL products pose a threat to this healthy competition by taking revenue from the national brands, without incurring the costs of innovation, development and launch. The brand manufacturer suffers disproportionate damage, over and above the effect of normal competition.
- Manufacturers will either reduce investment, or engage in continuous – and wasteful – differentiation. In the long run, the effect is that consumer choice is reduced (Dobson, 1998a and b).

It is, of course, possible to challenge these assertions: can we always rely on manufacturers to compete fiercely, since many of them are also oligolopolists? Even so, retailers may have started to recognize the force of the argument, since Asda says that it is not its policy to make look-alike products now, and Tesco made a similar commitment in April 1997; it remains to be seen how quickly and thoroughly that policy permeates the ranges, and how long it lasts. Sainsbury's has slightly reduced the share of OL in its sales mix (though it is still high at 60 per cent). It is perfectly acceptable for retailers to develop their OL range separately from their suppliers' brands, as with chilled prepared meals. The development of retailers' sub-brands, such as Sainsbury's Novon range of detergents, is also defensible. Manufacturers must continue to invest and innovate, ensuring that their brands are truly different, and do offer real consumer benefits. No one will benefit if the major national brands are gradually whittled away. OL will remain, however, a potent source of friction between suppliers and the powerful retailers. If true partnerships grow, perhaps some accommodation may be reached, allowing each its role, and its returns on investment.

FARMERS AND PRODUCE SUPPLIERS

Now that supermarkets sell the majority of fresh food, they exercise huge power here too. Suppliers are normally primary producers – horticulturalists and farmers – and some of them are relatively small. The retailers have been accused many times over the years of profiteering from this unequal relationship (the very large suppliers can presumably look after themselves, and we do not hear complaints from them).

> In 1993, British supermarkets were accused not only of failing to pass on the benefits of their huge profits to consumers, but also of condemning farmers and producers to their lowest farm incomes since World War II. According to Verdict Research, the gross margin of fresh foods increased from 21 per cent in 1986 to 28 per cent in 1990, while figures for the period 1982–92 suggest that farm incomes fell by 35 per cent. Over the same period, food prices to consumers rose by 52 per cent, but farm-gate prices received by farmers from supermarkets rose by only 18 per cent.
>
> (Raven and Lang, 1995)

In 1998, at the same time that the supermarkets were under attack for creating food deserts (see above), they were again accused of profiteering at farmers' expense. Farming was undergoing an unusually severe downturn, and many smaller farmers in marginal areas were going out of business. A programme on national television (*Newsnight*, 1998) claimed that lamb prices, for example, had dropped so far that many farmers could not afford to sell, or keep, their animals. Yet supermarket prices had not gone down at all. An animal that had fetched £42 last year would now bring only £28 – but appeared to be sold for over £75 on the supermarket shelves. *Panorama* added other, similar testimony from pig farmers, who were selling animals at a loss of £10 a head, though the retail price had not changed much at all (1998).

Part of the reason is that world agriculture was suffering a particularly acute cyclical downturn (*Financial Times*, 1999a), and hog prices in the United

States, for example, were at less than a third of their level in 1997. The pig industries of the United States, Europe and the UK had produced supply greatly in excess of demand, at a period when many export markets – in Russia and the Far East – fell sharply. At the same time, UK producers' costs have risen, due to factors such as the need to comply with new legislation, increased Meat Hygiene Service supervision, and loss of income from sales of offal (Asda evidence to the Agriculture Committee UK pig industry enquiry 1998). Asda also point out that abattoir costs are 54 pence per pig in the UK, against 9–17 pence in Denmark. The result, according to Asda, is that although the farm-gate price has fallen by 40 per cent since 1996, the cost to the super-market has gone down by only 21 per cent; as they have lowered prices by 25 per cent, their profit has actually declined by over 60 per cent. Tesco has produced similar figures, showing that they have passed on savings to shoppers, and that they are in fact losing money on beef and lamb (Tesco 1998).

The retailers' more general answer is that, firstly, they have many costs between carcass and shelf, and some of these have risen. Secondly, they say, they have made significant efficiency savings in their distribution chain (and so, presumably, are entitled to keep that extra margin). Finally, they argue that there are too many stages in the supply chain, and that farmers are too disag-gregated; they should co-operate more, as they do in New Zealand.

Accusations from others, such as suppliers of fresh vegetables, added to the charge of bullying and sharp practice. A grower of Brussels sprouts would be phoned by a supermarket buyer on a Thursday and told, 'We are running a promotion for the next two weeks, so the price is cut by £30 (or £40, or £50) a ton'. At the end of the two weeks, the price to the grower did not go back up, though on the shelves it did. Written contracts do not exist, even if suppliers ask for them (*Panorama*, 1998).

Other ways of increasing margin for the retailer included insisting that the grower used a particular maker of packaging, even though it was not the cheapest. The packaging maker was giving a kickback to the retailer, and there was nothing the grower could do about it. He has now left the business, which is why he was willing to speak out. In the climate of disillusion and fear that is said to exist, anyone who wants to continue to supply the supermarkets – and there is no one else to sell to – has to toe the line, and keep quiet.

The retailers either deny such stories, or claim that they represent a minority of cases (the 'odd bad apple' defence). They say that their relationships with suppliers are long-term; it is not in their interests to exert undue pressure. Of course there is conflict, as in any buyer–seller relationship.

Critics within the industry contend that the retailers are maximizing their short-term gains, but potentially harming the industry as a whole in the longer run. Food producers will not be able to compete internationally, claimed one (Michael Ullmann, Chairman of La Fornaia bakery products, *Panorama*, 1998). As he pointed out, Britain already imports a higher proportion of manufactured food than any other nation and, if the current trends continue, that can only get worse. (It is revealing that at least one of the supermarkets received a letter from the chief executive within days of the broadcast, disassociating himself and other directors from their chairman's remarks.)

Even those outside are worried. Sir John Harvey-Jones, asked how he thought the supermarket groups were exercising their power, replied in one word: 'Irresponsibly'. He explained that they are not concerning themselves with the health and profitability of the supply chain as a whole; they should be acting to maintain the health of the total food-supply industry, but they were threatening to destroy it. If, he suggested, they were damaging horticulture in particular, and agriculture to some degree, then the national effects were enormous. If you add that they are blighting many small towns in the countryside, their overall influence is worrying.

CONCLUSIONS ON SUPPLIERS

The discussion in this chapter may make it seem that we are being inconsistent. On the one hand, we admire the supermarkets as businesses, and argue that they have done a great job, reaching and even leading world-class standards in many areas of operation. On the other, we accept criticisms that their success has had undesirable effects, and that their business practices are not always perfect. This is true, and we accept the paradox. It is perfectly possible to admire Rupert Murdoch as a businessman, while deploring some of the results of his success. He is a global, strategic thinker and a major risk-taker who deserves the rewards that successful gambles produce – but we are appalled at the effect he has had on British newspapers. The analogy is not perfect, as we see the food retailers as having mainly – but not entirely – benign effects, but it shows that it is possible, perhaps common, to hold quite differing views about different aspects of the same organization.

The supermarket groups are, as we have said repeatedly, businesses, and they must act in the interests of shareholders. Within the industry as a whole, their success has led to a major shift in the balance of power, but this is not in itself a bad thing. There have been cases where they have abused their power, probably more often some years ago than now (one retailer told the author 10 years ago that 'some of our buyers have callouses on their knuckles from where their hands drag along the ground'). The stories in the press and on television have undoubtedly been one-sided, and have not put the retailers' point of view (even when it was offered).

In general, we believe that the retailers are to be congratulated on their strategies and operations. But they now have great power, and with that power goes responsibility. They will have to show that they can behave as industry leaders.

12

Future challenges

By the end of the 1990s, the big four UK supermarket groups (or Big Two plus two, to use David Webster's 1998 formulation), had achieved a position that was in some ways enviable, in other ways open to criticism. With some variations, they have been able to produce sales and profit growth consistently over many years. They are world-class in many aspects of their operations, and leaders in some. Consumers are generally happy with what they offer. They have built or taken advantage of barriers to entry, so that it is now extremely difficult for any new challenger to take them on directly. Suitable sites are now expensive and hard to find, and planning permission for development is difficult. The share prices of the companies makes them too expensive for most possible predators from within the industry; the major exception is Wal-Mart, which is big enough and rich enough to buy any of the British chains. While regulators might object to any merger between the home teams, they would probably not be able to resist any foreign takeover.

On the other hand, the firms may have reached a plateau. Today there are distinct and repetitive signs that we may be seeing them at the peak of their power and influence. Food sales are flat, and as a proportion of total consumer spending, have dropped by more than 10 per cent (to just over 10.5 per cent of all spending) in the past decade (Verdict 1998 data). They are likely to remain flat showing that this is indeed a mature market. There will be some continuing mileage in increasing the contribution from high-margin products, but there will be a limit to that, and US experience suggests that much of the ensuing gain will go to specialty niche suppliers.

Overall margins have been slipping in recent years, partly because of the entry of hard discounters and partly because the rivalry between the majors is now bringing them very directly into open competition between themselves. Long gone are the days of easy pickings from Co-ops and independents. The additional new formats that the major retailers have developed will certainly not improve margins. The barriers to entry that keep out new competition also affect the current players, as there are few sites left that are affordable and do not cannibalize sales from other stores. Public disquiet about the effect of out-of-town superstores on town centres has grown, and both current and future planning policies will severely limit further development. Conversion of existing stores allows some increase in selling space, but again it is limited. Smaller stores, whether in old high streets or market towns, will let them fill in gaps, but these smaller premises do not always offer the economies of scale that are so attractive in the superstores. New sectors (non-food, financial services, other services) offer some prospects, but it is not yet clear that the supermarket groups have the skills to do as well in these newer fields as in their core area.

Significantly, they have made little impact abroad, while major competitors such as Carrefour, Ahold, Metro and Aldi have been successfully building international businesses. If these international groups achieve real economies of scale and scope, that will deliver them a competitive advantage just as deadly as the British supermarkets developed against their smaller competitors at home. The British market has allowed, or forced, them to adopt a superstore model, when in the rest of the world the pattern of hypermarket/discounter seems to have been emerging as the norm. The supermarkets have been criticized for their effects on society, and are under investigation for allegedly monopolistic practices. They have reached a new stage: their existing strategies will allow them to continue on their current paths for a while, but there are many new challenges that they will have to meet in order to survive and grow. Some challenges are common to all, while others are specific to each.

In the short term – that is the next two to three years – the UK groups must keep their focus on current operations while also working out their responses to the longer-term challenges, and outlining a distinctive strategic vision for the global food-retailing market. The MMC investigation will not help them to concentrate on their business. They know from their own individual histories that each of the majors has, at some time, taken its eye off the ball, and each has paid the penalty, usually for quite a few years, in below-par results. In food at least, they are in a zero-sum game: any gain by a competitor has to come from someone else. They cannot afford a price war (given the high capital intensity of the industry), but they cannot afford to appear to offer poorer value than their rivals. The short-term challenges revolve around the fundamental operational retailing skills, of making their space work for them, squeezing out costs while maintaining availability, improving quality while preserving margins at attractive prices, innovating in the total mix of products and services. Perhaps the greatest (and least familiar) challenge is to make IT deliver real under-standing of consumers as a basis for marketing action. The longer-term chal-lenges – and to use the old cliché, the future starts tomorrow – fall into three broad categories: competition, changing consumer demands, and regulation.

COMPETITION

EXISTING

Among the current players on the British scene, a critical view would identify several issues which the supermarket groups have to tackle. Firstly, there is the lack of a truly distinctive personality. The chains may have persuaded them-selves that they are genuinely differentiated, but it is unlikely that most consumers would really agree. The reader is invited to try this test personally. If you were brought blindfolded into a town or area unknown to you, and into any superstore stripped of overt identification, would you really be able to say what store you were in? Asda claims to offer service with personality, but while the staff in their Leeds headquarters and store managers know the litany, there is little evidence of this on the ground, ie in the local store. How different, really, are Tesco and Sainsbury's, or is either from a good Safeway superstore? Is it not just that the newest store, or the most recent refurbishment, offers visible up-to-date features and the most attractive ambience? Waitrose and Morrison, in their different ways, have some penchant for distinctiveness, but they are relatively small players and make limited national impact.

The product range is not genuinely differentiated: in a similar way, the total product offering of the groups is hard to separate from each other. In fresh food Marks & Spencer and Waitrose have registered a clear lead, and in non-food Asda have pushed furthest, leading Tesco which leads the rest. But the differ-ences are not fundamental, and alternative profiling could change the respective rank orders quite quickly. With national brands – where by defi-nition they are all offering the same – only price can differentiate, and there the differences are a lot less than they used to be in the freewheeling days of the early 1980s. Not only are the chains uniformly determined not to go down the road of strong price differentiation; their discipline and control has removed many of the promotions that used to enliven store portfolios from the shelves in favour of the omnipresent 'multibuy' promotions that aim purely to load up forward purchasing. (Even Asda, which is slightly cheaper, takes great care not to open up large price differences on known value items, and are as disciplined as all the others in tightly limiting consumer promotions.)

Own-label is an important differentiator, one that in the past has made a difference. Marks & Spencer notably, and Sainsbury's for many years in the supermarket sector, were well ahead of competition. They opened up a gap against the whole of the rest of the world. Those who neglected the development of a worthwhile own-label brand – Tesco and Asda at different times – suffered. By now, however, all the groups are at a similar stage. Even the once-great Marks & Spencer is finding it increasingly difficult to show clear blue water between its offering and the leading rivals. Fresh food and meal solutions are the battleground, but any service innovation can be copied and usually is, if it is successful. All the groups are reintroducing craft skills across their product range but none can claim a great advantage. Indeed, despite the development of on-the-premises specialty bakery and butchery offerings, the present trend suggests greater unhappiness than ever before about the quality and safety of the UK market's food offering. Hence increasing consumer disquiet and the signalled intention to establish a national Food Standards Agency to create greater balance and to monitor food-quality issues for the country as a whole. In this regard it seems the UK does have more organic problems to deal with than other developed markets have had.

Secondly, the food-shopping process is the same as 10, 20, 30 years ago: self-service, the supermarket, the superstore all transformed our shopping experience in their time. Any subsequent changes have been at the margin. A modern superstore has more car parking, strives to be both emotionally warmer and physically more pleasant. It has a wider range of products – but the essential shopping experience is not really very different from that of 10 years ago. The food-shopping experience is clinical, unexciting, undifferentiated: for most shoppers, the basic weekly main shop is acceptable but a chore. We still have the same problems of car parking, finding a trolley, negotiating our way round the aisles, finding our way around with little assistance, shortage of meaningful information, queuing at check-outs, and so on. There are few positive or innovative experiences on offer (though we should stress that consumers find the overall experience acceptable; the sheer convenience outweighs the negatives).

The unavoidable impression is one of a mature industry, which has learned all the tricks, believes there is little objective difference between its companies but remains grimly determined to maintain its present satisfactory trading position for as long as it can. If this is true, it is a dangerous posture to take in any business, but especially one as well populated with global innovators as food retailing has been. The consumer–store relationship is dangerously monolithic, shallow and impersonal. At present, our relationship with the shop, and the store group is, and most certainly feels, one-way. (If you doubt this, those old enough should cast their minds back to the personal relationship they or their parents had with the high-street grocer. Younger readers will be considering the excitement of interactive browsing and shopping, eg for books or travel. Foreign travellers might reflect on a typical discussion of events at a French village butcher or baker.) In modern Britain the picture is one where 'they' decide what to offer, and arrange everything to suit themselves. We do a lot of the work, but are essentially taking what they give.

The fact that all the groups now make much more serious efforts to listen to customers and react to their needs and wishes, may take more time to penetrate. To date it has been a pretty defensive kind of recognition, arrived at perhaps with an unhappy sense of inevitability.

The Coopers and Lybrand study noted a further issue: 'not being near best in world operational standards' (1996). We disagree. The only evidence for UK food retailers' not being world-class is the failure of some, such as Sainsbury's, to operate successfully abroad; even the great Marks & Spencer struggled for years, though more in clothing than food. We see those as failures to adapt to a new culture and market. In future, the ability to operate in many countries *will* of course be an element of world-class competence.

Nonetheless, we believe that the current players recognize all these issues, and are confronting them. Differentiating a service business is difficult at the best of times, as ideas cannot be copyrighted. The development process of food retailing in recent years has been evolutionary, with the competitors studying each others' moves carefully and quickly. Perhaps indeed the basic retail offer now has to be similar, in the same way that most modern cars are very alike. The leading companies are all UK-based public companies with broadly similar access to capital for development. All competitors are using the same technology, and facing the same constraints, so different companies' solutions will invariably come out looking much the same. (Implementing solutions still takes great dedication and skill, so different companies do achieve different results. Firms rise and fall in competitive ranking in relation to how well they implement, as well as how good their strategy is.) Defining, communicating and maintaining a position will demand rigorous analytical skills, and creative innovation. And the protagonists must be conscious that they have to match not just the best UK-market potential standards, but those which could be imposed by new competition from different industries, different and more innovative parts of the world, and with greater access to capital as well as to skills in depth.

For Tesco, the challenge is to stay ahead. It must remain, if not all things to all people, attractive to all main segments. Its scale gives it the opportunity to do this, so if it stays humble, and innovative enough to lead as well as responding to consumer demands, using its still embryonic but growing IT and marketing skills, it should not be caught. Its international strategy is distinctly unproven, but there is at least a coherent philosophy behind its intentions; it has patently learnt from past errors and has an improving track record. Tesco would be a hugely attractive ally for any European major wishing to enter Britain.

Sainsbury's has an entirely different challenge. Having been leader for so long, then lost the plot a little (only a little, but that is all it takes), it has to engender new drive. It lagged in a whole range of key innovations, notably loyalty cards, and must rediscover the business authority and certain feel for food-standards leadership that once motivated it. Sainsbury's has an abundant need to insert humanity and warmth into its company, as well as genuine innovation in its consumer offer. Its international strategy, if it had one, is now in tatters and must be rebuilt from the ground up. Its scale and its still formidable skills make it a powerful competitor and should keep it in touch. Once again its size makes it a very worthwhile partner but it is not negotiating from strength to quite the same degree as Tesco is.

Asda has the clearest positioning of the majors, but has to deliver on its promises from a tightly controlled cost and staff base. Promising 'service with personality' and having all its many colleague-oriented practices will not help if staff shortages lead to poor availability. Its positioning also depended on having Kwik Save as a benchmark, and it will have to negotiate a clever course making sure the hard discounters do not grow but keeping close to its main rivals in pricing perception across the range. Asda is the most similar to Wal-Mart of any of the British retailers, a fact that cannot be lost on the US management.

Safeway, as we saw, has a strategy, but has a very mixed store base on which to operate. The revitalized Somerfield has some of the same location tactics (small to medium local stores), and threatens to overtake Safeway in sales unless the latter can speed up its climbing sales density. That means attracting more main shoppers, and that entails offering and communicating a competitive price level. Targeting the same family shopper as Asda, which has a good price perception, will not make it any easier. Safeway has always been willing to be the most innovative in shopping experience, and in principle related well to consumer requirements – self-scanning, crèches, are recent examples – but it will need to keep innovating with the pressure now very much more on the level of results it can achieve in a tougher market. Survival will be a challenge.

NEW COMPETITORS

While the store groups have to fight hard against each other, they must keep an eye on new competition. Some have already arrived, while others may be lurking.

Discounters have never had much impact in Britain, but the invasion of successful, professional operators from abroad may change that. In Germany, an astounding 90 per cent of food shoppers visit an Aldi within a six-month period (a higher figure than for any single British chain). It is too early to say whether Aldi, Netto and Lidl will be able to change the British preference for higher prices and a more pleasant shopping environment. They will at least constrain the majors' pricing freedom, and exert downward pressure on margins.

Other possible foreign invaders are the expansionist Europeans such as Carrefour and Ahold. Starting a new superstore group in Britain from scratch is unlikely, for the reasons set out earlier, but it seems very probable that one or more European groups will be looking for partners or acquisitions. In the current state of play, few if any of the Europeans have the cash or capital-raising potential (with the possible exception of Ahold) to make a straight bid for any of the four UK majors – but that may change. Some alliance, however, may be attractive to both partners. Some of the followers – such as Morrison or Somerfield – could be bought, and the latter have nearly 100 high-quality big stores, so any such purchase would change the competitive map.

Wal-Mart's menacing sword of Damocles has been hanging over the entire market's collective head. Nobody could afford to ignore it or the effect that its entry would have on what would thereafter seem to have been a quiet and gentle meander through the placid and predictable fields of the UK retail market. It has been expanding abroad, and with some speed, bearing in mind that while founder Sam was alive, its ambitions were pretty much US-based. Since they are in Germany already and a wide range of other foreign markets, then Britain would unquestionably represent a reasonable next step – the issue to us was not any longer whether but how (ie for whom it might bid) and when (ie where is Britain on the list of attractive world options). Whether or not it bids would have depended on how it views the payback from what would be, even for Wal-Mart, a substantial investment. In April 1999, it said that it would not buy in Britain in the near future. It said that it would not be in shareholders' interests: UK margins are too high to make an acquisition attractive. 'In the UK, eventually, margins will move closer to the levels in the rest of Europe. And if you buy a company with high margins which then fall, it will be difficult to make it work for shareholders', said a senior Wal-Mart manager (*Financial Times* 29 April 1999).

Few doubted that Wal-Mart would continue to expand in Europe, and eventually in Britain, so the question remained what, and when. There seemed little point in buying 'small' in the UK market – the evidence is against this working. If it took a long view, and bought a worthwhile British chain, that would completely change the industry structure, and all bets would then be off. Its buying power, operational efficiency and everyday low pricing would alter the UK scene radically, and the remaining supermarket groups would have to look very hard indeed at how they could respond. As we now know, Wal-Mart bought Asda in June 1999, and the remaining British groups must now be thinking about contingency plans. No doubt they are, but thinking needs to turn itself into action plans for the would-be survivors and they can't afford to wait around. We do not know exactly what Wal-Mart will do, and its freedom of action will be affected by site and planning availability, but it is certain that its presence will have a downward influence on prices. Given the publicity surrounding supermarket prices in 1998 and 1999, both public and government will no doubt welcome this. If an all-out price war occurs, then Wal-Mart's deep pockets (turnover of $137 billion or £86 billion, compared with Tesco's £18 billion) would guarantee it victory. We do not think it will come to that, but all the relatively small British groups will now intensify their search for a European partner.

Finally, new competitors may appear from outside the industry. The most likely at present would be a logistics/IT-based firm offering some form of remote shopping. Although no such operation has yet been shown to produce a profitable long-term outcome, or even the prospects of one occurring, the possibility must be taken seriously. It is not yet clear that the present British retail players really believe this is likely to make serious impact within 5 or even 10 years; their experiments are still at the micro-learning levels, designed as 'add-ons' to a powerful, structured superstore base. (In the United States, the experiments have so far been largely alliances between operators and systems developers but there is no reason why this should always be the case.) This might not be the appropriate way to regard such potentially hostile and highly disruptive moves.

Another possibility is what Americans call a 'foodservice' store, combining a fast-food restaurant, meal-solutions retailer and perhaps narrow-line grocer. The danger of these or any specialist cherry-picking is that it could take away the top end, high-margin sales and affect overall profitability more than proportionally. In addition, this would be a threatening move for the superstore locations, if town centres were to prove supportive, and if they proved ready to create the necessary amount of parking. The current retail leaders need to watch carefully for the early signs of such initiatives and the presence of the relevant innovative mentalities with new food-service ideas for entering the game in new and profitable ways – much less dependent on high levels of fixed assets.

CHANGING CONSUMERS

We know that consumers are changing – they always do. After 30 years of steady evolution in UK food retailing, they may now be ready for more radical change than anyone can currently predict. There are also plenty of prophets to tell us what is going to happen. Here we will concentrate on views directly related to food shopping in Britain and the United States. In Britain, the important trends identified fall into three areas which can be summarized as:

- polarizing consumers;
- the rise of the prosumer;
- new and continuing consumer realities.

POLARIZING CONSUMERS

It may not seem like it when you visit your local Tesco or Sainsbury's, but the mass shopping constituency is fragmenting rapidly, representing a huge issue for major companies, which have excelled in welding together large audiences of consumers with common aspirations and behaviours from single localities. Working women have now become the norm in the UK, the nuclear family is experiencing savage decline and perhaps even seeing its demise ahead; the population ages visibly, and simultaneously becomes more extreme, in divisions between rich and poor, healthy and sick, time-rich and time-starved. Social norms disappear, mealtimes fragment yet expand, and across the entire spectrum hovers stress from increasing work (for those lucky enough to be working), congestion, travel times, competition and personal insecurity. This is a different world from the adventurous and unifyingly positive 1960s in which the supermarkets and earliest superstores made their mark across the national community.

THE RISE OF THE PROSUMER

Not everything is divisiveness, insecurity and bad news ahead, however. Consumers have become more discriminating, more knowledgeable about the brands and offers available, more capable of rejecting apparent authority and more confident about making individual choices. The environment has surfaced as a major issue in its own right, somewhat more slowly in the UK than elsewhere, but there is no doubt it is now here to stay. Enhanced consumer knowledge now extends deeply into the food market, where diet requirements, concern for food safety and an awareness of real food-quality differences now exist at levels that were unheard of just one decade ago. Nightly food and cookery programmes on radio and television, and column inches in the daily newspapers spread the information more and more widely.

The existence of powerful individual consumer groups, determined to drive single issues forward, is another new factor – vigilante consumers now exist in numbers, and the frenetic activity behind animal rights is a clear indication of the pressure that can be exerted by small but committed groups of single-issue zealots. Criticism of existing food lobbies – ministries as well as retailers and suppliers – is rampant and uninhibited, and is making ever-increasing demands on the participants. Powerful new regulators arrive on the scene confirming increasing levels of public anxiety about what they are buying, what they are eating, and what they might not know about either or both. Everyone seems to need some kind of help with food these days, and more and more people and organizations stand ready to provide it.

NEW AND CONTINUING REALITIES

The role of government has altered out of recognition. Alongside the British so-called 'death of deference' is rapid growth in levels of European integration. Meanwhile the boundaries of food technology themselves expand in response to scientific development and ever more sophisticated consumer demand. Foods development must now address the delicate issue of genetically modified (GM) foods. Equally conflictual are such social 'time bombs' as the well-documented growth of the underclass, and the related issues of rising crime and of 'food deserts'. It is not at all easy for traditionally responsible companies to pilot an ethical and economically effective route through these complex social issues. Mistakes, based often on intelligible but ultimately incorrect judgements, are easy to make. Inevitably they will become more frequent.

An American analysis is similar: see Table 12.1. Most of these patterns in both countries – and indeed elsewhere – are well established and uncontroversial, but it is worth commenting on some of the lifestyle trends in particular.

Perceived time poverty

Americans are working longer hours, and think that they have less free time. Paradoxically, they have, in fact, twice as much free time as they think. To resolve this conundrum, we have to understand that the hours devoted to activities such as housework and meal preparation have declined significantly, creating more free time. But new technologies such as the fax, e-mail and the mobile phone have invaded the home, leading to less perceived free time, and more stress (chiming with the British analysis).

Table 12.1 *The consumer of 2005*

Today's Trends	Consumer Attitudes: 2005	Business Implications: 2005

Demographic trends
• Ageing America
• Greater diversity
• Income polarity
• More working women
• Non-traditional
  households
Lifestyle trends
• Time poverty
• Health consciousness
• Networked consumers
• Employee scarcity
	• Shopping seen as a chore
	  or as entertainment
	• More choice in meal solutions
	• Increased food diversity
	• More "wellness" and health-
	  enhancing foods
	• Continued growth in away-
	  from-home meals
	• More choices, less time
		For retailers
		• Increased consumer power
		• Convenience focus
		• Low prices on
		  replenishment items
		• Tight labour market
		For manufacturers
		• Many channels to market
		• More innovative products
		• Local, custom promotions
		For wholesalers
		• Low-cost distribution
		• Assist retailers with
		  perimeter development
		• Provide manufacturers
		  with better information
		  and execution

Source: A T Kearney (1988)

Health consciousness

Americans are increasingly interested in their health, in information about health, in self-diagnosis, in alternative treatments, and so on. They spend twice as much on health as do the British. Some exercise fiercely, but paradoxically the proportion of Americans who are overweight is going up. We know that, in both countries, attitudes towards a healthier diet do not always lead to changes in buying and eating habits (Kearney, 1998).

The fact that we can identify trends does not mean that we can say, simply and unambiguously, what exactly will happen. The consumer attitudes relevant to food retailing were summarized for the United States as broadly, a lot more choice, but simultaneously, a lot less time.

Shopping segments the US population and is seen by some as a chore, by others as entertainment. But increased choice is accelerating, offering consumers more choice in prepared-meal solutions, more diverse foods available, more foods that overtly set out to enhance health and well-ness, and a continuing growth in meals taken away from the home.

Coopers and Lybrand's European study confirms a comparable trend towards more complexity in shopping behaviour and choice of store, with consumers benchmarking their foodstore against the best service they can find anywhere. Standards of expectation are rising – zero defects and more for less are the expressions used. Customer loyalty is harder to maintain, and stores need to work more innovatively to fit their offers to the consumer's agenda – this idea seems quite a change! Mass-market appeal is on the decline, pressure on margins is unrelenting and consumers expect not just good food quality and value, but ethical standards and an acceptance of social responsibilities from their food-store proprietors (adapted from Cooper and Lybrand, 1996).

REGULATION

We have seen how regulation against a particularly free-market background in Britain has begun to move against unfettered superstore development – the worm has finally turned. While it has manifested itself late in the day, it is unlikely now ever to revert to previous patterns. The core issue would seem to be the maintenance in British society as a whole, but particularly in urban and suburban environments, of coherent communities of people, linked by common interests but operating in physical proximity and association one with another. The negative effects of car-borne, out-of-town shopping – on excluded social groups such as the poor and the old, on high streets and communities, and on the physical environment – have led to new restrictions. These are indeed new to Britain, but are more commonplace in other European countries. If current trends in growth of car- and road-use continue, and there seems no reason to suppose they will change by themselves, then further regulation may appear desirable, even necessary. For example, Robert Rowthorn, Professor of Economics at the University of Cambridge, makes this suggestion:

An adequate policy for dealing with these problems would:

- aid those presently excluded (the poor and the old) and
- make consumers pay the full cost of all the negative externalities they impose on others.

Use of out-of-town facilities should be taxed to reflect the full cost of these negative externalities. At the same time it should be a requirement of local authorities to ensure that neighbourhoods and villages have adequate local shopping facilities, just as they must ensure the provision of adequate local schools, and health authorities must ensure adequate medical facilities. This does not mean that shops should be publicly run. The provision of adequate local shopping facilities could be franchised to some private individual or even to a supermarket chain. Central government funding could be available to subsidize rents for local shops, using the money raised by taxes on out-of-town facilities. There could even be a local shopping inspectorate and league tables to ensure that local authorities were meeting their obligations. If this idea caught on, the existing supermarket chains would probably take up the challenge in a big way. It could be very profitable for them, and they could use their distribution and marketing expertise to make their local shops very attractive. Moreover, with home deliveries for bulk items, many shoppers could manage quite well without their cars. (Rowthorn, 1998)

It has become increasingly clear that something will have to be done if Britain's city centres are not to clog up with traffic completely, and many high streets and villages are to survive as coherent entities in any shape or form. While Rowthorn's prescription may seem extreme to some, to others it is simple good sense, and nothing more than an extension of existing policies in this and other areas. That some further regulation will happen now seems certain. While it might not yet enjoy the support numerically of a majority of the community, thinking consumers are much more conscious now of the trade-offs that out-of-town shopping has forced in their lives.

REACTING TO CHANGE

All this looks very threatening to companies with billions of pounds tied up in well-constructed modern shops. But then the scenario of developed societies where consumers no longer do their food shopping in out-of-town stores, or indeed in stores with fixed locations at all has been addressed by some of the most authoritative scholars, eg MIT's Lester Thurow (in a keynote speech to the 1998 UK Marketing Forum). Thurow suggested that retail fixed assets in the United States would be seen as an acute liability within the next few decades. Alternatively, of course, it could represent terrific opportunity to a company that is genuinely flexible and innovative. The precise amount of potential change that actually happens will depend not only on what customers want, but on what retailers are prepared to consider offering. For decades, customers have been happy to accept what they were given, because on the whole they bought perceptibly better convenience. Range and quality steadily improved year by year and most importantly of all perhaps, there was virtually no alternative. If they did not shop at the supermarket, where could they go? If they were not satisfied with Sainsbury's, would Tesco offer them anything radically different? If the British food retailers, constrained by their existing structure (and especially by their freehold estate) changed very little over the next five to ten years, would the consumer be able to do anything about it?

The answer lies in competition and the free market. Accepting that the

British food-retailing market might not meet the economist's definition of perfect competition, (whether any industries do is a legitimate question), it is still competitive. The existing players have always played to win, and still want to very badly. They will take any opportunity to gain an advantage over their rivals. If they do not, new competitors may enter, and given a market that is now global in scale, there are plenty of these waiting in the wings. If conditions change radically then, on Gary Hamel's argument, the current leaders are unlikely to be the winners of the next phase, but at present we cannot see who might be. What do the current players have to do to stay in the game?

STRATEGIES FOR SUCCESS

Let us talk first in general about what an ideal strategy might look like. The winner in the next century will have:

- broad geographical coverage, within a national market and internationally;
- sufficient scale to achieve economies in buying, and in investment in areas such as IT as well as store, product and brand development;
- a range of formats from hypermarkets (or supercenters in the United States) to medium-sized stores in local markets to convenience stores;
- the ability to use IT to maintain high product availability (95 per cent plus) at lowest cost.

Up to this point, you could argue that any firm that survives as a leading player will need all of these: they are the givens, simply an entry fee for playing the game. That does not mean that all the present British supermarket groups will be playing at the top table – they certainly won't. If they do not achieve all the standards listed, they will have fallen out of the leading pack, and, to change the metaphor, be back in the *peloton* (the terrifying mass of riders bunched together in the cycling *Tour de France*). What skills will really discriminate future winners? Here is our attempt to answer the question:

- the skill to use customer data to understand the market at increasingly fine levels of detail, and to find new ways of segmenting and serving customers;
- the ability to define a brand with unique meaning and appeal to consumers, and the skill to translate that into the reality of stores, product ranges and services;
- the ability to communicate with and build relationships with customers in an increasingly complex, fragmented world.

Winners will have to work at the leading edge of operational competence in all fields. We believe that British retailers have been doing this, at a national level, so their challenge is to keep doing it in more and more difficult circumstances.

They will also have to compete on price: not necessarily the lowest price available in the market, but certainly within reach of that; they may have to offer different levels of price; for any gap above the lowest price, they will have to offer clear, desirable added value. They will have to offer customers a range of ways of shopping.

We cannot say what a successful food retailing brand may look like, though we feel that it must set out to have more functional difference as well as more emotional warmth, and have more depth of personality than the current firms provide. A comparison would be the American bookshops that offer comfortable sofas and armchairs, coffee, and the opportunity to browse. Going to such a shop becomes an experience much richer than merely going to buy a book (which you can do more cheaply and conveniently via the Internet now). Similarly, FNAC, the French chain, offered competitive prices on electrical goods, music and books; more importantly, it created a culture of its own, so that visitors were encouraged to linger, to ask advice, to socialize; it became a club and place to meet friends. In both cases, sales and profits increased, too.

The challenge for the supermarket operators is to find a way of creating something like this – as an experience, not as an exact replication – without compromising their efficiency. Many of them now claim to offer superior customer service in one way or another, but the distinctions are marginal. Frankly, it is easier for them to see these differences than for their consumers, and in no sense can they be said to form part of a long-term conceptually driven programme of advantage with which consumers can identify. No group is yet delivering the truly outstanding service of, say, Nordstrom in the United States, whose reputation really is legendary.

The leading retailers already do have strong brands, in the sense that consumers know and trust them. Sainsbury's was the first (apart from Marks & Spencer) to build a strong retail brand, but it demonstrates the difficulty of the game that Tesco has certainly caught up, and in a series of recognizable ways has overtaken that brand strength. The temptation will be for the firms to use consumers' trust in the brand to offer a wider and wider range of services. They successfully provide many retail services outside food, and their extension into financial services seems to be succeeding – but there is a clear danger of over-stretch. The retailers who have done it believed that the apparently ossified group of UK clearing banks were a soft target and results have proved their judgements were right. Yet some retailers already prefer not to use their brand for a bank, as they do not want to have to say 'No' to customers and in any case, there will be few such easy pickings around in the years ahead as the high street banks offered. And while Sainsbury's and Tesco both offer great rates for overnight deposits, how do consumers perceive the banking brands as different?

There is no reason why the leading grocery retailers should not offer gas and electricity, for example, now that those are deregulated. Should they? Some combinations with food shopping are naturals, such as petrol (though the offer is comparatively recent in the UK; so like so many things, it seems obvious only when someone has done it successfully). Even here, reputable players, Waitrose for one, do not feel petrol integrates with their vision of their food offer, and they may be right. Other areas will be a lot more questionable. There needs to be an objective process – a test, and we suggest the test should be:

- Does it fit the brand?
- Can we add value (compared with existing competition), and can we then stay in the game (have we the resources and skills to do so)?
- Will we make an acceptable margin?

The brand does not end there. Consumers increasingly want a relationship with the company that stands behind the brand, and they are more demanding as to what the company should be. One model elaborates the different roles that a food store fulfils, and the different levels to which an individual brand might aspire (Table 12.2).

The elements are product range and added value, product origin and integrity, personality and service, and social responsibility/corporate mission. As there are many different levels of attainment possible under each principal heading, there are literally hundreds of possible separate combinations. What this points up is not that all of these will exist in any specific situation, but that there are many possible individual solutions. Each company will have to work out for itself what its role should be, and how it should evolve over the years. It is a careful, long-term and strategic process. The role should distinguish it from competitors, and be as difficult to copy as possible.

When considering the following examples of role combinations, the reader should consider how very different these are from today's more composite and therefore anonymous food-retailing realities, and this is as true in Europe and the United States as it is in Britain:

- the expert high-interest food company, concentrating on leading food values across retail, eating out and catering;
- the specialist in a particular type of shopping trip (top-up, bulk-buy);
- the food and skills educator;
- the world's favourite food store, or the European store;
- the spine of the local community (such as Hemshop in Sweden);
- the integrated life-support company, providing everything needed for day-to-day living;
- the innovative 'making life easy and interesting' company;

Table 12.2 *Generic food-store role model*

	'From ethics to ethics' Role		
Product range and added value	**Product origin and integrity**	**Personality and service**	**Social responsibility/ Corporate motivation**
1. When a basic range of food products is provided efficiently and conveniently at prices representing good value	1. When the food store is only interested in profit maximization regardless of all other product considerations	1. When the concern is entirely with shifting stock of food products quickly and cheaply	1. When the retailer is only concerned with selling SKU's profitably and legally
2. When the range is significantly extended and developed through own-label or other means	2. When the food store provides a deliberate choice of ethical/environmental/ organic products even if the direct profit justification is unclear	2. When there is a commitment to making the shopping process reasonably efficient, pleasant and convenient for the shopper and competitive for the locality	2. When the retailer does the minimum to avoid unwanted criticism or engages in charitable acts very much as tactical marketing ploys
3. When through own-label or otherwise the range becomes genuinely differentiated or unique and geared to wants as well as needs	3. When the retailer additionally provides information and education to enable consumers to make informed choices, even if this may impact short-term profitability	3. When the store strives to add a series of customer service, image building and ancillary facility initiatives whose short-term direct profitability is difficult to gauge and which give the store a 'just noticeable' competitive edge	3. When the foodstore takes on a level of social/corporate/environmental responsibility that involves some sacrifice of short-term profitability and investment back into society/ charity on a level that matches the prevailing norm for a large business
3a. When the range is additionally tailored to meet local or even individual requirements			
3b. When the range is extended to cover a coherent set of additional services and categories			
4. When significant value is added through the provision of added value solutions or advice/education	4. When the retailer elects not to stock certain profitable goods within categories on ethical/	4. When the store invests more heavily in substantive longer-term service and branding campaigns,	4. When the foodstore takes an 'upper quartile' but still business-like (eg 'we have to remember we are here

Table 12.2 *continued*

'From ethics to ethics'

Product range and added value	Product origin and integrity	Role		Social responsibility/Corporate motivation
		Personality and service		
	environmental/consumer safety grounds	with a particular emphasis on staff empowerment, based on a long-term judgement of their impact		to make money') approach to its investment back into society/charity and its lead on the environment
	5. When the retailer exerts pressure down the supply chain, on environmental/ethical/consumer safety grounds, to influence how some products are produced even if this involves short-term cost increases	5. When the store makes a major investment with missionary zeal in defining a unique brand personality and service standard and aims to make the shopping trip a positive leisure/social/educational experience – the service ethic/level of staff empowerment being recognized as excellent by the standards of any sector		5. When the foodstore is famous for its sponsorship and advocacy of particular social causes or issues and environmental policies in a way that clearly transcends any immediate cost-benefit consideration but where it is clear that the main purpose is still to maximize shareholder value
	6. When the retailer sets particularly exacting environmental/ethical/consumer safety standards across all products			6. When the food store is motivated by a higher sense of mission and broader responsibility that clearly overrides the profit motive and involves pioneering/evangelical campaigning
	7. When the retailer decides not to stock whole categories (eg tobacco) on environmental/ethical/consumer safety grounds			

Source: Coopers & Lybrand (1996)

- the committed environmentalist;
- the quirky personality;
- the guardian of the food chain, the crusading campaigner, or the consumers' champion (adapted from Coopers and Lybrand, 1996).

The final implication is that branding is a top-management responsibility (see Randall, 1997). It involves all aspects of the business, and should drive the strategy. That demands leadership, careful analysis, and creative innovation. The brand values must be adopted throughout the organization. This is necessary in all organizations, but especially so in service businesses when it is the people on the ground, in the stores, who have the day-to-day responsibility to deliver most of what the brand is. It has been fashionable to talk about empowerment of staff, but many firms that talk about it also try to exercise strong managerial control. Achieving a balance between the two is one of the leader's key tasks. Our own belief is that this is the area of differentiation that will ultimately matter most of all to tomorrow's successful retailers, and that it is this combination that can produce long-term success – a leader with a clear brand strategy and a supporting staff that collectively appreciate what the strategy means for the customers, and contributes day by day to its delivery on the ground with individual belief and passion.

This book has asked many questions. In many respects we seem to be at a stage of potentially massive market change in a society that itself sees change in retailing, and specifically in food retailing as more significant than at any time in the past half century. If we have asked more questions than we have provided answers, perhaps that reflects the complexity of the world the retailers are now entering. There are no simple answers, and what is right for one firm will emphatically be quite wrong for another. Not everyone can be one of the few big global winners and not all will compete for the biggest prizes. There will be room for niche players, certainly at national level for a while; as in other industries, there is no reason why a successful niche strategy should not be extended globally. Such niche players will depend more on innovation and flair, less on scale and sheer power; but they will still need to operate at near to world standards of efficiency to compete. There will be no easy hiding places in the future.

Our view is that those that emerge as leaders will have:

- international scale and scope, to benefit from economies and to provide cash, but also to transfer learning between countries;
- strong leadership, with succession planned well ahead and executed;
- clear strategy understood and operated by a team of learning individuals;
- well-defined brands with functional difference and emotional warmth;
- brilliant marketing knowledge to target and build customer relationships;
- real innovation in fields valued by consumers.

Appendix

AGB FIGURES

The following figures are published by kind permission of Taylor Nelson AGB plc. They are taken from the annual survey of consumer grocery shopping undertaken by AGB's Superpanel. A panel of 10,000 homes measures their spending on fast-moving consumer goods and fresh foods over an eight-week period, by means of an in-home terminal connected to the telephone network. Panel members use an electronic wand to record their purchases from the bar code of the products bought. The respondent then records (again from a bar code) the shop from which the goods were bought, and the total amount spent from the till roll statement. The data cover all consumer spending in the grocery outlets patronized, and are taken from the total till roll figures.

The figures show, for all the chains that we are concerned with:

- spend per visit, 1997 and 1998;
- retailer penetration and average spend per shopper, 1998;
- retailer penetration levels, 1997 and 1998;
- retailer visits and spend/visit 1998;

- retailer loyalty and grocery shares 1998;
- loyalty breakdown;
- retailer turnover demographic profile;
- retailer demographic map, social class versus age;
- demographic signatures: Tesco, Sainsbury's, Asda, Safeway.

The figures are discussed in the relevant chapters, but here we pick out some key patterns:

- Tesco, Sainsbury's and Asda show similar levels of spending by consumers, but Safeway lags them.
- Tesco and Sainsbury's have the highest penetration, with Asda and Safeway significantly behind, reflecting the gap between the big two and the followers. Tesco increased its lead in 1998 over 1997.
- Tesco, Sainsbury's and Asda account for 50 per cent of their shoppers' total spend, but Safeway lags with under 40 per cent.
- Tesco's shoppers are closest to the social-class profile of all grocery shoppers: they appeal equally across the board. Sainsbury's, Marks & Spencer and Waitrose have an up-market profile, and Asda a slightly down-market one.
- Age and social class taken together show strikingly that Marks & Spencer and Waitrose attract an up-market and old group, while the discounters, particularly Netto, are at the opposite corner of the map. Sainsbury's is towards the up-market and old position, Safeway and Tesco better positioned, and Asda in the middle, slightly younger.

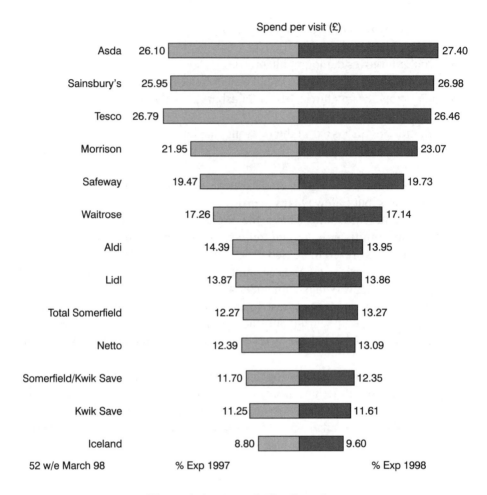

Figure A.1   *Annual till-roll totals*

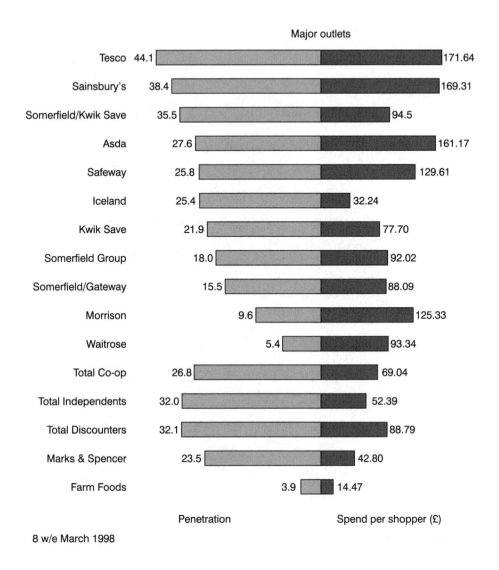

Major outlets

Tesco	44.1		171.64
Sainsbury's	38.4		169.31
Somerfield/Kwik Save	35.5		94.5
Asda	27.6		161.17
Safeway	25.8		129.61
Iceland	25.4		32.24
Kwik Save	21.9		77.70
Somerfield Group	18.0		92.02
Somerfield/Gateway	15.5		88.09
Morrison	9.6		125.33
Waitrose	5.4		93.34
Total Co-op	26.8		69.04
Total Independents	32.0		52.39
Total Discounters	32.1		88.79
Marks & Spencer	23.5		42.80
Farm Foods	3.9		14.47

Penetration   Spend per shopper (£)

8 w/e March 1998

Figure A.2   *Retailer penetration and expenditure*

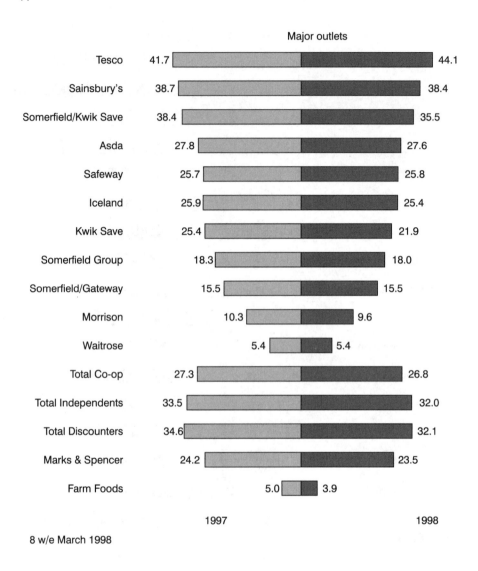

Figure A.3 *Retailer penetration trends*

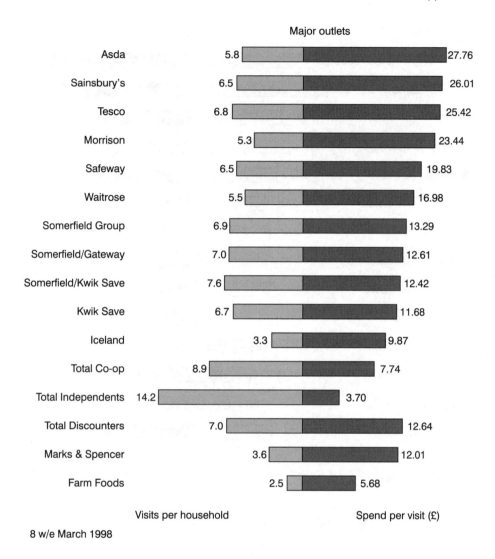

Figure A.4 *Retailer visit and spend/visit*

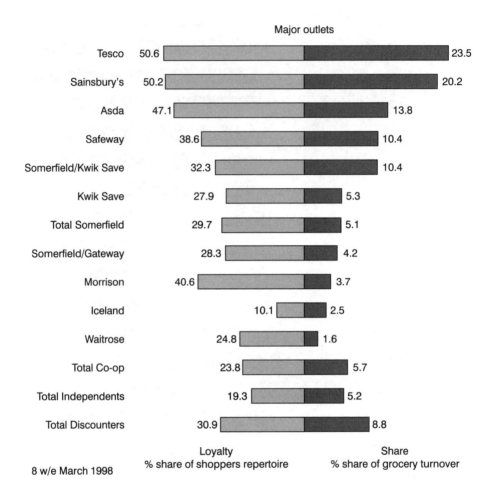

Figure A.5 *Retailer loyalty and grocery shares*

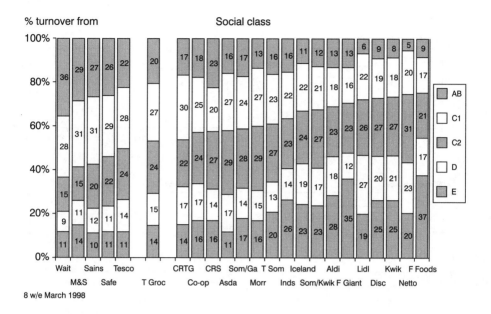

Figure A.6 *Retailer turnover demographic profile*

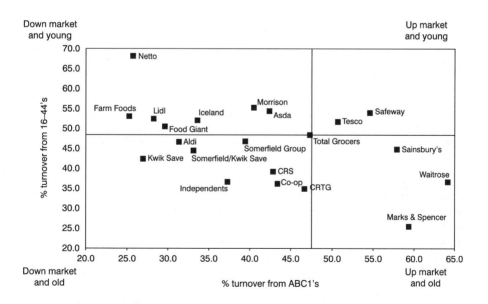

Figure A.7 *Retailer demographic map*

313

% Share

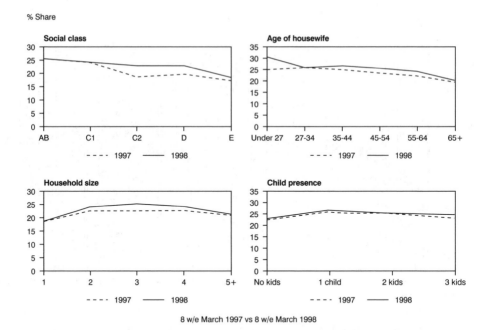

8 w/e March 1997 vs 8 w/e March 1998

Figure A.8   *Demographic signatures Tesco*

% Share

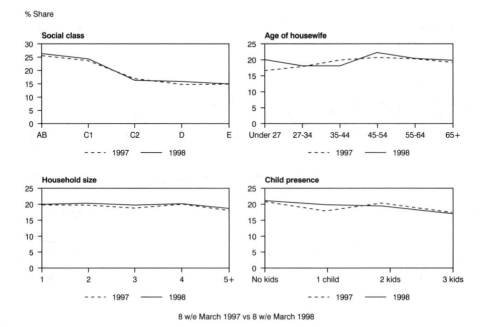

8 w/e March 1997 vs 8 w/e March 1998

Figure A.9   *Demographic signatures Sainsbury's*

% Share

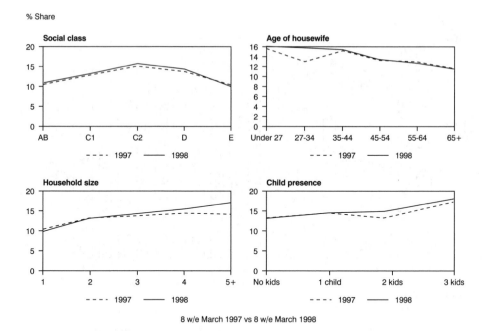

8 w/e March 1997 vs 8 w/e March 1998

Figure A.10   *Demographic signatures Asda*

% Share

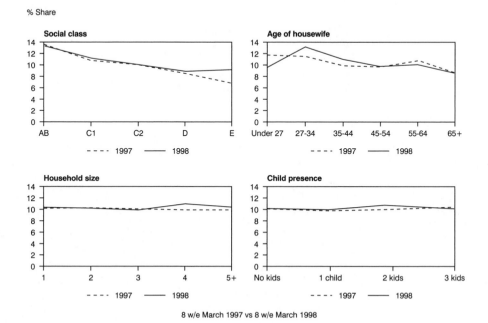

8 w/e March 1997 vs 8 w/e March 1998

Figure A.11   *Demographic signatures Safeway*

% Shoppers by loyalty

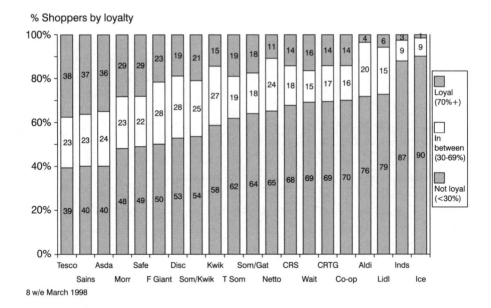

8 w/e March 1998

Figure A.12 *Loyalty breakdown of retailers' shoppers*

References

Abt Associates/FMI (1998) *Trends in the United States: Consumer attitudes and the supermarket*, Food Marketing Institute, Washington DC

ABN AMRO/Hoare Govett (1997) *Tesco: The ABF deal*

Asda (1998) *Evidence to the Agricultural Committee of the UK Pig Industry Inquiry*, Asda, Leeds

Ballington, J (1997/98) Interviews with author, London

BDP Planning and OXIRM (1992) *The Effects of Major Out-of-Town Retail Development*, a literature review for the Department of the Environment, HMSO, London

Beaumont, J and Webb, S (1982) *The Development of Multiple Retailing in the UK*, Institute of Grocery Distribution, Letchmore Heath

Bernard, D (1998) *Financial Times*, 4 December

Bookbinder, P (1993) *Simon Marks, Retail Revolutionary*, Weidenfeld and Nicolson, London (Marks & Spencer)

British Retail Consortium letter (1999) re Peter Welch, *Transnational Margin Comparisons*, 1 February

Burt, S and Sparks, L (1997) 'Performance in food retailing: A cross national consideration and comparison of retail margins', *British Journal of Management*, **8**, pp 133–50

Business Week (1999) 25 January

Cable and Wireless Research (1999) 'How long do people spend in supermarkets?', quoted in *Today*, BBC Radio 4,12 January

Carsberg, B (1997) Interview with author, London

Clark, R (1999) 'Loyalty cards: Upping the stakes in the loyalty game', *Evening Standard*, February

Coker, A (1997/8) Interviews with author, Cheshunt

Coker, A (1999) Memorandum on consumer pricing, monopolies, manufacturers, externalities, farmers (Tesco)

Consumers' Association (1997a), *The Food Divide: Eating on a low income*, The Consumers' Association, London

Consumers' Association (1997b) 'Never mind the price, feel the quality', *Which?*, London, July

Consumers' Association (1997c) 'Comparing customer service standards in supermarkets', *Which?*, London, December

Coopers and Lybrand (1996) *The Future for the Food Store: Challenges and alternatives*, Coca-Cola Retailing Research Group, London

Copestake, S (1998) *Home Shopping*, Added Value Group, Hampton Wick, Middlesex

Corstjens, J and Corstjens, M (1995) *Store Wars: The battle for mindspace and shelfspace*, John Wiley, Chichester

Dale, J (1998) Interview with author, London

Davies, N (1996) *A History of Europe*, Oxford University Press, Oxford

Department of Health (1996) *Low Income, Food, Nutrition and Health: Strategies for improvement*, part of *The Health of the Nation* project

DETR (1998) *The Impact of Large Food Stores on Market Towns and District Centres*, The Stationery Office, London

Deutsche Morgan Grenfell (1998) *Analysis of Food Retailer Results in Britain, France, Belgium, and the USA*

Dobson, P (1998a) *The Economic Welfare Implications of Own Label Goods*, School of Management and Finance Discussion Papers, IV, University of Nottingham

Dobson, P (1998b) *The Competition Effect of Look-Alike Products,* School of Management and Finance Discussion Papers, VIII, University of Nottingham

Dobson, P and Waterson, M (1996) *The Public Policy Implications of Increasing Retailer Power*, School of Management and Finance Discussion Papers, VI, University of Nottingham

Dobson, P, Waterson, M and Chu, A (1998) *The Welfare Consequences of the Exercise of Buyer Power*, Office of Fair Trading, London

DoE (1994) *Vital and Viable Town Centres*, HMSO, London

East, R and Hogg, A (1997/98) Interviews with author, School of Business, Kingston University

Economist (1996) obituary of Lord Alan Robert Sainsbury, 21 October

Economist (1996) 'Troubles at the checkout' (Sainsbury)

Evening Standard (1999) 'Upping the stakes in the loyalty game: Leah, Petra', February

Feldwick, D (1998) Interview with author, London (Waitrose)

Financial Times (1998a) 'The Carrefour revolution', April

Financial Times (1998b) 9 September

Financial Times (1998c) 'Carrefour offers cut-price telephone service', 27 October

Financial Times (1998d) 'Shopping around for global status', November

Financial Times (1999a) 7 January

Financial Times (1999b) 15 January

Financial Times (1999c) 19 February

Financial Times (1999d) 'Carrefour performance', February

Financial Times (1999e) 'Expansion pays off at Walmart', February

Financial Times (1999f) 'Ahold buys Pathmark', 10 March

Financial Times (1999g) 11 March

Fitzgerald, N (1998), Interview with author, London

Forbes, A S A P (1998) 'NetGrocer Net vs. Norm: Foodfighter business at web speed', *Forbes Magazine*, 23 February

Fowler, A (1997) Interview with author, London

Fry, D (1998) Interview with author, London (Sainsbury)

Goldenberg, N (1989) *Thought for Food*, Free Trade Press, Orpington

Grant, A (1996) James G Gulliver CVO, memorial service, author's typescript, 30 October

Gribben, R (1999) 'Tesco dips its toe into the grey motor market', *Daily Telegraph*, March

Halberstam, *The Best and the Brightest,* Fawcett Books, London

Halstead, R (1998) 'Sainsbury checks out £20 billion tie-up', *Mail on Sunday,* 18 October 1998

Hardy, L (1997) 'Discussion of brand and retailing strategies', in *Successful Business Strategies*, Windrush Press, Kingsbridge

Harvard Business School (1986) *Wal-Mart Stores discount operations case study N9–387–018*, Harvard Business School Publishing, Boston

Harvard Business School (1996) *Wal-Mart Stores Inc case study N9–974–024*, Harvard Business School Publishing, Boston

Harvard Business School (1998) *Asda (A) case study N9–498–005*, Harvard Business School Publishing, Boston

Hawkins, K (1999) 'Memorandum: USA and EU supermarket profits', Hayes, Middlesex (Safeway)

Heathcoat-Amory, E (1998) 'The end of the supermarket queue', *Spectator*, May

van der Hoeven, C (1998) *Financial Times*, 20 November

Hollis, J (1997) Interview with author, Windsor, 24 October

Hughes, B (1998) Memorandum and 'Tesco: Notes on Supermarket Margins', Cheshunt

IGD (1980) *The Grocery Business 1970–1980*, Institute of Grocery Distribution, Letchmore Heath

Independent (1998a) 15 October

Independent (1998b) 16 October

Independent (1998c) 21 October

Jefferys, J B (1954) *Retail Trading in Britain 1850–1950*, Cambridge University Press, Cambridge

Kapferer J-N (1995) 'Stealing brand equity: measuring the perceptual confusion between national brands and copy-cat own label products', *Marketing & Research Today*, **23** (2), pp 96–103

Kearney A T (1998) *Strategies 2005: Vision for the wholesale-supplied system*, Food Distributors International, Falls Church, Virginia

KPMG/OXIRM (1997) *Home Shopping across Europe: Experiences and Opportunities*, KPMG, London

KPMG (1991) *Comparison of Food Supply Costs in Four European Countries*, KPMG, London

Lang (1997) Dividing up the cake: food as social exclusion, in A Walker and C Walker (eds) *Britain Divided: the growth of social exclusion in the 1980s and 1990s*, CPAG, London

Leahy, T (1996) Speech to LE Retailing Conference, London, 28 February

Leahy, T (1997) Interview with author for Richmond Events Marketing Forum, Cheshunt, May

Leahy, T (1998) Interview with author, Cheshunt, May

Leighton, A (1998) Interview with author, 7 April

Lewis, N (1998) Summarized articles from *Time, Nation, Forbes*, and *Fairfield County Journal* on Stu Leonard stores, New York, September

Locke, S (1997) Interviews with author, Consumers' Association and Andersen Consulting, London, September

Locke, S (1998) Interviews with author, Consumers' Association and Andersen Consulting, London, June

London Economics (1997) *Competition in Retailing*, Research Paper 13, Office of Fair Trading, London

LPAC (1994) *High Accessibility and Town Centres in London*, London Planning and Advisory Committee, London

LPAC (1997) Interview with author, London, September

McAnena, F (1998) 'Proposals for Tesco clubcard: the next generation', Added Value Company, Hampton Wick, Middlesex

McCarten, K (1997) 'Marketing retail vs. manufacturer brands: is there a difference?' Marketing Society speech, 23 September

McCarten, K (1998) Interview with author, London, June

McCausland, R (1980) *Supermarkets: 50 years of progress*, Food Marketing Institute and Progressive Grocer, Washington DC

McKechnie, S (1997) Interviews with author, January

McKechnie, S (1998) and CA research findings, London, September

McKenney, J (1998) E-mail conversations re Marks & Spencer with author and case references on logistics and category management, Harvard Business School

MacLaurin, I (1997) Interviews with author, London, October

MacLaurin, I (1998) Interviews with author, London, December

MacNeary, T (1998) Interviews with author

MacNeary, T (1999) European Forum retailer presentations, London

Management Horizons *FDM Perspectives 1996–97*, Boston

Management Horizons Performance Reviews 1996–97 *USA: The emerging competitive edge*, Boston

Mason, T (1996) 'The best shopping trip', address to the Marketing Society, London

Melmouth, Graham CEO (1997), Speech to Cooperative officials, quoted in Verdict on Grocers and Supermarkets (1998)

Meyer, M (1997) Interview with author, London

Millen, J (1998) Interview with author, Egham, Surrey

Mitchell, H and Peck, H (1997) *Does Tesco Hold All the Cards? Case study*, Cranfield School of Management, Cranfield

MMC (1981) *Discounts to Retailers*, Monopolies and Mergers Commission, London

Morrison, K (1998) Interview with author and memorandum, Bradford

Murcott, A (ed) (1998) *The Nation's Diet: The social science of food choice*, Longman, London

New York Times (1998) 'Supersizing the supermarkets', 13 November

Newsnight (1998) BBC2, 16 October

Norman, A (1997) Interview with author, Leeds

O'Connor, D (1997) 'Major developments in the discounters, clubs, and supercenters: the "numbers" and what's behind them', Management Ventures Inc presentation to Lever Brothers Co, New York

OFT (1985) *Competition and Retailing in Great Britain*, Office of Fair Trading, London

OXIRM/Jones, Lang, Wootton (1996) *Retail Planning Policies: Their impact on European retail property markets*, Jones, Lang, Wootton, London

Panorama (1998) programme on supermarket pricing, BBC1, 23 November

Payling, D (1998) Memorandum to author on European retail competitors, Kingston-on-Thames

Peston and Ennew, C (eds) (1998) *Neighbourhood Shopping in the Millennium*, University of Nottingham Business School, Nottingham

Powell, D (1991) *Counter Revolution: The Tesco story*, Grafton Books, London

Randall, G (1990) *Marketing to the Retail Trade*, Butterworth Heinemann, Oxford

Randall, G (1997) *Branding*, Kogan Page, London

Raven, H and Lang, T (1995) *Off our Trolleys? Food retailing and the hypermarket economy*, Institute for Public Policy Research, London

Rowthorn, R (1998) Private communication to the authors, December

Sainsbury, D (Lord David of Turville) (1997) Interviews with authors, London, April, June

Sainsbury, D (Lord David of Turville) (1997) Memorandum and performance information, London

Sieff, M (1986) *Don't Ask the Price: The memoirs of the president of Marks and Spencer*, Weidenfeld and Nicolson, London

Silver, C (1997) Interview with author

Simons, D (1998) Interview with author, London

Simms, J (1998) 'Top Marks', *Marketing Business*, **71**, July/August

Tanburn, J (1974) *Retailing and the Competitive Challenge*, Lintas, London

Tanburn, J (1981) *Food Distribution: Its impact on marketing in the 80s*, Central Council for Agricultural and Horticultural Co-operation, London

Tedlow, R S (1990) *New and Improved: The rise of mass marketing in America*, Harvard Business School Press, Boston

Tesco (1998) *Pricing and Profits: Setting the record straight*, Tesco, London

Tordjman, A (1994) 'European retailing: convergence, differences, and perspectives', *International Journal of Retail and Distribution Management*, **22** (5) pp 3–19

Tweddell, C (1997) Interviews with author, London, October

Tweddell, C (1999) Memorandum, London, February

de Vault, K (1997/8) Interviews with author, New York

de Vault, K (1998) Memorandum, May, New York

Vyner, T (1998) Interviews with author and memorandum, London

Watts, C (1999) Memorandum, and Asda's evidence to the Agriculture Committee of the UK Pig Industry, Leeds

Webster, D (1998) Interview with author, London

Welch, P (1999) Interview with author, and memorandum, London

Wildstrom (1998) '"Bots" don't make great shoppers', *Business Week*, 7 December

Williams, B (1994) *The Best Butter in the World: A history of Sainsbury's over 125 years*, Ebury Press, London

Williams, B (1998) Memoranda on Sainsbury Board members, policies and photographs, London

Wrigley, N (1993) 'Abuses of market power? Further reflections on UK food retailing and the regulatory state', *Environment and Planning A*, **25**, pp 1545–57

Wrigley, N (1994) 'After the store wars? Towards a new era of retail competition?' *Journal of Retail and Consumer Services*, **1**, pp 5–20

Wrigley, N (1996) 'Sunk costs and corporate restructuring: British food retailing and the property crisis', in Wrigley and Lowe (eds.) *Retailing, Consumption and Capital: Towards the New Retail Geography*, Longman, Harlow

Wrigley, N (1997a) 'Exporting the British model of food retailing to the United States: implications for the EU–US food systems convergence debate', *Agribusiness*, **13**, pp 137–52

Wrigley, N (1997b) 'British food retail capital in the USA: part 1, Sainsbury and the Shaw's experience', *International Journal of Retail and Distribution Management*, **25** (1), pp 7–21

Wrigley, N (1997c) 'British food retail capital in the USA: part 2, giant prospects?' *International Journal of Retail and Distribution Management*, **25** (2), pp 48–58

Wrigley, N (1998a) 'Understanding store development programmes in post-property crisis UK food retailing', *Environment and Planning A*, **30**

Wrigley, N (1998b) Memorandum to author re USA consolidation processes, School of Geography, University of Southampton

Wrigley, N (1998c) 'How British retailers have shaped food choice', in Murcott, 1998

Yarrow, S (1992) 'Are UK supermarket prices competitive?', *Consumer Policy Review*, **2** (4), pp 218–25

Young, H (1998) *This Blessed Plot: Britain and Europe from Churchill to Blair*, Macmillan, London

Index

Visit Kogan Page on-line

Comprehensive information on
Kogan Page titles

Features include

■ complete catalogue listings,
including book reviews and
descriptions

■ special monthly promotions

■ information on NEW titles and
BESTSELLING titles

■ a secure shopping basket facility
for on-line ordering

PLUS everything you need to know about
KOGAN PAGE

http://www.kogan-page.co.uk